Shanghai

Shanghai

Life, Love and Infrastructure
in China's City of the Future

STEPHEN GRACE

SENTIENT PUBLICATIONS

First Sentient Publications edition 2010
Copyright © 2010 by Stephen Grace

A paperback original

Cover design by Kim Johansen, Black Dog Design
Book design by Timm Bryson
Photos by Stephen Grace

Library of Congress Cataloging-in-Publication Data
Grace, Stephen.
  Shanghai : life, love and infrastructure in China's city of the future / Stephen Grace. — 1st ed.
    p. cm.
  Includes bibliographical references.
  ISBN 978-1-59181-095-7
  1. Economic development—China—Shanghai—21st century. 2. Cities and towns—
Growth. 3. Shanghai (China)—Social life and customs—21st century. I. Title.
  HC428.S53G73 2009
  951'.13206—dc22
                        2009023857

Printed in the United States of America

10 9 8 7 6 5 4 3 2 1

SENTIENT PUBLICATIONS
A Limited Liability Company
1113 Spruce Street
Boulder, CO 80302
www.sentientpublications.com

By the time this book is published, most of Shanghai's traditional *shíkùmén* lane houses, the city's signature architecture, will have been razed. But this book is in no way meant to be a dirge for what's been lost. Rather, it is intended as a celebration of what remains. *Shíkùmén* are made of brick; my friends in Shanghai are made of something stronger. This book is for them.

Come, let us build ourselves a city and a tower with its top in the sky,
and so make a name for ourselves . . .

—GENESIS 11:4

The 21st Century Starts Here

—FROM A HEADLINE FOR A FEBRUARY 18, 1996
New York Times Magazine ARTICLE ABOUT SHANGHAI

CONTENTS

AUTHOR'S NOTE

Does the world need yet another book about China? I asked myself why I should add my voice to the chorus, sometimes shouting, about this country that has of late been the focus of so much attention.

During my work and travels in China I consumed every bit of information I could find about the country. Often I was left wondering about the people behind the avalanche of statistics and the endless parade of predictions about China's rise. The more time I spent there, the more people I met who had nothing to do with tainted milk, or the controversial train to Tibet, or multibillion-dollar businesses run by corrupt government cadres. Most of the people I met in Shanghai were simply doing their best to survive amid an urban overhaul taking place on a scale and at a pace unprecedented in human history. And some of these people became my friends. Like the nation of which they are a part, their lives did not want for problems. But I found them to be filled with hope and humor, with warmth, and with lovely, quirky individualism that was fiercely at odds with the recycled stereotypes.

This book is not about China. Nor is it about the Chinese. It is a book about people I met in Shanghai whom I first thought of as my Chinese friends and in time came to see as friends who happened to be Chinese. As I read endless accounts of rising dragons and waking giants and a billion plus consumers, I began to believe that making this distinction was worth exploring in a book. What separated my Chinese friends and me was obvious. What we had in common took some work to discover. But in time, through countless urban adventures, the differences between us started to seem as transitory and unimportant as the ever-changing skyline of the metropolis through which we traveled.

I am not a Sinologist. I am not a scholar. This book is not about history, though I have included history when I felt it was appropriate to do so. It is not a political treatise, though I have probed the politics of China's past and present. It is not straight reportage, though I have used many of the techniques of journalism to ground the story in fact. It is not a novel, though I have employed some of the methods of fiction to shape the story. It is certainly not a memoir, as the focus of the book is, fortunately for you, not my life. It is not a travel guide, and if one were to use it as such, one would become very lost. Nor is it a travelogue, for my journeys in Shanghai were often scattered and aimless.

What follows is an account of people making lives for themselves in a city with a storied past—a city that is also a hypermodern cosmopolis, fast and bright, and often referred to as "the city of the future," or simply "the future." Surrounded by a whimsical world of architectural designs run riot and by infrastructure projects of such scope and ambition that their construction seems reminiscent of raising the Great Wall, my friends in Shanghai led me into their world. Together we traveled past the city's fantastic skyscrapers and absurdly long bridges, beyond its lightning-fast trains and vast expanses of neon, deep into the little lanes where people cooked their meals, loved their children, argued and laughed as the city was ripped apart and shining towers filled the sky.

Except for a few well-known place names (such as the Yangtze River) and people (such as Sun Yat-sen), I have used the standard *pīnyīn* system of romanization. I have changed some people's names and other features that could be used to identify them.

To build the background for this book, I relied heavily on the excellent body of work created by China specialists such as Jeffrey Wasserstrom and Anna Greenspan; journalists such as Adam Minter and Paul French; scholars such as Mark Kingwell; artists such as Edward Burtynsky; and writers who bridge the gap between scholarship and art, such as Peter Hessler.

I also borrowed from writers whose work has no relation to China, such as Ernest Hemingway, Cormac McCarthy and Dave Eggers. I lifted words from a song by The Police. Any bad puns in the book are entirely my own fault, as are any errors.

This is not a book about China's choking pollution and every imaginable social problem. It is not about its myriad business opportunities and their pitfalls. Nor is it about Shanghai's manic buildup to the 2010 World Expo—which in all likelihood will be as spectacular as the 2008 Olympic Games in Beijing—though the transformation taking place in preparation for the event does serve as backdrop.

This is a story of people trying to navigate the tumultuous present in a city of the future. This is a story of my friends in Shanghai.

STEPHEN GRACE
Shanghai
March 30, 2009

The Towers of Pudong

Fighting my way down a thronging street, I lunged toward any bit of open space between people. But before I could relax into each sheltering void, I found it filled with arms and legs, torsos and heads. It was impossible to tell where one body ended and another began. I had a sudden sensation of being a single cell, a minute part of a many-headed, many-limbed organism oozing its way through the city. I fought this feeling and convinced myself I was an individual with a will of my own. Instead of going wherever the enormous creature of which I was a part moved, I tried to go where I wanted, lurching this way and that, bumping flesh on all sides, my heart rate nearing cardiac emergency pace. Zhang Li, who'd told me to call her Jennifer, moved through the crowd in front of me as though she did this every day. She did, of course. But it seemed unthinkable to me that a person could actually get used to this. Wasn't there some ancient and irrepressible part of the brain whose job it was to register panic when the body was squeezed and deprived of air? Mixed with the sensation of suffocation was the realization how truly meaningless I was, a single body among 1.3 billion bodies. To distract myself from feeling crushed physically and existentially, I focused my attention on the harsh orchestra of horn blaring. Along with bicycles and the handcarts of peddlers, cars and motor scooters pushed through the crowd. Each driver made enough noise with his horn to wake ancestral spirits.

Puxi ("west of the Huangpu River")

My ears clanging, my eyes stinging in the corrosive air, my skin sopping with sweat—both my own and that of the thousands of bodies I'd been pressed against in the seething streets—I followed Jennifer through crowds of increasing density to a viewpoint along the Huangpu River. In this city that makes Los Angeles seem like a sleepy suburb, we managed to scavenge a patch of empty pavement, a resource as rare and precious in Shanghai as water in the desert.

Above us hovered kites, their wings tearing the air. Long rays of the dying sun glanced from the river as it slugged its way toward the sea. Jennifer pointed across the water at a cityscape bristling with buildings and burning with light. "I remember pulling my father's shirt when I was a little girl and asking him what was on the other side," she said. "It was so dark. He told me there was nothing there. Maybe some farms." She was talking about Pudong, a Manhattan-on-steroids district of skyscrapers rising from the east side of Shanghai's Huangpu River.

Jennifer pushed an errant strand of hair back into the shiny black curtain around her smiling face. Tight jeans rode low on her hips, and her black boots would have blended well in the trendy streets of Rome. "Shanghai is called the Paris of the East," she said. "Is it like Paris?"

The Pudong skyline is dominated by a tower of enormous silver and pink balls attached to a slender spear poking into the perpetual haze. At night the balls light up with blinking bulbs of every hue. Perched upon tripod legs, the structure seems some sort of zany school science project run amuck, or something from an old science fiction movie portraying a tasteless space-age future. This Flash Gordonesque monstrosity, named the Oriental Pearl TV Tower, is the world's third-tallest communications tower. But in twenty-first-century Shanghai, third place simply will not do. The city was well on its way to building the largest urban mass transit system on earth, the world's biggest shipyard, and the largest sewage treatment plant in human history. Shanghai already boasted the world's fastest train, the world's largest cargo port, the world's longest arch bridge, the world's longest transoceanic bridge, the world's longest shopping district, the world's largest bus, even the world's largest skate park. (Plans to build the world's largest Ferris wheel were being discussed.) And to this long list of superlatives accumulating as the 2010 World Expo in Shanghai approached, the city had been planning to add perhaps the most pride-inducing biggest-tallest-longest distinction of all: the world's tallest building. More than one New Yorker, when confronted with the skyline of Pudong, has said something along the lines of, "This is the first time I've felt out of my league in a city. My god, this is a city." Texans have been heard to grudgingly admit that Shanghai has taught them the true meaning of *big*. Las Vegans, after visiting Shanghai, have described their own city as understated and subdued.

"It is not like Paris," I said to Jennifer.

"But all the lights?" She pointed across the river. "Shanghai is a city of lights."

A Parisian could not argue with this. A kaleidoscope of color spread across Pudong as building after building lit up, brightening the frothy wakes of barges in the river below. Trails of neon blinked their way up and down the sides of buildings, casino style. I pointed at the Oriental Pearl TV Tower, or the OPTV Tower as I had started calling it, and said, "That is quite possibly the ugliest building on earth."

"You think it is ugly?"

"Maybe not ugly, exactly. Maybe just weird. That is quite possibly the weirdest building in the history of human civilization. What would inspire someone to build something like that?"

Jennifer said, with complete seriousness, "The design of the tower is based on a Tang dynasty poem about the sound made by a lute."

"A lute?" I tried to recall the sound of a lute. If the OPTV Tower looked the way a lute sounded, I was completely at peace with the possibility that I had never heard lute music.

Jennifer said, "It is supposed to look like the haunting sound of a lute. I read that, but I'm not sure exactly what the 'haunting' means."

"Neither am I," I said, shirking my duty as Jennifer's language partner. The deal was this: I was supposed to help her polish her English, which seemed to need very little polishing; in return she was supposed to help me with my Mandarin, which needed far more than polishing. If her English were a sculpture that required a bit of smoothing, my Mandarin was a chunk of jagged rock yet to be hit by a sculptor's chisel.

"Do you really think a lute inspired someone to design that . . . that whatever it is?" I said.

"Um." She bit her lower lip and stared across the water. Then she said, "What do you think the inspiration was?"

I gazed for a moment at the tower in all its light-flashing, gaudy-baubles-skewered-by-metal-poles glory. "I don't know. Acid?" I offered.

"What is acid?" asked Jennifer.

"Acid feels like that tower looks," I said. We were both quiet a moment and I wasn't sure where to go next. "Acid," I said in English, and then switched to Mandarin, "is a kind of drug."

Jennifer blew at the bangs that fringed her forehead, as I was learning she did when thinking hard. And lower lip chewing was often a prelude to hair blowing.

"I'm sorry," I said. "I'm definitely not helping you with your English. I'm not even sure what I'm talking about. I'm just excited to be in Shanghai, I guess."

"I think the tower is beautiful," Jennifer said. "It is supposed to look like twin dragons playing with pearls."

I said this in Chinese, "twin dragons playing with pearls," and Jennifer corrected my pronunciation. "Do you really think that's what it looks like?" I asked.

"Perhaps not. That's what the city tells tourists."

"Do tourists believe that?"

"I don't know what tourists believe."

"But you think it's beautiful? Really?"

She was silent a moment. There was lip chewing and hair blowing. "Nothing was there fifteen years ago. That side of the river was empty. Now Shanghai has more sky . . ." With her right hand she patted the air in front of her to show me she was looking for a word.

"Skyscrapers?" I offered.

"Yes. Skyscraper. The Oriental Pearl Tower was the first building on that side of the river. Now Shanghai has more skyscrapers than New York City. I think that is beautiful. Do you think so?"

"It's impressive," I said.

I looked back across the dark water slipping past us, splashes of neon moving in trippy patterns along the far side of the river. Nothing had been there fifteen years ago—nothing but the black night and empty swampland stretching out to sea. The Chinese government had decided to turn Pudong into the nation's financial powerhouse and had spared no effort in doing so. Pudong now sported towers and trade zones, financial districts and metro stations, even a magnetic levitation train. While Pudong was being built, Jennifer had been studying in one of China's best universities, where she had to bathe with cold water every frost-crusted winter evening, her breath puffing whitely in the air as she gritted her teeth and turned on the tap. The idea of a steaming shower was a luxury she could image only because she'd seen them in the pirated American movies she watched on weekends with her friends. And now some of the world's tallest buildings were being raised across the river from where she'd grown up. With Shanghai as the neon-sparking showpiece of its newly attained modernity, China had reinvented itself, undergoing a transformation as dramatic as any before it in human history. The dragon of China's past now wore pink and silver baubles and spewed not fire or Tang dynasty lute music, but flashing light into Shanghai's electric night. And for one clear moment as bright as the lightshow raging across the river, I glimpsed the OPTV Tower through Jennifer's eyes. I saw not horribly imagined architecture but China's bright future, and it was indeed beautiful.

From that day forward Jennifer would guide me through the tonal tangle of the Chinese language and the concrete wilderness of her hometown streets, offering me a glimpse into the megalopolis of Shanghai. She was proud of its development, but she did not shy away from the costs of that progress, not least of which was the air we breathed each day, tasting sometimes of chemicals, sometimes of coal smoke, and always of shattered concrete's fine grit. As we became friends, Jennifer began to drop the city booster optimism that made her sound like a Shanghai Communist Party official and clued me in to the consequences of the most rapid period of industrial development the world has ever known. One of the costs was a program of massive relocations as entire city blocks of low-slung residences were razed to make way for tall buildings. Jennifer's family lived in one such area slated for demolition and they were fighting to stay in their home. Each day as bulldozers pushed down brick walls and construction cranes lifted their burdens of steel skyward, Jennifer's parents inched closer to eviction. But I didn't know that this first night that Jennifer and I met to practice language together on the bank of the Huangpu River. I had no idea what her family stood to lose as Shanghai's progress pushed relentlessly forward. I was drunk on neon, high on diesel fumes. My bruised and frantic brain, bombarded by more sounds and sights in a few furious Shanghai hours than it normally processed in an entire American month, perceived the urban mayhem as some vast and hopeful poem of which I was thrilled to be a part.

"Why are you smiling like that?" Jennifer asked.

"I'm just happy to be here," I said. "I feel like . . . I guess I feel like what's happening right now in China, all the development we hear about in the news every day in America, is really happening right here, in this city, at this point in time, and more people are being lifted out of poverty in a few years than in the last several centuries, and it might be one of the most pivotal points in human history and . . . well, I'm here to see it." I looked at Jennifer, her face tense with concentration. "I'm sorry, I'm talking too fast, right? And using too many idioms? And not really making any sense?"

"I think I understand," she said, and smiled.

"That's the other thing," I said, pointing abruptly toward her grinning mouth and startling the smile right off her face. "There's something about the way a lot of people in China smile that seems like they're actually expressing something, a real emotion . . . . Okay, in America you see these smiles that are . . . professional smiles. People smile because they have to, because their jobs require them to. It's weird and disorienting because it means nothing. But in China, when people smile it's because they want to, not because they have to . . . . You have no idea what I'm talking about, right?"

Jennifer again smiled, and said, "I think you like Shanghai very much."

"True," I said in Chinese. "I like Shanghai very much."

There were times when I wanted to hate China. I knew people had been massacred in Tiananmen: as a teenager I had followed the news as the tanks crushed the students. I understood that disastrous policies of the past had caused the death of millions. I knew that Mao had been a tyrant and a madman who had instigated measureless amounts of human misery, yet to this day the people still loved him, still praised his name, like traumatized children who idolize an abusive

Pudong ("east of the Huangpu River")

parent. I knew that dissidents were imprisoned and tortured every day in the People's Republic for questioning the status quo. I knew that the industrial revolution was creating so much damage to the environment it would take a century or more to reverse the destruction. I wanted to hate China but I could not. I could not, because of a certain Chinese smile that makes me believe all is right in this crazy nation and in my soul. That smile, the warmth of it, I saw every day in China, and I saw it now on the bank of the Huangpu River. I smiled back at Jennifer and asked her how she'd chosen her English name.

"Friends," she said.

"Your friends gave it to you?"

"No, Rachel, from *Friends*."

"The TV show?"

"Jennifer Aniston is very beautiful, do you think so?"

I stared across the river at a skyline that looked like a nightmarish dreamscape from a dystopian future, but I loved it anyway. This was all very strange to me, very disorienting. I had never been friends with anyone obsessed with *Friends* before.

We started walking again, and following the human tumble down into an underpass, we were disgorged on the other side to thread our way through a long line of neoclassical buildings. They looked like a staid backdrop snatched from London and set down amid the scorched earth of this madcap metropolis where towers torch and flare. I palmed one of the building's surfaces, feeling soothed by its density. This solid stonework was craftsmanship from a vanished past. Most of the new structures stacking up in Shanghai are cavernous and intimidating, but because of the hurried pace of construction and the shoddy quality, they can also feel temporary and frail. Shanghai sometimes seems a mighty city, sometimes a fragile shell.

To escape roads encumbered with cars, we ducked into a narrow alley where vendors nestled in every nook, speaking to passersby of deals on watches and shoes, and prostitutes huddled beneath floodlights, painted fingernails combing through glossy hair. On a backstreet we passed the UCool International Hostel, with décor so outlandish, even in the middle of the daily carnival that is Shanghai, it made me stop and stare. One could get a dorm bed and free wi-fi in a building that boasted tall spindles, in a pale shade of peach, holding giant spools of yellow, red and blue. Streaky paint the color of wet blood ran down a wall in dripping lines that spilled across windows of asymmetrical design. Black-and-white checkerboards edged the doors, and the building's façade boasted random rectangles in various hues of mint green. Send Dr. Seuss down the rabbit hole, hand him a hookah, and ask him to collaborate with Alice to design a building, and there you have it: Shanghai's UCool International Hostel.

Beyond the hostel lay Shanghai's Old Town, its ancient roofs of graceful curving eaves awash in neon. At a food stall we stopped to eat *xiǎolóngbāo*, Shanghai's most famous treat. Inside the soft skin of each dumpling is a piece of pork afloat in broth. Devour these tasty morsels whole and you'll scream with the pain of a burned throat, for the delicious liquid inside is scalding. One must eat them like a local, Jennifer taught me: Lower your face to the bowl and nibble a hole in the edge of a xiaolongbao. Then, before you eat the dumpling, drink the soup inside in small slurping sips. If anything on earth tastes better, it has yet to pass my lips.

"Do you know how the soup is put inside the dumpling?" Jennifer asked.

"How?"

"I won't tell you. You have to guess."

"I give up. How does the soup get inside the dumpling?"

"I told you—I won't tell you."

We tossed our paper bowls and flimsy wooden chopsticks into windrows of rubbish; the street beneath our feet was slippery with grease. Workers in orange

In Shanghai's Old Town, the elegance of traditional Chinese philosophy is manifested in the built environment and stands in stark contrast to a hypermodern skyline.

safety vests, pushing brooms, piled the trash on carts each evening, purging the alley of the day's activity, wiping it clean for the next day's feast. Beyond the food stall were glass-fronted massage parlors where women clad in lingerie lounged on couches and beckoned with outstretched hands, slender fingers slowly moving, eyes downcast, hair aglow in gauzy light, like sirens in a dream. People bedded down in blankets rose up from the shadows. On homemade crutches they tottered toward us in their rags and brandished the stumps of severed limbs, thrusting them at us as they pleaded for money. One woman, with a face that seemed made of melted candle wax—all her dental architecture exposed to the light of day where her flesh had burned away—sat unmoving on the ground. We filled her cup with coins.

As this megacity of the East wheeled its way toward night, the last of the long day's light stretched into molten bands of orange, mixed with seething red, creating a cataclysm of color in the west. Evening breezes stirred the roasting air. We wandered a street yellow with puddles of piss and brown with the spatter of bowels. We pushed through clouds of tiny black flies rising from mounds of rancid fruit and sloshed through stagnant water shimmering with reflected neon, and ended up back on the Bund, the city's celebrated strip along the Huangpu River.

Again we stopped on the promenade and stood looking across the river's rippled skin at the freaky lightshow of the OPTV Tower.

"Have you been inside it?" Jennifer asked. "Have you been to the place where you can go up into the sky and see the city?"

"Do you have time to go now?" I asked. "I haven't been to that side of the river yet."

My first night in Shanghai was like a honeymoon, everything fresh and perfect, any flaws registered in some deep recess of awareness so distant from the buzz of blissful excitement that they don't diminish it one bit. I couldn't wait to get inside that hideous tower and look out into the hopeful night.

To cross the Huangpu River, options abound—bridges, subway lines, car tunnels, and even an underwater "sightseeing tunnel." The latter offers a lightshow right out of Laser Floyd: video footage of lava, inflatable dolls that drift eerily in front of the silver sightseeing cars, neon animals cavorting on the walls, and a soundtrack that features a man speaking English and a woman Chinese, babbling about outer space, heaven, and hell, with maniacal laughter throughout. And as if this weren't enough excitement, at the terminus of the tunnel is an aquarium featuring "strange sea creatures" and the Sex Culture Museum, which purports to provide a look at five thousand years of Chinese sexual history. Seriously. That's pretty much the description someone gave me, and I thought he was joking until I went to see for myself what multitudes of tourists before me had spent six bucks on. If someone tells you something strange about Shanghai, it is safe to assume that the truth is even weirder. After finishing my mind-altering trip through the sightseeing tunnel, I was too confused by the commotion of lights and punishing sounds to spend much time at the sex museum studying thousand-year-old jade dildos. Shaking my head, I wandered from the dank tunnel into the polluted light of day wondering what the hell had ever happened to baggy blue Mao suits and good old-fashioned Chinese repression and restraint. But I digress.

In our many travels throughout the city, Jennifer and I eventually exhausted every possible means for crossing the Huangpu, but on this, our first excursion across the river, we chose the ferry and coughed up U.S. fifteen cents each for roundtrip tickets. The wide and lazy waters of the Huangpu were jammed with traffic. Even the rivers offer no relief from the clustering humanity. China's largest city is now the world's most densely populated metropolis. Central Shanghai is home to ten million people; another ten million live in the suburbs, and the headcount climbs each day. All around our ferry, sightseeing boats lined in neon plied the river among a mess of barges hauling toys and textiles, toasters and tennis shoes away from factories toward the East China Sea, where the products of countless millions of Chinese laborers would be loaded onto container ships and sent across the world.

"Shanghai is the largest seaport in the world?" I asked Jennifer as I leaned over a rail. She raised up on her tiptoes to lean along with me but looked uncomfortable trying to reach the top rail. She couldn't have been an inch over five feet or weighed more than eighty pounds soaking wet, but she seemed larger than her physical size, somehow, perhaps because of her confidence. That, and the fact that she stood incredibly straight. She had posture right out of a chiropractic textbook: look up "perfect posture" and there she was.

"World's largest seaport," she said. "Perhaps that's true. There are many boats."

"Many boats," I echoed several times in Chinese. How stupid I must have sounded, and how gracious she was to refrain from pointing it out to me. A man within earshot of my parroting said, "*Nĭ Zhōngwén shuō de hĕn hăo.*" You speak Chinese very well.

Would a Chinese person in America be given encouragement by a stranger on a boat for uttering "many boats" in English? I gave a standard response to the man, "*guò jiăng le,*" meaning "I'm flattered": a polite way to deflect a compliment and display the humility integral to Chinese culture. My humility had many times been false. I'd thought, "Yup, that's right, my Chinese pretty much kicks ass—so much, in fact, that I'm going to give you the standard humble Chinese response so you can further see the extent to which I kick ass." But right now I felt something closer to true humility. I felt embarrassed by how shitty native English speakers often are toward foreigners struggling to learn the language, and how absurdly generous the Chinese could be in contrast. But to further complicate matters, many Chinese were astounded to hear a Caucasian mouth form Chinese words because they considered their language the most sophisticated form of communication the human species had ever devised. They believed only Chinese brains could truly comprehend it and produce it—foreign brains simply not being up to the task. Sometimes from their effusive praise came a whiff of superiority; sometimes their condescension was so powerful it seemed a rancid wind. No one group has monopolies on arrogance or graciousness when it comes to the weird and often messy collision between China and the West.

So what to do, other than offer my *guò jiăng le* to the man and continue to stretch my brain around the tongue-twisting pronunciations and acrobatic tones abruptly jumping and falling, running along a high level plain, dropping down and then leaping back up. What to do but keep working toward fluency and helping Jennifer polish whatever needed to be polished of her English, which was so good that were my Mandarin ever to approach that level, I would have to be slapped repeatedly to remove the satisfied grin from my face. I liked the Chinese language because I was curious about the intricate history of the culture, which I'd been drawn to because I had many Chinese friends; I'd made many Chinese friends while studying the language so I could become immersed in the culture . . . or something. It all fit together, though I'd lost track of exactly how. But I knew that working my way across the gap between our worlds was as rewarding as anything I'd ever done, and that I'd be a student of Chinese for a long time to come. Fumble the tones of *guò jiǎng le* and instead of "I'm flattered" you've said "fruit jam." How could you not fall in love with a language like that?

Wǒ shuō de bù hǎo, I told the man on the ferry. "I speak very badly." A stock sentence that expresses the humility Chinese expect from each other but not from foreigners, who they assume will swagger. By nimbly sidestepping compliments, a foreigner becomes a bit less foreign in their eyes, perhaps a bit more Chinese. With a burst of satisfaction I thought that my Mandarin was far from perfect, but it really wasn't half-bad, and I was sure that he and Jennifer both understood this to be exactly what I meant.

Our ferry drifted across the river, Puxi behind us, Pudong in front. *Pǔ* refers to "Huangpu River," and *xī* means "west." So, Puxi means "west of the Huangpu River." The *dōng* in Pudong means "east," so Pudong is "east of the Huangpu River." Much of what initially seems mystifying in Mandarin to Western minds becomes manageable when broken down into simple chunks of meaning. A kangaroo is a *dài shǔ*, a "mouse with a pocket." A computer is a *diàn nǎo*—literally an "electric brain." Robots are *jīqì rén*, meaning "machine people." If language is a window into how a people thinks, methinks the Chinese are very logical indeed. If architecture is a reflection of a nation's psyche, I look at the Pudong skyline and think the Chinese are stark raving mad.

Many of the barges chugging along the Huangpu carried video screens as big as billboards, enormous floating advertisements that passed up and down the river flashing corporate logos. The bright lights of this clever marketing innovation, however, paled in comparison to the electric advertising bonanza on the buildings of Pudong. Each evening when the sky went black, the sides of entire skyscrapers turned into gargantuan LCD screens that bled their messages in vivid colors across the night. Among the blazing lights I glimpsed the Jin Mao Tower, a tiered pagoda-like skyscraper created by Skidmore, Owings & Merrill, the Chicago-based architectural and engineering firm that designed the Sears Tower. Depending on the time of day and one's state of mind, the structure either had an Art Deco-ish Empire-State-Building look, or seemed like something out of *Lord of the Rings*, a jewel-encrusted tower home to wizards hurling lightning bolts at all who dared approach. Official descriptions claimed it resembled a bamboo stalk. The architects insist the tower's base is an open book, the tower itself a pen that draws ink from the Huangpu River. I thought of a new city slogan: "Shanghai: World's Largest Mixed Metaphor."

Whatever the architectural inspiration or intended effect, Jin Mao was elegantly understated when compared to the OPTV Tower, which was beginning to cause random scenes from *Blade Runner* to race through my mind, as I'd been warned it would by many who'd come before me to Shanghai. Along with the OPTV Tower, Pudong's Jin Mao had been part of the vanguard of progress on the east side of the river. From the farmland of Pudong had sprung what until just recently had been the tallest building in mainland China, and the third-tallest skyscraper in the world. Jin Mao, completed in 1998 and 1,381 feet tall, had anchored the endless flux of Shanghai's skyline in the building boom that followed.

"What do you mean you've never been inside Jin Mao?" I said as we stepped off the ferry's gangplank and finally set foot on Pudong—this shimmering land of fantasy covered in pixilated advertising, this mystic city of the new world.

"Jin Mao is for tourists," Jennifer said. "Shanghai people don't really go there for fun." Airborne pollution clung thickly to every bit of my bare skin, as though I were wearing garments made of soot. It stuck to my face like a mask as we wandered the streets at the base of a vertical world. The city of Shanghai now has more skyscrapers than the entire West Coast of the United States, and the bulk of these tall towers rises from Pudong.

Jennifer tilted her face skyward and looked up at the Jin Mao Tower, a pillar of light in the dark night. "Perhaps I should go there one time."

Jennifer used the word *perhaps* constantly when she spoke English. In time I learned to translate her *perhaps* as "definitely." This wasn't exactly her intended meaning, but it was much closer to what she meant than what I normally took *perhaps* to mean.

"Then perhaps let's go," I said, and soon we were inside a structure that was in the running for the title of world's tallest building, an accolade that had recently created ferocious competition. Mainland China had briefly snatched the title with Jin Mao's neighbor, the just-finished Shanghai World Trade Center, only to have it taken away by the uppity island of Taiwan and then by that pushy upstart United Arab Emirates with its Burj Khalifa rising from a sea of oil money. But China will be back in the running with the completion of the futuristic Shanghai Tower, twisting like a dragon as it rises, its core curtained by a glass wall open at its apex. The tower's 128 stories will soar more than two thousand feet. Disagreements about whether rooftop antennas and spires should be included in a building's height are rife, as are arguments about whether buildings differ from towers and whether structures under construction should be included in the rankings. I had wearied of the my-building-is-bigger-than-your-building dispute and had given up my goal to thoroughly investigate and apply rigorous analysis to each country's claim to the world's tallest building. They were all tall, and impressive all of them. In 1931 when the Empire State Building was completed China had been too plagued by famine and war to worry about erecting tall towers; now it boasted two of the world's loftiest and had announced plans to raise many more. The skyline of Pudong is a mere beginning, harbinger of a future in which altitude-defying towers in China will be as common as tea.

I was delighted to learn during my exploration of Jin Mao that the Shanghai Grand Hyatt Hotel, located on the fifty-third to eighty-seventh floors, claimed the world's longest laundry chute. In faltering Chinese I asked a hotel employee if I could see said chute, and maybe even drop something down it.

"Perhaps we should not ask that," Jennifer said as she steered me away from the confused employee. We went back down to the basement and then learned of an observation deck: "a definite must-see" according to an American clad in a business suit, BlackBerry in hand, Bluetooth behind his ear. He stared at Jennifer as if undressing her with his eyes, slipping her into a sleek *qípáo,* and slowly undressing her again, while he explained to us that the building had been designed by structural engineers to withstand typhoon winds and earthquakes, and the swimming pool on one of the middle floors acted as a passive damper to absorb vibrations. I asked him if he'd read about that in a guidebook, and he gave me a look that said "guidebooks are for losers" as he pointed at his laptop and uttered one word: *Wikipedia.*

An elevator with a speed of nearly thirty feet per second slingshot us up to the sightseeing deck, perched on the eighty-eighth floor. The building had been designed around the number eight, an auspicious digit in this country. The Olympic Games in Beijing had, of course, begun at eight minutes past eight o'clock on the eighth day of the eighth month of the eighth year of the millennium. The lowest portion of Jin Mao was sixteen stories high and each succeeding section was 1/8th smaller than the one below it.

The observation deck offered vertigo-inducing views of the city. I explained the word *vertigo* to Jennifer; she had me write it down in her notebook. We each kept a notebook and pen handy to record new words, though my pages had remained clean and white throughout the night while several of Jennifer's were already crammed full of neatly printed words with diacritical clues to pronunciation and the definitions I'd offered. She'd been a top student at her high school and had studied diligently for the insanely competitive *gāokǎo*, China's National College Entrance Examination. I had gone to college because I'd had nothing better to do.

After gawking at the cityscape from on high, we made our way to a bar on the fifty-sixth floor and bought drinks for the cost of dinner and a bottle of *báijiǔ* in other Chinese cities, which is also roughly the amount a Chinese laborer makes in a week. The experience was worth the bloated prices, though, because above the bar was an open circular space that extended ever upward and ended in diaphanous light. It seemed Jennifer and I were standing at the bottom of some boundless well gazing toward an aperture in the heavens above.

"The Great Well of China," I said to Jennifer. She asked me to define *well*, and then she wrote the word in her notebook. I said, "Great Well of China" in Chinese to the Chinese bartender, who tipped his head to the side and slowly poured my drink while staring at me as though I were painted green.

"Perhaps he doesn't understand," said Jennifer.

When we finished our drinks, we lingered to look up at tiny people leaning over the railings of the atrium that rose some thirty-three floors, and watched them watching us. Camera flashes fired in the upper reaches, the bursts of brightness small against so much luminosity, so much dizzying space. I wondered if there was a single sight in Shanghai that was not absurdly tall or filled with brilliant light.

As we walked outside, I turned my face to the sky and thought of the Chinese word for faith. The word is built of two characters: *yǎng*, meaning "to look up," and *xìn*, meaning "to believe." Faith: to turn one's face skyward and believe. Beautiful, whether one believes in faith or not.

Perhaps no view in Shanghai is more arresting than this one, looking down into the atrium of the Jin Mao Tower.

My eyes felt as though they were bleeding. I blinked back pollution tears and studied the Jin Mao's latticework. Made of aluminum alloy pipes, the shiny cladding gives the tower a silvery sheen. The pagoda-inspired structure tapers upward in successively smaller tiers, its many flaring eaves more Gothic than Chinese. East meets West. I wondered aloud if *gothic-pagoda* was a style of architecture and decided it most likely was not. Jennifer wrote down *gothic* next to *vertigo* in her notebook.

And speaking of vertigo, the Jin Mao had been scaled by the real Spiderman, French urban climber Alain Robert. I had watched the gravity-mocking escapade on YouTube and felt a sickening jolt of vicarious vertigo. *Vicarious* was duly logged in Jennifer's notebook as I described the superhuman feat.

In 2001, Robert had made his first attempt to climb Jin Mao, but Shanghai authorities put a stop to his fun by denying his official request. Shortly thereafter, a Chinese shoe salesman dressed in street clothes and acting on a whim successfully ascended the building, plunging a razor-sharp bamboo shaft through Robert's ego. Authorities halted Robert's second attempt as well. The third time, in 2007, he went for it sans permission. Also sans ropes, anchors, safety gear— he didn't even wear gloves. During this carefully stage-managed assault, eager onlookers crowded around the tower's base, and Robert, sporting a Spidey suit, climbed to the eighty-eighth floor and returned to the ground in ninety minutes. He was promptly detained by members of Shanghai's police force, who jailed him for five days and then booted him out of China. "I've scaled the three tallest buildings in the world, so I reckoned I should also climb the fourth-tallest building," said Robert. "It's like there's something missing." Something missing, indeed. That part of the brain that says, "This is a bad idea. A really bad idea."

And speaking of bad ideas: During the Chinese National Day Holiday in October of 2004, a group of BASE jumpers was officially invited by the Shanghai Sports Bureau to leap from Jin Mao. Rumor has it the bureau had compared the sensation of BASE jumping to the free-falling thrill of Shanghai hurtling itself with ever-increasing speed toward the future. The jumpers hurled themselves from the top of the tower. The parachute of "Slim" Simpson, an Australian jumper, failed to deploy properly and he crash-landed on a nearby building, crushing his skull. He later died from his injuries. (This accident is in no way symbolic of Shanghai's reckless plunge into the future.)

I'd been told by the American who'd clued Jennifer and me in about the observation deck that Jin Mao officially contains the world's highest hotel rooms, and is officially, he insisted, the world's tallest building with a hotel inside. Who keeps track of these things? Or, more important, who takes them seriously, I thought derisively—while at the same time committing these factoids to memory and realizing to my chagrin that I would someday utter them in public and would most certainly be stared at with derision. And this: The Jin Mao Tower boasted the world's highest post office. I made a mental note to send a postcard to my wife from said post office as Jennifer and I headed toward Pudong's latest supertall scraper of the sky: the Shanghai World Financial Center.

Jin Mao lost its status as mainland China's tallest building when the Shanghai World Financial Center was topped off at 1,614 feet in September of 2007. Financed by a Japanese firm, the 101-story tower had originally been slated for construction in 1997, but plans were interrupted by the Asian financial crisis of the 1990s and design changes. The tower is as smooth and shiny as a knife blade, but its most striking feature is a trapezoidal hole at the top. This wind-pressure-relieving aperture was originally meant to be a circular "moon gate," but citizens of Shanghai, including the city's mayor, protested the design, arguing it was too similar to the rising sun of the Japanese flag. Architects settled on a trapezoid-shaped hole to puncture the top of the tower and allow the wind to pour through.

The towers of Pudong force you to tilt your face skyward.

An observation deck being built on the one hundredth floor, I had been assured by the American connoisseur of building-height rankings, would be the world's highest public observation platform. When finished, the tower would have seventy floors of office space for twelve thousand people, and would house a hotel even higher than the one in Jin Mao (no word yet on the length of its laundry chute), as well as restaurants, conference centers and shopping malls. A city inside a tower in a city of towers.

In 1978, China's supreme leader Deng Xiaoping, at the 11th Party Congress meeting of the Central Committee, introduced his policies of openness and reform that marked the beginning of China's rise. Part of Deng's strategy involved establishing Special Economic Zones (SEZs) where market reforms could be tested. Shanghai was not initially given SEZ status. It sat out the first round of growth because it was deemed too important a city to be a subject of economic experimentation. In the early 1980s, 70-80 percent of China's total tax revenue came from the municipality of Shanghai, and the city's enormous tax burden stymied its growth, according to China specialist Anna Greenspan in an Asia Times Online article titled "Shanghai, The Becoming Thing."

In the early 1990s, China's central government, led by the "Shanghai clique"—as the Party members from Shanghai advocating its development into an economic hub came to be known—began reducing the tax burden on the city and vigorously encouraging investment, both domestic and foreign. With its enormous potential unleashed, Shanghai's economy boomed, and towers rose like generously watered weeds. On a trip to Pudong in 1992, Deng told local officials, "Waste no time. Do not waver until the development of Pudong is complete." Pudong was granted SEZ status, and the showpiece district metastasized as more than six thousand foreign-funded businesses set up shop along its swelling streets. Deng's words are now on a monument across from the Jin Mao Tower.

There is no monument to free-market economist Milton Friedman in Pudong. Denounced by the late Nobel laureate as a "statist monument for a dead pharaoh," Pudong, like most of Shanghai, was financed with government money and built according to a government plan. The plan, essentially, was this: build big, fast, and high; light up the sky, and they will come. If China had juries, one of them would still be out on whether this massive gamble with public money has paid off. Many of the city's megaprojects cost far more than the revenue they will ever generate, but this doesn't dampen the enthusiasm of the government officials who give them the go-ahead.

I pointed at the Shanghai World Financial Center and said to Jennifer, "I wonder if building something like this, something so ridiculously big, makes financial sense." And then I wondered privately if it made sense for an American to question the sanity of building ridiculously big things.

"How much it costs isn't important," Jennifer said. "That isn't the . . . " She patted the air in front of her and said *point* before I could offer any help. "Tallest building, longest bridge, fastest train—these are face projects."

"Face projects?" I said.

"You know about face in China? What that means—you know?"

I did. Face is an essential part of Chinese culture that cannot be easily explained because no exact equivalent exists in English. To substitute words such as *reputation, honor* or *prestige* for *face* would not be entirely wrong, nor would these simple substitutions be entirely correct. Face causes endless confusion for Westerners when they first stumble into China, especially if they end up working with Chinese. To address a Chinese colleague's mistake without making him lose face is as easy as standing on a greased beach ball while rubbing one's belly and reciting the "Star-Spangled Banner." Backwards. Try it if you dare, for causing someone to lose face can ruin business deals and destroy friendships, abruptly toppling what you have worked so hard to build. I've done my share of toppling by acting like an American who translates *face* as *reputation* and doesn't see that they are almost the same, but altogether different.

Face is at the center of the cultural divide between the West and China, a divide that sometimes seems to me a chasm, at other times a fracture fine as hair. Admitting a mistake or apologizing causes one to lose face, and a reluctance to own up to errors infuses every facet of Chinese culture, from business transactions to the way the nation's leaders comport themselves when interacting with their citizens and with the outside world. Many American business students have complained to me that the concept of face is simply too foreign. How can they be expected to do business in a country led by people who never admit fault or say they're sorry for the damage they've done?

I never pass up an opportunity to discuss face with a Chinese friend, as each time I understand the concept a bit better and can perhaps avoid causing offence in the future. "Can you give me an example of someone losing face?" I asked Jennifer, expecting her to tell me about a business deal.

"Okay." There was a lot of lip chewing, a bit of hair blowing, and then she said, "In an episode of *Friends*, Chandler and Monica were invited to dinner by Chandler's boss. At dinner, Chandler laughed really loud at his boss's jokes even though they weren't funny. Monica thought this was weird and asked Chandler why. He said because the man was his boss, he wanted to flatter him. So the next time his boss told a bad joke, Monica laughed really loud too."

"So Chandler and Monica *gěi* Chandler's boss *miànzi*?"

"Right. They gave Chandler's boss face."

"But if the boss knew they were faking their laughs? Then they would be *pāi mǎpì*—patting the horse's ass?"

Jennifer formed her hands into little fists of triumph and shook them in the air. "Yes, you understand!"

I don't know if I understood face any more than I had before, but I certainly was beginning to look at *Friends* in a different light.

"I thought of another one," said Jennifer after we'd walked for a few minutes around the base of the tower. "In another episode of *Friends*, Rachel and Phoebe took a literature class together. One day the instructor asked Rachel what the book they were asked to read was about. Rachel didn't read the book, so she didn't know what to say. So she stole Phoebe's idea, which she had told her before class. Then the teacher asked Phoebe what was her opinion. Phoebe didn't know what to say. The whole class looked at her, waiting for her to talk, but she just mumbled something that didn't make any sense."

"So Phoebe *diūliǎn*?" I asked.

"Yes, Phoebe lost face."

"Why is the word for *face* when you say *lose face* different from the word for *face* when you say *give face*? I've never understood that."

Jennifer was silent a moment and then shook her head. "I can't explain it so you can understand. It is too hard for you to understand because you are a foreigner."

"Even *Friends* can't help us across this cultural impasse?"

"What is an impasse?"

"What we have arrived at just now."

"I don't understand."

Of course she didn't. And I didn't feel like simplifying my speech patterns and removing the GRE words from my vocabulary. For a moment I longed to be in the company of someone to whom I could say *impasse* without defining it. And Jennifer's tone (when speaking English, not her Chinese tones) told me her patience with my incessant questions had a limit to which I had strayed perilously close. Altering one's tone of voice to express emotion while maintaining the separate clarity of Mandarin's four tones (five if you count neutral as a tone) can give one a headache that even a latte with a fat dose of caffeine can't cure. My head was ringing and I was as tired of speaking Chinese as I'd ever been. All around us towers slanted upward, with windows like countless eyes empty and gleaming as they gazed into the night. Pudong suddenly seemed to me not a technicolor dream of hope but a bright nightmare.

We walked a few minutes in strained silence; then I remembered my favorite Mandarin sentence, grinned, and said to Jennifer: "*Wǒ shuō Zhōngwén de shíhou wǒ tóu dà.*" When I speak Chinese, I get a headache.

Jennifer smiled and pointed up at the Shanghai World Financial Center, all that shiny steel reflecting the lights of Pudong like the world's largest mirror. She said, "China wants face. These projects, they give China—"

"Mad face," I said, and then spent several minutes explaining the slang intensifier *mad* and how she should learn it because it was supposed to be cool, but if I had caught on and was using it then it was almost certainly past its prime and most likely highly uncool. I was having fun again and Jennifer was laughing.

Welcome to the future. A future of bizarrely conceived architecture covered in kooky lights.

We left the Shanghai World Financial Center and finally made our way to the OPTV Tower, the architectural wonder bedecked with silver and pink baubles, flashing lights in patterns that shifted so quickly and chaotically I thought they might cause seizures. The world's largest rave lightshow. If Shanghai has an official song, surely it is some sort of throbbing techno beat.

"Well," I said, standing beneath the legs that radiated outward from the tower like appendages on a lunar landing module sixty stories tall. "Well," I said again. I wasn't sure what else to say. The spheres surrounding the tower's central pillar appeared to have been speared, as though the pillar were a swizzle stick and the spheres olives. Olives painted iridescent pink and covered in giant Christmas lights. The sheer insanity of the structure killed my buzz. My enthusiasm waned for a brief and sobering moment; then I stared into the flashing multicolored lights and let them dance my brain cells around and soon I was raving again along with the rest of the city. Who among us can look at pretty flashing lights and not feel good? Every day here is bright with Christmas lights. What's not to like?

"Let's go," I said to Jennifer as I forced myself to look away from the lights. "Let's see what this thing looks like from inside."

What I remember most from inside the Oriental Pearl TV Tower is not the Space Module at its top, nor the wholly ridiculous Space City display in its lower sphere. What I remember most vividly is the elevator operator who narrated something while we were being lifted up the central pillar toward an observation sphere. The reason I cannot remember the substance of her narration is her face. To say she looked bored is to stretch the word *bored* until it means "completely devoid of life; appearing utterly and completely dead." She was either the least enthusiastic person on planet Earth or in desperate need of a reduction in the dose of whatever her prescription-happy doctor was medicating her with. I was transfixed by the creepy blankness of her face as she rattled off something about the speed of the elevator in a monotone that would have put my high school geometry teacher to sleep. I was mesmerized, if not a bit unnerved by the whole thing, when the elevator finally came to a smooth stop and the doors slid open.

"I want to touch her," I said to Jennifer.

"Why?" Jennifer asked, looking surprisingly unworried.

"I want to make sure she's real."

"Perhaps you should probably not touch her."

"Okay," I said as we left the lift. But at the last second I reached back inside to stop the doors from closing. Then I leaned in and said to the operator in Chinese, "You speak excellent Chinese." In the past this had resulted in a laugh, if not chortles of laughter—or at the very least a confused look followed by a smile. Right now it earned me nothing. Not a smile, not a scathing look. Nothing.

"God, that was weird," I said to Jennifer as I followed her away from the robot in the elevator. "That was the most vacant look I've ever seen on another human being's face."

I would see many more looks like this as my days in Shanghai accumulated and more towers rose to slash the sky.

Staring out from the windows in the sphere atop the OPTV Tower at the liquid dance of lights across the city, I exhausted my storehouse of Chinese words that mean beautiful. *Hǎokàn, piàoliang, hěn měi.* Okay, so it wasn't a very big storehouse, but the sight inspired me to learn new ways to describe the sublime. It was the size of the place, the scale of it, the relentless headlong tumble of the accumulated human energy, twenty million plus people pulling together to grow a metropolis from farmland and swamp. The tower I was witnessing this from was certifiably ugly, the pollution that cloaked the city in a perpetual stench was unquestionably foul, the human density of the urban madhouse was undeniably nerve-wracking, but through it all coursed an energy that was nothing less than magnificent. There were cities, and there was Shanghai. Gazing out at this spectacle from the OPTV Tower, it seemed less like a city and more like a crazy collective psychedelic trip into a future pulsing with light. Lights dripped and blended and morphed like plasma, sending bursts so bright into the night they erased the stars from the sky.

I circled around the observation platform, and for a few unsettling moments as I gaped at the view, felt totally disoriented, though all the buildings I saw seemed oddly familiar. This would happen to me many times in the coming months. I would find myself wandering around Shanghai in an area that was new and strange, yet I would feel I had been there before. This was because I had already seen the spires and towers and domes that surrounded me. I had seen them when I'd read H. G. Wells stories, when I'd watched *Star Trek* movies, in *Jetsons* cartoons, in video games, and in the Legos and Erector Sets and Tinkertoys I had played with as a boy.

Shanghai was at first a blast, but after the initial cheap rush wore off I came to believe this: it is a city of allusions to things we have already seen, whether in the real world we've constructed, or in the many futures we've imagined. We look to it to glimpse the future, but what we see are merely our dreams, lonely dreams of towers in the sky, made real in glass and steel. Shanghai is not so much a trip into the future as it is a flashback. There is nothing new in Shanghai.

In the basement of the nuttiest tower on the planet, Jennifer and I discovered, to my complete astonishment, a trove of black-and-white photographs in the compelling and tastefully designed Shanghai Municipal History Museum. Exhibits were based around exquisitely detailed miniature dioramas and strikingly realistic life-size wax figures in bars, brothels and banks. Both of these formats recreated the Shanghai that arose after China came out on the losing end of the Opium Wars.

"Face," I said aloud when I finished studying an exhibit of wax figures in which a British gentleman in a clean suit was being hauled in a rickshaw by a Chinese man in rags, who seemed about to collapse beneath his burden. Chinese people lay destitute in the street, writhing in the muck through which the struggling coolie pulled the pristine rickshaw. Face, I thought. China had lost face on a monumental scale during the Opium Wars and their aftermath. To understand why

Shanghai viewed at night from on high is a mind-altering experience.

China would go to such lengths to construct the Pudong skyline in less than two decades, it is necessary to travel into the past, back to the Opium Wars of the mid-nineteenth century.

To Americans, the period from 1839 to 1860 might seem like ancient history; to the Chinese, whose nation's past spans millennia, events in the 1800s might as well have happened yesterday. And those events have everything to do with what is happening today in Shanghai. In the early 1800s, Britain, hungry for China's tea, porcelain and silk, found itself on the low end of a massive trade imbalance. The frustrated empire hatched a plan, and in an act of narcotics criminality that makes crack dealers in inner cities look like saints, Britain began smuggling opium into China. Soon, millions of loyal customers were clamoring for more, and much to the delight of the British government, the dreaded trade gap narrowed. American merchants got in on the action, sending clipper ships loaded with opium from Turkey into China's ports. Many Americans, including the maternal grandfather of President Franklin Delano Roosevelt, made fortunes in the opium trade, the profits from which were reinvested in the United States, bolstering the nation's economy. Chinese leaders, watching silver disappear from their national coffers to pay for the drug and witnessing the human misery that addiction was spreading throughout their land, tried to put a stop to the opium trade. Britain responded with military might, and China, weak internally from a collapsing dynasty, was no match for the overwhelming force of Britain and her Western allies.

Perhaps the dream to build the towers of Pudong began when British gunboats first fired into China, forcing China to give the West what it wanted. At the close of the Opium Wars, China was strong-armed into signing treaties that ransacked its economy and devastated its pride. The cowed nation had been made to open the ports of Shanghai to please the imperial powers that had pulverized its defenses, and the British, along with the Americans and the French, were allowed to live in special zones in Shanghai beyond the rule of Chinese law. Shanghai's streets were crammed with bars and brothels that catered to the colonial marauders, along with Western banks that bulged with treasure extracted from the Chinese economy. Rudyard Kipling, while touring China in 1889, surveyed the cultural destruction and economic chaos caused by the Opium Wars. Assessing the spirit of a nation humiliated by the West, he wrote, "What will happen when China really wakes up . . . and really works and controls her own gun-factories and arsenals?" Before Kipling, Napoleon had weighed in on China's slumber, stating, "When China wakes, she will shake the world."

To say that China has awakened has become a cliché, so I say this: The only way it could possibly be more wide awake than it is now is if amphetamines were pumped into the nation's water supply. The China that the West once beat down is now rising. It is determined to never again be bullied. It has grown into a robust nation determined to raise metropolises from the ruins of colonialism, to build cities where once were swamps.

The wax figures and dioramas in the museum showed how Shanghai had been ground zero for the blows that had devastated the country's pride. Shanghai was the place where China had again and again lost face in front of the world. But now it boasted the world's fastest train, the planet's longest arch bridge. And in sight of the shores where British gunboats had once fired into an impotent nation, some of the world's tallest towers had been erected. Those towers stood stiff and tall like defiant middle fingers pointed out to sea, toward whatever threats would dare to visit a country that had vowed to never again be beaten down. To never again lose face. In a couple of years Shanghai would host one of the biggest face projects of them all: the 2010 World Expo. The world would come to Shanghai, and it would show the world that British gunboats blasting their way into its harbors was a thing of the past. The world would see China's new face. The world would see the towers of Pudong.

Of Narrow Lanes and Stone-Framed Doors

S everal weeks later we walked down a lane so skinny, when I spread my arms
my fingers rubbed brick walls on both sides. Above us power lines hung in
serpentine coils and crisscrossed the alley in random slants. Women leaned
from windows, chatting back and forth. Jennifer and I were in one of Shanghai's
traditional *shíkùmén* neighborhoods heading toward her parents' home.

In order to hold a World Expo, a city needs space for the venue, and infrastructure to support the event. Empty space was in short supply in Shanghai, so
city planners were knocking down old buildings to create new fairgrounds, and
infrastructure projects were underway throughout the city. Razing old structures
in order to raise new ones was nothing new in Shanghai, but Expo planning had
accelerated the process. Aside from being the largest World's Fair in history, The
2010 Expo boasted the distinction of being the first to be held in a developing
country.

Development was definitely in the air as Jennifer and I walked through a
checkerboard of lanes. Clouds of powder from smashed concrete sifted into my
nose and chalked my throat. I stopped to wipe my eyes. In a row of low-slung
houses lay an empty gap, like a mouth with a missing tooth. I walked closer to
investigate. Twisted grids of rebar and shattered slabs of brick slumped in smoking ruins. Demolition workers sporting red hardhats surveyed their work as they
rested their sledgehammers on their shoulders, and children climbed to the high-

est points of each miniature mountain of debris, scaling slopes of rubble, pushing each other back down as they scrambled to be the first to the summit. There was no construction tape marking the scene, no warning signs. No one seemed concerned about the children exploring this new urban wilderness.

"What happened?" I asked Jennifer.

"The people who lived there all accepted the money from the developer," she said. "So it was broken down."

"Knocked down," I said.

"Knocked down?"

"Demolished. Smashed."

"Smashed," she repeated.

Smashed: I repeated it too a few times and the word began to sound strange, as any word does when said again and again. "Smashed," I said, staring at the debris in front of me, dust settling on my skin. I leaned to rest on a broken wall bristling with bars of iron and heard a patter of small feet, the click of a rat's toenails against stone. Fat as a housecat, it ran across the ground and then ghosted through a crack, lizardy tail following the furred body into darkness.

"This one was smashed first," Jennifer said. "The rest of them will be smashed soon. When everyone agrees to the price, they will all be smashed."

"And if someone doesn't agree?" I asked.

"They have to agree."

"But if they don't?"

"The government needs this area for the Expo. It has to be empty so there can be grass and trees here."

"In America people protest destroying a park or historic buildings to make homes."

"There are too many people in China," Jennifer said. A common refrain: Throughout China you hear people say *Zhōngguó, rén tài duō le.* In China there are too many people.

"So there will be a park here?" I said.

"Perhaps there will be a new metro line, I think."

"The city needs a new subway here for the Expo?"

"I'm not clear what will be here. Maybe a park, maybe a metro. Maybe both. Someone said it would be a parking lot. There are so many rumors."

"So where will these people go after their buildings are torn down?" I asked.

"They will go to new buildings. Bigger buildings."

"*Mótiān dàlóu?*" Jennifer had taught me earlier that day the Chinese word for skyscraper.

"Yes," she said, smiling. "They will live in buildings that touch the sky."

And then she taught me a new phrase, one that could very well be the motto of Shanghai: *jiùchéng gǎizào.* Transforming an old city into a new one.

In the far distance beyond the narrow lanes, towers stood in serried rows like headstones in a cemetery. We left the remains of the smashed homes, our clothes dusty with their demolition, and tread a tight path between row houses that looked distinctly Western. No roofs with curving eaves graced their tops, no dragons soared above their doors. The stone lintels of the entryways were carved with flowers, birds and vines. The buildings looked more like nineteenth-century tenements in London than like Chinese domiciles.

From the 1850s to the 1940s, masses of Chinese had fled the chaos that reigned in the Chinese portions of Shanghai and flooded into the areas of the city controlled by Western powers. In order to accommodate them, thousands upon thousands of these Western-style residences had been built in mazes of intersecting lanes. This type of house is known as *shíkùmén.* The term is composed of three characters: 石库门. The first character means "stone," the second "storehouse," the third "door." Westerners refer to the shikumen as "stone-framed door" homes.

In the backstreets where we walked, stone archways held burly wooden planks that looked thick enough to withstand a battering ram, and each door was fixed with a big bronze ring. Impressive doors aside, in a city where on a rare clear day you can look out from the top of a tower in all directions and see tall buildings as far as the earth's curvature allows, the shikumen seem by comparison small and unimportant. They are often enclosed by a ring of shops that buffers them from Shanghai's bustling streets, and the stone entranceways to narrow lanes that connect the shikumen lie hidden between storefronts. When you do stumble upon these lane houses in your wanderings, the modest structures of gray brick are hard to notice against a backdrop of elevated freeways and high-rise tower blocks bathed in neon. The shikumen rise to two stories, three at the most, and have no neon. Many of them have no plumbing, and some even lack electricity. Each residence is part of a row and connected to its neighbors, much like townhouses in the West. What makes them unique are their elegant courtyards guarded by brick walls.

Whereas the row house style was a nod to the West, traditional Chinese architecture received its due in the enclosed courtyards, which have been integral to Chinese homes through the ages. Courtyard homes, known as *sìhéyuàn*, have been the dwellings of choice throughout Chinese history. Because Shanghai's shikumen were built to house people in a densely populated urban setting, their courtyards were small by comparison to their Chinese historical precedents— but they were courtyards nonetheless, providing a safe haven from the clatter and push of the streets outside. Shikumen dwellers could retreat behind their sheltering walls of sturdy brick to relax with their families amid the serenity. Rain splashed onto the uncovered patios to grow trees that branched their way toward the light, while fresh air and sunshine poured into these pleasing spaces, wafting through windows into the homes.

The courtyards served as buffers, both social and physical, from the outside world. During the mid-1800s, the walls of shikumen served literally as fortified defenses when rebels, bandits and thugs roamed the streets. In 1853 a secret society known as the Small Swords tried to take over the Chinese-controlled portions of the city, leading to warfare in Shanghai and its surrounds. Chinese fled to the relative safety of the foreign settlements, creating a bonanza for real estate developers who raised compounds of shikumen to rent to desperate refugees. An uprising led by a Chinese Christian convert, who claimed he was the younger brother of Jesus Christ and who aimed to abolish the Qing dynasty imperial government, spread civil war throughout southern China in the Taiping Rebellion. With a death toll of twenty to thirty million, the so-called Rebellion of Great Peace ranks as one of the bloodiest wars in world history. And this civil war was just one episode in a prolonged period of turbulence that sent people from all over southern China scurrying into the sections of Shanghai controlled by the British, the Americans and the French. These self-governing enclaves were insulated from the mayhem consuming China by their armies and police, and their streets were stacked with shikumen. The thick wooden doors framed by heavy stone gateways gave residents a sense of security. The lovely lintels with baroque carvings above the doors and the shiny bronze knockers provided them with a sense of status, and the common walls and tightly clustered alleys offered them a feeling of belonging, a sense of community.

Fleeing the Japanese army that stormed Shanghai in 1937, more Chinese piled into the foreign quarters of the city, which the Japanese neither invaded nor bombed. By World War II, more than three quarters of Shanghai's residents lived in shikumen, and the surrounding alleyways were busy with cobblers, barbers and convenience stores. Hawkers walked the narrow lanes selling everything from rice to roasted ginkgo nuts, and tinkers traveled door to door mending and

In the past, more than three quarters of Shanghai's population lived in row houses
with stone-framed doors. These *shíkùmén* have all but vanished.

repairing. The lanes were the heart of the city, each narrow artery filled with
coursing life.

Some of the shikumen had been sketchily built by dubious developers and
were little more than slums. Others were designed of more sturdy construction
for wealthy families, and British row house met Yangtze River Delta courtyard
home in a handsome fusion of East and West. In the wake of Word War II, peasants swarmed the city looking for work. A massive swelling of Shanghai's population and a citywide housing crisis resulted, and many shikumen, if they hadn't
already been subdivided and sublet during previous waves of population influx,
were modified to accommodate multiple families. When the Communists took
power, they furthered this trend, forcing affluent owners to turn their residences,
however elegant their architecture, however fine their French doors and Victorian
furniture, into cramped tenements for laborers. Large rooms were sectioned into
several smaller rooms, each housing a separate family, and all of them sharing a
communal kitchen. Indoor toilets were not the rule, and wooden chamber pots
were still in use in many of Shanghai's remaining shikumen.

When we reached her parents' home, I breathed deeply with relief as Jennifer
pointed me toward a bathroom that boasted a toilet. But breathing deeply proved

a bad idea, as the stench made my stomach heave and my eyes go watery. The toilet was a squatter: no stool to sit on, no lid to lift, just a hole in the floor that held a porcelain bowl with a rim where one could place one's feet and stand or squat down—depending, of course, upon one's gender and the business at hand. But the toilet did flush. Well, in theory it flushed. A sick trickle of water issued weakly from a corroded spout when I pushed a button on the tank. I pushed again, pushed a few more times, and a thin wash of water sloshed sadly in the bowl and then dropped down into the lightless depths below. No cleansing swirl, no satisfying suction. One must leave the precise and efficient toilets of one's own developed country behind and survey the myriad ways the developing world deals with human waste to truly appreciate the chrome and copper conduits, the plastic passageways, the matrix of mains and branches of the piping inside our homes that constitute the miracle of modern plumbing. Beneath every city on earth swirls a river of shit, but in the West this unhappy fact is flushed from our minds each time we pull the lever. In China—even in Shanghai, the nation's most developed city—images of endless streams of human waste surging through the subterranean world below the streets, bubbling up through clogged sewers and spewing through broken pipes, can haunt one's waking moments and surface in one's dreams.

As I left the bathroom and returned to the place where Jennifer's parents sat on a sofa smiling at me, I wondered if the people advocating the preservation of the shikumen for their historic and cultural value had set foot in one of their bathrooms. There was history here, to be sure; there were also foul smells and living conditions so cramped they made the cages of lab rats seem palatial by comparison. And the alleyways were fun to explore, but don't even think about fitting a fire truck in one. This is precisely where a grand and noble ideal—saving a vanishing portion of a city's past—slams up against reality. Poverty is not pretty, however deep its historical roots, and endeavoring to preserve structures with inadequate plumbing and unhealthy living conditions raises some uncomfortable moral questions. What is good for the culture of a people might not be good for some of the people in that culture.

We were all wearing slippers and our empty shoes lay paired by the door. Next to Jennifer's pumps and my running shoes were her parents' identical black canvas footwear with rubber toecaps and rubber rands around the heels, a few eyelets holding short and simple laces. Jennifer's mother wore her hair carried up in combs of jade with a few loose strands cascading down her cheeks. Elegant coiffure and the plain shoes of the proletariat.

I wandered my eyes across the jumbled room. A bed was crammed next to a table, where people I hadn't been introduced to perched on tiny rectangular stools playing mahjong. They sat halfway in a makeshift kitchen stuffed with piles of newspapers and stacks of clothing, among a riot of pots and pans. Atop a hotplate a teapot shivered and sang, steam issuing from its spout. I could feel the humidity of it on the other side of the room, so small was the space. The place was not messy—quite the opposite. It was extraordinarily clean, far cleaner than my town-house in Boulder. There was no dirt or dust, and each bare piece of flooring and furniture shined as if recently polished. Everything was tidy, but there was just so much of everything that it all bumped together; and people, when they moved around the room, also bumped together. Elbows were constantly poking torsos, toes were forever stepping on toes. Did the residents of the shikumen want to continue living like this? Did they want to stay here?

"Do you want to stay here?" I asked Jennifer's mother, a woman even smaller than Jennifer. She showed me the same smile Jennifer had the first time we'd met. Equal parts nervous shyness and friendly gesture, and as genuine as any smile I had seen. I had never been a big hugger, but something about the way Jennifer and her mother smiled made me want to hug them and squeeze them, to some-how get closer to the warmth that came from them in their smiles, to hold that warmth and shore it up against the cold stares and glacial smiles I knew would greet me in the city streets beyond this little lane.

Jennifer's mom shook her head when I spoke and looked at Jennifer. No sur-prise there: I was used to Chinese people not understanding my rudimentary Mandarin. I began to repeat the question, paying careful attention to my tones until Jennifer informed me that her mother didn't speak Mandarin, only the local dialect, Shanghainese. Ditto her father. He nodded to me when I glanced his way and we exchanged smiles; then he handed me a cup of steamy tea, curled loose leaves unfurling in the water. I nodded my thanks. How easy it is to express grat-itude without words, and the same with fear and anger. But to get answers to my questions, Jennifer had to translate.

"We don't want to leave," Jennifer's mom said. Her husband sat nodding in agreement as he blew into his tea and listened to his wife talk. What hair he had left was cropped close to his balding crown and his face was round and friendly. I smiled at him and again he nodded and smiled back. "Both of our parents lived in this neighborhood and this is where we have always lived," he said to me through his daughter. "This is our home."

China's Communist Party (*gòng chǎn dǎng*) literally means "public property party." Nevertheless, in 2007 the right to own private property had been written into the Constitution of the People's Republic of China. Designed to prevent rampant property seizures and to move China away from collective ownership of assets, the legislation had been fiercely debated, many in the Chinese government arguing that the protections would irrevocably erode the nation's socialist principles.

Most families living in shikumen, Jennifer's included, owned the usage rights to their homes, but they didn't own the actual homes, which were still controlled by government-run work units or government housing administrations. And in China the state still owned all the land: One could purchase a long-term land-use lease, but the land itself that one's property stood on could not be bought or sold. And when the government decided one's house stood in the way of progress—a superhighway or a shopping mall, World Expo fairgrounds or a subway line—it would fall, regardless of whether one owned property rights or usage rights. Despite the new legislation, the system of selecting dwellings for destruction and rebuilding on the land they occupied still involved a byzantine network of government officials in cahoots with private demolition companies and private development corporations, these parties operating in a manner that was positively opaque. China was passing private property laws, which was a good thing, but it lacked the independent judiciary and free press necessary to ensure that the laws were implemented correctly and transparently—which was, if you held the usage rights to a shikumen in Shanghai with the wrecking ball swinging outside, a bad thing.

Plastic mahjong pieces clacked together with staccato sound. I glanced at two women playing solemnly, heads tilted toward their task as they ticked and reshuffled their tiles. The holler and screech of children playing outside lifted up from the alley and entered open windows of the home. Against one wall of the room stood an enormous bureau of such sturdy construction and ornate design I imagined it had been brought on a steamer from Victorian-era London to Shanghai. Atop this handsome piece of teak sat a TV that was switched on, its programs providing background noise, people paying scant attention to the pictures flickering on the screen.

"We went to court," Jennifer said. "The court said we had to leave."

I asked if they'd had a lawyer.

They had. But he had been appointed by the government.

"Did the lawyer try to help you?" I asked.

There was discussion back and forth between Jennifer and her parents. "He did not really help us."

"Will you try again?"

"After these things are decided, they cannot be changed. They are final."

"But you can go to court and argue your case?"

"Yes, you can argue."

"Does the government put people in jail for arguing?" I asked Jennifer.

I knew full well they did. More famous than the shikumen neighborhoods of Shanghai were their counterparts in Beijing, the *hútòng*. Beijing's traditional residences were, like shikumen, based around courtyards and joined together in narrow alleys. Beijing's hutong had received a lot of press recently because of the orgy of construction that was a buildup to the Olympics. Old hutong throughout Beijing had been leveled to make way for the new tower blocks and commercial development that showed the world while it was watching the Olympics that China was now a prosperous and advanced nation. Its capital city boasted broad avenues lined with high-rise buildings of steel and glass—not ancient narrow alleyways with low courtyard dwellings that had remained essentially the same since they were built many hundreds of years ago during China's dynastic past.

Some of the hutong residents were not happy with this urban makeover and had demanded to stay in their homes. A few evictees had been so distraught they'd committed suicide to highlight their cause: one man had lit himself on fire, another had jumped from a bridge. Others had taken their fight into the courts of Beijing. The government was becoming more sympathetic to their plight, though it rarely allowed the protesters to win their cases against corrupt officials who condemned their homes and lawless developers who demolished them. According to Amnesty International, a Beijinger named Ye Guozhu had been convicted of "picking quarrels and stirring up trouble" and sentenced to four years in prison for peacefully protesting the razing of his family's home and restaurant. The case had made headline news around the world, though hundreds of thousands of people were being forcibly evicted from their homes throughout the country, and in all likelihood there were many Ye Guozhus shackled in prisons all over China.

"Usually people are not put in the jail for complaining," Jennifer said. "But sometimes, if they argue too much, they can go to the jail."

"On what charge?" I asked, before realizing the meaninglessness of my question. Of course the charge didn't matter. Though Shanghai boasted many of the accoutrements of modern Western life, it was still part of the Chinese authoritarian state. The Shanghainese drove Volkswagens and carried Prada handbags and wore Italian shoes; they ate at McDonald's and watched James Bond gun down villains and bed international beauties. But the progress that had granted people the freedom to purchase and sell consumer goods and see Hollywood movies had not gone hand in hand with the freedom to stay in one's home when it stood in the path of progress. Of course, in the West we have our own laws of eminent domain, and when someone's house is blocking an interstate highway expansion program, that house will fall, regardless of how many generations have lived there, regardless of the skills and lack of bias of the lawyer retained to try the case. People cannot stand in the way of progress anywhere in the world, though in the West those who are pushed aside by the greater good are generally compensated handsomely.

"The government offered you a new apartment?" I asked.

"At first they offered us money," Jennifer's mother explained. "But the government can set the price, and the price was not fair to us. After we went to court they offered us a new apartment. But we don't want a new apartment. We want to stay here, in our home."

That there were courts in place in Shanghai providing an opportunity for people to air their grievances was no small thing. However glaringly imperfect the system was, allowing the family a means to make their case seemed a step forward. A small step, certainly, but twenty years ago one would have been immediately locked up and prodded with electric batons or worse just for disagreeing with the government. My initial burst of optimism for China's progress toward reform, fairness and openness was smothered beneath a heavy cloud of cynicism, however, as I thought about what Jennifer had just said: people were jailed if they complained too much. In contemporary Shanghai one could complain—just not too loudly.

"Will you keep resisting?" I asked.

"What is *resisting*?" Jennifer asked.

"Fighting. Not giving up."

Now Jennifer's father spoke and her mother fell silent. "They have said we can go to court again. We will tell them we don't want to leave."

"And if you have to leave?"

"We will ask for what is fair. Enough money so we can buy a good apartment. One that is worth as much as our home. Most people who live in shikumen have to share bathrooms and kitchens. We are very lucky because we have a bathroom and a kitchen. So our home must be very valuable."

"You'll be happy if the compensation is fair?" I asked, glancing at the kitchen that seemed like something jury rigged in a college dorm room. A rubber hose snaked through a window and into a plastic bucket that formed a basin with no drain. A large wok hid the little hot plate beneath it.

"We won't be happy to leave here, but if the compensation is fair we will feel okay. We will not feel cheated. It is not good to feel cheated."

Through two small windows on a west-facing wall slats of afternoon light entered the darkening room. Jennifer spoke with her father for a few minutes and then explained to me that it was difficult for him to communicate with government officials and the development company because he didn't speak *pŭtōnghuà*, literally "common speech," known in the West as Mandarin. The Chinese government, in an effort to make Mandarin the official language of China, had tried to silence the cacophony of tongues across the nation's vast geography. Shanghainese had been banned in schools, and the local media had been encouraged to broadcast in Mandarin. Jennifer's generation had learned Mandarin in school and they used it, along with English, in the workplace. But her parents, whose native language was as different from Mandarin as French is from German, could understand some Mandarin but couldn't speak it fluently, which put them at a distinct disadvantage when airing their grievances to government officials who either couldn't, or wouldn't, converse with them in Shanghainese.

Someone flipped a switch and a bare bulb dangling from the ceiling glowed to life within the murk. The space was small, the bathroom stank. Why fight to stay here?

"Why is it so good to live here?" I asked. "Why not move to a new apartment?"

Jennifer spoke with her father a moment and then said to me, "He says *wulixiang* is a word you should learn. It is the Shanghainese word for *home*."

Jennifer's mom suggested we go outside to enjoy the cool breezes.

We passed down a flight of steep and rickety stairs, each board creaking in the dark hallway as we descended. Outside we crossed a courtyard, sprouts of grass growing between the bricks of the floor, the walls pleasant with hanging flowers. From pots arranged in neat rows grew onions, garlic and chives. We walked be-

Many residents of shikumen have lived in lane neighborhoods all their lives. Relocating in tower blocks can be a jarring experience. Some welcome the change in lifestyle; some do not.

neath the archway of the shikumen, its stonework carved in elaborate scrollwork that would not have looked out of place on a Parisian cathedral, and then we passed into an alleyway bustling with bikes and people. One motor scooter zigzagged past us, horn screaming. Rain had pelted the city while we'd been inside. The streets gleamed like platinum in the new sun and puddles steamed in the heat.

A wrinkle-faced woman with bright eyes greeted us immediately, as though she'd been standing there waiting for us to enter the alley. Old Wang, she was called. Old Wang chattered at Jennifer's mom and Jennifer's mom chattered back, and it seemed the two women were jumping back into a conversation they'd been having all day. They had, in fact, Jennifer explained to me, been having a conversation all their lives. They had both grown up here and had spent their childhoods and their adult years talking with each other every day.

"*Nǐhǎo*," I said to Old Wang, and in Mandarin I told her it was nice to meet her. She nodded and smiled, but that was about as far as her Mandarin went, and my Shanghainese went nowhere, so Jennifer translated. Or rather, she tried to translate, eventually giving up when she was unable to keep up with the flow of information. Old Wang told Jennifer's mom about a foreigner who had been lost in the alley that morning, having wandered away from a shopping district to take pictures, and there was a new restaurant around the corner where a block of buildings had recently been knocked down and rebuilt, and the price of fresh fish in the market had risen that day, and a baby stroller had been stolen from the Shen family but then was returned to their courtyard, so maybe it hadn't been stolen at all and had been a mistake, and on and on.

The smell of burning coal—I swiveled my head to sniff its source. A man stood hunched over a grill, black honeycombs of charcoal sending little clouds of smoke into the air as skewers of meat dripped fat in a hissing drizzle toward the flames. Women sat around a low table playing mahjong beneath a simmering sun, and cicadas chirred in the trees above. Mops hung from a balcony, water dripping from their frayed strands. To chipped and cracking walls clung advertising posters. I watched a corner of a poster peel away from the plaster and curl in the heat.

Eventually Old Wang turned her attention toward me, her eyes opening wide beneath the wrinkles of her face as she looked me up and down. When she asked who I was, Jennifer said I was her friend and was helping her learn English while she helped me learn Chinese.

Why had I come to China, Old Wang wanted to know.

I asked Jennifer to explain that I worked with a company that brought groups of American university students to China.

"Why?"

"They want to learn about China," I said.

"They like China?" Old Wang asked after offering me a chair that seemed suited for a hobbit. The tiny chair's backrest was carved with flowers and birds.

"Many of the groups are business students, and they don't really like anything except making money," I explained as I sat carefully in the little lap of the chair, afraid my weight would snap its legs in half. Old Wang sat down in another miniature chair. With a table between us that rose no more than two feet from the ground, we seemed giants in a storybook.

"The business students just want to learn about doing business here," I said, pausing to let Jennifer translate. "Some of the groups are engineering students. They want to learn about engineering projects like the Three Gorges Dam." I thought for a moment and then said, "Some of the people come because they are very rich and very bored and they don't know what else to do. Somebody told them they should come here, so they do, and I bring them."

Old Wang gave me a small nod, but she looked as though she wasn't quite sure yet what to make of me, this tall foreigner who'd wandered into her neighborhood with her best friend's daughter and was now sitting opposite her in a tiny chair.

Old Wang asked me if I liked Chinese food and I told her I most definitely did. She grinned a toothless grin and then led me down the alley. From a street vendor we bought one of my favorite foods: *jiānbǐng*. A crepe of lacy thinness is painted with egg and cooked on a sizzling griddle. Dab it with chili sauce, throw in some scallions and cilantro and a stick of crispy fried dough, fold it like a map or roll it up like a scroll, and there you have it: one of China's tastiest foods, and one you will not find on the menu alongside kung pao chicken at your local Panda Express. To say that Chinese food in America is different from Chinese food in China is to say that a Boeing 747 is not the same as a bar of soap. Chinese restaurants in America should be ashamed of themselves for using the word *Chinese* with the food they serve.

I ate my jianbing, pausing to smile at Old Wang, who nodded and smiled back, her mouth now full of teeth. She'd slipped her dentures in. She watched me closely, making sure, it seemed to me, that I was really enjoying the food and wasn't just pretending.

In America we tend to think of foods in terms of the protein, carbohydrates, vitamins, and other nutrients they contain; in China people often think of foods in terms of what they mean. Fish are served in one piece because a fish unbroken from head to tail indicates wholeness, a beginning and end. (More disturbing to Westerners than glassy fish eyes looking back at them is a chicken chopped up and served with its head and feet included. Many people on board for the whole fish—and who don't balk when encouraged by their hosts to eat its head because they are honored guests—find the chicken with its scorched beak and gnarled claws to be taking the concept of wholeness a bit too far.) Meats are served in bite-sized chunks because to slash at food with knives and forks is barbaric, as these sharp tools are similar to instruments of war and not suited to civilized dining, which must be done with slender, graceful chopsticks. But chopsticks must never be stuck into a bowl of rice and left to stand upright, because doing so symbolizes the incense sticks one burns at a relative's tomb, and food should be about life, not death.

Almost everything you need to know about Chinese culture you can learn at the meals. Every meal includes many dishes, and each dish means something. Food is so much more than sustenance, so much more than flavor. Food has profound social dimensions. It is money and sex and power. It is medicine. It is friendship and acceptance. It is a gift shared between friends, a bond within families. Food is everywhere—not just in the restaurants and street stalls, but on the minds and in the conversations of the Chinese. From the pithy wisdom of Confucius ("Everyone eats and drinks; yet only few appreciate the taste of food.") to modern-day slang such as *chī dòufu* (literally, "to eat tofu," but meaning, depending on whom you ask, to chase women, to cheat on one's wife, to grope someone, to lick or nibble a woman's white skin—or something racier yet), food finds its way into the language with remarkable frequency. Food terms that serve as slang for sex acts abound. Speak of "eating meat dumplings" or "licking the plate" and hear the hysterical laughter. *Zāogāo* (literally "rotten cake") is the most common way to say *Damn!* in China. If you stub your toe, "rotten cake." If you arrive at a store too late and find its doors locked for the night, "rotten cake."

"Have you eaten?" is the normal way to greet someone in China. It is more common, in fact, to ask someone if he has eaten than it is to ask him how he is doing. *Nǐ chī le ma?* If a person answers that he has eaten, then his interlocutor can conclude that the person being asked is doing just fine. "I've eaten" means "No problem, I'm well, everything's good." Whenever I've struck up conversations with cab drivers, they have asked me what I've eaten in their city. And it is not at all unusual when chatting on a subway or train with a complete stranger to be asked a few sentences into the conversation if you can eat spicy food. *Wǒ bù pà là*: "I'm not afraid of hot food." I learned to say this sentence before I learned how to explain what I did for a living. What you do for work matters less than where you are from, and where you are from often matters less than what you eat. And if you are a foreigner who loves to eat Chinese food and to talk about it, you are sure to make friends wherever you go.

People at a Chinese meal eat directly from communal plates in the center of the table. Tables traditionally are round because a circle symbolizes the wholeness of a group, its unbroken continuity. A circle means family and community—it signifies inclusion. People sitting in a circle can all participate fully in the fellowship of a meal; people at rectangular tables cannot communicate equally with everyone who is eating, because the straight lines and sharp corners inhibit the social flow. So entrenched in the culture is sharing food, so foreign is the idea of

Food in China is always best when eaten with friends, and there is no better way to dine than by sharing a meal with a family in a Shanghai alley.

individual portions, even during the SARS scare when everyone in Shanghai knew that sharing food was dangerous, tradition trumped hygiene and people still ate from communal dishes.

Dumplings are served on special occasions because they are round, like the bond of a family, like a wedding ring. *Tāngyuán*, a ball made of glutinous rice flour and holding a sweet treat inside, reminds the Chinese of their families, a Chinese friend in America, her eyes moist, told me during the Spring Festival—a time of year when families in China gather as we do in the West at Christmas and Hanukkah. *Yuèbǐng* ("mooncakes") are eaten during the Mid-Autumn Festival, the roundness of the cakes and the whole egg yolks contained in their centers mimicking a plump harvest moon. Noodles are served on birthdays because noodles are long, and there is no better wish on one's birthday than to have many more birthdays over the course of a long life. Fish are lucky food because the Chinese word for fish, *yú*, sounds like a Chinese word for *abundance*, and fish serve as a central symbol in many meals. I can't recall ever attending one of the feasts that masquerade as business meetings in China without a fish on the table. What better way to start a business relationship than by devouring a symbol of abundance.

As Chinese foods have special significance, so Chinese dishes often have attached to them elaborate lore. Crossing the Bridge Noodles, for example, takes its name from an ancient story of a scholar who, in order to study diligently, secluded himself on an island. Each day his wife would cross a bridge to the island to bring him a dish of rice noodles and tasty morsels in hot chicken broth topped by a layer of duck fat to keep the soup warm until she reached his hideaway. And there are dishes with names more evocative yet, names born of myths and poems and legends. A dish of chicken and soft-shell turtle is called Xiang Yu the Conqueror Says Goodbye to his Concubine. Some of the names of dishes are flat-out pretty: Butterflies Swarming the Peonies, for example. Some are just plain weird. An ancient concoction of camel's foot simmered with hearts of rape is named Desert Boat Sails on Green.

Businessmen ordering dozens of costly dishes to impress their clients; friends fighting each other in restaurants for the honor of clearing the tab (I have watched men literally wrestle on a restaurant floor, upending tables and chairs, while they sorted out who would pay the bill); college students away from home for the first time mumbling the names of dishes they miss in their sleep; mothers searching markets for fresh ingredients to recipes with origins receding deep into China's past; families honoring their ancestors during holidays by offering them plates of delicacies: food is forever finding its way to the center of Chinese life. And eating in China is almost always about more than just consuming food. It is about nourishing relationships between people. Hugging and kissing are unheard of in public life in traditional Chinese culture; even shaking hands is uncommon. In place of all this physical contact we use to communicate our feelings in the West, the Chinese use eating to show how they feel. To taste all the dishes ordered by one's host is to show respect. To leave some food on the table when one is finished eating is to give the host face, for it demonstrates that plenty of dishes were prepared and there was more than enough to eat. To praise the host not just for the quality of each dish, but for the balance of the overall selection of several dishes, to comment on how their colors, textures and tastes complement each other to create a satisfying whole, is to fully participate in the elaborate ritual that is a Chinese meal. Slurp your soup as loudly as you can, for your noisy enjoyment signals your satisfaction with the flavor. And to be happy with the soup's flavor is to be happy with your host. Share a feast with potential business partners and begin to build trust. Treat a friend to a meal and your friend will never forget. As the Chinese have a long memory for slights, so they long remember favors, and their memory for food shared between friends knows no end.

Every meal in China is a banquet, and the fare of each street vendor is a moveable feast. Eating is always on the minds of people in this food-obsessed nation, and what one eats, and how one eats it, often says so much. Right now, gleefully devouring spicy crepes allowed me to show Old Wang, in a way that was far more potent than using words, that I was comfortable in her world and happy to be a part of it.

Aside from the elaborate social dimensions of food, what has always struck me most about the nation's cuisines is their staggering diversity. To say you like to eat Chinese food is as vague as saying you enjoy European food. Traditional Shanghainese cuisine is not known for being spicy. Sugar more than chili pepper flavors many dishes, and Shanghainese food is often served at banquets where foreign friends are guests, as the mild dishes won't sear their delicate palates and sting their gentle tongues. People throughout China have told me that food in Shanghai is *tài tián le*: too sweet. In general it holds none of the fire of Sichuanese cooking or dishes from Hunan. But these crepes with their chili sauce put a little heat in my belly and beads of sweat on my brow. Old Wang watched me closely as I ate, nodding and nodding, her nodding growing more vigorous, more definitive, with each bite I took of the spicy street food. I finished my jianbing and tried to buy another round for everyone, but Jennifer's father would have none of it and insisted on paying. I handed a jianbing to Old Wang, and as her weathered fingers brushed my hand I felt the years she'd accumulated in this neighborhood in her cool and leathery skin. She'd lived here all her life, she told me as the food passed between us, and she knew everyone—every single person in every subdivided room of every shikumen in this alley.

"It's true," Jennifer said. If you wanted to know anything about anyone, you asked Old Wang.

I looked at Old Wang and she nodded that it was so, pride beaming from her seamed and sunken cheeks.

"Old Wang helped raise me," Jennifer said. "She looked after me for a long time. My mom was sick for a year when I was a girl and my father was sent away by his work unit to work in Hefei. But it was okay because Old Wang was here. She took care of me when I was little and she knows all my secrets." Jennifer translated this for Old Wang, who said something that made Jennifer laugh, but she didn't translate it for me.

When we finished our jianbing, Jennifer said, "He likes xiaolongbao," referring to the Shanghai specialty we'd eaten the first night we'd met. Jennifer had hardly finished explaining to Old Wang where we'd eaten the dumplings filled with delicious pork and broth before I was being led down the alley and directed to step over the threshold of a restaurant. Barely bigger than a phone booth, the room held but two tables and was filled with a chaos of voices, everyone wanting to know where I was from and what I was doing in the neighborhood. The close air was heavy with cooking smells so thick and rich I sniffed my shirt hours later and was reminded of the food they put before me now. In a little basket, xiaolongbao (which is literally translated "little bamboo basket buns") lay in steaming bamboo tiers. One tier of the basket was removed and Old Wang showed me the right way to eat the dumplings, a technique more refined than what Jennifer and I had improvised on the street. With her chopsticks Old Wang gently gripped a dumpling and lifted it from a bed of crinkled cabbage. She dipped the dumpling in a bowl of black rice vinegar laced with little shreds of ginger; then she transferred the slippery treat to a soupspoon and nibbled near the top, where the smooth, translucent skin was gathered up in folds. She slurped the hot liquid inside and lapped the overflow from her soupspoon, and then she ate the dumpling as quickly as she could. Had I ever seen a happier face I couldn't remember where.

"You cannot eat the xiaolongbao whole before you drink the soup inside because the xiaolongbao is too hot," she said through Jennifer, "but after you drink the soup, you can't wait too long or it will be too cold. The temperature must be just right."

I followed Old Wang's example, lifting a xiaolongbao from the bamboo basket with my chopsticks, moving carefully so as not to tear the dumpling's delicate skin. Then I dipped the dumpling in vinegar and transferred it to a soupspoon while a pack of people looked on. The owner of the restaurant sat down at my table and the cook came out from the kitchen to watch. Stage fright made me fumble the slippery little soup dumpling a few times but it didn't fall to the table, much to the delight of the onlookers, who appeared as nervous as I felt when the dumpling slid dangerously around my soupspoon. A hot bit of broth trickled from my lips and down my chin when I nibbled through the dumpling skin, but I swallowed most of the soup and then gulped down the dumpling and proclaimed it utterly delicious to my audience, who nodded and smiled their approval. The mob dispersed, some returning to their own baskets of xiaolongbao in the restaurant, others going back into the alley, where word was circulating that there was a foreigner in their midst.

"I think everyone in every shikumen for a mile around knows I'm here," I said to Jennifer.

"It's true," she said. One couldn't creep around unnoticed in these tight warrens. There was none of the anonymity one expects in a giant city, and crime in this neighborhood was rare.

A man I hadn't met pushed his way through the cramped restaurant, and with two hands he offered another basket of xiaolongbao, laying his steaming gift upon the table. His eyes smiled as I nodded my thanks. I was stuffed already, but to refuse the food he'd gifted me would be to punch him in the face. In America I would have wanted to punch him in the face because of the cigarette dangling from his lips and spilling flakes of ash on my arm. When I waved his smoke away he shifted the cigarette to the other side of his mouth and blew smoke in a different direction. His plume merged with many others, the upper reaches of the room as thick with smoke as if the restaurant had caught fire. Duck into a diner in Shanghai to escape the air pollution outside and be choked by cigarette fumes. Signs proclaiming NO SMOKING are suggestions in Shanghai, nothing more. What could I do but eat soup dumplings? The man's eyes grinned with each bite I took, his face glowing orange as he sucked his cigarette, its tip burning bright in the room's smoky light.

"You still don't know how the soup gets inside the dumpling?" Jennifer asked.

I studied the xiaolongbao snuggled in the bamboo basket and whiffing steam into the air. "Someone makes a tiny hole in each dumpling and fills it with soup, then closes the hole back up?"

"You are wrong."

"Are you going to tell me?"

"No, I will not."

When we left the restaurant, my belly bloated with delicious dumplings that held mysterious soup, I saw a woman squatting next to a stone basin in front of a doorway framed in stone, her bony hands kneading gray water from a mound of clothes. I imagined women in Shanghai had been doing the wash this way for countless generations. Dynasties had ascended and collapsed, the Europeans had come and gone, some of the tallest towers on earth had surged into the sky, and this woman squatted next to a stone basin, the tendons in her forearms standing in stark relief as she squeezed the suds from tattered underpants.

Old Wang asked Jennifer's mother if they had accepted the offer to tear down their home. She answered that they hadn't, and they wouldn't. Old Wang had already accepted her offer, she said. She had been promised an apartment in a brand-new building. The apartment would be bigger than her home in the shikumen, and best of all, it boasted a washer and a dryer. Washers were becoming common appliances in Chinese apartments, but dryers were almost unheard of, and most families in Shanghai, a city studded with high-rises and girded with superhighways, still hung their clothing outside to dry in the sun.

"A drying machine," Old Wang said to Jennifer. "A drying machine," she repeated, shaking her head with the bemused amazement of one who has received an unexpected bounty.

Beneath balconies strewn with soggy clothes, children climbed atop a wall. Instead of offering each other a helping hand, they pushed each other back down as they struggled toward the top. Mark one up for capitalism.

In the alleyways, options for play were limited. No kicking soccer balls within the narrow slots of the lanes, no flying kites among the crisscrossed power lines. When the kids tired of climbing the wall, they began a new game of chasing each other through the alley, running in and out of the stone-framed entrances of homes, dodging and darting between the legs of grownups. A man with skin mapped by myriad wrinkles sat in a chair. He angled his face toward a weak sun, a pale place in the watery sky. One of the children broke away from the pack and climbed onto the old man's lap. The man shifted in the chair to make room for the little boy and together they napped in the sun.

Past this place of pleasant napping was a storefront filled with foodstuffs. Next to the store, tradesmen sat on their heels in the alley mending shoes, rethreading wires, and fixing broken clocks. Across from them, a woman sold socks. While Jennifer talked with Old Wang, I explored a side alley and found scattered between the shikumen residences storefronts that displayed bolts of cloth and handmade brooms, batteries and bottles of water, bagged snacks and jugs of cooking oil. I weaved my way between pushcarts filled with fruit and sellers sitting on blankets surrounded by their wares. Sunglasses and CDs, leather belts and neon sponges: an overload of items, too many for my brain to process. I passed a dentist's shop showcasing spiky tools that seemed medieval instruments of torture, though the smiling dentist in the doorway had a fine set of pearly whites and he seemed nice enough. In nooks of the alley were tucked a barbershop and a laundry, a tailor and a store that sharpened knives. A butcher with joints of ham hanging from the ceiling. A fishmonger. For a shikumen dweller, all the goods and services necessary for daily life could be purchased, it seemed, within a block of one's home.

I walked back toward the dentist and struck up a conversation with him. He looked at me a moment as though he'd just heard a monkey speak, and then he asked how it was that I had come to be in China and learned to speak Chinese. I

Vendors selling everything from tofu to toys wander Shanghai's alleyways singing out their wares. The city's new tower complexes echo with the sounds of traffic, and the calls of roving peddlers are absent from the streets.

gave one of my standard lines in Mandarin: one day I woke up in my bed in America and suddenly I could speak Chinese, so I thought I better go to China. He laughed, and when I laughed with him he moved in close to look at my teeth. I glanced at the dental tools in the window of his shop and resisted the urge to run.

We chatted a bit about Chinese culture, and the conversation soon came around to "five thousand years of history," as it always does. Ask anyone in China and he will tell you: China has five thousand years of history. He will also tell you China has the longest continuous civilization on the planet. And Westerners who fetishize Chinese culture will agree. But there are some problems with these statements, not least of which is their veracity.

In the enormous area we today call China, human civilization has developed for millennia. But Justin Crozier, in an essay in *China in Focus Magazine* titled "5,000 Years of History," argues that a large stretch of this "five thousand years of history" is actually prehistoric, and some of it even recedes into dynasties for which there is no verified archeological evidence, dynasties that might be mythological. The Jews, Egyptians and Indians have histories of at least five thousand years, and the archeologically verified culture of the Celts goes back as far as that of the Chinese. A case could be made for the Western culture of the present, which the Chinese decry as short and shallow, tracing its roots back five thousand years to Egypt and Mesopotamia. China is a trove of cultural treasures, to be sure, but it is merely one nation among many with thousands of years of history.

When analyzing the claims "five thousand years of history" and "world's longest continuous civilization," the terms *China* and *Chinese* become problematic. The vast majority of Chinese people are identified as belonging to the Han ethnicity, but *Han* only came into use after the Han dynasty—founded a mere twenty-two hundred years ago. The Chinese will tell you their country is now and has always been *Zhōngguó*, which is translated "Middle Kingdom," but the word *Zhōngguó* first appeared in *Classic of History*, a book published just a few centuries prior to the Han dynasty. Does China's "five thousand years of history" refer to the history of the Han, or to the history of *Zhōngguó*—or rather to the history of the disparate peoples and warring states that were constantly moving around throughout the enormous region we today call China and were forever changing their names and their rulers before the concept of *Zhōngguó* originated and the term *Han* was first used? This is a slippery slope of semantics: If *China* and *Chinese* are applied retrospectively to a span of five thousand years, they refer not to a distinct culture, but to a broad geographic area. Modern Iraq, Egypt and Pakistan could use the same semantic trick and claim they own the world's longest continuous civilization.

Crozier notes that the concepts of *China* and *Chinese* become even more elusive when the Mongol conquest of China is considered. The Mongols, who founded the Yuan dynasty, were partially assimilated into Chinese culture before they were overthrown by the Ming, but large Mongol populations outside of China have never been under Chinese rule and have a distinct culture. The elastic concept of *China* allows China to assert that the Mongol conquests of Asia and Europe were a highpoint for Chinese civilization. Chinese history textbooks make this claim regardless of the discriminatory policies the Mongols adopted in China, which treated Han Chinese as conquered subjects and placed Chinese Confucian scholars in a social position below prostitutes and just above beggars. Ask any Chinese student and he or she will tell you: Genghis Khan's conquests were part of China's glorious five thousand years of civilization. It's on their government-approved multiple-choice exams, so it must be true.

The same confusion over what *China* and *Chinese* really mean surrounds the conquest of China by the Manchu, who conquered the country in the seventeenth century and founded the last imperial dynasty. The Manchu are often denounced by the Chinese as barbarian invaders. But mention the destruction of the Manchu Summer Palace by Anglo-French troops in 1860 to a Chinese and he will tremble with rage at this national humiliation at the hands of foreigners. The Manchu are simultaneously seen as foreign invaders of China and as Chinese wronged by foreign invaders.

Linguistic aside: One of my favorite words in Chinese is *máodùn*. *Máodùn* is translated "contradiction," but like so many Chinese words, it has a wonderful story that explains it. *Máo* means "spear," *dùn* means "shield." Once upon a time, a man in a market sold spears. He called out to passersby, telling them his spears were so sharp they could pierce anything in the world. The man also sold shields—his shields were so strong, he told everyone within shouting distance, that nothing in the world could penetrate them. So one day a clever passerby asked the man what would happen if one of his spears (*máo*) was thrust into one of his shields (*dùn*). Maodun.

Claiming the reign of the Manchu as part of China's five thousand years of continuous civilization while condemning the Manchu for ruling China as foreign barbarians is a maodun. A really big maodun.

None of this messy history and linguistics meshes well with the simple but powerful Chinese foundation myth, which is taught through the government's history textbooks to make the Chinese people believe that they are special. They are told in schools, in universities, and in the media that their culture is more ancient than any other in the world. With five thousand years of history behind it, how could China not have a grand destiny to develop into the world's next superpower. And how could people who are part of a rising superpower be unhappy with the government restoring their nation to its rightful place of greatness among the world's other countries, all of which have lesser cultures with paltry spans of history.

Five thousand years. Listen to a Chinese person say it. It sounds harmless enough. But words mean so much, and stories mean everything.

Coded deep in the language is the concept of *Zhōngguó*. China is the Middle Kingdom, and anyone from outside China is a *wàiguórén*, a "person from an outside country." It is impossible to speak Chinese without being Sino-centric, without participating in the story that China is at the center of the world. But China is still poor by the standards of developed countries and everyone in China knows this. Taught that theirs is a history longer and more sophisticated than any other on earth, and that China has been egregiously wronged by other countries and is now a developing nation struggling to catch up with the rest of the world, the people see themselves both as the bearers of a superior culture, and as tragic victims of barbarian aggression. Bo Yang, a Taiwanese author, published a book in Chinese in 1985 titled *Chǒulòu de Zhōngguórén* (published in English in 1992 as *The Ugly Chinaman and the Crisis of Chinese Culture*) that weighed in on the tendency of the Chinese people to waver between two extremes: "In his inferiority, a Chinese person is a slave; in his arrogance, he is a tyrant. In the inferiority mode, everyone else is better than he is . . . Similarly, in the arrogant mode, no other human being on earth is worth the time of day."

Take many centuries of isolation, mix these centuries with the humiliations caused by foreign nations and the social catastrophes of the nineteenth and twentieth centuries, add in the cultural barrier caused by the difficulty of translating the Chinese language, and you have the perfect recipe for China's tension between an inflated sense of self-importance and a national inferiority complex.

"Five thousand years," I agreed with the grinning dentist, "is a very long time."

I found my way through an enchanting maze of narrow lanes that seemed some puzzle in a dream. I turned down one little pathway after another, following clefts between buildings standing so close together the sun never reached the ground in these places of perpetual shadow, these tight spaces where brick walls squeezed neighbors together in a hug. When I finally arrived back at the spot where Jennifer and Old Wang stood talking in a gaggle of women, I remembered what Jennifer had told me earlier that day: the shikumen neighborhoods were referred to as *lǐlòng*. *Lǐ* means "neighborhood," *lòng* means "lane." A lane neighborhood. There were no cars in these brick-paved passageways, only bikes and the occasional motor scooter. People, more than machines, defined this public space. All the people knew each other, and they were all carrying on conversations that had begun when they were children and would last throughout their lives. I watched the adults corralling and herding children who ran around them in hyper loops, the children chasing each other and shouting, their voices bouncing from the alley walls and mingling with the gentle scolding of the men and women who watched over them as though they were their own. I felt warm, not from the steamy Shanghai heat, but from the closeness of this group, these people whose lives had twined together. I could not tell where one family began and another ended.

One of the boys chasing and being chased through the alleyway ran into my leg. He ricocheted off me and shook his stunned head. His mouth crinkled at the corners and his eyes pooled with tears. I scooped my hands beneath his armpits and lifted him high. "Don't cry," I told him in Mandarin. "Don't cry, little friend." In Chinese, children are called *xiǎo péngyǒu,* "little friends." Each time I say this to a child I can't help but smile.

Old Wang took the boy from me. She cradled him in her withered arms, and as his eyes leaked and his body shook with sobs, she hugged him to her chest.

By the time the Expo begins in the spring of 2010, less than 5 percent of Shanghai's population will

Children are called *xiǎo péngyǒu,* literally "little friend."

live in traditional lilong. I gazed up and down the lane. The walls of so many shikumen pressing against each other blocked the sights of the city. There were no panoramic views to be had from this lilong, and the alleyways were claustrophobically tight. But this small world was home. For now it was separate from the changes sweeping Shanghai. For the time being it was filled with love, and it was safe.

"This must be so different from where you live," I told Jennifer later that day as we walked down the alley outside her parents' home. Her mother and father had gone back inside and we'd said goodbye to Old Wang. I knew that Jennifer lived in a high-rise in a trendy part of town but I hadn't been there.

"It's dirty here, don't you think?" Jennifer said.

From bamboo poles, pants and shirts flagged gently in the breeze. Air conditioning units chugged and hummed overhead, condensation dripping from their underbellies and pooling on the ground. In a group kitchen, women hunched over the blue flames of burners. Broth bubbled and pans hissed, and from open windows spilled garlic and cilantro smells and pillows of puffy steam.

"I like it here," I said.

"If this was in your America you would tear it down and build something better, right?"

I thought for a moment and then agreed that in our America we probably would. We would tear it down, and we would build something we thought was better—a suburb with strict zoning codes that separated living areas from work areas and kept homes apart from stores. And the sprawling mess would be connected by a snarl of roads filled with harried commuters sealed cruelly in their cars. And then we would decide we had made a mistake and needed something better, namely neighborhoods where people could live and work and play without endless hours of commuting; and we would look around the world for inspiration, and by then the shikumen of Shanghai would be gone, and in their place would be towers and highways and shopping malls—and the fairgrounds for the World Expo. And at the Expo, which boasted the boldest ideas in the world, a concept called New Urbanism would be touted: the idea that the suburban-sprawl commuter culture of the United States is unsustainable and less than human, and there is a desperate need for communities that avoid the hell of endless parking lots, clogged roads, and soul-sucking commutes. Called by the *New York Times* "the most important collective architectural movement in the United States in the past fifty years," New Urbanism promotes the creation of compact, walkable, mixed-use neighborhoods as an antidote to empty lives lived among mindless mega-malls and the loneliness of asphalt deserts. I'd read that New Urbanism aims to create "human-scale communities" and "more livable communities." I hadn't fully understood what those statements meant until I explored the lanes of the lilong. Compact, mixed use and pedestrian friendly: the shikumen neighborhoods were all that. They were the very antithesis of auto-centric culture and vacuous suburbia. And after they'd been leveled, citizens of the world would peruse the pavilions at the Expo in Shanghai to learn about the evils of sprawl and the virtues of New Urbanism.

"What a world," I said aloud.

"What?" said Jennifer. "What is your meaning?"

"What do you mean, you mean."

"What?"

"It's better to say 'what do you mean,' than 'what is your meaning.'"

"Oh. So, what do you mean?"

"Never mind—I can't remember now." I stopped in front of a noodle stand to sniff the delicious vapors rising from simmering pots. After a moment I said, "You seem to like coming here." I'd noticed that Jennifer had moved a bit slower and had appeared more relaxed in the lilong than she did when we were racing around the city on subways and buses, jumping in taxis and riding elevators to the tops of towers. "You like seeing your parents, I think."

"Of course. But I'd come here anyway, even if they didn't live here anymore."

"To see Old Wang?"

"To see everyone." Jennifer was quiet a few minutes as we made our way between bikes parked in an alley so narrow two people could not walk side by side. Frames of flimsy bamboo held awnings that stretched over windows to block what little sun leaked between the walls. Power lines hung in tangled knots from metal poles that reached out from the sides of buildings. One frayed line spewed showers of orange sparks that landed hissing in a puddle. A herd of people stood massed around the spectacle, staring. Jennifer and I stopped a moment and watched everyone watching. No one made a move to call the power company, no one took the initiative to block off the area. I had been in China long enough to not register surprise that no one was doing anything other than staring. We walked on.

"It is dirty here and old-fashioned," Jennifer said. "But I come here when I feel afraid."

"What do you mean?"

"Sometimes I worry about so many things. There is so much . . . *yālì hěn dà*."

"So much pressure," I said.

"Yes, pressure. My job—I don't know if I should have a better job. Maybe I need to make more money. It is so expensive to live in Shanghai. And my boyfriend—when we broke apart I was sad and I thought I might be alone forever and never get married. And then I would be old and not married, and that is not good. When I feel pressure and I feel bad I come here and then I don't feel bad anymore."

"Do you talk with Old Wang about your problems?"

"I tell her everything."

"Does she give you good advice?"

Jennifer laughed. "What she tells me doesn't make any sense. When I broke apart with my boyfriend she told me to move back here and she would find a

Shanghai's traditional lanes offer no eye-popping sights of soaring towers seething with neon or multilevel highways arrowing off into eternity. Instead, the views from within the brick walls of a lane are close and tight, and the beauty is in the details—in the unglamorous but essential accessories of daily life: parked bikes, rows of outdoor sinks, mops drying in the sun, bedsheets freshening in the breeze.

husband for me. But I like telling her my problems. Telling her helps. She listens to me. No one listens at my office. And where I live no one listens. Sometimes in Shanghai everyone is talking and there is so much noise but no one is listening."

"Will you show me more of the lilong?" I asked.

"Why are you so interested in this place?"

"I guess because it is so different from where I grew up."

"When I was little, early in the morning the man who came to the lane to collect the . . . how do you call it . . . the chamber pots—the man yelled to let everyone know it was time for him to empty their chamber pots, and that is how I woke up every day." Jennifer patted the air a moment, her tiny hand telling me she was thinking. "You had hot water inside your house and you had your own kitchen that you didn't have to share . . . and you had big roads where you could drive your car? And shopping malls?"

"Yes, we had all those things."

"Then why do you want to see this?"

"Because we had everything, but something was missing. And I guess a part of me believes what was missing—maybe I'll find it here."

"I don't understand."

I looked around the lane and thought a moment. "When I'm in an American city, I feel like I could be anywhere. And when I'm in Shanghai's shopping malls, I feel like I could be in an American city. But here, in this neighborhood, I feel like I'm someplace. I feel like I'm actually in a particular place. Does that make sense?"

"No."

"No?" I said.

"Chinese people go to America because they want to see the things you have— the big cars, private homes, swimming pools, all these nice things. And you have these things, but you want to come here to see a place that doesn't have these things. I think this is very strange."

"Yes," I said.

"Yes?"

"Yes, you're right. It is very strange."

I spied a grocer selling his produce in the open air. One crate held a heap of *yòuzi*, my favorite fruit. Like a grapefruit on growth hormones, youzi are giant, and when you peel away the heavy skin there is a sweet and bumpy pulp within that holds delicious juice with a hint of sour tang. I bought one and peeled it, and we ate it while we wandered, pausing to toss the empty rind in a rubbish tin that stood between potted flowers and beneath a hanging plant. We made our way into a space between walls holding trellises twined with vines, this lane as green and leafy as a jungle path. After passing through an archway with a massive stone lintel split by cracks shaped like lightning bolts, we entered a rotting mansion, where one rich family had once lived in opulence and now a dozen families occupied the crowded rooms. The doors held grilles of ironwork in fantastic swirling shapes. Jennifer introduced me to people she knew as we climbed a staircase of riven stone, its balustrades beautifully carved with fishes, birds and flowers now thick with dust. Along the ceiling stretched an intricate maze of pipes scaled with rust.

On the second floor, elbows propped atop a splintery sill, we leaned from a window and looked out across roofs, watching the daily theater of life in the lanes.

People peeling vegetables over community sinks, a woman in pajamas washing greens. A fishmonger wrapped in a black rubber apron tossing stiff corpses of carp into a wheelbarrow. A man piloting a three-wheeled bike-cart through a cluttered alleyway stopped to collect a stack of bundled cardboard and plastic bottles tethered with twine, and then he rang his bell as he pedaled down the lane. Wandering vendors called out their wares: used clocks and sacks of rice, slabs of fresh beef and jars of handmade beer. Lining one alley wall were cages of chickens and ducks, and an old man wearing slippers spoke to a mynah bird walking in circles at his feet. A small owl with big blinking eyes stood watching from a perch. Smells of seafood rose to the window and I flared open my nose to sniff the source. Jennifer pointed out the hair salons that were fronts for prostitution. Where the alley opened onto a street stood a kiosk selling cigarettes and newspapers. A butcher spattered in blood walked outside his shop to drop the severed head of a pig on the wet brickwork of the lane. A man carrying a sack laden with tools advertised his services in a lilting song. He could fix your furniture, he said, could repair your damaged woodwork.

Waves of red-tiled roofs washed away to a place in the distance where they abruptly stopped against a huddle of towers shoving their way above the shikumen in blocky shapes of concrete, glass and steel. Tall buildings of modern design were encroaching from all sides, eating away at the red expanse of roofs, gnawing at its edges and spreading toward its center, its historic core.

We went back downstairs to explore a courtyard fallen into decrepitude, bricks spilling from the walls. "Do you see that bucket under the faucet?" Jennifer said. "The family has a water meter and they get charged by how much they use. But if the faucet drips, the meter doesn't record it. So they put a bucket under the faucet and when it is filled after many hours they have free water."

We pushed our way down a crumbled lane, through heaps of broken stone and mounds of shattered glass. On walls of gray brickwork, the Chinese character *chāi*, which means "to tear down," was painted red and surrounded by a red circle, marking the shikumen that were slated for destruction. A red banner bright as wet blood and encouraging residents to "Sell early and benefit early" spanned the alley, and bamboo scaffolding was everywhere. Ads for fake passports and television repair had been stenciled with phone numbers on places of bare plaster that coated the walls. Glass-covered display boards held community newspapers, free for all to read. Wooden mailboxes painted green hung from lacquered doors. Men in pajamas lounged in the alley playing cards.

"This is where I went to kindergarten," Jennifer said as we turned a corner.

"You went to kindergarten in a hotel?" I stood blinking in the sudden brightness of this place where shikumen had been ripped away and the alleys exposed to the light of day. A giant building wearing what looked like metal skin rose before us. A fringe of manicured bushes and burbling fountains surrounded it.

"My school was here," Jennifer said. She explained that it was not uncommon to arrive at a favorite restaurant or market that one had visited a few days earlier and find it gone. That the place where she'd attended kindergarten was now a four-star hotel did not seem to bother her a bit.

We tread a narrow path between tightly packed homes, heading back into the dim clutter of the alleys, where walls of brick crowded out the world, and the shining hotel we'd seen seemed but a momentary illusion. My eyes adjusted back to the shadowy spaces of the lilong and my brain recalibrated, bouncing between a zillion details, all of them arguing for attention. What to focus on? Shopfronts stuffed full of goods. Noodle stands filled with smoke, the sounds of slurping, and savory smells. A bent-backed granny with a handmade broom, cleaning a bit of alleyway outside her home. A woman cradling in one arm a little fox-faced dog. An entire interior wall covered with electrical meters with boxes and circuitry so complicated and densely clustered, the wall seemed a computer chip writ large. The clop of a knife falling into a heavy wooden block as an onion cleaved in half. The contented look on a woman's face while a hairdresser massaged her temples. An oval window framed in elegant stonework among the collapsing ruins of a lane. Discovering this window in the dust and rubble was like finding a rainbow in a morgue.

In an alley festooned with laundry, where a man and woman sat outside in their pajamas, we ran into a group of white-skinned tourists snapping pictures, lenses pointed at the pajama wearers and the drying clothes. It seemed Jennifer and I had wandered onto the set for a photo shoot about shikumen life. With my cell phone I snapped pictures of the tourists taking pictures of the streetscape. I stopped when I realized that one of them was taking a picture of me taking pictures of them taking pictures of the laundry and the people in pajamas. Jennifer said she'd seen it all before. Unflustered, she walked beneath the colorful banners of drying clothes, past the people in pajamas reclining in their chairs, through the mob of camera-toting tourists.

At the center of an empty lot where shikumen had been razed I stopped to join a group of children playing *jiànzi*. Similar to a hacky sack, a jianzi is more

As you wander these narrow lanes, be prepared for tight turns and dead ends, and be ready to press yourself flat against a wall to let a person on a wobbly bike pass by.

colorful and easier to kick. Feathers sprout from a springy weighted base. You kick the jianzi in the air and pass it back and forth. You can use your head and shoulders, your chest and knees if you have to; just don't use your hands, and never let it touch the ground. I'd first played with one in Vietnam and had become instantly addicted.

In Chinese I asked the kids if I could play with them, and they giggled and hid behind each other save for one bold boy who walked toward me and offered his hand, introducing himself as Roger. I shook his hand and asked him his Chinese name; I repeated it after he told me and then promptly forgot it. The rest of the crew gradually joined Roger and me as we kicked the jianzi back and forth, counting out the kicks before it touched the ground. The shuttlecock arced into the air, the feathers slowing its descent as we lifted our feet to tap it toward a new trajectory. Part of me—a very small part—felt that I should interview these children and ask them how the transformation of their neighborhood was affecting their lives, but most of me just wanted to play jianzi.

Jennifer ignored my invitations to join the circle, insisting she didn't know how to play. She stood off to the side, the circle growing larger as more children joined. At first they asked me questions about America (how much did a Wii cost in the States, did I have a gun and had I ever shot anyone, what was it like to have sisters and brothers) and they tried to practice their English, but soon all of us were focused on the task at hand—keeping the jianzi afloat. We took turns shuffling our bodies beneath the falling feathers, kicking the heavy base and hearing the satisfying pop as it sprang into the sky, its brilliant plumage leaving red, yellow and blue tracers in my eyes as it rose and fell, rose and fell above the rubble and the dust.

Jianzi has a history of two thousand years, dating back to the Han dynasty. The Chinese think they invented everything, and hacky sack is no exception. One of the boys, when I told him how we have a game similar to jianzi, called hacky sack, which uses a footbag instead of a shuttlecock, informed me that imperial Chinese guards had stayed alert during their overnight watches by kicking a small round sack stuffed with hair, and that's where the hacky sack had come from. But what of the frisbee? Surely China didn't invent the flying disc. He told me they had, but he couldn't tell me how. He asked me if I had one we could play with. I patted my pockets and told him, sorry, no I didn't have one with me.

I waved goodbye to the kids, and then Jennifer and I stepped back into a maze of lanes that held so many corners and dead ends, as we backtracked I listened for the roar of the minotaur and searched for Ariadne's string. Eventually we approached a stone archway marking the main entrance to the neighborhood. In order for shikumen residents to monitor who came into the lanes, the network of alleys connecting the homes had been designed to have few openings onto the city streets. By controlling who passed beneath the archways, the families that settled in lane houses could guard their neighborhoods from the armed gangs and bandits that had plagued the city when China seethed with chaos. By offering the outside world few entryways to the neighborhood, the community could protect the dwellers within from the mayhem without.

Next to the archway stood an old man with crinkled parchment skin. A sagging blue Mao hat sat crookedly on his head. His hands held the knob of a cane and his back was pressed flat to the wall. His eyes followed us as we approached him but his head didn't move. Though no part of his body or face budged, he watched us closely as we passed. Finally he gave Jennifer a small nod, a discrete movement of his chin. And once again he stood as motionless as the stone slabs around him. He seemed a sentry in some ancient story, gatekeeper to a closely guarded world. I stopped to stare at him. The watery orbs of his eyes gazed back at me. For a moment there was no sound in the alley nor was there movement of any kind and I thought the old man in the Mao hat had been standing there forever and would stand there forevermore.

"Who is that?" I asked Jennifer as we paused under the archway at the end of the alley. From the city streets beyond came the low thunder of traffic.

"We call him Old Xu."

"What does Old Xu do?"

"He stands there."

"He just stands there?"

"He retired a long time ago. I think he was a carpenter. Now he stands there all day and watches people come into the neighborhood. If strangers come in, he tells people." Jennifer nodded at Old Xu. Without swiveling his head he twisted his eyes to the side to see her. He gave another small nod. "He keeps us safe," said Jennifer.

"Is he like a security guard? Does somebody pay him to do that?"

"Old Wang told me that during the Cultural Revolution he was a Red Guard. His job was to spy on people who lived in the neighborhood and . . . rat out . . . I think you can say *rat out*—I heard it on *Friends*. He'd rat out the capitalists and the artists and anyone who was an enemy of the people. He'd find out if someone had a shrine in their home, or books, or gold—anything that was forbidden— and he'd tell the Party member in charge of this district. He became good at watching people to learn what they were doing. He knew where everyone was and what was happening in the lilong. No one could hide anything from Old Xu."

"And those people he turned in—what happened to them?" I asked. "They were beaten, put in prison, tortured? Sent to reeducation camps where they ate gruel and were brainwashed for ten years?"

"Yes, perhaps maybe they were." Jennifer nodded a moment. "That was a long time ago. Now he makes sure no thieves or bad people come into the neighborhood. When the government officials who are planning to smash the neighborhood come here he tells a family that they have arrived. Then that family tells everyone else, and everyone knows that they are here." Jennifer fell silent a moment, then said, "Old Xu is sad about what's happening to the neighborhood. He doesn't like the government planners who want to smash the neighborhood. He doesn't want to move to a new apartment. He won't have anything to do if he leaves here."

I tried to imagine Old Xu standing at the entrance to a sleek high-rise apartment building, his wet eyes studying young hipsters with PDAs in hand as they passed in and out of pneumatic glass doors.

Behind Old Xu stood cozy rows of shikumen snuggled wall to wall. Beyond the stone archway in front of us stretched wide streets filled with cars and commotion. The sound of horns, the stench of exhaust. And mixed with the everyday urban mayhem were the noises, sights and odors of the building binge that was remaking Shanghai. Within the confused soundscape I heard the stammer of jackhammers and the groan of dump trucks as they released their loads of rattling gravel. Construction cranes hung suspended from the metal spines of girders and beams, stacking the new towers higher. When I swallowed the grit lodged in the back of my throat I could taste the construction: the hot metal flavor of sparks fanning away from welding guns, the cool dampness of freshly poured concrete.

I took one last look behind us. I gazed past Old Xu standing guard and stared back into the little world of the narrow lane. Then Jennifer and I walked through the stone portal that marked its entrance, and as if passing by means of time travel from one century to the next, we left the lilong and plunged into the city's great gaping maw. We were instantly swallowed by an anonymous mass of crowds and cars, and within this tangled mess we wandered a gleaming wasteland of pavement, glass and steel. All around us twelve-lane boulevards spread outward and towers stretched upward. This was not a city made for humans. The new Shanghai was being built for some future species evolved in sterile spaces, a form of life suited to a world of gigantic scale. This was a city designed for dinosaurs with innards of cold circuitry, creatures that needed neither wildness nor warmth.

New Heaven and Earth

Later that day we stopped at Xintiandi, which is literally translated "new heaven and earth." It certainly looked new; I was a bit fuzzy on the heaven and earth part. Designed by American architect Ben Wood, Xintiandi is a hip shopping district in a swanky section of Shanghai. Because it holds the meeting place of the First Conference of the Communist Party of China, the Xintiandi area has major historic value to the Chinese, and city planners responsible for commercial development didn't want to raze it. So, what better to do with the birthplace of China's Communist Party than to turn it into a showpiece of Shanghai's new love of capitalism. The building where Chinese Communism had begun was preserved as a museum; the shikumen surrounding it were transformed into what in the parlance of developers is labeled a "lifestyle center." No mere outlet mall, Xintiandi boasts chic cafés, upscale restaurants and performance venues, even art galleries. In short, one came here not only to buy things, but to see the elite of Shanghai society and to be seen. One could learn about the history of Communism in China while drinking a Starbucks latte and pondering which pair of Italian shoes to purchase. And one could be seen in those fine shoes and sipping said latte by the expats and the moneyed Chinese who flocked to this new mecca of commerce where Mao and his cohorts had once denounced the evils of bourgeois living and had plotted China's course toward decades of deprivation.

I had several weeks previous been to Xintiandi, had drank a latte while watching a friend buy a pair of Italian shoes, but I hadn't really understood the context of the place. It had just seemed to me a bland mall like one would find in America. I thought that now with my newfound insight into shikumen, the Xintiandi communist homage shopping center would make more sense to me, and perhaps I'd appreciate it more. . . . Nope. Jennifer and I sat down at an outdoor beer garden and ordered a couple of brews, and I thought for a moment I'd been teleported out of China.

Xintiandi was cleaner and less cramped than the lilong neighborhood of Jennifer's parents. Gone were the sewer smells that drifted through the alleyways. Gone, in fact were most of the alleys. The old narrow passageways connecting Xintiandi's shikumen had been widened to shopping-friendly pathways that seemed as broad as superhighways after a day of dodging bikes and children in the narrow slots of lanes. This was a sanitized version of a shikumen neighborhood, and while I had to give props to Mr. Wood for preserving and repurposing the traditional architecture, I thought I could have been sitting at a piazza in Italy, or worse, at an upscale shopping center in St. Louis. The buildings looked like shikumen but I sensed none of the human warmth I'd felt in Old Wang's neighborhood.

I had become a big fan of converting moribund city districts into new commercial centers after watching downtown Denver rise from the ashes of urban decay based largely on historic preservation and retrofitting handsome brick buildings—steeped in the city's history but abandoned—to house sports bars, lofts and shops. The realization that rampant demolition is not necessarily the best solution to blight is essential to sound urban planning. The kind of smart, historically sensitive development that had taken place at Xintiandi could preserve the unique character of a city while stimulating its economy. And Xintiandi was arranged along a two-block pedestrian street. Pedestrian malls are without doubt a vast improvement over car-friendly shopping centers with the black-topped hell of parking lots the size of Lichtenstein. So what wasn't to like about Xintiandi? I couldn't put my finger on it, but there was something here I most definitely did not like.

Our waitress, a young Chinese woman who spoke sparkling Mandarin as pure and lacking in accent as that of an instructor on a CD I'd listened to when first learning the language, was nice enough, but she was no Old Wang. We ordered from a menu with laminated pages bound in a faux leather binder. I don't remember what we ate, and I guess that was the point precisely. We could have eaten anything, and I'm sure it would have been fine. It would have been prepared in a hygienic kitchen under the direction of a chef who had trained at a culinary institute, and it would not have tasted bad. But it would not have been *jiānbǐng* street food. I remembered clearly the tasty crepes we'd eaten with Old Wang. The soft shreds of egg, the lip-tingling chili sauce. The paper-wrapped snacks passing from the hands of the man who'd cooked them into my own and then into the hands of Old Wang. Watching the wrinkles of her face stretch apart and then bunch back together as she munched the spicy treat. Watching her small nods of approval growing into larger nods as we polished off a round and asked the vendor for another.

Xintiandi was without question a fine architectural achievement, and the beer garden where Jennifer and I sat and watched Shanghainese hipsters in their pumps and knee-high boots, their Armani and Gucci, their manicures and carefully groomed hair spiking its way upward, was a fine and decent place, but I felt as lonely there as I ever had in China. Xintiandi, designed by an American architect, could have been in America. And the one feeling I always associated with America was loneliness. In the St. Louis suburbs where I'd grown up, everyone lived in a house set off from other houses by the buffer of a sprawling yard, and people spent their lives in those houses and in their cars and in their separate office spaces, and when their lives bumped up against each other, as they surely must in the grocery store or at soccer practice for their children, they smiled and they were polite, but they were alone. I had felt the isolation of the suburbs as some sort of disease and I had fled as fast as I could and had gone as far as I could in search of something else. The closeness of the neighbors in the shikumen had been as near to the diametric opposite of a socially sterile American suburb as I'd found anywhere in the world.

I was glad Jennifer was with me at Xintiandi, but she seemed different now than she had in the alleyways around the shikumen. She smiled at someone she knew who walked toward our table, a man wearing a shirt with a satiny sheen, but the smile she gave him was not the same one she'd given Old Wang.

"This is Marcus," Jennifer said as her friend sat down to join us.

I greeted him in Chinese; he answered in English, showing me that his English was infinitely better than my Chinese, and why even bother with the charade of trying to carry on a conversation in his native tongue. Or that's how I took his meaning on this, our first meeting. Maybe I was feeling a bit oversensitive. Maybe he was speaking English because he assumed I would prefer to speak English. I took in his shoes, which seemed to me very much like shoes I had seen on the streets of Florence a few months previous. His briefcase was so new its leather scent filled our place on the patio, and I was willing to bet our bloated beer tab that his briefcase held a slim laptop. His hair had product in it. Lots of product. Slim laptop, stylish shoes, slick hair. I added it all up and gulped my beer.

Marcus and Jennifer had worked together at an advertising agency. They talked about former colleagues and they discussed their new jobs and their salaries and where they lived now. They spoke of saving up for cars and complained about how much it cost to buy a license plate. The Shanghai government had jacked up license plate fees in an effort to slow the number of new cars surging onto the streets, and there was now a bidding system in place. First you had to buy a car, and then you had to bid on a license plate. Bids were averaging around eight thousand U.S. dollars, and some license plates cost more than the cars they were attached to. In Beijing one thousand new cars enter the roads every day and the streets are clogged beyond belief. No one at our table knew the figure for Shanghai, but surely it was similar. This couldn't go on, we all agreed. The roads could not possibly sustain more cars. Traffic was unbearable already.

"What kind of car will you get?" Marcus asked Jennifer.

"A Passat," she said. "I want a Passat."

Marcus was planning to buy a Buick. Buicks in China confer serious status. Unlike in America, to drive a Buick is not to drive the crappy car your parents had driven; to drive a Buick in China is like cruising around in a sleek Mercedes (while your parents fill their stupid Buick with groceries). When General Motors reintroduced its Buick brand to the Chinese market a few years back, its advertising experts positioned it as a car for executives and high rollers. Shrewd marketers stressed that China's last emperor, Puyi, had driven a Buick in the 1920s, and so had modern leaders such as Sun Yat-sen, the father of the Republic of China, and Zhou Enlai, the first premier of the People's Republic. Many of the Buick models boasted sticker prices topping those of BMWs, and nouveau riche Shanghainese bought them up as fast as they rolled off the assembly line of the GM joint venture factory in Shanghai.

"Definitely a Buick," Marcus said. He was waiting for a raise; if he got the raise, he would buy a Buick.

Shanghai has made great strides in catching up to the West. Soon the lives of its citizens will be as barren and pointless as our own.

I drove the conversation away from cars and steered it toward shikumen, curious to hear Marcus's take. Jennifer shifted around in her seat and fingered a cardboard coaster on the table when I talked about her parents' place and how much I'd enjoyed meeting Old Wang and playing jianzi with the kids.

"The shikumen are so dirty," Marcus said. Jennifer continued to stare down at the coaster and said nothing. Marcus had grown up in Beijing, he told me. He'd moved to Shanghai after college. "Shikumen are like hutong in Beijing. We've gotten rid of most of those now."

"You think that's good?" I asked. "Getting rid of the hutong?"

"I think it's better to have modern cities. China needs to be a modern country like America. We need to be developed like America, and rich. There are no shikumen in America. Right?"

"True," I said. "Our poor people in cities live in big concrete boxes. And China will, like America, be very modern, and very rich, very soon, I'm sure."

"Thank you," Marcus said, as though I'd paid him a personal compliment. It was the first time since he'd sat down with us that he smiled at me.

"So, Marcus," I said, "you and Jennifer used to work together." Jennifer had gotten up to go to the bathroom.

"You understand Chinese?" he said in English that he seemed to be working very hard to make sound casual. "You understood our conversation?" Behind every syllable he lofted toward me I felt the strain of his purposeful relaxation, felt the effort he was putting into loosening his mouth. Watch Chinese people when they speak Mandarin and see the tightness of their lips, the narrow range of the movement of their jaws. As speaking their tones demands of us that our lips and tongues do things we have never before done with them, so our language challenges Chinese people to relax their vocal architecture and move their mouth muscles in ways that seem so physically improbable to them, it is as though we have asked them to jump up onto a table and do a back flip, then throw a forward flip onto the floor and walk on their hands out the door.

In Chinese I told Marcus his English was excellent; in English he told me my Chinese was terrific, and we locked swords and sparred there on the patio in the center of Xintiandi. His vocabulary was much larger than mine, as he had lived in America for two years to earn an MBA at Stanford, so I had to pay special attention to my pronunciation. He had me beat on vocab, but maybe I could out-pronounce him. He threw English at me, I hurled Mandarin back at him, and we punched and kicked and thrust and parried, battling back and forth until Jennifer returned from the restroom.

I called it a draw; though months later Marcus told me he'd been sure he'd won the first day we met. He did concede, however, that although he had believed he was victorious he had emerged from our battle bloodied and viewing me as a worthy adversary. What exactly we were both trying to prove has been lost to me, and it is possible I didn't even know it that day at Xintiandi. But of two things I am certain: language can be a weapon, and boys will be boys, forever competing in the strangest ways. In China as in America, men take the measure of other men from the moment they meet. The cultural differences that exist— Chinese men being more courteous and less obvious in assessing the strengths and weaknesses of each man they encounter—are but surface gloss. We are beasts, all of us, beneath the various trappings of our cultures. Geneticists tell us that people who hail from northern China have more genes in common with Caucasians than they do with people from southern China. Marcus, born in Beijing, had a genetic blueprint closer to my own than to that of a person born in Shanghai. And those genes drove us to immediately mark our territory, to settle the score as to whose cave belonged to whom and who was the mightier hunter. I'd been rumbling with men to determine who was the best mountain biker and snowboarder for many years, but the battle over who held the better language skills was new to me. And I would be damned if I was going to let Marcus best me.

"I was just telling Marcus how good his English is," I said to Jennifer as she sat back down at our table.

"His Chinese is really amazing," Marcus said, nodding his head my way.

"*Guò jiǎng le*," I said. "*Nǐ de Yīngwén bǐ wǒ de Zhōngwén hǎo de duō.*" You flatter me. Your English is much better than my Chinese. That last bit was meant to be the final blow—not just better, but *much better.*

Marcus produced the perfect, meaningless smile of a CCTV anchorman and sipped his beer, a mustache of froth forming above his lips.

I don't like to lose in any arena, but on occasion I do enjoy being outmatched—I like being the underdog and surprising people with my tenacity. Sometimes it feels good to go down swinging. "I think Marcus is really smart," I told Jennifer in absolutely the finest Mandarin pronunciation that had ever flowed from my lips, hitting Marcus with one last strong punch before we ended this match and moved on to the next. What a child I am, how young we all are.

"How did you like Stanford?" I asked Marcus. I was trying to be a grownup and leave our little game behind. "Did you like living in America?"

"It was good for my English and my career, but I didn't want to stay there."

"You missed living in China?"

"America is too boring, too old-fashioned."

"That's interesting, Marcus," I said, emphasizing the sounds of his name, giving equal stress to both syllables.

It is not unusual for a Chinese person to adopt an English name. *Marcus* seemed a bit banal in comparison to the myriad of strange monikers to which I'd been exposed in China. While teaching English in a rural province I'd met dozens of Apples, several of them Green Apples or Sweet Apples. I had even met a Sweet Green Apple. It had been difficult to teach these children, as it proved virtually impossible to say their names without cracking up. "So, Sweet Green Apple, can you please read the sentence aloud?" Stand in front of the class and say it with a straight face—go ahead, try. I had met Garfields and Snoopys. I had met Brad after Brad Pitt. My friend Jennifer was not the first Jennifer I'd met honoring Ms. Aniston, and I had met Chandlers of *Friends* inspiration. I had met Hank Manning, who had named himself after the mighty Colts quarterback Peyton Manning. And I had met people with names of invented origin, just sounds, really: Blarth. Blarth? *Méiyǒu yìsi, hǎo tīng,* I'd been told. (It doesn't mean anything, it sounds good.) *Blarth?*

In Shanghai, English names tended more toward the conservative. I had met no Blarths in Shanghai, no Sweet Green Apples. Marcus seemed a perfectly reasonable name for a marketing professional in a multinational company based in Shanghai. It seemed to fit him, really. He looked like a Marcus. "What's your Chinese name?" I asked him.

Wang Wei, he told me.

I worked with a Wang Wei; I had another friend of a friend who was Wang Wei; I met Wang Weis nearly every day in China. You couldn't throw a dumpling in a Chinese city and not hit a Wang Wei. Wang Wei was the Bill Smith of China. Or Bill Smith was the Wang Wei of America. Although, when I thought about it, I couldn't recall ever having met a Bill Smith in America, or anywhere else for that matter. Chinese people were forever asking foreigners their opinion about what they should choose for their adopted Western name. Perhaps to the next Chinese person who asked me to weigh in on his name choice I would suggest Bill Smith. It's a classic American name, I would tell him, though I don't know a single person who has it.

While Jennifer and Marcus talked about their jobs and the friends they had in common and who was dating whom, I thought I could have been eating in any bland beer garden anywhere in the world listening to the same pointless conversation. Another term developers use for a place like Xintiandi is "festival marketplace." A concept used to revitalize American downtowns, festival marketplaces such as Boston's Quincy Market and New York's South Street Seaport are equal

Where once families of working poor Shanghainese lived in shikumen, now wealthy Chinese and foreigners spend money at a combination shopping mall and theme park built from the shells of historic buildings that have been emptied of their original residents. This development, known as Xintiandi, also contains a museum where the First National Congress of the Communist Party of China was held.

parts theme park and shopping mall. The architect responsible for Xintiandi once worked for the company that created the yuppification of Quincy Market. During his first trip to the area in Shanghai slated for redevelopment, Mr. Wood had recognized the value of the existing architecture and convinced the Shui On Group, the company overseeing the project, not to raze the buildings but to retrofit them. Interiors were gutted and scrubbed clean; glass storefronts were placed in the stone frames so shoppers could see shoes on display. But before all this happened, something had to be done about the people inside the shikumen. Ancient grannies could not play mahjong outside the Christian Dior store. As the area's purpose shifted from housing families to providing upscale shopping for the upwardly mobile, the sanitization process that helped create this change involved relocating families. Lots of families. All told, when Shanghai's New Heaven and Earth complex was completed, between two to three thousand families, depending on who was doing the math—either government cadres overseeing the project or housing rights activists not happy about the new heaven morphing overhead and the new earth shifting beneath their feet—had been relocated. One enormous housing unit, where thirty families resided before the redevelopment, was cleared of its tenants and turned into what is now referred to as *The Clubhouse*. The Clubhouse contains a conference center where corporate types meet and toss around terms like "festival marketplace," and it boasts private dining rooms where the price of an appetizer could keep a shikumen family in dumplings for a week.

I wasn't necessarily against all this. I had met none of the people who'd been relocated, despite trying to track a couple of them down. And I had read no reports of their discontent. For all I knew they had been compensated handsomely, had landed windfalls that made them happy to move from their scruffy low-slung neighborhood into a gleaming tower in the sky. (Those gleaming towers were visible all around Xintiandi, a constant reminder that one might have been in the Xintiandi theme park celebrating a historic way of life in Shanghai, but the theme park was surrounded by the all-encompassing cyberpunk movie set that is the Shanghai skyline.) I was all for free markets, I was an unabashed fan of progress. China had in the past couple of decades succeeded in pulling more people out of poverty than at any other time in human history. Millions of Chinese were having wretched destitution replaced with a standard of living that offered them comfort, health and happiness. This was no small thing. And for the people being lifted up, the Chinese people riding the economic wave all the way from the rural poverty of the rice paddies to the sparkling towers in the sky, it was a very big thing. It was everything.

Isn't it easy to criticize a country for their poor record of human rights when one has a full belly? But full belly or no, you say, human rights must be respected! Our luxurious lifestyle is not the point, you insist—China treating its people badly is. And maybe you are right. But there is a saying in China that only when your stomach is full can you know right and wrong. Poverty breeds desperation, the thinking goes, and desperate people will do anything to escape their poverty. Morality is a luxury of the wealthy, and China can start to really focus on human rights after its people are fed. Many Chinese believe this. Can we categorically reject this premise if we have never felt our stomachs twist and cramp with hunger?

On October 1, 1949, Mao Zedong announced the founding of the People's Republic of China with this statement: "The Chinese have always been a great, courageous and industrious nation; it is only in modern times that they have fallen behind. And that was due entirely to oppression and exploitation by foreign imperialism and domestic reactionary governments . . . . Ours will no longer be a nation subject to insult and humiliation. We have stood up."

Soon after Mao took power he launched what became known as the Great Leap Forward. It was aptly named, albeit ironically: it was a great leap forward not toward progress, as Mao had claimed it would be, but toward the abyss. Initiating what might very well be the most disturbing episode of collective madness in the history of humankind, the Communist Party made to the people of China promises of wealth and plenty. Mao melded Soviet pseudo-science with his own dunderheaded beliefs to develop agricultural directives that created the greatest famine the world has ever known. Applying his understanding of communist "class struggle" to crops, Mao decreed that plants of the same species should be planted closely together because, being from the same class, they would not compete with each other and would cooperate. The densely packed crops died, whole fields went to rot, and the peasants who followed this directive went hungry. In another ludicrous scheme, citizens were forced to build backyard furnaces to make steel. Born of Mao's metallurgical moronity, these furnaces consumed peoples' knives, bicycles and woks—and every other bit of metal they could muster—and they denuded landscapes of trees and bushes that were used to fuel the fires. The ridiculous contraptions produced lumps of worthless pig iron. The list of the chairman's follies would be comical were it not that his slapstick antics killed millions.

While Mao was destroying the Chinese economy with his lunatic policies, officials across China, afraid of being punished if they questioned government directives, announced absurdly high grain targets for the 1959 harvest. When the amount of crops that were harvested fell far short of the inflated goals, officials, fearing for their lives lest they incur the wrath of Mao and his minions, made up phony figures, often tripling or quadrupling the size of the actual harvest in their district. Attached to the impossibly high targets were quotas of grain that had to be delivered to state authorities. If the officials failed to meet their targets and deliver their quotas, they would be highlighting the failure of the Great Leap Forward. So they seized from the peasants in the districts they controlled every grain of rice they could grab, desperately trying to meet the bloated quotas they owed the state. The quotas were met, but at the expense of the peasants—who were left with nothing to eat. With all the grain they had grown taken from them, the peasants and their families began to starve. If they complained about having their grain taken away or about being hungry, they were denounced as enemies of the Communist Party and tortured or killed. In what eminent China scholar Jasper Becker calls a "climate of megalomania, make-believe, lies and brutality" in his book *Hungry Ghosts: Mao's Secret Famine*, the Communist Party, which had ridden to power largely on the backs of the peasants, pretended the famine didn't exist. When government cadres went to the countryside to observe the progress of the Great Leap Forward, local officials orchestrated carefully staged shows complete with bountiful piles of grain, fields thick with crops, and ruddy-faced, smiling peasants. Bark that had been stripped from trees and boiled by starving peasants was painted over so that Party leaders would have no clue as to the desperation of the people. Senior officials toured the towns and discussed the nation's new economic policies over feasts fit for emperors. Leaders from Mao on down observed the sham displays of agrarian paradise and proclaimed the policies of the government a great success. The Communist Party spouted bogus propaganda, local officials lied and concealed their crimes, and the peasants starved in droves. Becker discovered officials in one district had tried to hide the rising death toll by issuing regulations that made "crying and wailing" illegal. They banned traditional mourning clothes and ordered peasants to plant crops in the fresh soil that blanketed endless acres of graves.

A few cadres confronted Mao about the famine, but anyone who spoke up was quickly denounced, demoted, tortured or killed—or some combination thereof. Eventually the evidence of the misery being caused by the Great Leap Forward became impossible for Mao to ignore. Perhaps this was because 30 million of his people were missing. Thirty million corpses might have gotten his attention and clued him in that something was wrong. Some estimates of the death toll caused by the Great Leap Forward dip as low as 14 million, some range higher than 40 million, but Becker, who has devoted many years to painstakingly researching this brutal episode of history, has determined that at least 30 million people perished. Thirty million people. Sometimes I say the number aloud and it never fails to make me slowly shake my head. The entire population of California, dead. Combine the buffoonery of the Three Stooges with the cruelty of Attila the Hun, and there you have it: China's Chairman Mao.

And the Great Leap Forward was but the beginning for Mao. He was just getting warmed up. Jung Chang and Jon Halliday, in *Mao: The Unknown Story*, their epic biography that aims to slay China's myth of Mao as a great man once and for all and to expose the naked brutality of his rule, argue convincingly (though some

China specialists have criticized the authors' selective use of sources and sensationalistic tone) that the true creed to which Mao devoted himself was not communism but the pursuit of personal power at any cost. That cost, according to Chang and Halliday, when Mao finished with his grisly work, was more than seventy million Chinese, making Mao responsible for, by far, more deaths than any other twentieth-century leader; some argue he was the greatest mass murderer in history. When it comes to wanton slaughter in the names of communism and socialism, Mao makes Stalin and Pol Pot look like wannabes.

"What do you think of Mao?" I asked Marcus.

"He made China into a strong country." Marcus took a drink of beer from his mug, and with a manicured finger he wiped a bit of froth from his lips.

"Mao was good for China?" I said.

"Of course," Marcus said. "He created a new China."

"At what cost?" I asked.

"He made mistakes. All strong leaders make some mistakes."

"Seventy million of them?"

"Chairman Mao," Jennifer said, "he is like the George Washington in your America."

I studied her face. She wasn't kidding. Here we sat on a patio of a modish mall built on the skeletons of homes that had been emptied of families and scrubbed clean to make way for marketing professionals who wore fashions from Versace and Vera Wang and quoted *Friends* and told me that Mao had made their nation strong. Beyond the patio and the pretty brickwork of Xintiandi rose surreal spires and shiny glass pillars through endless scrims of haze. It all seemed some strange mirage that could vanish in a moment, as a vision from a fevered dream swiftly fades when the boiling heat and sickening chills subside. I looked around me at Shanghai. This place of shapeshifting towers. This collective hallucination gathering itself into a sprawling, formless city. I ordered another beer and drank it from the bottle in a few long pulls. I could not purge Mao's murderous reign from my mind when all around me stood towers built of bones.

I struggle constantly with Mao. I tell myself I shouldn't be too judgmental about him, because doing so makes many Chinese people very angry. But I like Chinese people quite a lot, and Mao was responsible for the death of so many of them—which makes *me* very angry. What a mess.

Was Mao simply a moron, hatching what were arguably the dumbest economic policies ever devised by a human, or a madman addicted to murder? Or was he something even worse, something like the Judge in Cormac McCarthy's *Blood*

Meridian, an agent of chaos loosed upon the earth from some dark and nameless netherworld? Perhaps he was a mix of all these things: a policy dunce who liked a good slaying as much as the next bloodthirsty tyrant, and on his best days he approximated a demon spat forth from the fiery bowels of hell. But this was certain: images of Mao were displayed from one end of the country to the other. And rarely with ironic intent. Chairman Mao was a deity that filled the vacuum of the modern Chinese soul. The Chinese people, stripped of emperors and religion, were left with little to revere other than a tyrant, a butcher, a madman. Long live Chairman Mao.

"Do you know why Americans are coming to China to adopt Chinese girl babies?" Jennifer had asked me earlier that day.

"Why?" I'd said. Because they felt sorry for them, of course. But I hadn't said this, not wanting to offend her.

"Because they know that Chinese are smart."

"They're adopting Chinese baby girls because Chinese people are smart?" I'd said.

"Of course. They want babies with high IQs."

China has made some progress in coming to terms with its past, acknowledging the mistakes and excesses of the Cultural Revolution (which followed the Great Leap Forward and affected the educated classes), but the Communist Party has had little to say about the tens of millions of anonymous peasants who died because of the Great Leap Forward. Mao medallions dangle from the rearviews of cabs, and Mao pictures hang framed on families' walls. And every school in Shanghai displays a picture of the beloved chairman—a potent clue to how a twisted tyrant bent on bloodlust could be a national icon. The Communist Party controls the schools and indoctrinates the children, teaching its future leaders that their great Chairman Mao had basically been good for China. He had been, as official government calculations reckoned it, 70 percent correct and 30 percent wrong. How bureaucrats had computed this metric was a mystery, but these numbers rang in the ears of schoolchildren throughout China. 70/30. Ask any Chinese child and he or she will tell you. And these children will tell you their beloved chairman made China into a strong country, heroically ending their nation's "century of humiliation." He sent the Chinese army into battle against the Americans in Korea, they will remind you, and he fought the most powerful nation on earth to a standstill.

One thing Chinese children are not taught in school is this: So desperate with hunger were peasants during the holocaust of the Great Leap Forward, they resorted to boiling grass and to eating roots, bugs, weeds and mud; and when these measures failed to sate their hunger, they became more desperate yet, and some of them began eating the flesh of human babies. Families horrified at the thought of eating their own babies traded babies with other families so that the meat they consumed in order to survive was not of their own child. The first time I read this, I put down the book that told this gruesome tale and I sat very quietly for a very long time, until my wife called me down from my office to eat. That night at the dinner table I looked at the chicken leg on my plate in a way that I had never looked at a chicken leg before.

After reading about the carnage and cannibalism of the Great Leap Forward, whenever I grew baffled at contemporary China's policies that seemed so harshly repressive toward its people, I thought of parents eating a baby's flesh so that they would not starve to death. I tried to imagine their desperation, the craziness of their hunger. And then I thought of a rising nation so hungry for better lives for its citizens that it would do whatever it had to do to lift its people out of poverty, hundreds of millions of them, even if doing so meant that it had to devour its young. People eager for freedom are consumed by the Party in China each day; but each day the Communist Party of China progresses toward its goal of boosting a nation bloated with people into a prosperity in which its citizens dine on crab roe at Xintiandi. And then these happily bloated citizens jump in taxis with Mao medallions dangling from the rearview mirrors.

My goal in learning about China had never been to judge it. China is far too complicated for me to understand, let alone criticize or condemn. I have met legions of China lovers; I have met hordes of China haters. Their world views are completely opposite but the same with regard to the childish simplicity of their certainty. China isn't good or bad. It is massive; it is endlessly complex; it simply *is*. How can one make a blanket statement, a simple value judgment, about one fifth of all humanity? With 20 percent of the planet's population, China must contain multitudes of motivations and behaviors, must hold every single thing available in the human heart. And now it has Starbucks.

"How about a latte?" I said to Marcus and Jennifer.

Before we left the beer garden, there was the bill to settle. Marcus and I argued over who would pay the tab; I let him win so he would earn face in front of Jennifer. This in turn earned me respect from Marcus—we were off and running in the Chinese relationship-building face game. Business in China is all about what the Chinese call *guānxi*. Relationships. Connections. Think good-old-boys network in 1950s America—but more pervasive, and more important when it comes to getting things done. *Guānxi* is the people you know, and how you know them, and what you have done for them, and what they can do for you. To get anything done in China you have to know people. You must have pull with people who can do you favors. The more people the better, and if these people are important, all the better. And if these important people happen to be government officials, that is the best scenario of all. Guanxi.

Maybe this isn't so different from how business is done in America. Graduates of America's most prestigious MBA programs have told me that the most important lesson they learned in their studies was that one's network is everything, and cultivating the right connections is the single most important skill one must possess in order to succeed. The main difference, in my experience, regarding business relationships in China and America, is this: China's fledgling free market economy is riddled with corruption, and contracts aren't worth the paper upon which they are printed. Many new business tycoons have old connections—connections to the Communist Party. To enter a new market, to open a store, to import items or ship goods from the country, you must have a permit or permission, and government bureaucrats are the gatekeepers who grant permission and regulate access to permits. The best way to succeed in the contemporary climate of gangster capitalism is to have guanxi with Communist cadres.

But back to Marcus. He seemed a bit vacuous to me and I thought maybe I didn't want to have anything to do with him. He could keep his guanxi. He was a type and I recognized him instantly. His English was as crisp as the upturned cuffs on his designer jeans. He was young and he wanted it all: powerful position in a powerfully branded company, bucks, Buick—and a hot girlfriend who hung out with him for his bucks, Buick and powerful position in a powerfully branded company. He'd studied marketing in college, he told me. Not that there was anything wrong with all that. The pursuit of the material good life is a valid way to live; I just found myself uncomfortable around people who'd devoted their college years to learning how to shill crap to the masses. Of course, my job title was now Marketing Director for a travel company. But I liked to think I was above it. It was just my day job and I had never taken it seriously. I wasn't really into marketing and selling. It's not like I liked money or anything. Okay. So I liked the money that went with my cushy job, and maybe I was happier working in the travel business than I had ever been as a starving writer. Maybe Marcus and I would get along just fine. Besides, I was toying with the idea of writing this book, and Marcus had access to an inside world of which I very much needed to become a part were I to write about the city. I was a bumpkin out of my league in this newfangled metropolis, no more comfortable among the beautiful people of Xintiandi than a peasant rice farmer from the countryside would be. I needed a guide. I needed someone to teach me what kind of shoes to wear. I glanced down at Marcus's footwear, which looked as if it could be displayed in a store window of Xintiandi, and I scooted my running shoes, torn and stained, into the shadows beneath the table as I pocketed my wallet and Marcus laid bills bearing Chairman Mao upon the glass-topped table.

The tab paid, we set off to explore the alleys of Xintiandi. These were not the lilong Jennifer and I had visited earlier that day. We saw, instead of old women playing mahjong, young women in wedge heels with yoga bags swinging from their shoulders. Instead of little boys playing in the street, men with briefcases hurried into bars. One bar had minimalist décor so spare it seemed the bar had closed and the owner had sold off all the furniture and fixtures, and people were now standing around in an empty room to celebrate one last time before the door was locked forever. Minimalism so minimal, if one didn't know any better, one would think there was nothing there. Apparently plenty of trendsters had clued in to what was there: the empty space was packed with people. I had so much to learn about this edgy urban world. And I definitely needed better shoes.

But it was all good when we finally made it to Starbucks and I swilled a latte and the caffeine coursed through my veins and lifted me above my morose pondering and up toward the pleasant plane of heightened senses that comes with a caffeine blast, and soon I was tapping my tattered shoes to the urban tribal beat of Shanghai.

"I usually don't drink coffee," Jennifer said as she took a sip from a cup the size of a soup bowl.

"I drink coffee every day," Marcus said. I raised my cup to his and proposed a toast to this brave new world of coffee and Buicks. He grinned and nodded.

One fun thing about being an American in China is that one is afforded a delicious bit of freedom to say ridiculous things. Things that would not pass muster most other places in the world. One could say something along the lines of "Let's toast this brave new world of coffee and Buicks," and Chinese people would smile and nod and assume the fault was on their end, and they were missing some important cultural clue, and what you had said surely made perfect sense. Of course this only worked when there weren't other Americans around to brazenly articulate what the Chinese were quietly thinking: something along the lines of *"What the fuck are you talking about?"*

Speaking of marketing and coffee, on my first trip to the Forbidden City in Beijing, where Chinese emperors had lived and reigned in perfect splendor and complete isolation from the common people, I had, while exploring the purported 9,999 royal rooms, run smack into a Starbucks. I had downed a latte and then complained to everyone who would listen how crass it was that Starbucks was in the Forbidden City. Was nothing sacred? On my second visit to the Forbidden City, while escorting a group of MBA students from UCLA, I had drank a latte with them in Starbucks as we discussed branding in China and how for many decades the only brand the Chinese people had known was the CCP, and now, thanks to savvy marketing, they couldn't get enough of KFC. But on my third visit to the Forbidden City, I had encountered trouble finding said Starbucks because the corporate logo, that green and white circle that beckons caffeine addicts in caffeine-deficient China (*What do you mean you don't have coffee in this restaurant? What's wrong with you people?*) like a shining beacon in a dark and perilous sea, was nowhere to be seen. The Starbucks store was still there, I found out later, but had been forbidden from blatantly advertising its presence. The sign had been removed to appease Chinese citizens vexed by a symbol of corporate America adorning the Forbidden City, where their emperors had once banned them from entering. The Forbidden City was for emperors, not American brands. Eventually, bowing to pressure from angry Chinese, Starbucks shuttered the shop.

Marcus and I, buzzing from our second latte each, talked about all this, and we talked about Buick's marketing campaign in China, how they had diluted their brand image when they leveraged their success to start selling lower-end models at lower price points; and we talked about how Lays had adapted their brand to Chinese tastes by offering potato chip flavors such as fragrant red chili and blueberry; and we talked about Pizza Hut going upscale in China to build a high-end brand, waiters in white gloves opening the doors for young Chinese professionals and pizza chefs dishing up delicious pie instead of the greasy slop Pizza Hut serves in the States; and we were having a grand old time talking shop until I noticed that Jennifer looked a bit green around the gills.

"It's the coffee," she said after I explained the saying "green around the gills" with mixed success, Marcus nodding his understanding, Jennifer just turning a deeper shade of green and looking more confused.

"You really don't drink coffee very often, do you?" I said.

"This is perhaps the second time."

Jennifer and I had drank tea together, but not coffee, I realized. "Wow," I said. She did not look well. "Maybe you're allergic to it?"

"Maybe it's because we drank beer over there and now we're here drinking coffee," Marcus said.

This sounded plausible. I fetched a cup of water and handed it to Jennifer. She took a few sips and then said she needed to walk.

So we quit Starbucks and continued wandering the new heaven and earth. Jennifer picked up the marketing discussion where Marcus and I had left off and said, "My company works with some of the tents . . . tem . . ." With a fingertip she began to draw the letters on her palm.

"Tenants?" I offered.

"We work with the tenants here. Some of them have to leave because the rent is so high now." Jennifer explained that when Xintiandi had first opened, the developer had offered low leasing prices because no one knew about Xintiandi yet—it needed to build brand recognition. That Jennifer knew terms like "brand recognition" was surprising to me, until I remembered she worked with foreigners who flung terms like "brand recognition" around her office every day. I had to teach her what a mug was, as in "coffee mug," but she didn't miss a beat when someone said "brand recognition" or "market penetration." Why that brought silly smiles to the faces of some foreigners was something I hadn't figured out a tactful way to explain to Jennifer. She was Western in so many ways, her Ralph Lauren jeans and Gucci handbag, her encyclopedic knowledge of *Friends* episodes, the plasma TV she'd just bought that she spoke of in a manner nothing less than reverential, as if she burned incense in front of it and chanted its praise as her parents did at their ancestors' altar. ("The picture is so clear and so big it's not like watching TV, it's like watching the world," she had said to me with so much furrowed-brow sincerity.) She spoke of her wish to move to America for a few years to perfect her English; she spoke of American movies; but she never spoke of sex. (For people who have created a country absolutely crammed full of whorehouses, the Chinese can be remarkably prudish about discussing sex.) Many things Jennifer guarded, and her love life was one of them. She occasionally asked about my wife, and I asked her if she was dating anyone or had a boyfriend, which made her blush and put a hand in front of her mouth, but the discussions seemed perfunctory, something etiquette dictated we do.

The truth was this: The only heat between us came from the friction of our cultures rubbing against each other—this friction made a flame that flickered in intriguing shapes but not a fire that would cause our relationship to combust. I saw in our future together nothing more than teasing laughter and friendly language lessons, and this seemed to me a gift. I knew more about Jennifer than I did about any other Chinese person, and I was grateful she had let me into her life. Seven years separated us, as did at least a foot of height. When Jennifer's shyly grinning Chinese friends asked her if I was her boyfriend she told them I was her big American brother. Her friends seemed to like that. When my American friends asked me if I was bedding Jennifer I told them they were idiots: she was my little Chinese sister. My friends said I was an idiot for spending so much time with a Chinese girl who was just a friend.

I could think of no better use of my time. I had been to China on many occasions, under the auspices of a nonprofit global leadership organization, working for a travel company to bring American university groups to China, and traveling on my own. But all of that had been surface: whether developing immersion programs for young leaders, or escorting tours for universities, or backpacking around China with a *Lonely Planet* guidebook in hand, I had skimmed across the surface of the country, had skated past people's lives with little more than a glance at the things that mattered. I had been a tourist gaping at China from behind the windows of a bus. I had been a tour leader with a phrasebook and a camera. When I was with Jennifer, I felt for the first time that I was sinking below the surface. She was fixing my gaze on the things that were important to her, drawing me down into her world. And all I had to do was teach her that *mug* was another word for coffee cup.

Marcus walked with a confident gait and I noticed Jennifer watching him walk. Jennifer said, "Rents here are now ten or twenty times as high as when Xintiandi opened. They had low rents at first because they wanted to make it easy for international brands like Häagen-Dazs to move here. But because Xintiandi is a big brand now, they can charge much more. Now everyone knows the brand and they all come shopping here. It's expensive for the tenants to stay here, but if they don't want to pay the new rent it doesn't matter because there are so many businesses waiting to move in here."

"Häagen-Dazs can afford to stay here, I'm sure," I said.

"But perhaps for the Chinese companies it's not so easy."

"Soon Chinese companies are going to be as big as American companies." This from Marcus. "Chinese brands will be all over the world just like American brands."

I asked Marcus to name one Chinese brand he thought would spread throughout the world.

"A lot of them," he said, not naming one.

One of the great debates going on in the Chinese Communist Party is how to foster innovation. China is, of course, good at copying things. Pirated CDs are sold on street corners throughout Shanghai; knockoff name brand clothing and fake Rolex watches fill the markets of the city. QQ, the Chinese answer to MSN Messenger, is essentially MSN Messenger with Chinese characters and, inexplicably, a winking penguin wearing a scarf that serves as a mascot. Sometimes it seems there is nothing new under the Chinese sun, just infinite replicas of ideas created in the West, with a winking penguin thrown in. For China to move beyond its economic base of manufacturing plastic crap and trinkets, it has to produce original creative content. To do this, it has to nurture innovative thinkers. But the children in its schools, the future creators and inventors who would lead the nation beyond an economy based on sweatshops and into an innovation-based economy, study beneath portraits of Mao, cramming their heads full of gibberish and regurgitating pointless facts that their teachers tell them. Mao was 70 percent right, 30 percent wrong, kids—repeat after me. Now, go have an original idea, go create something.

It is true that Chinese children spend many more hours in school studying than their American counterparts do, a fact that some in the West find a disturbing indicator of China's coming superiority on the world stage. But those children spend endless hours memorizing nonsense. China's government, true to form, experimented with addressing the dearth of innovative minds not by eliminating the nonsense in the educational system, the blind conformity fostered in students taught to never question their teachers or the Party, but by mandating "innovation sessions." For a fixed period of time each day, schoolchildren would be forced to practice in the classroom, under the watchful eye of their teachers, "innovative thinking." Those who speak of the inevitability of China's global supremacy in the coming years really should spend some time in China.

China has potential, mad potential, massive potential—that much is certain. Whether it will be realized or not remains to be seen. Some days I think they have a 70 percent chance of success; some days I believe it's 30. Some days even less. As you stare at the freakish pastiche of the Shanghai skyline, remember that the country has not produced a single invention or idea of global importance in the past few hundred years. Tall towers do not a vibrant civilization make, and most days I believe this: reports of the death of the West have been greatly exaggerated, and predictions of China's impending world dominance are breathless pap.

But enough of that. Back to the matter at hand: What to do in the consumer paradise of Shanghai's new heaven and earth? We ducked into a café advertising free wi-fi and Marcus powered up his laptop of exceptional slimness and logged on and opened a browser in less time than it took me to send a text message. We Googled Xintiandi and read one of the hits. We learned that Xintiandi is where "yesterday meets tomorrow in Shanghai today."

"Who knew," I said.

"I know the person who wrote that," Marcus said. "He was in charge of making this site."

The site seemed some sort of portal for hotel bookings. "He must be very proud," I said.

"Our company bid for the contract but we didn't get it," Marcus said, missing the smart-alecky intent of my comment.

Sometimes the utter soul-sucking vacuity of marketing punched me right in the gut, and my only response was to make fun of everyone who sold things for a living, to excoriate every single person who'd sold out to make a buck, including myself. I salved my own wounded conscience by reassuring myself that my job had little to do with marketing (our company's website and brochures, written by someone for whom English was not a native language and editing was not a strong suit, were superfluous, as we sold trips almost exclusively by word of mouth). I brought groups of the best and brightest in America to China, and I told myself there was value in sharing China with Americans, letting them experience it for themselves and make up their own minds about the country and its people independent of the relentless barrage of sensationalistic stories in the Western media. Poisoned toothpaste, dangerous toys, end-of-the-world pollution, red tape wrapped so tightly around every business opportunity that no company could ever hope to cut through it. Behind the stories were people, but those people seldom appeared in the news, just the problems—and to be sure, China did not want for problems. But I wanted Americans to meet Chinese people, not just read about their problems, and my job allowed me to send groups to China to do this. Though I had been issued, for reasons unclear to me, the title of "Marketing Director."

But what of these people who lived to sell, who sold to live? Surely they could find a higher purpose than writing insipid prose for websites, surely they could come up with something better to do than blathering on hotel booking portals about "yesterday meeting tomorrow today."

Marcus was reading through the site, commenting on the copy, praising what he liked, mentioning what he would have done differently. When Marcus had been studying marketing in college I had been reading Nietzsche. But what a luxury, to be able to lounge around and learn about philosophy knowing full well I could always find a job and I would always have food.

"What was it like for your parents?" I asked Marcus.

He looked away from the computer to stare at me. "What?"

"Your parents—what were their lives like? They must have been alive during the Great Leap Forward, and they must have been about your age during the Cultural Revolution, right?"

"The great what?"

"The Three Years of Natural Disasters," Jennifer said.

Chinese students are taught that the mass starvation during the Great Leap Forward was the result of natural disasters, not flawed economic policies and the incompetence of the country's leaders.

"Oh yeah," Marcus said. "Yeah, I guess."

He swiveled his face back toward the computer screen. His cheeks and eyes glowed bright with the light of a thousand pixels.

"Xintiandi is divided into a North Block and a South Block," Marcus said.

"Who knew," I said again, disappointed that I couldn't engage Marcus in a discussion about his family's past but not terribly surprised. Most young Chinese people I knew didn't want to dig through the sordid strata of their country's history, whether because they didn't want to unearth unpleasant memories and reminders of their nation's failure, or because they simply didn't care. Like American youth who want to shop and find jobs that make them a lot of money and drive sexy cars and surf the net and listen to their iPods and go clubbing every weekend, and who could not care less about America's legacy of racial separation and injustice, or the shaky moral questions of how we conducted the Vietnam War, or the role of the U.S. in supporting dictatorships in Latin America, or any number of other things buried in the past and not relevant to the pursuit of their material comfort, most young professionals in Shanghai such as Marcus just wanted to go after the good life now and not look back. And who could blame them.

Looking back is painful—especially when what is lurking in the rearview is tens of millions of dead bodies and parents who somehow survived the carnage, perhaps by selling out their principles. Perhaps they'd turned in their neighbors and watched them bleed to death at the hands of a mob. Perhaps to survive they'd eaten tree bark. Or worse. If I were Marcus, I probably wouldn't be looking back either.

I leaned over and together we stared at the computer screen and read endless inanities about Xintiandi, while all around us young men and women opened their laptops and shouted into their cell phones, the din of the café rising as manic voices spoke of money, sex and power. How much this cost, how much that was worth, who had gone home with whom, who had started a new company.

Xià hǎi, "jumping into the sea," is what the Chinese call starting your own business. In the West we have been jumping into the sea for a long time, have enjoyed the freedom to start a business if we choose to, have enjoyed a rich material life and sexual freedom for many decades. But it is all new to the Chinese. They are jumping into the sea, plunging into the unknown, buoyed by the dream of American-style pleasure and wealth while they swirl in risk.

"Do you want to start your own business someday?" I asked Marcus.

"Of course," he said.

"A marketing company?"

"My own marketing consulting company. But it will be a long time before I can do it."

"*Xià hǎi*," I said.

Marcus grinned at me. "Yeah," he said in English. "It will be a long time before I jump into the sea, but I'll do it."

"I hope you get rich," I said.

"Me too," Marcus said.

"What will you do after you get rich?" I asked.

"What do you mean?"

"What will you do after you have started a successful marketing company and you have so much money you don't have to work anymore, and after you have bought everything that you want—then what will you do?" I queried almost every Chinese person I met in this way, and often their answer was to stare at me without answering, or to say they didn't understand the question. Sometimes their response was "get more rich." A few of them said "travel all over the world."

"Teach," Marcus said without hesitation.

Had he told me he would become a nun I would not have been more surprised. "Teach? Like what, teach school?"

"Education is the most important thing. There is nothing in the world that is more important. I like to teach kids, but I don't want to be poor. I want to get rich. Then I'll retire and be a teacher and give students good educations so they can be rich, and then China can be a rich country."

He'd clearly thought this through. "And what will China do when it's a rich country?" I asked.

"Why do you ask so many questions?"

I stared a moment at the creaseless tapers of his eyes. "I'm just curious," I said. "What will China do after you've gotten rich and helped other Chinese people get rich and the whole country is rich. Then what?"

Marcus nodded and smiled and seemed to get back into the fantasy game. "Okay," he said. "When China is a rich country it will help people in poor countries like in Africa have better educations and get rich so they can make their countries rich."

"Okay." I nodded. "And after China has helped all the poor countries in the world get rich, then what? What do all those rich countries do with all their money? What do they do after they've become rich?"

Marcus looked away from Jennifer and me. He stared into a crowd of Chinese hipsters in boots, jeans and T-shirts as though their fashion choices might offer him the answer. After a moment he said, "If all the countries in the world got rich there wouldn't be wars anymore. Countries make wars because they are poor."

How exactly America fit into this scenario I wasn't sure nor did I ask, and left it at that. World peace through marketing. Why not.

Together Marcus, Jennifer and I scoured the Xintiandi copy on the website, analyzing the marketing jargon, doing our part to lift the nations of the world up from poverty and foster world peace.

We learned that the South Block of Xintiandi is modern and boasts the best boutiques; the North Block holds the shikumen lanes that make the shopping complex unique. I told Marcus and Jennifer I wanted to explore those lanes. We looked at Xintiandi on Google Earth, zooming in on the maze of alleyways. I had become a full-fledged Google Earth addict requiring at least one weekly fix of floating digitally over Shanghai's topography, dropping down on points of interest, swooping toward the details on the ground. To use Google Earth is to be a god surveying one's domain from the heavens above.

After enough gazing down from the heavens to set our heads spinning, Marcus stashed his laptop in his briefcase and we headed into the labyrinth of Xintiandi.

Setting foot on the flagstones of an actual alley was a bit of a buzzkill after the high of Google Earth. It was as though we'd been flying in a dream, detached from the ground but able to reconnect with any part of the planet whenever we chose, dipping down to see something up close, zooming out to scope the big picture. The beauty of computers is that they can create worlds not subject to the boring rules of physics, and there is no more potent fantasy than to be outside the law of gravity or to exceed the speed of light. But that was over now; that limitless world was shut down in the laptop in Marcus's briefcase and lay dormant in the crystal of a silicon chip. I felt the hard stones of the alley beneath my feet, felt the bricked walls graze my shoulders. I sniffed the chemical reek that infuses Shanghai's air. It is the scent of frantic industry, the odor of a city building itself into a behemoth. The opium smoke that once wafted through the hedonistic alleyways of old Shanghai has been replaced with a narcotic more powerful yet, the delirious dream of creating the world's leading twenty-first century city. The smell is not pleasant at first, but one gets used to it, and in time one even begins to crave it. The sky in Colorado is too clean, and on bluebird days at my home in Boulder I long for my next fix of Shanghai sky, my next hit of the city's chemical air. There is cocaine in Shanghai's air, there is ecstasy in it, I am convinced. When your brain is sizzling from a dose of pure Shanghai, you have a blast while the wild ride lasts; but as with any drug, once it ends you are back where you started, and you feel emptier than before you began.

We passed a club with music blasting through an open door and the thumping base echoed in my bones. Outside the door we paused to peer in at a stage where a wisp-thin Chinese man with a Yankees cap perched crookedly on his head and his mouth curled to one side in a snarl made Chinese rhymes that Marcus told me translated loosely as "I need more money" and "I need more bitches." One has not truly experienced weirdness until one has witnessed the jaw-droppingly bizarre clash of cultures that is Chinese gangster rap.

"What kind of music do you like," I asked Marcus in Chinese.

"His Chinese is good," he said to Jennifer, and then in English he answered me: "I like hip hop. But not this hip hop. This is crap. I'll take you to a good club where we can hear some good music."

We were back to our old games and I wondered would they ever end. Marcus's compliment seemed a sort of backhanded insult when coupled with his insistence on continuing the conversation in English. His English was so much better than my Chinese, he seemed to be saying, why even bother trying to talk in Chinese. It was a pat on my head and a slap in the face. "Your Chinese is cute, but if we really want to talk about anything of substance, let's give up the charade and just talk in English, okay?" That this was entirely true didn't lighten the sting of the slap. More face for Marcus in front of Jennifer, less face for me. No worries. This was Marcus's country, this was his city, this was his life; I was a visitor here, an observer. I didn't need face. I needed information. I needed to get below the surface of Shanghai, to move beyond the spectacle of flashing lights and goofy Chinese gangster rap. I needed to know what was at stake in a city that was being razed and rebuilt at a pace and on a scale unknown in human history. More people were on the move than at any time before—hundreds of millions of peasants giving up their lives in the countryside to swarm the cities in search of work, millions of them heading toward Shanghai. More people being lifted out of poverty than at any point before. More construction cranes working round the clock, more tall buildings crowding the sky of this new world composed of towers in their countless thousands. And I was here to see it, to watch it all happen as Shanghai launched itself toward modernity and the largest Expo the world had ever known. Who needs face when one has a front-row seat at one of the most monumental events taking place on the planet, a change that might affect the human species for millennia to come. I lifted my Starbucks to-go cup to Marcus's and we tapped together our paper rims and plastic lids. "I definitely want to see that club," I said.

"I'll take you," he said, stuffing a business card into my shirt pocket. This was a decidedly Western thing to do. Chinese people usually hand and receive business cards with great delicacy, as though passing back and forth fragile eggs. Two hands give the *míngpiàn*, or "name card," as they're called, each card displaying the bearer's honorable name and deserving undivided attention. Two hands receive the card, and the receiver must scrutinize every English word, every Chinese character. Anything less than this careful attention, and the giver of the card loses face. Marcus slipping his card into my shirt pocket as though he were an American was either meant to put me at ease or to show me that he was comfortable with Western ways; or maybe he was telling me he was so modern he'd given up all vestiges of traditional Chinese decorum. I slipped my own card into his shirt pocket but he immediately fished it out and studied it with much head nodding. I smiled as I studied him studying the card. Our cultural roots lie anchored deep beneath the surface. I stopped at every Starbucks I passed and Marcus couldn't help but study a mingpian. But I had grown fond of the name card ritual, had begun to take great pleasure in the careful scrutiny to which every card is subjected, and Marcus knew the Starbucks menu more thoroughly than I.

We passed through a food court, where Marcus and Jennifer indulged my curiosity as I popped into restaurants and cafés to survey the fare. German, Italian, French, Brazilian, American, Korean, Japanese: the Benetton of food courts. We wandered down backstreets, walking past doorframes of elegantly carved stonework and heavy lacquered doors. Past boutiques selling purses and shoes, belts and hats. There were shikumen here, to be sure, but they were shells of their former selves and there was none of the messiness of lives being lived within them. This was a dead museum. A sanitized marketplace where things were bought and sold.

"Seems like shopping is the favorite pastime of people in Shanghai," I said. "Buying things gives people face?"

"You know about face?" Marcus asked.

"I'm trying to understand it. I've had some help from friends."

"I call this city Shang*buy*," Marcus said. "It's the capital of the Cha-Ching dynasty." He pointed at a Louis Vuitton label on his briefcase. "Buying expensive things gives people—"

"Mad face," Jennifer said, giggling so hard she turned green again. She stopped walking and took a few big breaths and then we were on our way.

Flyers advertising a new nightclub were thrust toward us by two women dressed schoolgirl style in short skirts and knee-high socks. Men clad in crisp white cooking smocks squatted in an alley sucking on cigarettes, heads wreathed in smoke. Electric bicycles glided silently by. We shuffled through drifts of dust and trash, wandering from a tight alleyway into a tall world of glass and steel, everything shining dully in the ashen light cast by a banished sun. Buildings shrouded in distant murk loomed and vanished like things imagined, and all objects in this stark otherworld seemed but pale copies of themselves beneath a sky that smothered the earth with heavy sheets of grit. The taste of it never left your mouth. The smell of it never faded from your clothes, your hair.

Inside the ultra-cool TMSK we sat on crystal stools at a crystal bar and the walls were crystal too. The throbbing music seemed the pulse of a frightened beast, and the cocktails came in every color in a crayon box. Because of the financial success of venues such as this, where the powerbrokers of the new Shanghai play in the prettified shells of shikumen, the value of the surrounding property was soaring, ensuring that the last of the adjacent lane neighborhoods would be scrubbed of their residents and rebuilt into lifestyle centers for the rich. Perhaps a few of the original families would be allowed to remain to help create the stage set of an idealized past—as had happened in other upscale shikumen redevelopment zones, such as Tianzifang. And grandmothers in pajamas would trudge past trendy bars and play badminton in the glow of electronic billboards as the high-rises that ringed their new world twinkled in the night.

"What a world," I said as I drained my crystal glass of a sticky purple substance.

"What do you mean?" Marcus said.

"He is always saying that," Jennifer said. "I have never heard it on *Friends*. Is it something Americans say?"

"It's something this American says."

We quit TMSK and journeyed back into a crowded colony of alleys where narrow brick walls blocked the sky. After wandering through this bewildering world of cramped and airless passageways, we turned a corner, and as though we'd passed from the wardrobe and into Narnia, the lanes abruptly ended and the walls vanished. All around us spires and cylinders and tall glass towers tumbled upward. As the gray day dissolved to grainy dusk, pulsing lights beat back the blackness of the night, and onward through the city streets we walked. Eventually we found ourselves in Tomorrow Square at a Ferrari dealership.

After working our way through the crowd outside and finally finding a place free of people, we gazed through spotless glass into the soft blaze of the showroom lights. More interesting to me than the candy-apple-red and sky-blue cars displayed inside were the faces of the people outside staring at the Ferraris. Some seemed so stunned by the sight of cars that cost three to four hundred thousand U.S. dollars they looked as though they might need to sit down and take small sips of air to keep from hyperventilating. Others seemed to glow with rapture, as though they were gazing upon a sacred icon in a church. A few looked as though they were in the throes of making love. I finally forced myself to look away from the people looking at the cars, and I looked at the cars themselves. They were beautiful indeed. They were breathtaking. They were sexy. So sleek, so modern, so brightly colored with coats of paint that looked as though they would neither rust nor fade, would never succumb to weather and time. They seemed eternal, these cars that sold at a rate of one or two a month to the moguls of Shanghai. These were objects that could defy decay—as if the wealthy could fend off death by sealing themselves inside these sparkling shells beneath the showroom lights. These shiny vessels of immortality.

Everyone in this city, it seemed, was moving toward this showroom window to stare with naked longing. None of them would ever be able to afford a Ferrari, but perhaps that was beside the point. Perhaps it was proximity to this extravagance that mattered most. For Chinese people to be in the presence of such bounty, such a costly prize, was to share in the experience of their nation's meteoric rise. Outside the showroom lay the dim alleys of Xintiandi, and beyond these gentrified lanes stretched alleys darker still, where globalization had yet to reach, where stores and houses slumped in benighted decay. Perhaps visitors to this temple of wealth in Tomorrow Square looked at the Ferraris and saw proof that the desperate days of the Great Leap Forward were far behind them. Or maybe they looked at the cars and saw reminders that they were poor peasants from the countryside who had come to this twenty-first-century boomtown to take dreary jobs and were now as far removed from the dream of driving a Ferrari as their ancestors before them had been from entering the Forbidden City. And maybe foreigners who came to this place to preach their platitudinous theories about what the Chinese people think and feel deluded themselves by believing that the questions they were seeking to the answers they had already arrived at would be found in the faces of Chinese people staring at these cars. Once upon a time in a land far away, foreigners looked to the Forbidden City to make sense of the great mystery of the Middle Kingdom; now they flock to the Ferrari dealership in Shanghai for clues to help decipher the riddle of modern China. And they are as clueless now as they were then. They return from the Ferrari showroom and proclaim some eloquent nonsense such as "China is a protean nation in the process of becoming." I am no exception. I pulled a notebook from my pocket and tried my damnedest to scribble some eloquent nonsense.

Marcus, Jennifer and I stood staring into the bright showroom at shiny cars, our backs to the dark, and for several minutes no one spoke or moved. The spell was finally broken when Marcus flipped open his phone to take a picture. A man in a black suit burst out of the showroom door and yelled that photos were not allowed. I asked him why, but he ignored me and went back through the door. Inside the showroom he leaned over the cherry-red hood of a Ferrari 575M and adjusted his tie in its reflection.

When we finally wrenched ourselves away from the surreal vision of transcendent light that was the Ferrari showroom, Jennifer and Marcus indulged my penchant for pointless wandering and we made our way back to the shadowy streets around Xintiandi. We ended up at the building where, on July 23, 1921, Mao Zedong, Marxist philosopher Li Da, and eleven others secretly convened the First National Congress of the Communist Party of China. A crowd of Chinese men, in business suits that would have blended in perfectly on the streets of New York or Tokyo, parted around us. As we stared at the Communist shrine, a family of three passed by on a scooter: dad driving, mom on back, baby girl riding in front. I looked at them and thought: "How cool would it be if a Ferrari drove by right now in front of the Communist museum and I could put that in my book!" No Ferrari drove by. Young people, many of them bespectacled, wearing ratty clothes and looking much like students making some kind of statement by wearing ratty clothes, milled around outside the museum. Chinese tourists led by a guide holding

Tomorrow Square boasts, among other modern marvels, a Ferrari dealership.

aloft a tall antennae that flew a triangular yellow flag walked in front of the building and then stopped, people circling around the guide until she disappeared and only her yellow flag was visible above the mob. I asked a man in the group where he was from: Jiangsu Province, he answered. They were all from Jiangsu. This was their first time in Shanghai. Like Midwesterners in Manhattan, the people in the Jiangsu group looked frazzled, a bit frightened, and utterly fascinated with the spectacle around them.

"We get these groups from the countryside every day in Shanghai," Marcus said, shaking his head. "They come in tour buses to see Shanghai and shop. Some of them save up their money for years so they can shop here."

"And they come here to learn about the history of Shanghai?" I asked. "About how the Communist Party started?"

"Mostly they come to shop."

First they would go inside the museum, their guide explained, and then they would walk around the stores outside. Several of them swiveled their heads to look away from the museum at the retail paradise of Xintiandi, which I took as confirmation that they were more interested in perusing designer brands than in paying their respects to the founding fathers of the Communist Party. But maybe I just wanted to believe this because it was so batty that in Shanghai people came to the birthplace of Communism to shop. Maybe I wanted to believe this because it would sound good in my book. So I asked the tourist standing closest to me this: "Learning about the Communist Party or shopping—which do you like more?"

She looked at me as though I were a ghost, her face twisted with what seemed fear mixed with deep surprise. I had gotten used to Chinese people who were accustomed to foreigners, who talked with them every day. Many of my Chinese friends in Shanghai worked with foreigners, hung out with foreigners, even dated foreigners. I was willing to bet this woman had never dated a foreigner.

"She's probably never even seen a foreign face before," Marcus said. "Except on TV."

Jennifer stood off to the side, shaking her head and laughing at me. "These people are from a little town," she said. "They've never been to a city. They've never seen an elevator."

"I am a foreigner," I said in Chinese to the woman.

"No shit," said Marcus, and Jennifer laughed so hard her cheeks burned red.

"I am your foreign friend," I said to the woman, who scurried away from me and merged into the group. I saw her lift up on her toes to give me a few peeks over someone's shoulder, her eyes darting away when I tried to meet them with my own. I waved to her and she pushed her way into the crowd of fellow tourists, as far from me as she could be.

"Stop bothering the peasants," Marcus said in English, assuming, I guessed, that no one in the group would understand him. To call someone a peasant in the cosmopolitan city of Shanghai is a grave insult. People from the countryside are considered backward and unrefined, an embarrassment to the sophisticated urban dwellers in the metropolis. The Chinese are as conscious of skin color as we are in the West. The darker someone's skin, the more likely that he is a farmer and spends his time outdoors, laboring under the sun. The whiter the skin, the greater the chance that the pale person works indoors, separate from the land, sheltered from the sun. I once asked a Chinese girl I'd met on a ski slope in Colorado why she had a scarf wrapped in several layers around her face and covering every bit of skin save a narrow slot for her sunglasses. The odd facemask made her look like a bandit and was completely unnecessary on such a warm and wind-less spring day. She had to protect her skin, she told me. Not from cold or snow but from the sun. If the sun touched her skin, it would darken and people might mistake her for a *nóngmín*, a peasant. Chinese people think white skin is beautiful, she told me. Remembering this got me thinking.

"Do you know any farmers?" I asked Marcus.

"Of course not," Marcus said, as though I'd asked him if he knew any lepers.

"Farmers come to Shanghai to make construction," said Jennifer.

"Your skin is so pale," I said to Jennifer, curious to hear her reaction.

She said something in an embarrassed mumble that told me she was flattered.

"In America people lie outside in the sun to make their skin dark," I said.

"It is very strange," said Jennifer. "In your America you think black people are bad, but you try to make your skin black."

She had me there. I dropped my dermatological inquiry. I was not willing to drop my interest in the disdain of modern people for peasants, though, and I wondered if Chinese prejudice against peasants based on skin tone was really any different from American urbanites dismissing farmers as brainless hicks based on the twang of their accents. Across the globe people in cities look down on those who grow the food to make it possible for them to live in cities. And in China, much like in America, people who live close to the land had once held a prominent and respected place in the national psyche. Mao and his cohorts had succeeded in defeating the Chinese Nationalists in large part because they'd won the hearts and minds of the peasants, and the urban elite that supported the Na-tionalists were no match for the masses of angry farmers who heeded Mao's call and rose up to fight their overlords. Chinese Communism had peasants to thank for bringing the Party to power. And Chinese peasants, under Communist rule, had suffered the most, bearing the brunt of each brutal starvation that had swept the nation. And now they were derided by educated people in cities who made fun of their dark skin, burnt by the sun as they labored in fields to feed a nation that seemed determined to fill every bit of open space with towers—which were built by peasants who migrated to the cities in search of work.

Shanghai and most of the other boomtowns of China lie along the crescent of the east coast. A thin rim of development in the east, a great undeveloped and poor expanse in the center, and a wilderness frontier in the west. This is a gross simplification, but it gives a fairly accurate snapshot of the state of development today in China. The Communist Party, for its part, had recognized the wealth disparity between the rural poor and the urban elite and had initiated a "Go West" campaign that aimed to shift development away from the eastern coastal areas and create new and prosperous cities in rural provinces deep in the poverty-stricken interior. Whether the Party was doing this out of genuine concern for rural people, or because it was worried about unrest in the countryside as more and more peasants protested their plight, and the Party saw this as a potential threat to its hold on power, was up for debate. But as long as the money kept flowing through Shanghai and the shopping spree continued, most people in the city didn't seem to have any interest in debating this or anything else.

Despite China's tremendous disparity in wealth, there is a growing middle class made up of people like Marcus and Jennifer. According to many Panglossian prognosticators, eventually the middle class—after enjoying the freedoms of choosing their career, buying whatever they want, going into business for themselves, after having tasted these freedoms—will want even more freedom. They will want freedom with a capital F. They'll want the ballot box. Let them choose their pizza toppings and soon they'll want to choose their leaders: so the thinking goes. But often times the people who think these sunny thoughts have failed to ask the Chinese what they think. So, let's ask Marcus.

"What do you think about the government?" I asked Marcus.

"The government?"

"Yeah, you know—the Chinese government. Do you think it's doing a good job?"

"China's an important country now. People in the world respect us."

"So you're happy with the way things are going in China?"

"Things are improving."

"Do they need to improve more?"

"There can always be improvements, but I think there has been so much change in China. If there's too much change, there can be problems. The government has to be careful to make sure there is change but not too much change. That's not easy. The balance isn't easy."

"What do you think?" I asked Jennifer. "About the government? What do your parents think?"

She looked at me a moment before answering. "Perhaps you're asking about democracy?"

I grinned and nodded. "Okay, you got me. Perhaps that's exactly what I'm asking. What do your parents think about democracy?"

"They don't think anything about it. They don't think about politics. To them politics is a piece of shit. Politics did bad things to them in the past. Politics got them nothing and hurt them very badly."

"What's your opinion?" I asked her.

"Maybe we will want democracy someday, but right now China has to develop. Making the economy rich and making the country strong is the most important thing right now."

"That's two things," I said, correcting her grammar, then realizing that, point of fact, it was one thing.

I had been shocked the first time I came to China and heard a conversation like the one we were having now. My shock had been two-fold: First, I was amazed that people could talk openly about the government, politics, democracy. I had imagined Chinese Communist goons wearing dark sunglasses, with discrete listening devices plugged in their ears, lurking on every corner. (I guess I'd gotten this image from our secret service, but my mind had somehow applied it to Chinese government thugs.) I imagined Commie thought police dragging people off to dank and lightless cells to reeducate them if they so much as questioned the perfection of the Communist Party. I soon learned the distinction between authoritarian, which is what China's government is, and totalitarian, which describes the governments of Burma and North Korea. Big Brother is a little more laid back in China. He rarely drags people off in broad daylight. But I remain deeply skeptical of this kindler, gentler version of Communist China. Just as a republic that prides itself on its tradition of liberal democracy can quickly shift toward authoritarianism when it is attacked, so an authoritarian regime, when its power is threatened, can quickly morph into totalitarianism and turn tanks against its people.

Second, I'd been surprised that people who had been allowed a measure of freedom to debate the merits of their government—which was clearly top-heavy with bureaucracy, riddled with corruption, and in the business of routinely interrogating, locking up and torturing its citizens if they organized groups that questioned its legitimacy—would say that sure, the government was good because China was becoming a rich and powerful nation. Well, they were probably just saying that because they were afraid of being interrogated, locked up and tortured, right? Nope. Most of my Chinese friends in America—in the States on student visas or living there permanently—said the same thing. Money was on the minds of the Chinese—money that would lead to national greatness, to China reclaiming its position as the Middle Kingdom. China had always thought of itself as the center of the civilized world, with backward and barbaric people lurking around the periphery of its empire. Now China was creating a new empire that was shaking the global order, and China was, if not the center of the world, certainly at the center of the news of every nation on earth.

If democracy was coming to China, it seemed to be coming at a pace so glacial I wondered if Jennifer or Marcus would live to see it in their lifetimes. And they didn't much seem to care. "What do you think about the American presidential race?" I'd asked Jennifer a few days previous.

She had laughed and then she'd said, "I don't care who our leaders are here— why would I care who is the leader of America? But I want Obama to win."

"You think he's the best candidate?"

"I think he is very handsome, so I hope he wins."

Jennifer had earned one of the highest scores possible on China's National College Entrance Examination, I had reminded myself after she said this. And then for a moment I had felt afraid. Very afraid.

Old people in Shanghai, still reeling from the ravages of the Cultural Revolution, believe that passionate debates about politics lead to social chaos and disaster; young people in Shanghai are too preoccupied with making and spending money to discuss China's political system. Producers of a PBS *Frontline* documentary (employing somewhat questionable methodology) concluded that undergraduates at Beijing University, which trains many of China's elite, didn't recognize the image of "The Tank Man," the young man with shopping bags in hand standing defiantly in front of a column of PLA tanks on Chang'an Avenue near Tiananmen Square in 1989. That iconic image, which is seared into our collective consciousness and continues to speak poignantly to the West of Chinese aspirations for freedom and democracy, cannot be found in newspapers or in magazines or on television in China. To find it online in China is not easy (thanks to American companies Microsoft, Google, Yahoo and Cisco providing the Chinese government with the technology it needs to police the Internet), but the image can be located with a bit of persistence and technological savvy by using a proxy server or encrypted virtual private network to breach the Great Firewall. Technological savvy is certainly not in short supply among the students at Beijing University, which boasts the nation's best and brightest—the "Harvard of China," it is often called. What is missing is motivation. This widespread indifference to China's political plight among students and affluent young professionals is due in part to censorship and fear. It is also due, in large part, to just plain old indifference. Most young people in Shanghai are too focused on the minutiae of their lives—their paychecks, their shoes, their cell phones, their dates—to debate the state of their nation. Perhaps China, in this regard, is becoming more Americanized than we know.

Free markets will lead to personal freedoms as China's middle class develops and gradually demands more and more liberty—so the theory goes. The problem with that theory is this: The people gaining wealth in Shanghai benefit most from the system as it is; therefore, they have the most to lose if it changes. If people are getting richer and richer, why would they want to rock the boat? As long as the Communist Party can keep the economy pumping smoothly along, the boat, it seems to me, is pretty damn stable.

If anyone is going to rock the boat while China's current economic system is creating massive wealth, it is the peasants, the great mass of whom (switching metaphors) have not been invited to the party in Shanghai. "A revolution is not a dinner party," Mao famously declared in a report on the condition of peasants in China. But the husband-and-wife team of Wu Chuntao and Chen Guidi in their book *Will the Boat Sink the Water?*: *The Life of China's Peasants* show that the Communist revolution has been a dinner party for cadres, whose lavish feasts are financed by plundering village treasuries and imposing unfair taxes on rural people—people who still, even in this age of Shanghai's glittering office blocks and elevated highways, constitute nearly two-thirds of the nation's population. Originally published in China under the title *Zhōngguó Nóngmín Diàochá*, which translates "The Chinese Peasant Survey," Wu Chuntao and Chen Guidi's exposé quickly sold one hundred and fifty thousand copies before it was banned by the Communist Party. An estimated ten million more copies sold on the black market. The book was published in the West in 2006 under the English title *Will the Boat Sink the Water?*, and it is essential reading. In rural villages outside Shanghai, Wu Chuntao and Chen Guidi chronicle the lives of peasants and government officials as they come into conflict during the crisis ripping across China's countryside. Peasants who protest the endemic corruption risk being tortured, even murdered.

The title *Will the Boat Sink the Water?* is a play on words of warning from Emperor Taizong of the Tang dynasty, who said, "Water holds up the boat; water can also sink the boat." China's vast rural peasantry is the water holding up emperors and government officials. Wu Chuntao and Chen Guidi's book argues that the bloated boat is now in danger of sinking the water that buoys it. Much of China's underclass in the countryside beyond the towers of Shanghai lives within a brutally unfair and repressive feudalistic system virtually unchanged for millennia. They are angry. And there are eight hundred million of them.

The Communist Party took notice. Though it banned *Will the Boat Sink the Water?*, it did take steps to address the problem of the rural poor. Following the book's publication, the government canceled China's agricultural tax—a stunning departure from a practice that had lasted two and a half thousand years. They also issued directives forbidding village cadres to charge other unfair fees, and they even made some efforts to enforce these directives. The government, it seemed, had heard the message of *Will the Boat Sink the Water?* and had taken steps to eliminate the crushing financial burdens on the peasantry. There is, however, a more cynical interpretation: eight hundred million farmers with disposable income means eight hundred million consumers to buy things, their purchases helping the economy to keep pumping. As long as money is flowing through the system and consumers can shop, the government's grasp on power will remain firm.

Whatever the motivation driving these reforms, the lives of the peasants have perhaps improved a bit, but people from the countryside are now moving by the millions into Shanghai, and when they arrive in the big city, what they find is not the urban paradise they might have imagined. The shining city that beckoned them from their lives of bare subsistence in the rice paddies presents them with a desperate struggle for survival. They are discriminated against by a residency permit system that forces them to live and work illegally in the city and prevents them from enjoying any of the benefits of the brave new paradise. *Míngōng*, the migrant laborers in the city, have no rights to education or health care. They cluster together in filthy hovels, forming shantytowns fraught with danger and disease. And as Shanghai cancers its way outward across the Yangtze Delta, government officials engage in land grabs, selling property that peasants' ancestors have worked for centuries to developers so that more towers can rise, and dispossessing powerless peasants of the only means they have to make a living. The government officials who snatch the land thereby gather the means to buy black Audis with tinted windows and send their sons and daughters to MBA programs in America. Throughout China, children from desperately poor families and adults with developmental disabilities have been kidnapped and carted off to brick kilns in distant provinces, where they are chained to cavernous ovens

Outside Shanghai's opulent buildings the destitute huddle.

and forced to work as slaves in factories so barbaric they seem something from the Middle Ages, and girls from impoverished villages are frequently sold to human traffickers who force them into lives of sexual slavery. In the countryside and in cities across China, measureless masses of the nation's poor are furious at the current corrupt government system in a way that in the past presaged the overthrow of an emperor. Beneath the euphoria of Shanghai's development lies the seething resentment of peasants supporting China's urbanization with their agricultural output, with their unfairly seized land, and with their construction labor. The towers of the metropolis are haunted by angry ghosts. Eight hundred million of them.

Whether the Communist Party will further implement policies to improve the lives of the peasants so that they are happy with the government or will crush the discontented masses of rural poor beneath draconian measures remains to be seen, but what's certain is this: The Communist Party will do whatever it thinks is most effective to retain power. A government losing power in China is not like a government losing an election in the West. Members of a toppled Chinese regime certainly lose their fortunes, and they might even lose their lives.

China has never had democracy, but to say that its rulers have always been unaccountable to the people is not correct. Chinese society hasn't had the ballot box, but it has always had the Mandate of Heaven, a traditional philosophical concept that has guided it through the ages. First used to legitimize the rule of the kings of the Zhou dynasty, the Mandate of Heaven was later applied to the emperors of China. The idea is this: Heaven blesses the authority of a fair and honorable ruler but withdraws its mandate when displeased with a corrupt, despotic regime. Throughout China's history, the people had risen up to over-throw rulers deemed to have lost the Mandate of Heaven, and the mandate had then been transferred to those best prepared to rule. When a rebellion succeeded, Chinese historians interpreted this as a sign that the overthrown regime had been unjust and its Mandate of Heaven had expired. The mandate had no time limit, and the standard of just conduct to which rulers were held was not clearly defined.

The Mandate of Heaven wasn't exactly the Declaration of the Rights of Man and of the Citizen or the United States Constitution, but it did in the past provide a brake on corrupt powermongers in the Middle Kingdom. Westerners (I include myself) often note that China's tradition of civic action is weak and we make disparaging remarks about the indifference of average Chinese people to their political plight. But civic action of *lǎobǎixìng* (literally "old hundred names"—the average Joes of China, the common people) has toppled dynasties throughout Chinese history. The Mandate of Heaven is checks and balances Chinese style. And like so many traditional Chinese concepts that the Communist revolution set out to destroy, it has, perhaps, persisted.

"What do you think about the Mandate of Heaven?" I asked Marcus.

He exhaled sharply in answer.

"Come on, I'm curious to know what you think."

"I think you've been reading too many history books."

"Does the mandate matter today? Do people still believe that?"

"Do Americans still believe in fairy tales? Look, I understand what you're asking. People in America when I was at Stanford asked me all the time: How can you stand your government? How can you stand not being able to vote? But if I could vote, how would my life be any better? Why should I care? Look at my life—it's good. I have a good salary and I can buy things that I want. I have enough money to take care of my parents and buy them things that they want. I live in an apartment in Xujiahui. I have an iPod and an Xbox 360. Next year I'll get a car. Someday I'll buy a home—a villa with a garage. Why do I need to vote?"

What Communist political repression couldn't quash, American-style consumerism has. Perhaps the Chinese government will maintain its mandate as long as city-dwelling citizens have iPods and Xboxes. But what of the peasants? Do they still believe in fairy tales? Eight hundred million of them don't have iPods and Xboxes, and when they go to bed at night their bellies are cramped with hunger.

We left the Communist Party museum, which seemed to interest Marcus and Jennifer even less than discussing democracy, and walked back into the bright lights and retail bliss of Xintiandi, which seemed to hold very much interest for both of them indeed.

> *In Xanadu did Kubla Khan*
> *A stately pleasure-dome decree:*
> *Where Alph, the sacred river, ran*
> *Through caverns measureless to man*
> *Down to a sunless sea.*

For no reason I could clearly explain, I said the first stanza of Coleridge's "Kubla Khan" as we walked by a store called Stella Luna. Inside, women's shoes stood perched on pedestals like works of art arrayed in a museum.

"They have the best shoes in the world," said Jennifer.

Marcus said they had the best marketing in the world.

Thousands of years of civilization and all we could talk about was selling shoes. It made me sad and I decided to call it a night.

"Do you want to come to my apartment?" Jennifer asked. "We can drink tea. I have the green tea you like."

Beyond Xintiandi rose buildings lined with neon and towers crowned with light. This was a city heaving itself upward as it convulsed in luminous spasms. Like an overwrought character in some outlandish story, Shanghai clamored constantly for attention.

I forced myself to look away from the lights and to focus on Jennifer, and I told her sure, I'd like to drink some tea. She invited Marcus too, but he said he had to get back home to catch up on his work. As he walked away, the footsteps of his finely tooled shoes ringing against the walls in the narrow lane of Xintiandi, I had one of those moments I sometimes have when I don't understand what is happening to me and I feel that I will at any moment be swallowed by something larger than I am, something filled with sticky darkness, and my last act on earth will be to help a friend. Jennifer's arms hung neatly in front of her, one hand atop the other. She looked so fragile, as though her bones were made of glass, and I wanted more than anything to keep the darkness from reaching her, but there was nothing to be done. I was a stranger here and I could not stop the future from taking away her family's past. Their home would be reduced to rubble and erased, and they would begin again in towers in the sky.

Shanghai is a gorgeously meaningless place, a dazzling shell surrounding nothing. It is a new city that demands a new way of living, one that borrows and blends, one that reaches high and ultimately comes crashing back down from the dearth of its freshness, the paucity of its substance. Shanghai is a hollow place. It is a hole at the center of the Middle Kingdom. It is a great emptiness filled with endless crowds.

"Are you okay?" Jennifer asked me. "You are crying?"

"I'm having trouble seeing. I think it's the pollution." I wiped at my eyes with the shoulders of my shirt. "I'm glad you're here," I said. "This is a lonely place."

"Yes, it's good to have friends in Shanghai. It's important, I think. Sometimes it is not good to be alone in this city. That's why I thought you should come to my apartment and drink tea." She stared at me, her face so serious. I smiled at her and she smiled back and I felt much better.

"The pollution is bothering you?" she asked.

"I'll be okay. *Wǒmen zǒu ba.*" Let's go. Let's walk.

Through the choking streets we will walk, blinking back pollution tears as we push our soft flesh through a monstrous wonderland of concrete and steel, a city built sky-high upon the starved and hollow bodies of the dead, a new heaven and earth.

A Home in the Sky

Jennifer's apartment building stood within a gated security compound. It was one of eleven identical buildings whose vertical stature was such that I tilted back my head until my neck felt the strain of staring upward. Before we went in we decided to get something to eat. We walked around Jennifer's neighborhood, which, disappointingly, held none of the street-market mayhem and comforting human chaos of a lilong. In this neighborhood built around broad avenues one could walk down the street without sliding on pavement greasy from food stalls or having one's face wrapped in delicious steam. We eyed a sterile restaurant opposite Jennifer's apartment block. The only activity inside seemed to be men sitting alone and smoking glumly. Next door was a massage parlor that looked upscale with its potted plants and hostesses sheathed smartly in body-hugging *qípáo* but which clearly sold services other than massages, and I imagined those men had either just come from said house of pleasure or were headed there after their lonely meal in the clean restaurant.

The area seemed disturbingly quiet after the festival of the backstreets we'd found in Jennifer's parents' neighborhood. I realized this place wasn't silent—far from it. Traffic roared from nearby highways but there were no sounds of human voices. The thunder of cars and trucks, loud enough to make your ears ache, was bland background noise and nothing more. There was too much time to think here, not enough distractions. I craved riotous human noise and I wanted to devour delicious, dangerous food, all the tastier for the knowledge that it might send me to the hospital the next morning. I wanted the real deal, a Shanghai night market, not a restaurant with molded plastic chairs and English menus. I talked Jennifer into taking the metro to Wujiang Lu, a winding lane tucked behind Nanjing Xi Lu, one of the glitziest shopping streets in China.

Gentrification threatens to spill over from Nanjing Xi Lu into Wujiang Lu and sanitize the dilapidated lane, crazy with cheap food stalls and dive diners, and any day now the wrecking ball will arrive and put an end to the fun. But tonight we could browse the stalls lining the ramshackle street, tasting skewers of quail and ribbons of tripe, wrinkling our noses at a dish aptly named "stinky tofu," devouring puffy steamed buns, slurping noodles laced with baby cabbage and shaved carrots, slipping into our mouths rolls of glutinous rice filled with shredded meat and salted mustard greens, and savoring chunks of mutton painted red with spices and barbequed over sputtering flames by Turkic Muslims from Xinjiang. And these foods were but a buildup to the pièce de résistance: at Yang's Fry-Dumpling, the specialty was pork-filled snacks that were first steamed, not unlike xiaolongbao, and then fried to crunchy goodness on their undersides and sprinkled with sesame seeds and scallions on their soft tops. The restaurant was claustrophobically crowded and filled with endless clatter and squawky chatter. After waiting for half an hour in a line that snaked down the street, constantly sniffing the delicacies being dished up inside, we were finally handed chipped enamel plates heaped with piping hot *xiǎoyáng shēngjiān mántou*. We sat at a communal slab of greasy wood using wooden chopsticks stained black from vinegar and wiping our dripping lips with toilet paper torn from rolls that were passed around the table.

"This is one of Shanghai's most special foods," said Jennifer as I bit into a crispy dumpling and sucked out the soup. "Is it very delicious?" she asked.

I slurped the scalding broth, cooling it on my tongue; then I swallowed and smiled. "It is very delicious."

Smile lines creased the corners of her eyes. "Does your city have special foods?" Jennifer yelled above the restaurant's din.

"Boulder? Well, we have hippie foods." I slurped the rich broth of another shengjian mantou and then ate the crackling skin and tender morsel of pork within.

"What is hippie foods? Is it delicious?"

"Not really, no."

There are few things more enjoyable than eating street food in Shanghai. This gritty lane, Wujiang Lu, is slated for redevelopment and will soon become part of a glitzy shopping district.

"Does it have special fried dumplings?"

"No. No dumplings."

"It must be hard to live in a place where there are no special dumplings."

We left the close and sweaty madness of the restaurant and walked into the relative coolness outside, but the noise was no less frantic, and we disappeared into a jostling crowd massing in the market and eating its way noisily through the night.

We wandered a few blocks away into a neighborhood made of little lanes, where the throbbing loudspeakers of shopfronts argued for attention. So clamorous was their shouting to announce items for sale, the competing sounds canceled each other out, and we passed through a place of loud silence as we journeyed deeper through knotted alleyways, heading toward the guarded heart of the neighborhood, as if wandering in a fable through a maze. We threaded our way between motor scooters parked at random angles, and a little boy in split-crotch pants squatted to poop on the pavement as the blaring beat of the loudspeakers drubbed on. Sesame cakes stood stacked on metal trays and people ate them on the go. Shirts and keys and sacks of tea were for sale. A woman who rose no higher than my waist and who had the shrunken face of a sorceress reached my way a withered hand that clutched in its rickety fingers an assortment of hard-core sex DVDs. On a table before this ancient peddler of porn were arranged boxes of dildos and one was on display, pointing upward and rotating in pulsing circles amid a whirling mass of flies. I noted a pair of panties with "all you can eat" printed on the crotch before we pressed on through the crowds in this close-packed maze of crazy commerce. Boxed electronics formed walls of impressive height and thickness, and one man was selling kitchen sinks. I stopped to take his picture but he was immediately in my face and filling my camera lens as he explained why his sinks were the best. They were fine sinks indeed, and I nearly bought one before Jennifer convinced me to move on, ending the first sentence of a story building in my head: You can buy anything in a Shanghai street market, even the kitchen sink.

A woman wearing pants that stopped just below her knees and tan hose ending midway up her shins took my attention in another direction, and soon I was staring at feet. Feet in black socks and sandals; slippers padding softly on flagstones; shoes with stiletto heels and straps and rhinestones, the feet in these sexy shoes sheathed strangely in nylon stockings that rose in crinkled folds no higher than the ankles. These mysteries of the Orient.

Thoroughly and wonderfully lost, we walked past the neon glow of karaoke bars, through unending tunnels where subway lines converged. We walked and walked, through streetscapes and through metro scenes, past myriad colors and a multitude of sounds. Within the ever-changing bazaar there wasn't a moment to think and I felt my brain go blissfully numb. When one wants to forget, sensory overload in Shanghai can be as potent as opium.

But when we bumped into a Legoland of high-rise apartment blocks painted shades of sorbet, I found myself standing still and staring up at a checkerboard of lighted windows in these strange towers built of little boxes where people lived, and I could not push from my mind the thought that had been bothering me all day. Everyone in Shanghai, it seemed, was still striving so hard to get a box in the sky that they hadn't yet had time to settle in and come to terms with the night-mare of emptiness and longing that begins when one's material ambitions are finally fulfilled. This is a city of postmodern architecture with a premodern lack of ennui. A city of people who still believe that to lift soaring towers into the fir-mament is the height of human ambition, a glorious achievement that will set them free. Who believe that living in such a tower will fill the hole at the center of modern life. Imagine people as earnest as your ancestors who survived the great wars and the Great Depression yearning not for a house with a green square of yard and a white picket fence but for a cube in a tower that rockets upward seventy stories. And in this cube close to the clouds lives a couple with a single child, this one child pampered and coddled and chubby with treats, inheriting a world of easy comfort much like his counterparts in American suburbs, his brain crammed with math and with government-approved mantras and with dreams of more money and a bigger cube in a taller tower, while peasants in the streets below spread out sheets and lay their wares upon the tattered cloth, hustling tourists who wander through the city of tomorrow, faces tilted toward the sky.

When we finally returned to Jennifer's apartment building, she showed an identity card to a doorman; I showed nothing but my white face. Jennifer didn't tell the doorman I was with her, and for all he knew I was just some random not-Chinese person wandering into the building among the crowd of Chinese people surrounding us, each person showing his or her card to the guard.

"How does he know I'm not a burglar or something?" I asked Jennifer as we walked inside.

"You're a foreigner, so it's okay."

I pondered this as we entered a lobby with a naked concrete floor that was about as inviting as a Greyhound bus station. Jennifer spread newspaper on a bench so we could sit down safe from whatever germs it held. Every stain tells a story, I thought as I studied the blotched surface of the bench. The exterior of the building looked hip and shiny; its interior was another matter. If Soviet Chic or Maoist Deprivation were interior design styles, this is how they'd look.

I stared at the doorman, who appeared unconcerned with who I was or what I was doing in his building—one in which, I gathered from Jennifer, foreigners were rare. His indifference startled me. China is, of course, notorious for its suspicion of everyone, and foreign journalists are often shadowed by Chinese minders, every move scrutinized. I had journalist friends whose phones had been bugged and who had been questioned for hours by Chinese police, the questioning sessions never amplifying into an international incident of incarceration or torture, but often veering dangerously close to a type of detainment that would be proper grounds for a complaint by the detained in any country on earth with due process and the rule of law. To be a white face in Shanghai opens some doors, such as the one to Jennifer's apartment complex, while closing others—such as the detainment room door when one asks too many questions.

All my life I had been asking questions. So many questions, people who knew me thought I was investigating something when I grilled them about their jobs or hobbies or where they lived. It was all harmless enough, just the product of a relentless curiosity. I was forever trying to understand what people wanted and trying to get them to tell me their stories. People in Shanghai seemed pleased that I asked so many questions about their city, and my interest in their lives had made me many friends. But I understood that were I to ask too many questions about certain things—mainly revolving around the human cost of progress in Shanghai—I could lose friends and make enemies. I could end up in a room behind closed doors being asked questions about why I was asking so many questions.

"Do you think I ask too many questions?" I asked Jennifer.

"Why do you ask me that?" Jennifer asked.

"I'm afraid maybe I'm asking too many questions."

Jennifer patted the air a moment while she considered what to say. Finally this: "I think you want to know a lot about China. A lot about Shanghai. I think you like Shanghai and you want to know more about it. Perhaps it is okay, I think."

"I think I want to write a book about it."

"About China?"

"China is too big. It will only be about Shanghai. Shanghai is big enough for a book."

"What will be in the book?"

"Maybe it will be about you. Is that okay? It will be about you and your family and your friends and your city." I was making this up as I went along. This was the first time the idea of writing a book about Shanghai had struck me as something I must do. I had been too busy learning Chinese and exploring Shanghai to worry about writing a book. All along I had been taking careful notes, but with no real purpose in mind—just to help me remember the overwhelming crush of experience, the riot of impressions in the wild frontier of China's fastest-growing metropolis as I engaged in aimless sleuthing. Wandering around the megacity had resulted in mega notes. I had already filled three notebooks and had started in on another. I was writing in one right now as Jennifer lifted her hand in front of her mouth and laughed.

"Why will that be a book?" she asked.

I looked up from my notebook and tapped my pen against its spiral. "Because I think it's a story worth telling."

Jennifer was silent a moment and then said, "You will tell about my parents? How they are not happy with the government for taking their home away? How they are protesting?"

"Will it cause trouble for them if I do?"

"It is better not to talk too much about it. In China we say that the nail that stands up, it gets the hammer. My parents are the nail standing up. The government is holding the hammer. The government will let them stand up for a while, but it must hit all the nails back down."

I studied Jennifer's face, which right now gave no clues to her emotional state. The saying "stoic as a stone Buddha" came to mind. "Are you worried for them?" I asked.

"Of course." No change in her expression.

"Could anything happen to you?"

Jennifer said nothing for a moment and then she took a small sip of air and looked away from me. "Some people came to talk to me. About my parents and their home."

"People from the government?"

"Developers. The developers from the company that wants to smash their home and make a new park or a subway."

"They aren't with the government?"

"Perhaps they are. Perhaps their company is owned by the government."

"Did they threaten you?"

"They asked questions. They asked me where I work and how much money I make. They said it would be better if my parents accepted their offer."

"Did they say what would happen if your parents don't accept the offer?"

"They said it would be better if they accepted it."

We both said nothing for several minutes. I smelled the metallic odor of air that issued soundlessly through vents above.

Finally I said, "So is it a bad idea for me to write a book that talks about your parents?"

"Perhaps it would be better if you didn't. They have already made so much trouble for themselves."

"And for you?" I said. "Do you wish they hadn't made trouble for you?"

For a daughter to criticize her parents is an enormous rupture of China's social norms. Filial piety, a value rooted deeply in Confucian thought, has been passed down through the ages, providing a consistent social structure for many generations. Parents are invariably right and it is the duty of children to respect the infallibility of their mothers and fathers. This concept had been attacked by Mao during the Cultural Revolution, when he instructed the sons and daughters of China to do away with old thinking and criticize the values and beliefs of the older generation. This new thinking reached its frenzied pinnacle when children snitched on their parents for believing in outmoded and dangerous ideas such as private property and religion. Children of the Communist revolution, arms sheathed in red bands of cloth to signify their disdain for the old, dragged their parents into public places and berated them for all to see. The lashings often escalated from verbal to physical, and for a few strange and fevered years, sons and daughters who throughout Chinese history had been taught to revere the sanctity of their family bonds and to look upon their parents as nothing less than minor deities, beat their parents in the streets, spilling the blood of their elders for the red flag of Communism.

China's Cultural Revolution, often referred to in China as the "ten years of chaos," occurred from 1966 to 1976. While American hippies were professing the virtues of pot and free love and decrying the materialistic morality of their parents, Chinese teens were beating the older generation senseless in the name of Mao, and sometimes pummeling them to death. The entire nation turned upside down and anarchy was loosed upon the land. Physicians swabbed floors while orderlies performed surgery, barefoot peasants posed as scientists, students tortured their teachers. Hundreds of thousands of people were murdered during the Cultural Revolution, often at the hands of China's youth. Filial piety, however, has made quite a comeback from the mayhem of the revolution and is once again a value many Chinese hold dear. They view our inclination in America to send our elders off to facilities where they live apart from the family as morally questionable, if not outright barbaric. Chinese people had treated me with what seemed like pity when I described the loneliness of an American nursing home. What kind of country expels the elderly from their homes, they wondered aloud. What kind of country tells its children to murder scientists and educators and then reveres the instigator of the movement as a hero, I would ask them in return. And what of your Indians, they would counter. And slavery?

There is no shortage of savagery in the world, and every country has its crimes.

But back to the matter at hand. Jennifer was looking away from me and not changing her facial expression, as was always the case when I asked her questions that I thought made her uncomfortable. "No," she finally said, without meeting my eyes. "I am not mad at my parents for protesting."

Would she tell me even if she were? Perhaps she would probably not, as she would say. At least not yet—not until we knew each other better. There was still something stilted between us, a barrier that made both of us bite our tongues at times. I hoped this barrier was permeable and would in time dissolve. I hoped it was not a bulwark built of the cultural differences between us that we would never breach.

"And the book?" I said. "I could change some things like names and places so that nobody would know who I'm talking about. If I did that, would it be okay if I wrote it? Besides, people don't really read books much anymore, anyway. Probably very few people will read it, and no one will pay much attention to it."

"You won't blog about us?"

"Not if you don't want me to."

"I don't want you to. Lots of people read blogs. The government reads blogs to find out who are the nails standing up."

"Okay, no blogging."

Jennifer swiveled her head to look at me, as intent now on staring at me as a moment ago she had been on averting her eyes from mine when I was asking if she was angry with her parents for involving her in their struggle with the powers that be in China, be they the government or developers, or government developers—whoever these people are with the power to find where you live and ask you where you work and tell you that it would be better for everyone if their offer was accepted.

"Nobody will know it is me and my parents in your book?" she said.

"I'll do everything I can to make sure nobody knows it's your parents and you. Thousands of buildings are being ripped down all over Shanghai all the time—and there'll be even more as the city gets ready for the Expo. Your parents could be literally hundreds, maybe thousands, of nails sticking up. The hammer won't know which nail they are."

"Let me ponder."

"Ponder?" I said.

"This means to think about something—yes?"

"Yes, it does." I laughed. "It just sounds funny, that's all."

Jennifer's mouth turned down and her eyes went small. "You are making fun of me?"

"Of course not. Listen, if I wanted to make fun of your English, you could have plenty of fun at my expense making fun of my Chinese. It just makes me smile when you say you will ponder my idea. *Ponder* is not a word I use often."

"Because it sounds stupid?"

"When I say it, yes, it does sound stupid. When you say it, it most certainly does not sound stupid. You can pull it off."

"Pull it off?" She smiled. "I heard this on *Friends*." Her face went bright as she retrieved a little spiral-bound notebook from a pocket of her low-rise jeans. "Right here," she said, after flipping to a section marked by a tab with *Friends* written on it that she'd taped to a page. "Yes, 'pull it off'—this was on *Friends*. Chandler said it. What does it mean?"

"It means you can do something. If you can pull something off, you can do it without any problem, even though it seems difficult or unlikely."

"Pull it off," Jennifer said, giving equal weight to each carefully spaced word she pronounced. "Pull . . . it . . . off," she said again.

"Like this," I said. "Pull it off." I said it quickly and casually, jamming the words together so it sounded authentic. "Say it like that," I said, "so it sounds real."

"Pull it off," Jennifer said, mimicking me, and it did indeed sound real.

"*Bù cuò*," I said. Literally, "not wrong." But "not wrong" or "not bad" in Chinese more accurately translates in English as "really good." Chinese humility can be a wonderful counterpoint to American braggadocio. I jumped up from the bench and raised my hand for a high five. Jennifer stood up; then she lifted up on her toes and slapped her hand against mine.

"Pull it off," she said as she pressed the button for the elevator in the lobby and the doors slid open. "I pulled it off. Can I say, 'I pulled it off?'" she asked as we entered a cramped compartment with walls of stainless steel and floors of glaring white. "Opening the elevator—I pulled it off."

"Let's not get carried away," I said as the elevator whooshed us silently downward.

"Carried away," Jennifer said beneath her breath as three men in suits and two women in smart businesswear entered the elevator at the basement level. We had gone down instead of up.

"I didn't pull it off," Jennifer said.

"You are definitely getting carried away," I said.

Jennifer wrote "carried away" in neatly printed letters on a page of her notebook.

I fished my own notebook from a pocket, found a pen in another pocket, and wrote: "Shanghai book—must have Jennifer's permission first. Must have her talk to her parents and explain what I am doing and that I will protect their identities. Then must be careful to protect their identities. Must do this the right way and not mess up. I absolutely cannot screw this up." I realized, while writing this, that if Jennifer agreed to let me move forward with the book, I would have to be brittle-eggshell careful with how I presented her story so that it could in no way damage her or her family.

"You absolutely cannot screw up," Jennifer said, laughing. She was reading over my shoulder.

A year previous I'd begun writing a magazine article that I hoped would turn into a book about my experiences in Tibet; I had abandoned the project after realizing that if I made a mistake in covering the identity of a Tibetan railing against the Chinese government, or were that monk even to be seen with me by a government spy, he could end up in prison. Or worse. I had seen a picture, procured by an elderly Tibetan man from a pocket of his yak-wool robe, of the bodies of Buddhist monks stacked like cordwood in a grave during the early years of the Chinese presence in Tibet; and my responsibility had weighed heavily on me, so heavily it eventually crushed my ambition to write a book about Tibet. In Tibet, informers had been everywhere, and many Tibetans snitched on their own to garner better treatment by the Chinese. Every interaction I had there had seemed fraught with treachery and disaster, and I had often been followed by Chinese men who hurried away when I doubled back to ask them what they wanted.

Shanghai was a world apart from Tibet, not just in terms of squat medieval architecture contrasted against ultramodern skyscrapers, but in terms of openness. There were a zillion foreigners wandering the streets of this supercity swollen with people, and no one seemed to pay much attention to what the *lǎowài* were up to in the heaving crowds. But for all Shanghai's modernity and openness, it was still part of a system that included government labor camps—to which anyone could be sent, at any time, for any reason.

The men and women who'd joined us in the elevator, clothes wrinkled from a day's work, stood without speaking as we were lifted toward the sky. I watched the floor numbers count upward as we rose. There was no fourth floor. The pronunciation of *four* in Chinese is similar to that of the character that means "death."

Some buildings in China not only don't have a fourth floor, they are missing all floors that end in four or begin with four, so profoundly unlucky is the number. And some modern buildings in Shanghai, in deference to Western ways, lack a thirteenth floor as well. As we rose I did the math: that adds up to a lot of missing floors.

"Marcus has a business partner that is selling phone numbers," Jennifer said in English as she watched me studying the numbers. "Chinese people pay a lot of money for phone numbers with no fours and lots of eights." Sometimes I sensed that Jennifer was speaking English with me around other Chinese people to show off. Now was one of those times. Everyone else in the elevator stared at the ascending numbers in silence, and I wondered if they'd understood what she'd said. She'd been deliberately offhand, as I had been teaching her to be—she had spoken quickly and had let some of the sounds blur together in casual chatter. "Your English is improving," I told her in my most casual-sounding Chinese. "It sounds authentic," I said in my most authentic-sounding speech, showing off to everyone in the elevator. I earned a few gracious smiles and approving nods and one compliment filled with lavish praise. Show me a foreigner in China who is learning Chinese and insists that his motivation is in no way related to the constant praise his efforts earn him, and I'll show you a lying foreigner.

We exited at the twenty-fifth floor, and after the elevator doors closed I asked Jennifer if she knew many of the people in her building.

"No, not many. Perhaps no one, actually." She stomped her little foot on the ground to trigger the hallway light and then she tossed her head to the side, flipping hair that had fallen in her face back behind her shoulder. She fake-coughed when we turned a corner, triggering another sensor to illuminate another hall, and then she opened her first apartment door, a heavy steel barrier that fortressed a wooden door within. "No one on my floor says hello to each other," she said. She twisted open the deadbolt on the inner door. She had lived in this place for more than a year, she told me.

Her apartment sported the wood floors common in upscale residences throughout Shanghai. Wood was everywhere—on the floors, that is. There were almost no trees around the high-rise apartment buildings in the city, just random patches of greenery in the occasional park, and a smattering of tree-lined boulevards in the old sections of Shanghai, quaintly out of place amid the maelstrom of development. No forests to be seen, even in the hinterlands beyond the outskirts of the city. It was hard to imagine where all the lumber for all the hardwood floors originated. Most likely it didn't come from China but was shipped in from the faraway forests of Borneo or some such place. Somewhere in a poor country rich with sprawling woodlands there were yawning holes in the canopy where timber had fallen for the floors of Shanghai.

"Nice floor," I said to Jennifer as I kicked off my shoes, as is the custom in Chinese homes, and proceeded to slide across the shiny wood floor in my sock feet— not the custom in Chinese homes. Jennifer opened the slatted blinds of a window that looked out upon the city. The dimensions of her apartment were positively ginormous compared to those of her parents' place. The Western-style toilet was certainly a dramatic improvement over the stinking squatter in her parents' home, but Jennifer's place struck me as depressingly spare in contrast to the comfortable chaos that had filled the main room in the shikumen. Here there was no bed next to a mahjong table shoved halfway in the kitchen. No piles of blankets and stacks of newspapers, no pots and pans and brooms dangling from the walls. Jennifer's kitchen was separate from the living room, and the living room (very sensibly) held a couch and two comfy chairs. There was a separate bedroom set off from the main room, and I guessed no mahjong was played in this apartment. Instead of portraits of Chairman Mao with his fat head and smug smile, black-and-white prints of the Brooklyn Bridge and the Eiffel Tower adorned the walls. The sofa, chairs and dining room table all had the sleek minimalist Scandinavian look of trendy but not terribly expensive furniture purchased from Ikea. A few questions later and my suspicions were confirmed: Shanghainese love Ikea as much as Seattleites. (I discovered some weeks later with Jennifer that Shanghai's Ikea even serves the same famously tasty meatballs dished up in the land of drizzle and rain.) Copies of *Cosmopolitan* lay neatly fanned on a low coffee table made of rich wood dark as chocolate, and a mod bookcase held several seasons of *Friends* DVDs. The apartment could have been that of a Seattleite, or that of a person living in a loft in St. Louis and desperately wanting to leave the Midwest and move to Seattle. We could have been anywhere in the world, but we were in China's largest metropolis.

I walked to the window where Jennifer had peeled back the blinds and I gazed upon a scene that seemed taken from the electronic world of *Tron*. Tubes of neon lined a tangle of elevated superhighways that stood above the ground on stilts, these roads dipping and swooping and curving like rollercoasters, and in the distance rose tower upon tower, each one straining to outdo the next with a random display of blinking, pulsing, swarming lights in a rainbow of artificial brightness so ostentatious one could not help but grudgingly admit that staring at the city's lightshow was, in its own kooky way, enjoyable and infinitely addictive, not unlike watching *American Idol* or reading a relative's blog. As with every other night I had spent in this city of lunatic lights, on this evening I was startled by how the critical faculties of my mind had been numbed to the point at which, instead of perceiving this cityscape as a hideous abomination—which it most certainly was—my overworked brain instead registered the pulsing brightness as flat-out gorgeous.

"It's a good view, yes?" Jennifer asked as she handed me a cup of *Lóngjǐng chá*, or "Dragonwell tea," a type of green tea she knew I liked. Grown in the misty hills of Zhejiang Province, Dragonwell is painstakingly processed: only young leaves slender as sparrows' tongues are plucked from the top branches of tea bushes, and then these tender shoots are roasted in a pan by the handwork of a master. Old Wang, whose parents had come from the area around Xi Hu, or West Lake, a famous lake near which the tea originated, had told me the legend of Dragonwell tea, which is as notable for its name as it is for its fragrant nose and the delicate sweetness of its flavor. More than one thousand seven hundred years ago a Daoist monk told villagers they could end a brutal drought that had settled upon the land by summoning a dragon that lived in a nearby well, a shaft so long it was thought to reach the sea. A dragon was believed to inhabit the depths of the spring-fed well because the water that bubbled up from beneath the earth was dense and heavy, and after a storm, rainwater, which was lighter than the well water, floated on the surface. When the two weights of water mixed, sinuous shapes appeared, and these patterns swirled like a twisting dragon. The villagers prayed to the dragon in the well, and the rains returned, greening the surrounding hills.

"Yup," I said, inhaling steam that smelled like honeysuckle as it rose from my cup and I looked out the window at the manufactured landscape of the city. "It is a good view." I blew the loose leaves away from my lips and sipped the bright green liquid, velvety against my tongue, its flavor similar to that of sweet chestnuts. I stared outside. The view was worth every RMB of the inflated rental prices Jennifer was paying, but I missed the snug jumble of her parents' home, that cluttered womb where families lived and played.

In the gaps between tower blocks of the brightly lit city lurked dark places of low-slung buildings that had yet to join the neon revolution. In each of these lightless chasms lay a lilong not unlike the neighborhood where Jennifer's parents lived. Shanghai's shikumen would never completely disappear, as they were honored in the architecture of Xintiandi, where we had sat in the bland beer garden and listened to Marcus talk about his dream of buying a Buick. And the lifeways of shikumen dwellers were frozen in time in the diagrams and exhibits of Shanghai's museums. The distinctive structures would still stand in one sanitized form or another, and the lives of the people in the lilong would be preserved in galleries like bugs pinned to boards and labeled with Latin names. But something would be lost when Shanghai's old neighborhoods fell to developers. The intangible networks that had been brought from the countryside when waves of Chinese refugees swept into Shanghai, the social filaments that joined families and friends: these would vanish along with the razed shikumen. And this rich webwork of connections that had been nurtured in the little lanes that lay in the heart of the city was not likely to reappear in the new neighborhoods built of separate boxes arranged in soaring towers.

Shanghai is not unique among the world's cities in implementing a controversial urban overhaul. Paris, for example, went through a process of renovation beginning in the mid-nineteenth century that caused fierce controversy throughout France. What we take today to be Paris par excellence—the boulevards, the parks, the monuments—did not result from the accretions of history, but rather was the masterwork of one planner commissioned by Napoleon III to build an entirely new city to replace the squalid tenements of the old urban core, to create something fresh that would demonstrate to the world France's greatness. This transformation ignited controversy so heated, the boulevards of the new city were built wide enough to facilitate troop transport if the citizenry rioted over the destruction of old homes in the medieval quarter that were being razed to make way for new architecture. And the Eiffel Tower, erected for the Exposition Universelle of 1889 to serve as an entranceway to this World's Fair and to announce to the world the glory of a rising France, was loudly denounced as a hideous abomination of good taste.

Who can now question Paris's place among the world's most beautiful cities. Could it be that someday Shanghai will be looked upon as a quintessential symbol of the twenty-first century, as charming as Paris, and the displaced dwellers of Shanghai's tenements that fell to progress long forgotten? Maybe. But the OPTV Tower is no Eiffel Tower, and there is no overriding aesthetic to guide development in Shanghai as there had been in mid-nineteenth-century Paris. Paris was created as a unified whole from the vision of one city planner. Shanghai is a hodgepodge born of the desperate desire of Communist bureaucrats to show the world a modern face, along with the unfettered fantasies of architects who have left the strict zoning codes of the United States and Europe to build amid the free-for-all of China's wild frontier. As in the boomtowns of the American West where wooden brothels, bars, and gambling halls were hastily slapped together, so towers of steel and glass rise in motley fashion from China's booming east.

And what of the people pushed out of their homes amid the pandemonium of development leading up to the Expo in Shanghai? Their struggles will, in all likelihood, within a few decades lie buried beneath the helter-skelter rise of Shanghai's tall towers—as the struggles of nineteenth-century Parisian tenement dwellers lie buried beneath the broad boulevards and pretty parks of La Ville-Lumière.

Expos, formerly called World's Fairs, have been organized for more than a century and a half—longer than the modern Olympic Games. The Great Exhibition, the first in a series of World's Fair exhibitions of culture and industry, was held in Hyde Park, London in 1851 as a celebration of modern industrial technology and design. Boasting a spectacularly futuristic building of cast-iron and glass known as the Crystal Palace, the event became a symbol of the Victorian-era United Kingdom, which boasted the largest empire in history and was the world's foremost global power.

One of the most memorable of all World's Fairs was held in Chicago in 1893 to celebrate the 400th anniversary of Christopher Columbus's arrival in the New World. The architectural centerpiece of this World's Columbian Exposition was the White City, a cluster of buildings made of pale stucco and illuminated by the cutting-edge technology of streetlights. The White City, in stark contrast to the dingy sprawl of the city's downtrodden tenements, shined a brilliant alabaster. The father of American landscape architecture, Frederick Law Olmsted, developed the layout for the fairgrounds, and renowned architect Daniel Burnham, guided by principles of European classical architecture, designed the buildings. Architectural luminary Louis Sullivan believed the style of the White City was too staid; he created as counterpoint to the pale city of classical design a polychrome Transportation Building in a forward-looking style that drew rave reviews from the international architectural community. The scale and grandeur of the World's Columbian Exposition far exceeded those of previous World's Fairs, and the event became a symbol of America's development into the dominant nation of the twentieth century in much the same way that the Great Exhibition had been emblematic of the United Kingdom's Victorian Age. The World's Fair held in Chicago in 1893 was an exclamation point on the accomplishments and wild aspirations of a young nation eager to demonstrate its rise from an agrarian society into an urban utopia. The World's Columbian Exposition was, in short, the creation of an emerging superpower bursting with ambition to lead the world.

China today in many ways resembles America in 1893, with all the optimism and excess that infused our nation when we began our rise. As Europeans at the time of the Columbian Exposition thought of America as uncultured and uncouth, so we view Shanghai with disdain for gauchely flaunting its wealth, and curse the Chinese masses for spitting in the streets. One of those streets will be the stunning Expo Boulevard. With the help of German engineers, Shanghai is creating Expo Boulevard as an architectural highlight of the 2010 World Expo. This multilevel megaproject boasts six gigantic structures built of steel and transparent plastic. Each one is shaped like an inverted horn with a narrow, tapered end aimed at the ground, and on top of each structure is the flaring rim of an orifice as big as two basketball courts that faces skyward to collect rainfall and sunshine; water and light funnel down the horns and spill into the underground level of the boulevard. These colossal cones, each standing boldly upright without support, have been dubbed "Sunny Valleys." Each Sunny Valley poses a monumental engineering challenge, but China is confident it is up to the task, measuring the dimensions of every portion of the massive structures to the micrometer. Crystal Palace and the White City might have met their match in Shanghai's Sunny Valleys when it comes to sheer outlandish grandeur.

Each day many thousands of workers swarm the 2010 World Expo site, the largest in more than one hundred and fifty years of Expo history. Hanging from girders, pouring rivers of concrete, burrowing their way beneath the ground, they labor to complete the largest construction project in China. When the Expo begins, if all goes according to plan at this "Economic Olympics," as the Chinese refer to the event, ideas will be exchanged, cultures will be shared, and a peaceful spirit of international cooperation will pervade the fairgrounds. All of this is good, and the Chinese are sincere in their intentions. At their towering national pavilion, another architectural centerpiece of the Expo, they will complete the process of rebranding their nation that began two years previous in Beijing at the Olympic Games. China will be presented to the world not as a downtrodden country filled with quaint relics from the past but as a strong and confident nation awash in modern wonders. Once the world marveled at Marco Polo's tales of cities so massive and so opulent they made the barbarian nations beyond the

Celestial Kingdom shiver with awe and envy; now citizens of the world will travel to the fabled city of Shanghai and their jaws will drop as they stare stupefied at the city of the future.

The Chinese are proud of the new China, and why shouldn't they be. From the ruins of foreign occupation, civil wars, disastrous economic policies, and calamitous revolutions, they have built a city of shining towers. The list of problems Shanghai faces is so long and depressing it's enough to make a Westerner pack his bags and leave Shanghai forever. Expats choking on pollution and foreign companies crumpling beneath the weight of corruption have done exactly that. But the Chinese carry on, and there is an exuberance in Shanghai as palpable as the polluted air. It is the giddiness of a giant waking from a long slumber. The giant is clumsy, but he is powerful, and perhaps he is dangerous if misunderstood. Above all, he should not be ignored—he is, after all, a giant.

For most of recorded history China was the wealthiest and most powerful nation on the planet. Chinese civilization has survived thousands of years; perhaps it will persist for thousands more. Some days in Shanghai, surrounded by every possible malady a city could muster, from unbreathable air to people so urgently poor they left their homes hundreds of miles away to make five dollars a day as they squat in rat-ridden middens and work at hazardous jobsites where they might be maimed, I feel the future will be as bright as the towers of Pudong. The Chinese have lost religion, but they have faith. The have faith that their country will persist and it will prosper. They have faith that their future will be better than their recent history and match the glory of their ancient past. This might sound silly and old-fashioned in our cynical postmodern world, but the people who live amid the postmodern skyline of Pudong possess an earnestness we lost long ago.

It is often said that there is no word for irony in Chinese. This was true in the past, as irony was a foreign concept with no equivalent in traditional Chinese culture. But ask a Chinese student now and she will tell you that *fěngcì* is irony. It is not. *Fěngcì* is more like satire, the closest concept in Chinese to irony, and *fěngcì* has become a stand-in for a word that does not exist. The Chinese prefer their humor with a punch line. China's state-run *Beijing Evening News* once republished a story from *The Onion* about the U.S. Congress demanding a new Capitol building with a retractable dome. Cluing in the rest of the world to the depths of its clueless earnestness, the Chinese capital's largest-circulation newspaper issued this statement as part of its retraction: "Some small American newspapers frequently fabricate offbeat news to trick people into noticing them, with the aim of making money."

Irony is a luxury of people who have had their basic needs met. What use is irony when one is starving? I'd grown up at a point when the United States boasted the highest standard of material living in the history of the world, and irony had seemed a necessary trope to help cope with the angst of modern life. Ah, what a luxury angst is. Only someone with a full belly can have angst, only someone who has eaten can savor irony. A person with an empty stomach feels hungry, and there is no irony in hunger—it just flat out sucks to starve.

Not one of my Chinese friends, no matter how advanced his English, thinks *The Onion* is funny. But perhaps in time, when China is rich and its citizens have wearied of wealth and power, the Chinese will learn to slay all that is sincere and earnest with their wit. Cynical postmodern people bemoan the state of things. The Chinese believe they are building something important, something glorious and good, in much the same way that Americans in the aftermath of World War II joined together to create something wonderful from the ashes of the war. Earnest people get things done: instead of finding sophisticated ways to whine, they change the world—for better or worse.

How China will evolve as it rises remains to be seen, and if all the China watchers and experts in the world were to put their heads together, they would make plausible arguments about what will happen, but the truth is, they would have no idea. Westerners who spend a significant amount of time in China are often surprised to discover how little control Beijing really has over the country's enormous territory—sometimes it seems every province, every city, is going its own direction. The people themselves don't know what their nation will become. China is simply too vast, too endlessly complicated, to change in any predictable way. Look out at the Shanghai skyline and make your best guess.

The Middle Kingdom might very well reclaim its place at the center of the world, and Shanghai could serve as China's most powerful economic engine beyond the 2010 Expo and far into the future. The city might even become, as many have predicted, an emblem of the twenty-first century in the same way that London represented the nineteenth century and New York the twentieth. But what's certain is this: the way in which Shanghai develops in the coming decades will help steer China's course, and whatever happens in China will ripple across the planet. See the cranes hovering over the half-finished towers. They are building, building, and they will not stop building until they have filled the sky.

Cranes are everywhere in Shanghai. Construction is constant, and new towers crowd the sky.

I remembered the boy who'd bounced off my leg in the alley and how Old Wang had cradled him in her arms. And I imagined him growing up in that neighborhood in Old Wang's firm grip and surrounded by her questions and her stories. The boy would feel smothered, perhaps, by the narrow alleys and the gossip in the small world of the shikumen lanes where everyone knew everyone's business and weighed in on what each member of the community should and shouldn't do, but perhaps too he would feel safe, and certainly he would feel loved. And I felt sad at the thought of that neighborhood vanishing and that boy growing up in an apartment as cold and barren and barricaded from its neighbors as the one I stood in now. But it wasn't my place to tell Shanghai what was worth preserving. It wasn't my right to tell its people how to live. Perhaps I felt bad for that boy because I felt bad for myself, for the lonely life I'd led as a boy in an American suburb where no one really talked to anyone else, where no one seemed to care what happened to the neighbors as long as they kept their yards neat and maintained their property values. Where no one played mahjong in the streets and shared spicy crepes and chatter on the corner. Where children were not routinely held by everyone around them.

Throughout the ages Westerners have seen in China that which was missing in themselves. In a culture so different from our way of life, in a country so alien to our understanding, it is easy to see whatever we want to see. The magic mirror of Shanghai. A mirror filled with omniscient old women and lurid lights that pulse like the breath of a space-age dragon. China is the Other, a world so foreign it often seems less a different country and more a different dimension. But perhaps the Other is simply the part of ourselves that we do not yet know or understand. On this night in Shanghai I felt a bit less like a foreigner and a little more Chinese. I felt as though I had been a Shanghainese forever. I felt I had been that boy running down the narrow lane; I felt I had known Old Wang all my life.

Wooden planking gleamed beneath our feet. What better use of a shiny floor made from a vanishing rainforest than a sock-footed sliding contest. If the world is falling down, why not make the best of what's still around. After I explained the rules to Jennifer, we each took three long running steps and slid across the polished flooring. With empty teacups we marked the endpoint of our slides, and then we took longer running starts for round two, setting new personal bests as we skidded past the teacup markers. Each time we ran longer and faster and slid farther, laughing, sometimes falling, bodies bruising as they collided with the floor and with furniture. I laughed and looked at Jennifer. Her flashing eyes, her floating hair. Outside, somewhere among dim alleyways Old Wang laid the children of the neighborhood down to sleep and listened to their softly spoken secrets in the glowing Shanghai night.

Pajamas

Soon my stay in Shanghai ended and I had to return to my life in America, but Jennifer and I spoke by Skype each day, Voice over Internet Protocol compressing our voice streams into digital packets and hurling these packets between Boulder and Shanghai. The telecommunications miracle of VoIP, sure to be as quaint as the telegraph in a few years' time but astonishing for now, eliminated the cost of transcontinental chatting, and because Jennifer and I could call each other for free from our laptops, we continued our language lessons as though I were still in Shanghai. Webcams made hanging out in cyberspace even more like spending time together in person. By Skype and sometimes by email so Jennifer could improve her written English, I followed the developments of her family in their shikumen home closely. I followed them very closely—from inside the home—because a broadband service provider offered Internet access in a neighborhood with plumbing that seemed so ancient and decrepit it could have been installed in the Shang dynasty, a neighborhood where I had seen laborers on bamboo scaffolding using tools that looked to have evolved little since the Bronze Age. Jennifer often took her laptop into her family's apartment and turned on the webcam. I sat at my desk in Boulder, the foothills of the Rockies rising into a blue vault of Colorado sky behind me, or into the star-spattered blackness of the night. Jennifer's mother and father sat on the edge of the bed in their home, clothes and cooking implements and newspapers piled all around them, the soothing cadence of mahjong tiles clacking in the background as two women in pajamas played and played without end, and they caught me up on the latest happenings in the neighborhood while Jennifer translated.

Old Wang had gone to the hospital with a pain in her abdomen; it was her gall bladder, and the swollen organ had been removed. Now she was back at home and as busy as ever, tending to the children in the lane, joining the neighbors when they gathered outside in the evenings to enjoy cool breezes, talking to everyone in sight to learn the latest gossip, burrowing her way into everyone's business. Three more families had moved out, and their homes had been smashed by bulldozers. The alley was too narrow to bring in cranes with wrecking balls; the demolition crews drove in small bulldozers to push at the buildings, or they swung sledgehammers into the bricks or poked at the walls with pickaxes. The air had been filled with smoke and dust, and Jennifer's parents had sealed their windows shut with duct tape and donned surgical masks to keep from coughing on the grit. Across the alley a red banner had been strung up. It read, "Thank you for peacefully leaving your homes." Representatives from the development company had visited Jennifer's parents, increasing their offer of compensation. They had written a number on a pad of paper and showed it to Jennifer's father. He could have that number if he and his family left, he'd been told. And they would give him a good price on a new apartment in a skyrise tower.

"And?" I asked. "Did he take it?"

He had not, Jennifer said.

Her father shook his head, the movement jittery on my computer screen. The picture broke apart, dissolving into random points of light and then reassembling itself back into a coherent image. What would the pointillists have made of computer pixels? Would Seurat have dipped his brush in paint had he been born, instead of in 1859, in the last quarter of the twentieth century? Or would he have looked at a computer monitor and thought, why bother.

"It wasn't enough money?" I asked, trying to focus on the topic at hand. The computer screen between us made the family's problems seem less real, less immediate.

"The apartment they said he could buy for a good price was too far away," Jennifer said. "My dad didn't even know where it was. Somewhere out by the airport—Pudong, not Hongqiao."

Pudong International Airport might as well have been in another city it was so far from the center of Shanghai. And not just distance separated the neighborhood lanes of Jennifer's parents from the frenetic air transportation hub of Shanghai—from the shikumen to Pudong was like a leap from the nineteenth century straight to the twenty-first.

"Your father doesn't want to be near all that air traffic and noise?" I asked.

"No, he likes airplanes. He's never flown in one but he likes to watch them and he likes the sound of them. Sometimes when I was young we used to go to Hongqiao to see them."

"So why doesn't he want to live there?"

Jennifer asked her father something and they spoke several sentences of Shanghainese.

Before I started learning Chinese, I used to say, "The hell if I know what that person said—he might as well have been speaking Chinese." Now I say, "The hell if I know what that person said—he might as well have been speaking Shanghainese."

Jennifer looked into her webcam. "He says this is his home. He's an old man and this is where he wants to live." She spoke with him a moment and then she said to me, "He doesn't know how else to explain it."

I had read somewhere that the Pudong International Airport had the only control tower in the world that was open to the public. I said I wanted to go with him to the airport sometime to watch the planes lift and land.

Jennifer translated and her father nodded and said okay, we could go together.

"Hey, can you do me a favor," I said to Jennifer. "Walk outside with your laptop."

"I might lose the signal."

"That's okay. Just see how far you can get."

"Why?"

"I want to see the alley. And Old Wang. Let's see if she's outside."

"*Nǐ fēng le.*"

Nǐ fēng le means "You're crazy." I told Jennifer I did not disagree. "Leave the microphone on and the webcam on and walk outside. Come on, please?"

"*Fēng le,*" Jennifer said a few times as she left the apartment and made her way down the twisty staircase and toward the courtyard. Images wobbled on my computer screen. The shaking caused both by Jennifer moving with her laptop and by the degradation of the digital signals passing through thousands of miles of fiber-optic cables on the ocean floor gave me jolts of vertigo. I saw random flashes of brick walls and Chinese faces until Jennifer passed through the stone-framed door of the courtyard and into the narrow alleyway beyond. The world steadied as she stood still, and Old Wang was there to greet her. Jennifer talked to her a moment and then Old Wang moved her face close to the cycloptic eye of the webcam, each wrinkle of her cheeks clearly defined on my screen.

"*Nong ho*," I greeted her, and with that I exhausted my entire lexicon of Shanghainese.

Each ridge and furrow of Old Wang's cheeks stretched apart and then reassembled into a new pattern as her face formed a smile that made me realize I had to return to Shanghai soon. Old Wang nodded at the webcam as she watched me smiling back at her on Jennifer's laptop screen. Behind her stretched an alley dense with detail.

"Hey Jennifer," I said, "walk down the alley. Please?"

"Walk down the alley?"

"With your laptop. Just hold it in front of you and pan the webcam back and forth as you walk down the alley."

"*Nǐ fēng le.*"

"I know, I know—we've established that. I just want to see the lane again. I miss it."

Outside my home in Boulder stretched a sky so impossibly blue and mountains so crisply defined in the high-altitude air of Colorado it seemed I lived in a CGI world of computer-generated purity. Springtime in Boulder is paradise. But perhaps it is too perfect and the world cannot possibly be as clean and green and beautiful as it is when the plump buds of May burst open and meadows combust with color. There is something a bit surreal about it. Too much beauty, maybe. One gluts oneself on it and forgets that the world that lies beyond the pristine skies and gorgeous mountain vistas of this storybook town is filled with grit and it is real. No computer-generated skies of spotless blue stretch over the shikumen of Shanghai.

Shanghai's lanes were a world apart from the orderly streets and healthful air of my home in the foothills of the Rockies. But those alleyways heaved with humanity and hummed with activity every day and night. There was so much life packed into those narrow spaces and I missed them terribly. Women clicking together mahjong tiles, men squatting on the street to rethread frayed wires for a few coins, or spreading the tools of their trade across scraps of cloth to resole worn-out shoes, or pushing handcarts to sell small piles of roasted potatoes. Hawkers singing out their wares. Families sleeping in the streets in the muggy heat of summer. Parents sipping chrysanthemum tea from sweating mason jars and fanning the moist faces of their children. Men soothing their bare bellies with the breeze made by giant paddle fans that they moved like metronomes through the broiling air. Children playing tag in the nooks and crannies of the alleys. People shuttling back and forth between their homes and the community sinks where they washed their faces and brushed their teeth. People clad in pajamas lounging in lawn chairs. I think I missed people wearing pjs in public the most.

Bored with my job in Boulder, tired of creating tours to China for American business students, I'd skipped out on work and sequestered myself in the Denver Public Library to research the history of public pajama wearing in Shanghai. Everyone needs a hobby, though my curiosity over the pj phenomenon nearly got me fired. When I should have been on the phone with professors and student trip leaders I was in the stacks searching texts for clues to why a person in Shanghai could leave his house clad only in a pair of comfortable pajamas and stroll down to the neighborhood store, buy some groceries or a newspaper, and then casually walk back home. I thought it would be fun to try this in America and see if I could pull it off without getting arrested, or at least evaluated in a psychiatric facility, but I lacked the guts to try it.

The answers I found to why this was so in Shanghai led me into the city's history, and then further afield into China's history, and soon I was spending so much time poking around in the library and looking in cyberspace I realized I was researching the background for a book about Shanghai that I would write; and I shaved my hours at work down to part time and kept just enough of a relationship with the travel industry to get business visas and plane tickets and to give me excuses to return to China and continue my connection with Jennifer and her family as I watched their story unfold. Skype was a brilliant invention, but there was no substitute for putting my feet on the flagstones of an alley, for sharing street food with Old Wang, for searing my lungs by taking in draughts of Shanghai's chemical air. Some things just cannot be replicated by digital means.

But back to the topic at hand, that topic being the sociological/historical/cultural inquiry into the question that intrigued me: Why did people in the most prosperous city in China wear their pjs in public? One reason for this phenomenon lay within the layout of lilong. Many shikumen dwellings had less-than-adequate plumbing, as I'd discovered on many occasions and had yet to flush the memories from my mind. Most shikumen residents in the past had shared communal toilets in the alleys with other families, blurring the boundaries between private space and public space. With so many families living together in tight quarters, and everyone knowing everyone in the neighborhood and sharing toi-

In Shanghai's traditional lane neighborhoods, residents share outdoor bathrooms and sinks. This has created a culture in which it is perfectly normal for people in pajamas to stand chatting alongside a busy avenue.

lets and sinks and kitchens, being seen in your pjs was no big thing. The extension of one's home into the streets beyond the threshold of one's front door had made it acceptable to don some jammies and go about one's business in the world.

All perfectly reasonable, it seemed to me. Many Shanghainese even separated the pajamas they wore to bed and slept in from the pajamas they wore around town. But why was the leisurewear of choice pajamas, I wondered. Why was it not, say, tracksuits and T-shirts—my favorite leisurewear in Colorado? Shanghai is brutally hot and sticky in summer; pajamas are lightweight and loose fitting. They are comfortable casual wear on a day so sultry the asphalt sticks to your shoes. But men in Beijing, when the mercury soars and the sky sweats humidity, take off their shirts and roll up their trousers. Something else explained the prevalence of pajamas in public in Shanghai, and the answer, this time, resided not in the arrangement of the shikumen neighborhoods and their poor plumbing but in Shanghai's obsession with wealth.

Shanghainese have been wearing pajamas in the streets ever since the Chinese economy started to take off. After the Communist Party embraced free markets and lifted the restrictive dress codes of the Cultural Revolution, residents of

Shanghai could add sleepwear to wardrobes that had consisted of little more than the baggy, bland Mao suits that everyone covered themselves with to show they were part of the proletariat.

The history of the Mao suit in China goes back to 1912 when Sun Zhongshan (known in the West as Sun Yat-sen), the provisional president of the Republic of China, modernized the clothing of Chinese men. Previously, the style of dress in China had been mandated by the Qing dynasty, made up of Manchus, and had been imposed on the Chinese people as a form of social control: the Han Chinese had been forced by their Manchu rulers to give up local traditions of dress in favor of Manchu-inspired fashion. The resentment of the Han Chinese toward their Manchu overlords, whom they blamed for keeping China weak and poor and making it easy prey for Western powers, culminated in the overthrow of the Qing dynasty and the founding of the Republic of China. Throughout Chinese history, a new dynasty had dictated a new fashion to the people as an emblem of its power and a symbol of the new regime. With the overthrow of the Manchu-led Qing imperial court, a new China determined to build itself into a strong modern nation needed a new style of dress.

Sun Yat-sen instructed a Chinese tailor in Shanghai to create a tunic suit based on a Japanese military uniform. The sleeves of the jacket, designed to cover the knuckle of the thumb, were longer than those of a Western suit, this loose fit allowing for more ease of movement and reflecting the style of the traditional Chinese long gown. The original Sun Yat-sen suit (or *Zhōngshān zhuāng*, as it is known in Chinese) had a collar that was raised straight up and five center-front buttons, which were said to represent the five powers of the constitution of the Republic. Changes crept into the suit, including influences of German military dress such as a turned-down collar and four symmetrically placed pockets. The four pockets, regardless of their Teutonic inspiration, came to embody the Chinese principle of balance, and they were believed to represent the four cardinal virtues of the *I Ching*, or *Book of Changes*, one of China's oldest classic texts. Though the suit boasted some distinctly Chinese symbolism, it stood in clear contrast to the Manchu clothing of the past and showed the world that the new China, while not adopting the fashions of the West in a wholesale manner, was open to contemporary ideas from overseas.

The suit that Sun Yat-sen popularized held patriotic significance for the Chinese people long after the founder of the Chinese Republic passed. Mao understood the power of clothing to project national identity and promote ideology. At the ceremony in Beijing marking the founding of the People's Republic of

China, he donned a modified form of the Sun Yat-sen suit. It was immediately adopted by the vast majority of the Chinese people as their clothing of choice. Throughout the rest of the world it became known as the "Mao suit," and this blue, baggy, sexless uniform with a lumpy hat became emblematic of the bland conformity of Chinese Communism.

In the People's Republic of China, Western-style clothing was seen as a symbol of depraved capitalist society, and Chinese citizens avoided it at all costs, lest they be labeled bourgeois enemies of the people and be tortured or killed by crazed mobs when Mao and his minions ordered purges. Only Mao suits were considered acceptable attire. The garment that Sun Yat-sen had intended to signal an openness to foreign ideas came to represent a statement of Chinese identity, ascetic devotion to Communist principles, and a stark contrast to Western decadence. Through a combination of government clothing prohibitions and poverty, the Chinese people for three decades following the establishment of the People's Republic wore little else than Mao suits. Everyone tried to look like workers, who were regarded as noble pioneers building a better society through their labor and solidarity.

After Deng Xiaoping famously declared "to get rich is glorious" and began opening China's economy, Shanghai's tradition of family life spilling out of homes and into the surrounding streets combined with the city's newfound fascination with material things and its burgeoning interest in individual identity. The newly rich Shanghainese had the money to diversify their wardrobes, and they had the freedom to wear what they wanted. And what they wanted to wear were pajamas. Strutting around the streets in pjs made a statement, and the statement was this: I've got money. The people of Shanghai had once put on matching Mao suits and formed mobs that ransacked the town rooting out capitalists; now they took to the streets of their city clad in comfortable cotton and silk, displaying pinstripes, plaid, and polka dots to show that they were rich enough to afford more than Mao suits. It seemed that public pajama wearing had less to do with dressing down, as I had assumed, and more to do with dressing to impress.

"Is this true?" I asked Marcus on a Skype call I'd made while I was supposed to be working. Bored and procrastinating, I had just called Marcus and shared with him the fruits of my research. I was hoping for validation from an insider.

"Yeah, I guess that's why they started wearing them. It's stupid."

I said, "Wearing jeans or dresses or whatever shows that someone has enough money to buy clothes that are better than a Mao suit. Why are people still wearing pajamas? Is it just habit now?"

"It's so stupid. Basically, some people think that if they walk around in their pajamas in the middle of the day, then everyone will think they're so rich they don't have to go to work. They want everyone to see that they're, like, just hanging out and enjoying the good life."

"Do you ever wear pajamas in public?" I asked.

"Are you kidding? In Xujiahui? Nobody in my neighborhood wears pajamas when they go out."

"So what do you wear when you're just hanging out or going to the grocery store or something?"

"What do you think I wear? The same stuff you wear, dumb-ass. Except my clothes are better than yours because I live in Shanghai and you live in America. New fashions come here first."

"I wouldn't pick up on new fashions wherever I live."

"I know—I'm trying to help you with that."

"It's not going to be easy."

"No, it's definitely not easy. Hey, check this out."

Marcus sent me an emoticon over Skype. In the chat box of the Skype window I saw not the flashing dollar sign he usually sent me but a little cartoon man giving me the finger.

"It's a hidden emoticon," he said. "There's a whole bunch of them. I found this website that tells you how to do it."

One after another he sent them my way. Instead of the smiley faces that Jennifer sent me when we were chatting online, a barrage of emoticons consisting of tiny cartoon people mooning, cussing, smoking, wobbling around drunk, and beating their heads against walls appeared on my screen.

"Cool, huh?" Marcus said. "I love emoticons."

"I think you've gone emoti-crazy," I said.

"I have a new business idea."

For the past few months Marcus had been talking about quitting his marketing job and starting a business of his own. Not a marketing business, though. His business ideas changed by the day. At first he wanted to get into parking—with all the new cars entering the streets of this Manhattan-on-Red-Bull city, parking was at a premium. But so was land to build car parks—scratch that idea. How about wheel clamping? The Denver boot had yet to make an appearance in Shanghai. He would get into towing and locking wheels. All the world's wheel clamps were being manufactured in China—might as well start using them there to make some money. Next he'd decided to introduce fortune cookies to China. While eating dinner in Shanghai together on my last trip, fortune cookies had come up. In conversation, that is. They had never shown up on a table in China as far as Marcus knew. I couldn't recall ever having seen one in China. Or in Chinese restaurants in Europe. Only in America. The fortune cookie, with its familiar crackly wafer, curved shape and ancient words of nonsense, had been invented by Japanese bakers in California, and there is no standard term for them in Chinese. Chinese tourists on their first trip to America are mystified by the crisp cookies with slips of paper bearing lottery numbers and profundities such as "Your bold adventures will bring you big rewards." With China's interest in American food, fortune cookies were sure to be a big hit, Marcus had mused. Would they be served in Chinese restaurants in China? You couldn't really say "Chinese restaurants" in China, because "Chinese" was, of course, the default. Or would they be served in American restaurants in China? Maybe American-style Chinese restaurants would go over well in China! Why on earth would Chinese people in China go to American-Chinese restaurants that offered bland interpretations of Chinese food created for the timid American palate? Maybe a restaurant that catered to American expats in China who were hungry for a taste of home? And it would be named "In Bed" after the American game of adding "in bed" to the end of each fortune to spice it up! And so on. We had gone through several of these brainstorming sessions in person and on Skype, though Marcus was no closer to having an idea compelling enough to make him *xià hǎi*, jump into the sea.

"X-rated emoticons," Marcus said.

"That's your business idea?"

"These ones are cool, the mooning and drinking and stuff, but if you had a set of really sexy emoticons, you know, like really X-rated emoticons doing crazy sex stuff, you could sell those. What do you think?"

"I don't think it's absolutely the worst business idea you've had, but it's probably in the top five all-time worst. Hey, how about pajamas?"

"You're still worried about pajamas?"

"I'll bet there's a business in pajamas—high-end designer pajamas. Pajamas as haute fashion. Pajamas in Shanghai say money. Take them to the runways of the world."

"That's the worst idea you've had," said Marcus.

"Says he who wants to peddle X-rated emoticons."

"Actually," Marcus said, "maybe that would work. Suits are out and casual clothes are in. My generation wants to wear relaxed stuff and express ourselves when we go to work. We don't want to wear business suits."

"So you want to dress like Bill Gates, not like Hu Jintao?"

"We don't want to wear sweaters like Bill Gates, we want cool clothes."

I told Marcus I'd already done the research and was a step ahead of him. When the Chinese business boom of the 1980s and 90s shook the country and entrepreneurs replaced workers as the pioneers of a new society, the Western-style suit had made a comeback, and Armani had trumped Mao. In 1984, the General Secretary of the Communist Party shocked Chinese TV viewers by appearing on domestic television wearing a business suit. This was the first tremor of a coming tectonic shift in national fashion: cadres began trading in their blue Mao suits for the Western-style black business suits and no-nonsense ties now in vogue with Party members. Occasionally, to show their solidarity with the people when they toured rural areas, Communist Party leaders would make appearances in Mao suits, and Chinese presidents might dust off their Mao suits when reviewing military parades, but for all intents and purposes the official dress code of the capitalist revolution in China consisted of the Western-style suit. As Marcus had mentioned, however, the venerable business suit was facing growing competition in the workplace from clothing that was more relaxed. Edgy young professionals in Shanghai had begun to view the business suit as too formal and too uncomfortable. I agreed completely. Down with ties, let the revolution begin!

Traveling to China was not the best part of my job; the best part was being at home in Boulder in my pajamas lying nestled on the couch between my two Labradors with a headset perched atop my unkempt head of hair while I talked with university administrators (who were surely wearing suits) about their upcoming travel plans, pretending I cared while I petted my dogs and winked at my wife.

"Pajamas in the workplace could be the next big thing," I said to Marcus. "You better ride that wave while you can."

Aldous Huxley, that inveterate globetrotter, described Shanghai's allure with a diary entry: "In no city, West or East, have I ever had such an impression of dense, rank, richly clotted life. Old Shanghai is Bergson's *élan vital* in the raw, so to speak, and with the lid off. It is Life itself." After investigating the pajamas-in-public mystery and delving into China's sartorial past, with Huxley's words echoing in my head and a picture of Old Wang as the screensaver on my laptop, I resolved to return to Shanghai as soon as possible. I finagled my way on to a trip with an MBA group, and after introducing them to the labyrinthine world of contemporary Chinese business, I pawned them off on a local tour guide so they could see the highlights of the city from a bus. And with Jennifer I ventured on foot back into the mazelike alleyways of one of the last remnants of old Shanghai, where rows of shikumen lay squeezed between skyscrapers.

It was a day of wicked heat and watery sun. Smog curled in dreamlike tendrils around the tops of towers, and through the hazy thickness of the air I glimpsed construction cranes. The ancient man who guarded the entrance to the lanes by the home of Jennifer's parents was standing next to the stone archway exactly as he had the last time I'd seen him. As if he hadn't moved in the months that I'd been gone. Once again his eyes followed me though his head did not. He gave Jennifer one small nod as she passed and she nodded back and then we traced our way toward the inner alleys of a neighborhood fortressed by an old man's stare.

When we reached the lane that held the home of Jennifer's parents, I saw, instead of a single demolished house amid the rows of shikumen, several empty places where brick walls and stone-framed doors had fallen. Previously, I had thought the tier of shikumen with one absent home had looked like a row of teeth with one tooth missing. Now many teeth were missing.

And speaking of missing teeth, Old Wang greeted us and caught us up on the neighborhood gossip. She talked too quickly for Jennifer to translate the Shanghainese into English, but later when we left the alley, stepping over a threshold and setting our feet on the flagstone flooring of the courtyard, Jennifer told me that Old Wang's house would be torn down soon—maybe within the next few weeks—and she had already started moving her belongings to her new place. Mostly she'd talked about the washing machine and dryer, Jennifer said. They were on an enclosed porch.

Shanghai had been trying to address its laundry-hanging-outside image that visitors to the city took away with them. It seemed so incongruously third world amid a cityscape of futuristic towers, and tourists were forever commenting on the phenomenon and photographing people's underwear flapping from bamboo poles against backdrops that seemed snatched from *Star Wars*. Shanghai is modern and ancient, they would tell their friends back home. Within sight of some of the world's tallest buildings, people hang their skivvies out to dry.

The leaders of Shanghai had in the past made attempts to ban hanging laundry from balconies; they had mandated adding enclosed porches to new apartment buildings so people could dry their clothes in spaces hidden from the prying eyes of tourists. Most citizens of Shanghai had ignored the rule, had defiantly dangled their wash from poles stuck out the windows of the private porches, and it seemed the government had finally given up: throughout the city of the future, undies hung steaming in the sun, stockings spiraled in the breeze, and the shutters of tourists' cameras clicked open and closed.

But Old Wang would be drying her clothes in a machine from now on, and she could not have been happier. She was one big grin when she spoke to Jennifer about the dryer.

Fighting for attention with the multicolored laundry were red banners. They webbed the alleyway outside the shikumen home of Jennifer's family. The silly sloganeering of the banners contained sentences such as "It is every person's duty to build a better China" and helpful phrases such as "Maintain harmonious society."

It has been said that China's Communist Party must continuously manufacture slogans, and what the actual slogans say isn't important, because if the government stops filling the streets with banners and its citizens' heads with gibberish, there is the danger that those citizens, in the absence of government propaganda, will come up with slogans of their own, will start to think for themselves. And citizens thinking for themselves is, of course, the last thing the Party wants. But what if all the propaganda were to suddenly stop? What would the Chinese people think—what ideas would fill their heads? Surely with five thousand years of culture behind them, they would have some pretty profound ones, thoughts that would change the world. Maybe. Or maybe there wouldn't be revolution in the streets. Maybe most people would carry on doing pretty much exactly what they are doing now, trying to get rich and not worrying about anything else. Perhaps this is the dirty laundry hanging in the breeze. Perhaps this is really where we should be pointing our cameras. Americans are convinced it is our mission to set people free from tyranny. Sometimes we forget to ask the people if they want to be free. And sometimes those people don't even understand the question.

A tattered flag of pajama bottoms stretched out from a bamboo pole and furled above Jennifer. Someone's underpants flapped above my head. Not one of the

Drying laundry festoons lane neighborhoods, adding garlands of color throughout the city. Residents relocated from shikumen to towers often continue to dangle their clothes from bamboo poles poking out of futuristic boxes stacked sky high.

American MBA students I had sent to China, not one of the administrators of America's elite business programs that had accompanied them, had ever asked me why in China they couldn't find pictures of the tanks rolling toward Tiananmen or footage of unrest in Tibet. And I had never encouraged them to look, for these things had no relevance to our purpose in China: to figure out how to make money, how to get rich. All around Jennifer and me, clothes and bed sheets cracked and curled, snapped and furled in the wind that filled the alley.

"Sometimes the people in charge of relocating will give a good deal to someone like Old Wang," Jennifer said. "They find out who everyone respects in the neighborhood."

"And they give that person a dryer?" I asked.

"If they make Old Wang happy, then she will tell people it's okay, they should move out of their homes and take the offers."

"And your parents?" I asked. "Do they get a dryer?"

"The apartment the developer will let them buy hasn't been built yet. I don't know if there's a dryer there or not. Perhaps there is not one."

"I thought the apartment was out in Pudong—by the airport."

"Perhaps that is where it will be built."

"Where are they supposed to stay while it's being built?"

"A temp apartment."

"A temporary apartment."

"You can't say *temp*? I thought this was an abbreviation for *temporary*?"

"It is for workers. Temporary workers, like people who work in an office temporarily, are called *temps*."

"Oh. So they will have a temporary apartment while theirs is being finished."

The pace of construction being what it is in Shanghai, a new apartment building could be raised in a matter of weeks. A fact often bandied about—though it might be an urban myth, as no one can ever seem to cite a source—is that a few years back one quarter of all the construction cranes on the planet were in Shanghai. Whether this is true or not is immaterial; the entire city is a perpetual construction zone and buildings grow as swiftly as bamboo in a Chinese jungle—in part because of all the cranes, and in large part because of all the construction crews that work around the clock. I knew this for a fact because of countless sleep-deprived nights. Jackhammers stuttering, rivet guns hissing, steel beams gonging together, construction workers barking commands at each other: no earplugs on earth could block the racket. I'd spent many nights in hotels and crashing on friends' couches throughout Shanghai with noise-canceling earphones covering the foam plugs crammed tight in my ear canals and a black sleep mask shielding my eyes against the glare of floodlights and welding torches. In boomtown Shanghai, buildings were constructed with blistering speed, but trusting the development company or government cadres or whoever was in charge of the relocation scheme to provide a permanent home somewhere down the line seemed sketchy to me. So much business in China is conducted with a handshake, and a handshake in China, in my experience, means virtually nothing. I had watched people in Shanghai swindle each other with startling regularity, and the promises broken by businesspeople and by government officials were legion. You Americans are like stone, Chinese had told me; we Chinese are like water—we change easily, we switch directions, we adapt. Call me stone, but I like a contract. And cultural relativity be damned: I like for people to follow the contract.

"Is there a contract?" I asked Jennifer's father when we got inside their home. As always, random people playing mahjong filled the small space. "Are these people related to you?" I asked Jennifer before her father could answer.

"They live downstairs. They play mahjong here because there's more space here."

I looked around the room and tried to imagine a home that was more cramped. I suppose the bed could have been in the kitchen, not just next to it. Or in the bathroom. It seemed a bit extravagant, all that empty space in the bathroom. Someone could be living in there instead of devoting those six square feet solely for toileting and washing. "Does anyone in a shikumen ever sublet their bathroom for someone to live in?" I asked Jennifer, forgetting that I had asked her father a question.

"We had a neighbor when I was little who shut off the water in her bathroom and let someone stay in there. The toilet didn't work right so she made it into a room where a person could sleep and she rented it to make money."

See, that was the thing about Shanghai. You could think up the most preposterous scenario, could postulate the goofiest idea your mind could conjure, and chances were it was true. A tower shaped like olives speared on a swizzle stick and covered in flashing lights. Yup, got it. People shopping in supermarkets wearing nothing but pajamas. Uh huh, you see it here every day. Boarders renting bathrooms to live in. Sure, it's been known to happen.

"My father says that there is a contract, and he says that it isn't important."

"It's not important because the developers might not honor the contract?" I asked.

"It's not important because he doesn't want to leave. He says he won't take their offer."

"I think he's a brave man."

Jennifer said something to her father; he shook his head hard and spoke softly to her.

"He's not brave, he says. He is just an old man who doesn't want to leave his home."

"Even if the offer is good? Even if there's a nice apartment with a dryer?"

Jennifer's mother shook her head when Jennifer translated.

"They don't want to leave. Besides, they don't like dryers. It is better to dry clothes in the sunshine. Hanging clothes to dry outside is *hěn jiànkāng*." Very healthy. "Clothes dryers are not good for health, because sunshine kills the germs." She listened to her father speak a moment, and then she said, "And he says it is not good for health to live in the sky. It is better to live close to the ground. People should be connected to the ground. It is healthy to be connected to the ground." Her father raised his shoe and tapped it against the floor a few times, putting an exclamation point on Jennifer's sentences.

We were one story up from the ground, but compared to the grotesquely towering high-rises that glowered from the sky, his home was as happily rooted to the earth as the tree in the courtyard with a trunk so wide I could not encircle it within the six-foot wingspan of my arms.

Jennifer's mother hadn't said much after greeting me when I came in. She sat on the faded cushions of an upholstered chair, her fingers working through the dark silk of her hair. Her eyes searched out my own. Each time they found mine she smiled, and in her smile was a glint of gold, the flash of a precious crown. Her hair was, as always, carried up in such a way, raven waves of it held in place with combs of jade, as to make her appear like an aristocrat of old. Her posture, whether sitting, standing or walking, seemed as studied as that of a runway model. Her beauty sometimes made me bashful, and right now I had to lower my eyes until my gaze fell on the shoes that sheathed her feet in simple cotton.

I could tell Jennifer's father was finished talking about the apartment, and Jennifer seemed distracted. Agitated. She forgot to finish sentences and stared at the TV, which, for once, wasn't on. Maybe she was worried about what would happen to her family, maybe she'd fallen in love.

In the crowded room of the shikumen we spoke of a few other things: the sticky summer weather, the Olympics coming to Beijing. I realized I'd never asked Jennifer's parents what they thought about the Expo. Jennifer's father grew more animated when we talked about the Expo. "It will be good for Shanghai," he said, "and good for China. Countries from all over the world will come to China and learn about China and see how advanced Shanghai is. They will see the most modern city in the world and they will be impressed."

His shift from grit-in-the-cogs-of-progress protester to city booster and enthusiastic spokesperson for modernity was as understandable as it was momentarily jarring. So many people in China had so little to believe in. The instigators of the Communist revolution had done their best to destroy every last trace of traditional Chinese culture. Confucian values that had instructed people for millennia how to live were gone and gone were the anchors of Buddhism, Daoism and any other ism other than Communism. And now gone too was Communism as an ideology that offered people solace in the belief that they were sacrificing for social justice and the greater good. Deng Xiaoping is credited with an aphorism that has become the guiding principle of China: "Economic development above all." Jennifer's father was too old to enjoy the to-get-rich-is-glorious adrenaline rush that helped propel Jennifer's generation through the void. An old man in Shanghai had little to believe in other than the comfort of his home and the greater glory of China. His eyes went bright when he talked about the Expo and about the world watching Shanghai as now it watched Beijing. He was too old to get rich, but he wasn't too old to feel his soul lift up as he witnessed China's rise.

Jennifer's father asked if I wanted to eat some Shanghainese food and I rubbed my belly and said of course I did. We left the house, walked to the end of the alley and turned into another alley, hooked a quick right into yet another alley, and soon I was completely lost within a latticework of lanes that held equal parts tightly clustered shikumen and gaping holes where homes had been destroyed. We crossed a dusty stretch of open ground where a woman stood amid a pile of debris with her head downcast and her arms outstretched like some humbled supplicant in a cursed and ravaged land.

When we reached a building with its upstairs ripped open and reduced to rubble but its downstairs still intact, we ducked inside and found a table. Next to the entranceway, aquariums slippery with algae held crabs and frogs, turtles and eels. In the largest glass case swam carp with pouting mouths and bodies shielded in scales of silver and gold, as if clad in regal chainmail. Because Shanghai is situated on the Yangtze Delta, its restaurants are rich with all manner of water-dwelling creatures. We ate braised turtle and stir-fried eels, focusing on the food and not mentioning that the top floor of the restaurant had been demolished and the room we sat in now might be gone tomorrow. There was nothing to be done but to enjoy the feast before us.

Platters of sliced lotus roots and lily bulbs were placed on our table. As I picked at a crab with my chopsticks, digging at its sweet flesh and creamy roe, I saw outside the restaurant a brick building shiver and fall a second before the shock of its collapse sent our plates and bowls sliding across the table and made our teapot's lid flip open and release a burst of steam. We rearranged our crockery and continued eating. Someone came out of a backroom bearing a platter with a fish that had been deep-fried whole in heavy batter. As it was set upon our table,

Jennifer, her father and mother and I all turned our chopsticks toward the giant fish in its pool of sweet red sauce, its crispy skin showered with pine nuts, peas and carrots. When it was nothing but bones and a head picked clean, we ate wedges of watermelon skewered with toothpicks and then we left the restaurant and traveled the knotted alleyways back to their home.

"I want to go shopping," Jennifer said when we reached their courtyard. "Are you ready to leave?"

She had seemed less happy today than during the previous times we'd visited her family together. After we said goodbye to her parents, I asked her what was wrong.

"Those men came to see me again. They came to my apartment and asked me why my parents are being so stubborn."

I stopped walking and turned to look at Jennifer. She seemed so small today. So filled with worry. Instead of displaying her usual enthusiasm for my city-wandering shenanigans and pointless questions, she was having none of it and simply wanted to shop. The wings of her shoulders fell forward in a slump. She seemed deflated, and she looked, for once, as small as she was.

"They weren't polite this time," she said a few moments later as we walked between bumpers and fenders amid stalled lanes of cars. All around us on burdened streets the traffic crept and crawled.

"Did they threaten you?"

"They said my parents should take their offer. They said it was a good offer and the new apartment they are building will be worth much more than their apartment now, but they will sell it to them very cheaply."

"Did they say anything would happen to you if your parents didn't take the offer?"

Jennifer was quiet a moment and then she said, "They told me that if my parents keep complaining it could be difficult for me to go to America to study."

A man pushing a fruit cart forced its wonky wheels alongside the road through piles of brick and rubble. I watched him a moment and then said, "How do they know you want to go to the U.S. to study?"

"Of course they know."

"When would you go?"

"I wanted to go in the fall next year."

"To graduate school?"

"MBA programs in China are not so good. I need to go to one in America. Then I'll work in America, learn good English and come back to China and have a good job."

"You have a good job now," I said. "And your English is amazing."

"I need a better job. It is expensive to take care of my parents. I don't have brothers and sisters to help me pay for them when they are old. Our government doesn't give us money like yours does in your America. There is only me."

China's iron rice bowl—the job security and cradle-to-grave benefits provided by the Communist Party—is, of course, a thing of the past. But sometimes I forget just how odd it is that contemporary China consists of a world of raw capitalism, a brutally competitive place of every man and woman for himself or herself, while in the West we enjoy the cushy benefits of socialist systems in which governments provide for their citizens an array of services so generous they are of almost unbelievable bounty to a Chinese person in Shanghai.

"I have to learn about teamwork in your America," Jennifer said.

"Teamwork?"

"We Chinese are taught not to trust anyone unless they are part of our family or an old friend—this is our culture. Chinese are smarter than Americans, but you are more rich because you have teamwork."

"Well, we are smart enough to value cooperation and trust."

"Yes, but you are still not as smart as Chinese." For the first time that day, Jennifer smiled.

I laughed. "You'll be a *hǎiguī*," I said.

"That's right. There are so many people here trying to get better jobs. Being a sea turtle is the best way to be successful."

Chinese who go overseas to study or work and then return to China are called *hǎiguī*. The characters that mean "return from overseas" form a homonym for the characters that mean "sea turtle." And not unlike loggerback turtles, *hǎiguī* disappear into the sea for a long time and then return to the land of their birth. What they learn while away—Western business practices and conversational English— sets them apart from their peers when they come back, providing them with a competitive advantage in the job market. Which, like everything else in China, is crammed full of people shoving their way toward the front of a line that is not so much a line as it is a frenzied mob. American MBA students flock to China to learn how they can make money in Chinese markets; Chinese professionals head to the States to learn from American MBA programs how to apply the wisdom of the West to Chinese business so they can survive the maniacal competition in their country.

"Do you think the developers are serious?" I said. "Or do you think they're bluffing? Can they really do that? Can they stop you from studying overseas?"

"Of course they can stop me."

A dog painted white with the dust of demolition wagged its way past us. In the distance stood slim towers, each one like an exclamation point rising from the rubble of a ruined neighborhood.

"You need a permit or something from the government?" I asked.

"If you cause problems, perhaps they won't let you leave."

"So even if you get a U.S. visa they'll stop you from going? Why can't you just go to the airport with your visa in your passport and get on a plane? Your name will be in the computer when you try to go through immigration?"

"I've heard that they have face scanners in the airport. If they don't want you to leave because you have caused problems, they know who you are and they will not let you leave."

"Christ that's creepy."

"What is your meaning?"

"What do I mean?" I asked.

"Yes."

"Here's a new expression for you: 'That makes my blood run cold.'"

"Your blood?"

"I don't understand what the developers have to do with the government," I said. "They have guanxi with the government?"

"Of course. How else would they get the permits to smash the buildings and make new ones?"

"Of course."

I felt a momentary burst of a nameless feeling, relief or perhaps pride, knowing that someone in the United States protesting his home being destroyed would not be denied permission to travel abroad—and his daughter would certainly not be affected by his civil disobedience. And if for some reason that were to happen in America, the press would have a field day exposing the scandal. For all our flaws and shortcomings, we have the rule of law and a free press, and these are not small things. Of course on some level I'd always recognized how important these things are, but not until faced with their absence in China had I appreciated them so fully and understood so clearly how they help form the deep foundation upon which the edifice of freedom stands. China had been a civilization of laws for millennia, but it had never enjoyed the rule of law. It had invented printing, though it had never had a free press.

There is a famous query known as the "Needham Question." Francis Bacon, born in the latter half of the sixteenth century, was an early advocate of the empirical method that helped give birth to the Scientific Revolution in Europe. Bacon credited Western Europe's rise to three things: the use of gunpowder, navigation with the compass, and printing with moveable type. Bacon had no clue where these things had originated; we now know all three were invented in China. Because China, unlike Europe, did not follow a path from scientific development to an industrial revolution, historians ponder why these inventions were so revolutionary in Western Europe, while China, which had been leaps and bounds ahead of Europe in scientific discoveries for many hundreds of years, failed to have a scientific revolution and an industrial revolution: the so-called Needham Question. A fascinating question, to be sure, and one that has proved elusive to answer. The person who originated this line of inquiry, Joseph Needham, created, along with an international team of collaborators, a twenty-seven-volume magnum opus, *Science and Civilisation in China*, but came to no definitive conclusions about why China (which not only came up with the compass, gunpowder, paper and printing, but a whole host of lesser-known inventions that were no less important, such as the stirrup, the chain drive and the grafting of fruit trees) had lagged far behind Europe in science and technology.

Another question, one perhaps more vexing yet, is why China, with thousands of years of social and political development, had failed to create a system of checks and balances on power and to form democratic institutions. There will probably never be a clear answer to either question, but some potent clues lie buried in China's past.

Confucian philosophy emphasized obedience to authority as the highest virtue. While Europe was entering the Enlightenment, undergoing enormous change and affirming the paramount importance of inquiry, China was stuck in the comfortable rut of a dynastic system that emphasized stability and continuity—and in which the individual's place was solely to serve the system. While Europe was waking up to the truth that the highest good was to seek the truth at any cost, China slumbered snugly in a value system that abhorred change, disdained the spirit of individual inquiry, and looked backward to an idealized past instead of forward to a future in which innovations in science and technology would raise its civilization to a higher level than any it had known before.

I had mistakenly believed bureaucracy to be some invention of Communism, some consequence of the clumsy state apparatus devised by Mao and his hench-men. But far back into the distant mists of Chinese history was evidence of a rigid system that placed the virtues of serving the system above all else. Whether by the decree of an emperor or by the dictates of the Communist Party, the system was superior and the individual was to be subservient to it—then all would be right on earth under heaven. I'm no Sinologist, but I'm confident in saying that maintaining social harmony through authoritarian rule has been a constant throughout China's long history. There had been the occasional blossoming of individual inquiry—such as during the Warring States Period, when the absence of centralized control led to multiple schools of thought engaging in open debate, and in brief periods during dynastic rule when the relaxation of repressive gov-ernance created a flowering of advances in the sciences and arts—but in the end China always reverted to its authoritarian ways.

China's Communist revolution had set out to destroy "feudal" concepts such as an emperor's role as the son of heaven maintaining harmony on earth, but the people loved Mao because he was their "red sun in the east." He had, in essence, crowned himself China's new emperor; and China, after a brief foray into repub-lican government under Sun Yat-sen, soon returned to the old order of authori-tarian rule, as it had throughout the millennia of its history. The Communist regime had in many ways, not least of which was its weighty bureaucracy that buried the individual and smothered innovation, been like a dynasty of old. Now, the new creed in China was the Communist Party's cult of wealth. Developing personal fortune one entrepreneur at a time is the way to make the whole nation rich, and a rich nation is, of course, a powerful nation. The Chinese now kowtow to a dynasty devoted to economic development. The individual's place in this system, as it has always been throughout China's past, is to perform one's role within the system and to never, under any circumstances, question the system. Creating a new idea in the new China is encouraged—as long as the new idea doesn't threaten the absolute power of the government, and as long as the idea creates wealth. Under the new dynasty it is one's duty to make money. To get rich is glorious, and there is no greater glory than a China that is wealthy and strong. All hail the new emperor.

Is the desire for democracy universal, or is it something specific to the West? The French and American Revolutions could look back to the classical civilization of Greece for inspiration about the participation of citizens in their governance and the value of independent thought; China has no such precedent in its long history, the history it loves to vaunt as evidence of its superior civilization. The Chinese could argue, and do, that an all-powerful system of government is preferable because democracy is messy and inefficient. To many Chinese, democracy seems a strange aberration of a state that wields absolute power and can thus prevent chaos and quickly implement the changes needed to create a harmonious society.

One of the most useful characters to learn in Chinese is *luàn*. *Luàn* means messy, chaotic, disorganized. It is the diametric opposite of order and control; it is the enemy. *Luàn* shows up everywhere. Jaywalking is *luàn chuān mǎlù*: literally, "messy street crossing." Littering is *luàn rēng lājī*: chaotically throwing trash all over the place. *Wǒ de nǎozi tài luàn le* means "my brain is a real mess—I am completely confused." And society can be luan—chaotic, disorderly, out of control. This is, to the Chinese mind, about the worst state of affairs imaginable. Order is always preferable, even if that order is obtained and maintained by an authoritarian government. If China's Communist Party were to lose control of the country, Chinese friends tell me all the time (and some Westerners witness to the daily mayhem in the store queues and subway scrums agree), China would shatter into a million messy pieces. The country would be *tài luàn le*. There would be chaos, and with chaos would come civil war. Think how many people would die, they tell me. Millions. To their way of thinking there are but two alternatives: absolute state control or complete chaos. There is no middle ground, no room for the controlled messiness of democracy. Democracy is *tài luàn le*. It is too messy to mess with. The truth of this to them is as clear and immutable as that of a mathematical theorem. They are my friends and I love them, but they have convinced themselves that their society is made up of disorderly children who must be overseen by a strong parent who can maintain discipline and make decisions. And on my worst days in China, I believe that they are right.

With the collapse of China's last dynasty leading to the thuggery of warlords battling in the streets, civil wars in which tens of millions perished, and the opportunism of the Western powers and imperial Japan carving up their collapsing nation, the last thing in the world the Chinese want is more chaos. Mao had killed millions of their fellow citizens, but he had been the Great Helmsman, steering China toward a course of building a nation that was firmly under control. The Communists had put a stop to the chaos, and they were keeping a lid on it now. Were the Party to collapse and that lid to come off . . . The Chinese didn't even want to think about that. *Tài luàn le*.

China's authoritarian form of governance was certainly not invented by the Communists; indeed, a cursory survey of Chinese history shows that it can be traced all the way back to the First Emperor of China, Qin Shi Huang. After ascending to the position of king of the state of Qin, located in what is now the province of Shaanxi in central China, he proceeded to conquer all neighboring states, creating what became known as the Middle Kingdom. From the middle of this brutal new kingdom Qin Shi Huang consolidated his power by creating a system of totalitarian rule based on Legalism, a political philosophy that taught that laws are obeyed out of fear, not respect, and called for a centralized military bureaucracy. The First Emperor, after uniting the Middle Kingdom, forcibly united its people by stamping out in the conquered lands all remnants of language and culture different from that of the Qin people. He standardized virtually everything, including currency, a writing system, weights and measures—even the width of axles on vehicles so that chariots could roll along in the same ruts of the imperial roads. He completely abolished feudalism, eliminating the privileges of the land-owning aristocracy; everything was owned by the state and administered by a system of laws enforced through fear by a centralized authority. Public meetings and organizations independent of the state were banned.

The First Emperor crushed all competing schools of thought, including Confucianism, which taught that rulers should be benevolent. Confucian thinkers were buried alive and their texts were torched to put an end to any ideas of benevolence. Terror was the tactic Qin Shi Huang used to maintain order, and it was highly effective. Surveillance of his subjects and manipulating them into informing on each other: these were the tools of his regime. Qin Shi Huang was considered the Son of Heaven, and anyone who questioned his authority was summarily executed. Though the First Emperor was regarded as the Son of Heaven, there was no God in the political system as there was in medieval Europe, and thus there was no church to check the emperor's power. The emperor was the only god the Chinese were allowed to worship, and the stability of society was valued above all else. Under the harsh reign of Qin Shi Huang, duties among the people were many but rights were nonexistent, and the absolute power of the centralized bureaucracy was questioned upon pain of death.

After the First Emperor established order in his dominion, his government embarked on a series of ambitious infrastructure projects, including a national road system and the precursor of the Great Wall. Qin Shi Huang ordered a mausoleum the size of a city built for himself and he filled this massive space with an army of soldiers crafted from terracotta to help him rule another empire in the afterlife. The Terracotta Army, as with the Great Wall and all other monumental projects undertaken by the First Emperor, was built at the expense of countless human lives.

In all of this it is easy to hear echoes of Mao and to see parallels with the contemporary Chinese Communist Party. Qin Shi Huang had been criticized by later dynasties that adopted Confucianism rather than Legalism and employed benevolent rule rather than tyrannical repression as their guiding principle—but these dynasties still maintained a centralized bureaucracy and absolute power. Mao publicly compared himself to the First Emperor and declared his admiration for the despot's effective techniques. Qin Shi Huang had, after all, united China and made it a strong empire. What isn't there to like about that? Across thousands of years there is a direct line between the cruel and ruthless tactics the First Emperor used to maintain China's empire at any cost and the Chinese Communist Party's strong-arm techniques it uses to prevent what it calls "splittism," or the fracturing apart of the motherland by renegade groups determined to weaken China. It is often said that China is less a nation in the modern sense of the word and more an empire held together by brute force.

China had, throughout its long history, when confronted with a choice between the messiness of freedom and the stability of authoritarianism, chosen the latter—this is clear from a brief overview of Chinese history. What is less clear, and what requires a more thorough investigation and yields more surprising results, is that China's one foray into a republican form of government, its one serious attempt to achieve democracy, ended badly in large part because of the United States.

The Xinhai Revolution of 1911 toppled the Qing dynasty, marking the end of two thousand years of imperial rule. Rather than democracy taking hold, however, chaos swept the fragmented country as warlords battled for control in a meritocracy of brute force. To defeat the warlords and establish democratic rule, Sun Yat-sen turned for help to foreign powers. Western democracies ignored his pleas for assistance. Nevertheless, China entered World War I on the side of the Allies under the condition that German spheres of influence in China, such as Shandong Province, the birthplace of Confucius, would be returned to China when Germany was defeated. More than one hundred thousand Chinese laborers were sent to France to work on the Western Front. When the war ended with the Allies' victory and it came time to craft the Treaty of Versailles at the Paris Peace Conference of 1919, China, believing very sensibly that it should be rewarded for its contribution to the war effort, made some very reasonable requests, including the return of Shandong to Chinese control.

At the conference, the United States promoted Woodrow Wilson's Fourteen Points, including the principle of national self-determination. America's advocacy of respecting nations' sovereignty was embraced by the Chinese, who thought America would champion their cause of returning Shandong to the Chinese motherland. But when faced with French and British opposition, Wilson abandoned his idealistic stance, and the Treaty of Versailles, instead of returning Shandong to China, turned over control of the province to Japan. China viewed the breach of the Allies' promise and the failure of the United States to follow through on its pledge to promote sovereignty as deep betrayals.

Western-style democracy had, prior to the Treaty of Versailles, been gaining ground among Chinese intellectuals. But after the treaty, Woodrow Wilson's principle of national self-determination was viewed by China as hypocritical hogwash, and many leading Chinese intellectuals suddenly wanted no part of Western political ideas, including democracy. As belief in democracy as the ideal form of governance waned, Marxism took hold in Chinese intellectual circles, and soon communism was seen by many of China's avant-garde thinkers as the best system to fill the political void left by the collapse of China's last dynasty. In short, a window had opened in China's long history, and Western nations—including the United States—instead of taking advantage of this opening to help spread the principles of liberal democracy in one of the world's oldest civilizations, slammed that window shut. And China, though it adopted communism as the official ideology of its revolution, reverted to its old authoritarian ways. It instituted the only form of government it had ever known: one in which power rested not with the people but with a centralized bureaucracy that was often brutal and always beyond the rule of law.

We decry the propaganda campaigns of the Chinese government, and rightfully so; but we should not delude ourselves into believing our media and our history textbooks are free of propaganda. Witness the conspicuous absence of any mention of China's unfair treatment in the Treaty of Versailles and the role of the United States in convincing the Chinese that communism was a more attractive ideology than democracy, that an authoritarian regime was preferable to a free society. Regardless of whether the silence in our media regarding this historical tidbit when discussing China's descent into the hell of communism is an honest oversight or part of our own propaganda machine that aims to convince us of our infallible righteousness, the omission is significant. Of course, that I can criticize our media for this omission and not have a bullet put in the back of my head, the preferred method of dispatching dissidents in the People's Republic, is evidence that the ideals of Western liberal democracy have tremendous merit, whatever the diplomacy mistakes of our nation's past.

I asked Jennifer if she was scared. "Are you worried about what will happen to your parents and what will happen to you?" I said as we walked.

"Of course."

"Do you want me to forget about writing the book? I will—all you have to do is say so."

"I thought you were already writing it."

"I am, but I can stop. I don't want to make any more problems for your family or for you."

We walked a few moments in silence. "I think perhaps it's okay," Jennifer said. "Just don't talk to the developers or anyone in the government. If you talk to them, if they know what you are doing, then that could make more problems. But if you don't talk to them, then it is perhaps okay. And no one will know who we are, right? In your book, our names—will they be different?"

"Definitely."

"And there won't be any pictures of us?"

"No pictures of you or anyone you know."

In the distance a cluster of towers hovered unmoored from the earth, bases lost in clouds of heavy gray. Like a floating city in a fantasy film.

"It's fun," said Jennifer.

"Fun?"

"It's like a game. We have to cover our tracks. In a movie I saw, someone said that: 'We have to cover our tracks.'"

"We'll cover our tracks," I said as we walked.

"Are you a spy?" Jennifer said. "Sometimes you look like a spy because you wear sunglasses and a long black coat."

"I am not a spy."

"We should not talk about it on Skype or on email."

I stopped walking and looked at her. "They read your email?"

"Perhaps they read everyone's email." She smiled. "Your blood is cold?"

"Very cold." I started walking again, and after a moment I said, "You weren't kidding about them reading your email, were you."

"No, I was not making a joke. But I was joking about you being a spy. I know you are not, because you are not smart enough to be a spy."

We picked our way across a swath of shattered homes where the remains of fallen walls lay wrapped in haze like the wreckage of a battlescape. Haze is one of the most distinctive physical features of Shanghai: it is always present in various degrees, and its origin is never certain. It could be caused by auto exhaust, industrial pollution, construction dust, effluvia from coal-fired power plants outside the city, water vapor drifting in from the coast—or some combination thereof. The city's pervasive air pollution is, of course, disgusting, but it can also be quite beautiful, lending a surreal, dreamlike appearance to city scenes, not unlike the fog that partially conceals mountain panoramas in classic Chinese paintings.

Ahead the ghostly hulks of buildings loomed. We rounded a corner, and where before there had been a dense network of lanes there was now an open lot. Reference points had vanished; I turned in circles trying to make sense of where I stood. I was astonished at the new towers that had heaved into being in the short time I'd been away. Though the city lay swaddled in smog, I could see the suggestion of tall towers, faint shapes in the mist, where none had stood before. In a few months the skyline had changed; I could hardly imagine the changes that would occur in two years' time when the Expo began. Through a thinning in the sky, hulking pillars of steel and glass suddenly appeared. The unseen sun cast no shadows from cranes that swiveled and lifted, and the half-constructed shells of buildings stood dim and shapeless in the murk.

In the 1920s, after skyscrapers had been raised in Chicago and St. Louis, a new vision of the future gripped America as New York architects and planners scrambled to create a modern urban center of soaring towers. In 1925, New York passed London to become the world's largest metropolis, and Manhattan grew into a vertical world as block after block of low-rise row houses was destroyed and assembled anew. We have razed and rebuilt our cities, we have had our skyscraper dreams. China is planning to build up to fifty thousand towers in the next twenty years, the equivalent of ten New Yorks.

I spotted the group of children with whom I'd played jianzi. They were once again kicking a jianzi, feathers bright against the bone-colored dust covering every surface. Shikumen had been bulldozed, but for the children of the neighborhood there was now no more open space where they could play than there had been

The last of the low-built shops and homes of old Shanghai are surrounded by lofty towers that power their way above the ground.

before, because the demolition site had been blocked off by a wall of blue tin sheeting.

I shrugged my shoulders out of the straps of the backpack I was wearing, and fished out a frisbee the color of a construction cone.

"I wondered why you were wearing a backpack today," Jennifer said. "I thought perhaps you had spy things in it."

I tossed the orange frisbee to the boy who'd told me that the Chinese invented the frisbee, and I told him to wait a moment as he fumbled the disc and dropped it into a pile of pulverized bricks. I wandered around the big blue fence until I found a door. It was padlocked shut. I paced along the perimeter of the fence, finally finding a point of weakness, a seam in the metal sheeting that could be pried apart. I wrenched the gap wide open and wiggled through, careful not to snag my clothes on jagged edges. I'd been worried that inside I might find a mess: broken boards and tilting walls, shattered glass and rusty nails—dangers of every description. Instead I saw a flat expanse of ground clear of debris. A clean slate for building. And the perfect frisbee field.

"Even if the Chinese did invent frisbee," I told the boy holding the disc, "which, for the record, I very much doubt, we still perfected how to throw it." I pried open the seam in the metal wall and let him wriggle his way in.

"Perhaps you should not go in there," Jennifer said as more children slipped through the slot and filled the frisbee field contained within the tall blue walls of tin.

"Perhaps we should definitely not go in here," I said as I widened the gap to let Jennifer in.

I pulled the seam of the sheeting shut when we were all inside, but a moment later someone was banging on the metal. I opened the slit back up and was scolded by a woman who looked old enough to be my grandmother. It was dangerous, she told us. What were we doing?

"Playing," I said, holding up the orange disc to show her.

She shook her head and asked if she could watch. She left and then returned a few minutes later with two other women with gray hair and sunken cheeks, each one carrying a small rectangular stool. I helped them through the cleft in the metal, and the grannies assembled themselves on their stools, backs bent by age, hands curled up in little fists that rested in their laps. The blue tin barrier blocked us from the sight of developers and police, and the metal walls shut out the wind as well. In this place of perfect stillness, on a field larger than any the children had played upon in their cluttered lanes, we threw the frisbee back and forth, and our audience of ancient women nodded their approval as we moved farther apart. Gradually the children's throws stopped wobbling and the frisbee flew in clean straight lines instead of skewing into random arcing curves. As the disc sliced through the air, the children's laughter filled the silence in this gap between worlds, where the shikumen of the past had fallen, where the towers of the future would be raised.

Rich Gate and *Rènao*

My next trip to Shanghai was my first time to visit the city in winter. Though not nearly as bitter as winter in Beijing or other places farther north, Shanghai's *dōngtiān* is a distinct season with weather cold enough to send me shopping for a fake North Face parka.

Everything about the parkas I perused in a crowded little shack of a store looked right except for the tags. The tags with pictures of mountaineers braving the icy slopes of Himalayan peaks had clearly been photocopied, a dead giveaway that the parkas I was eyeing were not *zhēnde*, as the shopkeeper with whom I was haggling insisted they were, but instead were *jiǎde*—fake. I pointed at a photocopied tag, told him the garment in question most certainly was not zhende and most definitely was jiade, offered him a third of what he was asking, began to walk away, and finally left his store wearing a red parka with a phony tag and Gore-Tex of dubious authenticity—but which did a fine job nonetheless of blocking the wind as I walked the winter streets of Shanghai beneath a gray and vaporous sky.

When I met up with Jennifer, she was on her mobile phone with Marcus and doing more laughing than talking. I asked her what was so funny when she finally hinged her handset shut. She said that it was nothing, Marcus just made her laugh. The way she said this made me think they'd been doing a lot of talking and laughing in the months that I'd been gone. She had her hair pulled back and her cheeks were pink from the cold. I stared at her and smiled.

"What?" she said.

"So you and Marcus are dating?"

For all Jennifer's worldliness, all her expensive shoes and familiarity with *Friends*, she blushed and stammered like a little Chinese schoolgirl who's been asked if she has a boyfriend. She looked so genuinely uncomfortable it wasn't any fun to tease her, and after a few minutes I quit badgering her about Marcus being her boyfriend.

After wandering the polished floors of an elephantine mall to window shop and people watch together, Jennifer went off on her own to buy shoes. Remembering that I'd packed hastily and had forgotten to bring my Speed Stick, I decided to play a little game I call "Let's try to find deodorant in Shanghai." To Chinese people, wearing deodorant is as foreign as eating with knives and forks. You could buy knives and forks in Shanghai, you could buy a Ferrari, but good luck finding somewhere to buy a stick of deodorant. When that game ended (no deodorant, no surprise), I began another game called "Try to find a bathroom with toilet paper because I made the rookie error of not carrying my own toilet paper with me at all times while walking around a Chinese city." Thank god for friendly Belgians and the ubiquitous golden arches. A handful of TP bummed from some helpful backpackers from Brussels, a clean restroom next to a Ronald McDonald statue grinning knowingly as if he understood I wasn't there for the burgers and fries but only to use the clean Western toilet, and then I was on my way.

I met back up with Jennifer, who was carrying a bag that held new shoes. I asked her if her shoe budget exceeded her food budget, and she answered, with total earnestness, that her grocery bills were larger than the amount she allowed herself for shoes. We rode a tilted moving ramp, Jennifer explaining that escalators with their constantly folding and unfolding steps confused elderly people. While we rode up Jennifer showed me the shoes she'd bought: bright tangerine plastic punctured with holes—a pair of Crocs.

"Those were invented in Boulder, where I live."

"So your city doesn't have delicious dumplings but it has cool shoes. What else does it have?"

"Clean air."

"That's all?"

"It's no Shanghai."

"I feel bad for you because you live in a boring city."

When we reached the top of the moving ramp and walked outside the mall, I stopped as abruptly as a character in a cartoon, and Jennifer skidded to a halt beside me. No one banged into the back of us, as would usually happen on a Shanghai street if one suddenly stopped moving and blocked the ceaseless flow of bodies. People all around us had paused and were staring upward. From the gray sky snowflakes whispered down, expiring on the pavement and on the palms of outstretched hands.

"I didn't know it snowed here," I said.

"It usually doesn't. But sometime it does."

"Does the snow ever stick?"

"Stick?"

"Ah, does it ever stay on the ground. And pile up? Or does it melt away?"

"Usually it melts and doesn't stay. But sometimes it stays for a few hours and it is very beautiful."

A light dusting skimmed the concrete around us, and in corners and against edges of walls drifts rose in little piles. I stuck out my tongue to catch a falling flake. I've surfed my snowboard through waist-deep powder every winter for as long as I can remember, and I've grown used to seeing slopes of purest white gleaming beneath aching blue skies in the mountains of the West. But never in my life have I been as moved by snow as I was that winter day in Shanghai, each flake a blessing on my tongue. Shanghai snow tasted different from Colorado snow. Not as clean. A bit of a chemical aftertaste. But still, it tasted pretty damn good.

Jennifer joined me, tilting back her head and opening her mouth to catch some drifting flakes. Snow vanished in her mouth and landed on her cheeks. White snow on the black silk of her hair.

"Marcus is lucky," I said.

She grinned and blushed, and then she tipped her thinness into the wind and pressed on. As we walked, gusts shrieked through the streets and so much snow clogged the sky our frosted lungs gasped for breath. We ducked into a coffee shop and found a seat by a window where we could watch the storm. After we ordered cups of wicked-strong java, I told Jennifer how much I missed snowboarding in Colorado. Shanghai has an indoor skiing area—a giant refrigerated tube—and this is one place in the city I have promised myself I will never go. Skiing is something that should happen only in the mountains. To do it indoors is like trying to enjoy a steak in a mortuary.

After much arm-twisting, I convinced Jennifer to join me in drinking a second cup of coffee, and after a bit more twisting of her arm, a third, and soon we were grinding our teeth like teenagers wired on Red Bull and ready to party. But there was nowhere to go in this brief blizzard and nothing to do but watch it while it lasted. As the snowfall thickened and the storm ramped up, we played a game of naming the shapes we saw in the swirling sky. I saw a baseball player swinging a bat, Jennifer saw a plate piled high with steaming *bāozi*. I saw a witch with a twisted nose, she saw a panda in a forest of bamboo.

When the flakes stopped falling and the sun burst through, we went outside and walked the streets. Pale drifts of snow lay melting beneath a sky of china blue. Gone was any trace of haze, any hint of smog. The gorgeous hue of the sky seemed the color of hope itself.

While we made our way to the lane where Jennifer's parents lived, Jennifer pulled plastic bags from her purse and wrapped the bags around her feet, protecting her shoes from the wet grime that coated the streets. I looked around us at the feet of people tromping through sludge and saw that using shoe bags was common practice. In the trendy metropolis, cool shoes condomed in plastic bags were preferable to the functional footwear of snow boots. I had so much yet to learn.

As we splashed through slushy streets beneath the gorgeous sky, I asked Jennifer about a word I'd recently learned: *rènao*. "This means hot, but it also means noisy?" I asked. "I don't understand. Why is this such an important word?"

"Noisy is good in China. It makes us happy. When there is lots of things happening in the city and the streets are very full and there is music and many sounds, we call this *rènao*. When we are with our family and our home is noisy we are happy, and it is *rènao*. Can you understand?"

"No, not really. The noise in Shanghai made me want to wear earplugs when I first came here. Now I'm used to it, I guess, but I still don't like it."

"Maybe Americans like *ānjìng*—calm and quiet. Peaceful. Maybe they like peaceful, not renao."

"Maybe this American does."

Depending on how demographers define city boundaries, Shanghai might be considered the largest metropolitan area on earth, but you'd never know it in the old neighborhoods laced with little lanes. You could just as easily be in a hamlet in the countryside. And the lane neighborhoods were arrayed in districts as distinct as separate cities. Some people grew up in one district and married there,

The openings to Shanghai's last lane neighborhoods are often squeezed between storefronts and difficult to find. But they are worth seeking out, for each stone entrance offers a portal into a lively world very different from the city's ever-increasing expanses of gargantuan tower blocks and glaring neon.

and they lived and worked and died there, never setting foot outside that one section of Shanghai.

As Jennifer and I walked, beneath our feet sheets of wrinkled asphalt peeled away from ancient slabs of rock. We passed Old Xu standing watch at the entranceway to the neighborhood, still as stone, and we found Old Wang, who told us we were idiots for wearing too few clothes. She shook her finger at me, and then with crossed arms she made a shivering motion. Children wearing puffy down coats tottered around the alley, bouncing off each other like little sumo wrestlers. Steam and cooking smells poured from windows. Old Wang led us to her home, through the gateway of a courtyard, which opened onto another smaller courtyard paved with crumbling stone, and then she took us farther into sets of interconnected spaces until we reached the two rooms where she had lived with her husband and daughter until her husband died from cancer and her daughter went away to college. Jennifer translated the stories from Old Wang's life as we sat beneath windows white with rime and she made us mutton soup.

"Lamb keeps you warm in winter," Jennifer explained.

Old Wang shared a kitchen with her neighbors, and in this kitchen was one of Shanghai's last remaining tiger stoves, or *lǎohǔzào*. Used to boil water for community residents, the enormous iron chamber had a long exhaust pipe that curled like a tiger's tail and windows shaped like tiger's eyes. Fueled with dirty coal, the stoves look very cool but are an environmental nightmare. Stare into the eyes of the tiger glowing orange and choke on the sulfurous fumes spat out by the beast.

Jennifer and I joined Old Wang as she shuttled back and forth between the communal kitchen, where there simmered a cauldron of bubbling broth, and one of Old Wang's rooms, which would not have been more tidy had it been owned by military personnel. A drill sergeant could have bounced a quarter from the taut sheets of her perfectly made bed, and the polished wood of the kitchen table showed a reflection of my face. Through the narrow doorway came neighbors drawn by the smell of grilled lamb. They filed in and stamped their feet and rubbed their hands, and breath billowed white from their mouths.

Old Wang's daughter was finishing her PhD in physics at Keji Daxue in Anhui province, one of the nation's finest universities, one famously focused on science and technology. She was married and had a teenage daughter of her own. Old Wang put pictures on the table before me. A growing mob of neighbors, including Jennifer's parents, crammed their way into the small steamy room, studying me as I stared at the pictures. I told Old Wang how beautiful her daughter and granddaughter were. She understood my Mandarin, as evidenced by her embarrassment at my compliments. "You should wear more clothes in the winter," she said through Jennifer as she took the pictures back from me. "And you should eat lamb and hot pot and stinky tofu to stay warm."

The Chinese traditionally believed that eating dog was a sure way to stay warm in winter, but dogs in Shanghai are now pets of the privileged. They provide warmth by snuggling with their owners, and they are rarely seen these days in soup pots in the city.

As the room filled with people, the temperature rose from so cold that it made faint plumes of people's breath to the sticky heat that I had always associated with the city. All these neighbors, by stuffing themselves into this small space to eat hot soup, replicated Shanghai's subtropical climate in the microcosm of the room.

Shanghai seemed to be curing me of my claustrophobia and my dislike of crowds. There were times early on in my visits to the city that I wanted to jump on a plane and fly back to Colorado, to put as much space between me and the human density of Shanghai's streets as possible, to lose myself in the boundless spread of the Rocky Mountains and never return to China. I still sometimes had brief yearnings for open space and privacy, but right now I felt happy to be in this room that was steamy as a bathhouse and populated with people cradling in their chilly hands bowls of boiling soup. Two more smiling people came in from the courtyard, chatting between slurps of piping broth. Neighbors leaned against neighbors, bodies pressed together in the tight space of the room. The windows were opaque with steam and rivulets ran down the sweating panes. And then four more people arrived, packing themselves into Old Wang's home, crowding around her soup. A dozen different voices filled the room. Everyone huddled together like a litter of puppies balling themselves into a warm and wiggly mass. So many lives overlapping in this shikumen room, so much friendly noise. I thought I was not in a mighty city but instead in a humble village that measures its wealth by the warmth of its citizens rather than the quantity of its skyscrapers.

"Renao," I yelled to Jennifer above the din. "Is this renao?"

"This is very renao. Now you understand? You like renao?"

A man with forearms that showed muscles raised and twisted like bands of braided steel, and who later told me he was a construction welder who never wanted for work in Shanghai, gave me a handshake so light it almost tickled. He said in the carefully pronounced English that he had been learning during weekend classes, "Warmly welcome you to China. Warmly welcome you to Shanghai. Eat more soup. Outside it is too cold."

I yelled to Jennifer, straining to make my voice rise above the happy bedlam of soup slurping: "I like renao very much."

My new friend told me he'd grown up in the courtyard next door and he still lived there with his parents. When I asked him if he liked living in a shikumen he answered that he liked the *rénqíngwèi*, the friendliness and hospitality of people in neighborhoods built of traditional homes close to the ground, but he liked central heating even more. The towers he'd been working on with his welding gun were equipped with central heat, and he hoped to live in one someday.

"When I get married to a wife and have a small baby," he told me, each English word crisply pronounced, "I want my small baby to live in a house with heat so that he will never be sick in the cold winter."

The Chinese government, when developing a national heating policy back in the days of a command economy, had bisected the nation roughly along the Yangtze River: cities north of the river could have central heat; cities south of the river could not. No matter that cities such as Shanghai in the winter months had snow and cold, frost and freezing rain. The government had mandated no heat, so in Shanghai's homes and buildings there was no heat, and citizens made do.

Old Wang showed me a hot water bottle shaped like Mickey Mouse that she took to bed with her, and Jennifer explained other tricks to stay warm. Heated toilet seats are a treat that make cold days in Shanghai bearable. Many air conditioning units, strangely, function as heaters. Look for the sunshine icon on the remote control, Jennifer explained. Crank the air conditioning unit's temperature as high as it will go and the machine will breathe warm air into the room. Who knew? Thermal underwear is worn throughout the winter in the city, and people fill the pockets of their shirts and pants with tiny bottles filled with boiling water, sometimes taken from atop a tiger stove. Floor heaters that resemble miniature car radiators burn what looks like motor oil and work wonders in the battle against arctic air that fills your drafty room. Curtains wrinkle in the wind that hisses through cracks and gaps, and your hair ruffles in the icy indoor breeze. Insulation in walls and caulking in window seals are not part of Chinese building codes. It isn't the temperature that feels so uncomfortable, it is the humidity. Thirty degrees Fahrenheit in Colorado's dry air and sunny skies feels positively tropical compared to thirty degrees in Shanghai's chronic dampness and winter gloom.

After the soup from Old Wang's pot was gone, a man with drooping eyes said, "Xiànzài xiūxi ba." Now rest. He offered me a chair and then leaned against a wall and closed his eyes. Xiūxi is siesta Chinese style, and I can't imagine there is better napping to be found the world over than in the drowsy room of a steam-filled shikumen while one's belly is full of homemade soup. After some delicious grogginess, I tumbled down into a place of deep and nourishing sleep cocooned in gentle warmth.

When we finished our xiuxi, Jennifer and I said goodbye to everyone and we thanked Old Wang for the hot lamb soup. Old Wang waved our compliments away and said it was nothing as she followed us out from her cozy room and into the cold little courtyard in front of her home, and then into the larger courtyard, where the temperature seemed to drop a few more degrees. And then, against my insistence that she didn't need to see us off, she followed us through the stone gate at the entrance and into the alleyway beyond, where the air was colder yet. "Wear more clothes," she yelled after us. "Don't forget to eat lots of lamb and hot pot and stinky tofu. And put on hats, you idiots." Her calls echoed through the back alleys, each pocket of them filled with human activity, revelry around every corner. Music blared from a storefront, drawing passersby like moths to light. A jostling, chitchatting mass of people huddled together in this place of noise and joy, thawing winter's freeze.

"Renao," I said, pointing at the crowd milling round the music.

Jennifer clapped her gloved hands, their padded palms muffling the sound. "Now you understand renao. Now you are like a Chinese." She thought a moment, one gloved hand patting the air in front of her, and then she said, "Do you have renao in your America?"

I thought of men in sport coats carving turkeys at Thanksgiving dinners, sock-footed children tearing into presents beneath a lighted tree, the sound of ripping paper blending with the voices of tipsy relatives who gather once a year. "I guess we have something similar to renao in our America," I said. "We call it *festive*, but it is not the same as in your China." Then I thought of the hubbub in Times Square, the buzz induced by the commotion and noise of a big American city, and I said, "And we talk about a city's energy, about the excitement of being in a city with all its activity, but American cities are quiet and calm compared to Shanghai."

Many of my Chinese friends had told me that of all the places they'd visited in America, the one in which they felt most comfortable was New York. The frenetic activity of Manhattan is the closest thing to the renao of a Chinese city, though the Big Apple's noise is a timid squeak compared to Shanghai's mighty roar. One of my Chinese friends who grew up in Shanghai and studied at a university in Kansas told me that he found life in New York so slow and quiet compared to a Chinese city, he could hardly tell Manhattan, New York from Manhattan, Kansas.

Shanghai's size and sounds are epic in scale, but these things do not engender affection for the place. Shanghai manufactures nostalgia and fantasy as though the city is scheming to flood the world nostalgia and fantasy markets. And there is no shortage of excitement in the city. But these things hold little interest for me. What draws me to Shanghai are the random instances of kindness, the accidental discoveries of human warmth, which amid the hulking buildings and hyperkinetic energy the city is creating, sometimes seem few and far between. Each instance perhaps more precious for its rarity. Each instance like a molten spark within the blackness of a cave.

We decided to walk to People's Square, once a horseracing track for rich Brits, now a handsome public parkland and showcase for new architecture beautiful and bizarre. We headed in that general direction anyway, but with no firm destination in mind. Jennifer and I both had all day free, and I believe there is no better way to see a city than to walk it. If I have viewed a city through the windows of taxis and tour buses and hotel rooms, it seems the same to me as watching it on a screen. If I really want to know a city, I walk it until my feet swell with blisters and the soles of my shoes rub smooth against the pavement. Shanghai is amazing in that it is the biggest city in China but one can walk safely through its streets. I suppose if you want trouble in Shanghai you can find it, but if you keep your head down and mind your own business, you can walk wherever you want and find no trouble at all. There are no sections of Shanghai where you shouldn't go. There are no shootings or carjackings; no tourists are raped or murdered in the streets. You can wander wherever you'd like and no Crips or Bloods will put a bullet in your brain.

In Shanghai, the biggest danger is not crime on the streets but crossing the streets. Traffic in Shanghai flows in an orderly way compared to many other places in China, but that is relative. Very relative. To a Westerner who visits Shanghai on his first stop in China, the scene is one of utter chaos. Drivers in China use their horns not to warn of potential collisions, but to signal their position. The horn is a safety tool that says, "Here I am, I'm driving on your right side, now I'm on your left side, I'm approaching you, now I'm passing you, now I'm in front of you." With countless cars clogging the streets, everyone is in a perpetual state of approaching and passing, and everyone blares his horn continuously. In the West we have been trained to register a bit of panic at the sound of a horn—*look out, something bad is about to happen!* It takes a long time on the streets of China to unlearn this conditioned response, to rewire our brains so that when a horn blares we register that, okay, someone is approaching or passing, no big deal, disaster is not imminent and there is no need to make an evasive maneuver to avoid a collision. There is that difference, and there is also the incontrovertible fact that all the horn honking is LOUD. My lungs have been altered for the worse by the time they have spent in Shanghai, I am sure; I am also certain my eardrums have been permanently disfigured. I imagine my poor abused tympanums have little tears that will never be repaired.

The pockmarked street we walked held puddles of oily water, surfaces shimmering with iridescence as we hopped across each one. From the ceiling of a butcher, carcasses hung shrouded in flies, and the smell of moldering fruit mixed with spicy wafts of incense being burned by a woman before a family shrine facing an open window. Next to the window was a pharmacy with mushrooms and bones displayed in glass jars, and in front of the pharmacy rested a cart piled with green tangerines. Before I could buy a couple of tangerines from the man sitting on his heels next to the cart, I was distracted by the sugary smell of *tángchǎolìzi*. Sweet roasted chestnuts, Jennifer's favorite snack. I bought a bagful from a peddler on the street and we peeled them as we walked, each one shaped like a little furrowed brain, the buttery nutmeat melting sweetly on our tongues.

To escape the monotony of otherworldly office towers, each one strangely shaped but dull as dishwater all the same, I ducked down a backstreet into the living world of a lilong, Jennifer yelling at me because her shoes were getting slathered in grime. Inside the narrow artery that led through the neighborhood, I ratcheted my brain into overdrive to take it all in. Laundry hanging in a hundred colors from the gray brick walls of shikumen. Prostitutes with short skirts and tall shoes lounging on couches behind the windows of shabby beauty parlors. Old women sitting on little stools in the street, cracking sunflower seeds between their teeth. Men playing cards, boys gathering round to learn their games. Storefronts offering every item except automobiles and every service under the sun save surgery. Arched stone gateways leading to narrower lanes, each one more friendly and chaotic than the last.

One passageway opened onto an empty plot of land where shikumen had been knocked down, dust lingering above the detritus of the demolished homes. Pile drivers and construction cranes were doing their work. Jennifer stopped a moment and then walked on. "I can't watch," she said. "It makes my stomach hurt."

"Because it reminds you of where your parents live?"

"The first time I saw *chāi* painted on the walls near our home, my stomach started to hurt. It still hurts. Sometimes I wish the developers would just hurry and finish, and maybe when it is over my stomach will stop hurting."

I studied her a moment and then said, "You never talk with your hands."

"What is your meaning?"

"You asked me earlier today to help you sound more natural when you speak English. Your hands and your head—they don't move when you speak. You don't talk with your hands," I said, demonstrating what I meant by using my hands to shape my words.

"That is not how Chinese talk," Jennifer said. "We talk with our words, not with our heads or our hands." When she said this she moved her head and her hands to make her point; her motions seemed so unnatural we both laughed.

"When you talk Chinese, it is too flat," she said. "You sound like a machine. If you want to talk like a Chinese, the emotion has to be in the words. Your hands and your head cannot help you." She made me practice a few sentences as I stood stock still, fighting the urge to move my hands and trying desperately to infuse the sounds that flowed from my mouth with nuanced meaning—and failing disastrously. We both ended up laughing so hard that it became a hopeless exercise, but one we would revisit many times in the coming months when we both needed to laugh.

We wandered into a dreamy maze-world where bikes tinkled and squeaked their way through slender lanes and what light there was came from narrow slots of sky. Everywhere brick walls tapered toward tight conclusions, leading us into nooks and shadows where broken boards scratched at our clothes and tiled roofs sagged on crumbled eaves. As we ducked and twisted our way through the ever-tightening spaces I felt neither the joy of a delightful dream in which one discovers a bounty of rewards nor the terror of a nightmare in which one must flee the menacing rooms and hallways of a doomed house. I had been to this place before, this place of endless passages and chambers revealed through restless wandering, and I would visit here again after the bulldozers laid waste to these bricked lanes from another age. Modern Shanghai is a crazed hallucination, its shikumen a dim and haunting dream.

We left the lanes and walked away from the dust and screech of the building site toward a main thoroughfare that held a calamity of traffic. I stopped at an intersection to open a map. Shanghai changes so rapidly maps of the city have to be constantly updated and redrawn. I'd heard that the government had issued a new map of the city eight times in the past year. The figure of two weeks was thrown around a lot as well: every two weeks a new map was released. Honest statistics are of course hard to come by in China, as the government manipulates numbers to fit its needs. The two-week figure might have been an urban myth, perhaps manufactured by the government to perpetuate Shanghai's legendary status as the fastest-developing city on the planet. What foreign business wouldn't want to jump into a market that is adding customers by the thousands every week? Millions of migrants had come to Shanghai, millions more were on the way, foreigners were flooding in, and the city swelled each day. A new map every two weeks might have been an exaggeration, but there was no denying the fervid pace of development.

Jennifer looked at my map and laughed. "Americans are so old-fashioned," she said. "We Chinese feel sorry for you," she added as she pressed buttons on her

A Shanghainese woman uses her state-of-the-art smartphone to photograph flowers in Lu Xun Park, a memorial to China's most famous author of the twentieth century, a writer who decried the nation's backwardness.

smartphone and used a GPS system to show us exactly where we were. After some digital assistance we recalibrated our directions and walked on. I tucked my paper map, which had turned as crisp and yellow as parchment from exposure to the city's pungent air, into a pocket that held a cell phone that Jennifer told me, shaking her head slowly as she studied it, had been popular in China two years ago. The way she sadly said "two years" made me believe I might as well have been using tin cans connected by wire to communicate.

"Do you want bags and watches?" a vendor yelled our way. His mundane query sounded gorgeous in Chinese. *Bāobāo shǒubiǎo, yào bù yào?* I repeated this as we walked. Ah, the music of Chinese. Every sentence a song, every paragraph a poem.

Down a blanched and treeless street we strolled. We walked and walked, past building sites with yawning holes. We crossed through forests of concrete pillars that lifted freeways far above the ground. Barbers crouched in shady places giving haircuts, their scissors scaled with rust, and workmen pushed brooms with straw-stiff bristles across the scratchy ground. The street we followed pinched down into a narrow straightaway of whizzing traffic and gaseous fumes, and as we skirted a blue tin construction barrier on a narrow ledge of sidewalk I had one of those moments you sometimes have in Shanghai when you feel so utterly small that you believe all of us are but nodes in a network and the network is evolving ever faster.

We walked between the legs of giants, the steel beams of electricity pylons standing ten stories tall, the lattice of their upper reaches lost in a lowering haze. Then we entered a world of whimsy: a huge expanse of tumbled blocks made of metal and glass, random facets flickering in the sun. I turned in circles and nothing made any sense. Beneath a cantilevered roof the size of Cleveland stood a man in sneakers and a greasy suit. Across his shoulders rode a nylon bag, stressed seams popping open: a peasant with all his worldly belongings in tow as he searched for work in the city. We traveled a maze of apartment blocks colored in pinks and pale blues reminiscent of Easter eggs, each vertical housing complex so large it held as many people as an American suburb. A businessman voided the contents of his nose with a bubbling ferocity that left me fighting the urge to retch, and crickets in little cages were being sold on the sidewalk. The odor in the air was equal parts burning tires and savory noodle broth, with a bit of frying pork and construction dust thrown in. A toddler sporting a surgical mask decorated with Mickey Mouse heads stopped to stare at me, and an old man slumping in a chair glared. I smiled at the little boy and he scampered away. I smiled at the old man and he glared harder. The little boy stopped and spun around to face me, tearing off his mask and flashing a smile that showed the bright pearls of his teeth. Jennifer and I wandered on, finding our way amid a silliness of skyscrapers, necks cramping as we stared at towers arrowing upward.

What is odd in this city of so many people and so much construction is that so many of the new buildings are empty. On the surface, things seem to be booming in Shanghai, but enter many of these shiny towers and you'll see that there is no one home. *Guǐ gòuwù zhōngxīn* (ghost malls) haunt the crowded streets. All prestigious global brands have opened stores in Shanghai's malls, but their stores are empty because so few Chinese people can afford to buy their products. But the stores don't close: the Shanghai marketing machine has convinced elite brands that they must have a presence in the city, even if they sell very little of their product, because Shanghai is a *world class city*. It seems Shanghai is being designed from the outside in, as if planners are more concerned with how the city will look to visitors than how it will perform for its residents. If America is the birthplace of conspicuous consumption, then China is the originator of conspicuous development, and Shanghai is its showpiece, its icon of progress. And in Shanghai, development for development's sake seems to pass for progress. Like so much else in Shanghai, the endless acreage of ghost malls shaped into giant spheres and soaring towers are enthralling spaces filled with questionable content. Shanghai is not a Potemkin village but a Potemkin supercity.

There is a little game I like to play when I'm wandering Shanghai that I call "Let's try to find a city block where there is no construction." The object of the game—to find a street in stasis surrounded by the seething upheaval and mutation of the city—is challenging. A variation of this game, "Let's try to find a piece of skyline without a construction crane," is even more difficult.

And what are all these cranes constructing? Imagine clever children with frantic minds doodling their daydreams of how they would like a city to look, madly mixing and matching every building style ever conceived, and then each fantasyland they sketch is in a matter of months constructed. No planning committees, no building codes, no environmental regulations, no prohibitive labor costs. Whatever their crazed and brilliant little imaginations conjure is suddenly real. Shanghai is a child's dream come to life not in plastic play blocks but in slabs of metal and sheets of mirrored glass. Shanghai is an adolescent city with ADHD, which is why I feel right at home walking its rambunctious streets. Architecture critics claim Shanghai's fanatical development has resulted in a skyline that is overwrought and ridiculous. Certainly no sober adult would declare the city tasteful. If China is the Kingdom of Kitsch, as so many who visit the hideous hodgepodge of its cities contend, then surely Shanghai is the capital of this modern-day empire of bad taste. But I believe this: no child can wander through Shanghai's dreamland of spires and cubes and spheres bright with every color and not take delight in these wacky fantasies and hyper imaginings brought into the world. And who among us has prohibited the child that still lives in the playground of his mind from occasionally peering out at the world, this strange world arrayed in every shape conceivable and covered in kooky lights. The adult's face is pinched into a stern frown in Shanghai but the child's eyes are forever smiling.

Another game I play when assessing the latest architectural additions to Shanghai's surreal skyline is called "Giddily Imaginative, or Just Plain Stupid?" That building over there that resembles an enormous bronze cauldron from China's ancient past: giddily imaginative. That tower topped with a retro-futuristic flying saucer disc: just plain stupid. Everyone's a critic in Shanghai but the city doesn't care; it just keeps building itself upward in stacks of dissonant shapes.

Shanghai's construction binge has resulted in a cityscape that can, by turns, seem a brilliantly shaped dream of hope and a ghoulishly twisted hallucination.

Jennifer and I spotted a man and woman of wizened appearance marooned in the center of a road. The man's eyesight was apparently poor because the woman led him by the arm. Where she led him was toward a construction barricade; then the pair swiveled and headed toward a new destination, straight into oncoming traffic.

"That doesn't look good," I said.

Jennifer was already running toward them, waving at cars and trucks to stop the speeding vehicles from smashing into the elderly couple. I joined her, and the mess we found ourselves in makes my head throb to this day whenever I revisit that zone of utter mayhem. There was a metal fence along the centerline of the road that the man tried to climb over while his wife and I helped lift him up and then decided that was too dangerous, for one slip of his frail body and his bones would crack. All around us cars and trucks raced past, the wind of their transit wrapping the woman's hair around her face, so pale with dust and fright she seemed to have just risen from the grave. Finally our haggard group returned to the side of the street from which we'd started. I convinced the couple to stay put and Jennifer waited with them, blotting sweat from their foreheads with the man's handkerchief while I went to scout a route that didn't involve climbing fences or heading into a whizzing rush of traffic. There was no way to walk alongside the road to a crosswalk because the shoulder was barricaded on both sides. I could find no clear path through the vehicles careening along the road, so I spoke with workers from a construction crew and they opened a barrier and let the couple through. Jennifer and I joined them, afraid they would disappear into a vat of wet cement or be bonged on the head by falling rods of steel. We traveled a gauntlet of chugging machinery and bundled sheets of metal, passing through piles of pipe and scattered stacks of rebar. When our journey finally concluded and we had crossed the death maze of the street, I asked the couple where they were from.

Shanghai. They had moved to Taiwan five years ago. "We don't recognize this place now," the woman told me. They were trying to make their way to a restaurant to meet their daughter for lunch.

Jennifer gave them directions and then said goodbye; I waved and watched them walk off, the man's hand resting on his wife's trembling arm as the couple tottered through a world of upended concrete slabs and endless barricades of steel.

While wandering the streets of China's largest metropolis, you might think you see relatively few pregnant women and what seems a scant number of children, and you might note that the alleyways and parks of Shanghai are packed with older people. Your observations would be borne out by Chinese demographers, who have demonstrated that China's population is graying, and that Shanghai is the fastest-aging city in the nation. I don't have a doctoral degree in city planning, but perhaps a prudent infrastructure strategy for the city of the future would be to shift funds away from supertall towers for young business tycoons and toward facilities for the elderly.

I glanced back at the construction crew. One of the workers nodded and smiled at me, and together we watched the aged duo born and raised in Shanghai, and now completely lost, turn a corner. When they were gone I stared a moment at the building site. Amid the upheaval of the streets I glimpsed the first sections of scaffolding rising from a pit. A construction site is a place of awesome beauty, where many hundreds of people join together to solve a staggering puzzle: how to raise a building so large it forms a world unto itself. And when the great structure is complete, its walls and floors layered with mazes of wires and pipes, it will bathe the streets around it in its light.

When I was a child, my parents had to pry me apart from the excavation pit near our home when old pipes were lifted from the earth on the yellow teeth of

Shanghai is a fantasy sprung from the mind of a child.

backhoes and the riddle of a building's frame was laid bare before my eyes as cranes assembled steel beams in interlocking stacks. In Shanghai I am still that little boy whose dream it is to build, to solve the mystery of how to reach further toward the sky. Building facilities for the elderly is no fun at all.

Shanghai is less a place than a process. It is difficult to believe that the city will ever be considered "developed." Almost all the Expo pavilions will be torn down after the six-month event. The largest World's Fair will be transformed into the world's largest demolition zone, and developers will race to fill the pricey river-front property with new structures. I imagine Shanghai will always be developing, will forever be in a state of becoming. Developing toward what, becoming what: These are the questions we should ask in this city of rabid change. But we don't have time to ask these questions; we have to cross another street.

I scanned my map and then read a street sign we were standing beneath. The name of the street didn't match anything on the map. I looked back at the map and then waved my hand around us and shook my head. "*Luàn qī bā zāo*," I said. I'd been looking for an excuse to say this. It translates, basically, "to be in a mess," but it is a *chéngyǔ* and thus means so much more than a simple translation can convey. *Chéngyǔ* are phrases whose characters individually might not amount to much, but when you put them together in a predefined pattern (usually four characters but sometimes more), you are uttering an idiom that Chinese people might very well have been using from before the birth of Christ. Throw around a little Latin in Europe and people look at you as though you are loopy; use an ancient idiom in China and no one misses a beat. It is this continuity that makes the Chinese language special. Dynasties have risen and fallen, emperors have come and gone, revolutions have torn down and rebuilt the social order, but a language with millennia of stories behind it remains. Many Chinese characters can be traced back more than three thousand years to the oracle bones of the Shang dynasty, when the first Chinese script was incised on ox scapulae and tortoise shells and used for divination. How could one not be filled with a sense of reverence when writing the strokes of characters that some calligrapher on a mist-shrouded mountaintop penned thousands of years ago? Provided one can write Chinese, that is.

My spoken Mandarin was becoming pretty solid, but my reading skills put me at about the level of a child watching Sesame Street and studying his ABCs. And my writing was even worse. If there is a task under the sun more difficult than writing Chinese characters, I have yet to discover it. In college I'd thought calculus was hard. Calculus is Sesame Street compared to writing Chinese. Fortunately, pity had been taken upon people like me, and romanization systems that assign letters to Chinese characters based on their pronunciation had been devised. The standard romanization system in China is called *pīnyīn*—literally, "spell sound." Pinyin is taught in Chinese schools to help small children master the pronunciation of spoken Chinese; it is taught to foreigners not up to the task of memorizing thousands of characters. One can learn pinyin, master pronunciation, achieve fluency of speech, and not be able to read a newspaper or even the simplest sign on the street. But the character-deficient foreigner is in luck because many areas of China with a lot of foreigners have street signs written both in Chinese characters and in pinyin. So, instead of just seeing a Chinese character that looks like something from the *Space Invaders* video game, a character that looks like a bunch of horizontal lines with a vertical line, a character that looks like a contorted stick figure with a dot and dash over its head, one sees something along the lines of "Nanjing Dong Lu." As crazy as this improbable letter salad might look, it is infinitely more understandable to one raised on the Roman alphabet than Chinese characters. You can easily write it down. You can match it against a street name in your guidebook or on your English language map the Shanghai tourist office has so generously provided. With a little pinyin practice you can even pronounce it in a way that doesn't leave Chinese people laughing hysterically at your pronunciation, which is worse than that of a small child studying pinyin in a Chinese school.

Actually, the Chinese almost never laugh hysterically at foreigners for butchering the pronunciation of their language. I don't know if they are just so used to it that it's not even funny to them, or they are naturally less critical of foreigners making the effort to learn. Try speaking French in Paris and hear the mocking laughter; speak a bit of Chinese in Shanghai and be lauded. Or at worst, get nervous giggles that sound very different from derisive laughs. Chinese people tend to smile and laugh when they are nervous or feel uncomfortable for someone; with a bit of practice you can learn to translate a Chinese tight smile into embarrassment, and a strained chuckle into the sound of empathy and distress.

I love to get lost in Shanghai. Often I don't have to try too hard, but sometimes, even when I am not lost, I ask people for directions because I like to talk with them, and I like to watch them smile when I speak Chinese. And though I seldom completely understand the torrent of directions that spill from their lips and I have to ask them to speak slowly and repeat themselves, these people I stop on the busy streets of Shanghai are very rarely anything other than friendly and kind.

What the language lacks in ease of acquisition is more than made up for by the warm encouragement of Chinese tutors, who are everywhere. Language lessons can be found on subways and in taxis, in supermarkets and in restaurants. Learning Chinese is one's passport to China: it helps one find acceptance, and it all but guarantees friendship. The effort to learn is appreciated; proficiency is almost incidental. That one tries to train one's vocal architecture to make those strange sounds means so much to the Chinese. And why not try? By saying a four-character chengyu one taps into a linguistic bounty. Each chengyu has its own history, its own story. Each chengyu is a gem worn smooth and shiny with use through the years. Say it and feel the ages on your lips; say it and add to its luster.

The Chinese have sayings with stories that stretch back thousands of years. We have sports analogies. I was forever explaining expressions such as "slam dunk," "home run" and "strike out" to Jennifer. She had a list of things she'd heard on *Friends* that she couldn't translate, and that list drove home the point that we use a lot of sports expressions in everyday speech. Try explaining "hit a home run" to someone who's never seen a baseball game and doesn't know a pitcher from a bat.

"*Luàn qī bā zāo?*" Jennifer repeated and laughed. "Where did you learn that?"

"Online. From a chengyu website."

"You taught yourself?"

"Is it too old-fashioned? It's like something Old Wang would say?"

"I say it sometimes." She thought for a moment, blowing at her hair, ruffling the straight curtain of her bangs. "But young people don't use chengyu much now. They like using English words. English words are *hĕn kù.*"

Kù is a transliteration of "cool," and *hĕn* is an intensifier: "very cool." Very cool Chinese kids aren't using chengyu; they are peppering their Mandarin with "email" and using "google" as a verb.

We passed vendors with their goods spread out on sheets selling DVDs and Chinese chotchkies, and then we wandered through a park where stark gray trees creaked in the wind and the turf had been worn smooth by shoes and was scabbed with brown denuded earth. Several men were carrying forward the ancient Chinese traditions of throwing trash everywhere and blowing smoke in people's faces. Jennifer and I coughed and kicked our way through the rubbish. My spirits lifted as I watched people practicing tai chi along a leafy promenade and women performing a fan dance, red paper unfolding like gossamer wings and then disappearing into bamboo handles as the dancers snapped shut the fans and pivoted on their heels, turning in practiced circles beneath the trees. Elderly men in tracksuits were walking backward and beating themselves with their slapping hands. Someone had once explained this form of exercise to me, something about stimulating *qì*, but it didn't make any sense to me. I just saw old men hitting themselves. Though I suppose it is no stranger than golf, and it is much more fun to watch. One man stood crouched over a sidewalk painting with a giant brush. He dabbed the brush in a bowl of water and then drew Chinese characters on the ground. His precise calligraphy lingered a few moments and then evaporated from the cement. This seemed an act so blatantly defiant of the world's rot and ruin, an act filled with a crazy faith that beauty, however temporary, is a triumph. While I watched his art emerge and vanish I felt an upwelling of affection for the city, for my friend Jennifer, for my life. China can do that to you, can knock you off balance: one moment it fills you with bile and spite, and the next moment it can purge your heart of poison. It can make your spirit swell with joy so expansive you swear you will never mention the moment at which the feeling occurred to another soul, for fear of being laughed at—and because you're afraid whomever you tell will see only the cement, not the gorgeous character that was there an instant before, steaming in the Shanghai sun.

I convinced Jennifer to linger and watch the people in the park with me. This place of spontaneous and genuine happiness for the elderly seemed so different from the forced joy of an American retirement home, with scheduled craft hours and sad bags of bones wrapped in suit coats and dresses eating dinner alone, pictures of their children tucked in pockets damp with drool. When finally we left the park, we stopped at a curb and looked out on a street so jammed with cars there appeared to be not an empty inch of pavement. It seemed the cars and trucks and taxis had been arranged by some grand design so that each bumper and fender matched up with every other bumper and fender in perfect symmetry: a giant traffic jigsaw puzzle.

And speaking of puzzles: "Now do you know how the soup gets inside?" Jennifer asked me. To our left was a dive serving xiaolongbao, waiters setting steaming baskets on outdoor tables in front of men who lifted open the bamboo lids and gripped the slippery xiaolongbao with their chopsticks. There was much slurping and happy nodding at the tables.

I said, "Okay, I've got it. The person who makes the xiaolongbao holds the sides of each dumpling open and pours soup into it, and then he twists the skin together at the top to keep the soup inside."

"That's not correct."

"Do you want to tell me what is correct?"

"No, I do not. Today I will not tell you."

Back to crossing the street. Sweat dripped down my sides, leaking from my deodorant-free underarms. I have kayaked the Zambezi surrounded by the saber-toothed jaws of crocodiles and the munching maws of hippos; I have been mixed up in a civil war in Kashmir with tracers lighting the night sky while I hid on a houseboat; I have been stalked by a grizzly in the Alaskan wilds. But I tell you this: crossing a Chinese street is the most dangerous thing I have done. Gone in Shanghai are the days of the ubiquitous bike. I had been raised on *National Geographic* images of the Chinese masses pedaling their way through city streets with not an internal-combustion-powered vehicle to be seen. But all over China people had traded their bikes for cars, and people-powered vehicles were now in the minority in Shanghai. Cars ruled the streets, pushing bicycles and tricycles to the edges of the boulevards, where riders of human-powered transportation took their lives in their hands as they pedaled between dump trucks and taxis, megabuses and minivans. Throw into the mix some motorcycles, motor scooters, motorized bicycles, motorized tricycles, and endless streams of pedestrians; cover it all with fumes so thick you can hardly see the other side of the street you are crossing while your eyes blink desperately to soothe themselves in the stinging air; fill the scene with a cacophony of revving engines, blaring horns and protesting brakes; and there you have it: a Chinese street. You can cross in the middle, you can cross at a light, you can run across, you can walk across, you can go halfway to an island of safety in the middle to take a few calming breaths and then cough out the pollution and continue, or you can go for it and cross in one continuous push, but however you do it you are rolling the dice with your life each time you cross the street.

Occasionally within the maelstrom of the streets are moments of pause and peace.

"In America, pedestrians have the right of way," I explained to Jennifer. "Not cars."

"That's strange," she said. "Cars are so much bigger—people who are walking should watch out for cars."

Might makes right on the roads of China, and to undertake the task of crossing a street is to feel the full fight-or-flight adrenaline blast that has aided in our species' survival from the time we dropped down from the trees and fled from the fanged beasts of the savanna. To cross a street in China is to enter into combat. One has to fight one's way across, gaining and giving up ground, always alert for danger, eyes peeled and head panning back and forth, lest one be attacked from one's unguarded flank as traffic curves in from the side.

When I prepped groups in the United States before they left for China about cultural differences, after talking about using chopsticks and surnames coming before given names and whatnot, I would always end with this: "Pedestrians do not have the right of way in China. If you don't watch out for yourself when crossing streets, you could be killed. If you get scared while crossing a street, don't panic—do not run. Keep making your way carefully across, watching out for vehicles coming at you from all directions, and remember to breathe. Just don't breathe too deeply or the pollution might impair your judgment. I'm not kidding." I wasn't kidding. Though everyone always laughed and no one ever believed me until faced for the first time in China with crossing a street. You weren't kidding, they'd tell me between gasping breaths when they arrived on the other side of the street, pupils dilated and pulses visible in their neck veins.

There is a method to the madness of traffic in China, as evidenced by the fact that there are not collisions on every street every few seconds—as it appears to the Western eye there should be. The traffic lights are mere suggestions and lanes are nonexistent. Everyone drives toward whatever open space happens to exist at any given moment. The first time I saw Chinese traffic I went rigid with the anticipation of an accident: I was certain the taxi I was riding in would crash into something amid the chaotically moving mass of metal in which we were im- mersed. How could we possibly not collide with all the other taxis and busses, cars and trucks? Everything was going every which way and there was no order, no scheme—it seemed complete and utter madness. But somehow we hadn't crashed then, and I have yet to be in an accident other than one scrape of the mir- ror on a bus I was riding in against a Range Rover.

There is some pattern, some set of rules to Chinese traffic; taxi drivers had tried to explain the etiquette of the road to me. It is something along these lines: Go where you need to go when you need to go there, and honk your horn inces- santly to let others know that you are going. Waiting one's turn is in no way part of the rules. Waiting is unheard of. One simply charges ahead into every space that momentarily opens, occupying it before accelerating into the next open space, and millimeters separate bumpers from bumpers, fenders from fenders. Chaos theory claims there is hidden order buried deep beneath the random sur- face of things. Wherever that order is in Shanghai traffic, I have yet to delve that deep. What happens in the streets still looks to me like unmitigated lunacy, though I've rarely seen a wreck. As miraculous as it is that there aren't smash-ups on every piece of pavement every few minutes, there is no shortage of cata- strophic auto accidents in China. The law of averages catches up with many of China's drivers who eventually succumb to the chaos.

I'm certain Chinese traffic is a metaphor for something. What the metaphor is exactly, I don't know.

Likewise, the new high-end, high-rise housing development called Rich Gate that Jennifer and I stumbled upon was surely pregnant with clues to Shanghai's identity, yet I was so overwhelmed by the sheer nuttiness of Rich Gate I failed to put it into any meaningful context.

Our discovery of one of Shanghai's most outlandish new developments went like this: We left a main thoroughfare to escape the traffic and wandered the al-

leyways of a lilong strewn with red government banners urging everyone to remain calm and act in an orderly way in the coming days as the neighborhood
was demolished. A World Expo poster proclaiming the motto of the event, "Better City, Better Life," was pasted to a wall at the end of the lane. A man standing
on a street corner checked his wristwatch. He was wearing gold pajamas and
carrying a briefcase. A motor scooter hurtled toward him and skidded to a halt,
leaving a black scuffmark on the pavement beneath the smoking tire. Covering
the driver's face was some sort of shield that looked as though its design had
been inspired by equal parts tennis visor and welding mask. I know this description doesn't make a lot of sense, but neither did the unlikely looking apparatus
perched upon the man's cranium. This headgear made the pilot of the motor
scooter look like a Jedi Knight, I thought, as we walked by him. The man in pajamas with the briefcase, who happened to be wearing loafers, swung a leg over
the saddle of the scooter and sat down behind the Jedi, and the two zoomed off
beneath red banners and through the narrow lane. I noted how preposterous it
was that I had just registered this scene as utterly mundane, just another day in
the life of Shanghai, but as Jennifer and I left the alley, I stopped in my tracks.
In front of me was a gateway not of stone leading into another alley, but rather
it was made of metal bars fifteen feet tall and flanked by walls that looked as
though they could hold Mongol hordes at bay. Behind the walls stood towers so
strange, even in Shanghai they made me stop (literally) and scratch my head
(figuratively).

"What is that?" I asked Jennifer.

"The English sign says it is Rich Gate."

The sign, indeed, did announce in English that this was Rich Gate.

"I know," I said. "But what *is* it?"

Atop soaring towers made of what looked like marble stood columns of classical design. As if a Roman temple had been built atop each tower. I had grown
used to pagodas topping futuristic skyscrapers—something of an architectural
cliché in Shanghai. But this was new. Fighting for attention with the Roman temple on the apex of each tower were the enormous golden columns at the entrance
to the complex. They gleamed richly in the sun as if advertising the gateway to
one of the lost cities of Cibola. I tried to imagine what Marcus with his keen marketing skills could do with this. "Like a conquistador enjoying the treasures of a
conquered Aztec palace covered in gold, you return triumphant through the gates
of your new home, watched over by the wisdom of the ancient Romans, whose
pillars rise above your roof."

"*What?*" I stood looking at Rich Gate and not saying much of anything save "what . . ."

"Are you okay," Jennifer asked?

"No, I am not okay."

"What is the matter?"

"These buildings are the matter." I thought a moment. "Do you think if the developers offered your parents an apartment here, they would accept?"

"Maybe. It's close to their neighborhood."

I looked at her to see if she was kidding. Hard to tell. What I could see clearly was that the beautiful blue sky scrubbed clean by the morning's blizzard had reverted to its old gray ways. Haze drifted between buildings of staggering height and bulk, and the magic of the morning snowstorm was but a quickly fading dream.

"Did we catch snowflakes on our tongues this morning?" I asked Jennifer. "Or did I imagine that?"

"I imagined it too."

I pointed up at the nutty tower. "Let's go check it out," I said.

"How? We can't just go in there."

"Sure we can. I'm a rich American—let's say, maybe, that I'm a senior vice president of an investment firm."

"Maybe we could pretend you are a movie star."

"No, they'd see right through that."

"See through that?"

"They'd know that it's a lie."

Jennifer studied me a moment. "Yes, they would not believe that."

"Senior vice president is more plausible."

"Plausible?"

"Believable."

"Oh." She looked me up and down. "But you are wearing jeans and tennis shoes. You look poor."

"True. Okay, I own a software company. Like Bill Gates. That's why I dress like this."

"How much do you know about software?"

"As much as I know about investing. How about this: I am the vice president of a travel company in America. If they ask questions, I can talk about travel."

"That is plausible."

"Nicely done. You are an excellent student," I said in Chinese.

"You are a good teacher," Jennifer said.

"I'm not a teacher," I said, embarrassed by this, perhaps the greatest Chinese compliment of all.

For all of China's fascination with all things Western, its citizens had yet to adopt Western-style indifference toward teachers. Teachers (*lǎoshi*) are held in high esteem in China. To be called a teacher is a high honor, and in my case, utterly undeserved. Many professions in China have names that connote the prestige they have in Chinese society. *Zuòjiā*, a writing expert, carries associations with literature and fame. To call oneself a writer in America is to say, "I am ill equipped to make a living doing anything even remotely productive in society, and besides, I am socially awkward and inept at performing any practical task in the everyday world—and I'm poor. Really poor." To call oneself a *zuòjiā* in China is to say, "I am a creator of literature, a contributor to culture." But one should never say this, because to call oneself a zuojia is considered conceited. It is best to simply say one writes things; others decide if you are a zuojia. In America you can say, "I'm an artist," and it doesn't sound pretentious; in China you say you paint pictures. It's up to others to decide if you are indeed an artist.

In China, it is proper to address people not just by their names but also their titles. Zhang *Lǎoshi* (Teacher Zhang), Li *Jīnglǐ* (Manager Li). The use of titles could pigeonhole people in their appointed places, could reduce them to roles; but by learning how to carefully address people in Mandarin, instead of limiting them to their function in society, you can lend dignity to their lives. To call a taxi driver simply "driver" (*sījī*) is considered rude. Taxi drivers should be addressed as *shīfu*—meaning essentially "master": a master of a particular discipline. Bicycle repairmen and street cleaners are masters of their trades. Call them shifu. Kungfu masters are also called shifu, as they are masters of the craft of combat. Every time you address a taxi driver as shifu, you are acknowledging that he is more than just a driver—he is an expert at what he does. A master. I like that. I like it because it is respectful, and I like it because in Shanghai's psychotic traffic, it is good to have a master at the wheel.

"So who am I?" Jennifer asked as we walked through the gigantic entrance of Rich Gate and into a splendid world of grass as green as a golf course, burbling fountains, and sculpted shrubbery.

"Maybe you are my wife?"

"That's plausible." She looked at me and grinned.

"Or my mistress."

"Yes, that's plausible too." And again she grinned.

With the loosening of social control by the Communist Party, divorce rates had soared and the incidence of affairs had skyrocketed. In part because of changing societal norms that removed the stigma of sleeping around and dissolving a marriage, and in part because of housing reforms, the institution of marriage in China, long lauded as a pillar of society as sturdy as the golden columns at the entrance to Rich Gate, is now as weak and wobbly as it is in the West. Before the Communist Party embraced capitalism, housing had been scarce. If a husband and wife separated, there was nowhere for them to go. Since two people were forced to share a space so small they literally could not leave each other's sight, divorce made little sense. And there was nowhere to go for a tryst, nowhere to house a mistress. But in the early 1990s, with privatization reforms sweeping many sectors of the economy, local governments were allowed to auction off land to developers, giving birth to a booming real estate industry. Lovers could consummate illicit affairs in apartments purchased as real estate investments, spouses could separate and stay in different spaces, mistresses could live in the luxury of a Rich Gate penthouse. With the advent of capitalist reforms, the Chinese had, along with a free market in real estate, adopted the Western tradition of widespread divorce.

Keeping mistresses has an antecedent in the Chinese tradition of concubinage. Chinese emperors housed thousands of concubines in their imperial chambers— by the time of the Qing dynasty (1644 – 1912) there were twenty thousand living in the Forbidden City. Lust was most definitely not forbidden to the emperor.

Every culture has its myths. We have cowboys and Indians, the Chinese have eunuchs and concubines. There are no more concubines in China. Officially, anyway. Mistresses, or *èrnăi*, are becoming increasingly common throughout China, especially in Shanghai, a city in which so much new wealth allows tycoons to support two wives. Perhaps because of the long-standing Chinese tradition of concubinage, keeping a mistress in China is not as taboo as it is in America. The Communist Party made a concerted effort to raise the status of women in society and erase concubinage, which it deemed a remnant of feudal Chinese society that would, if not destroyed, hamper China's modernization and progress. But among Shanghai's new elite, its businessmen loaded with money, keeping a hot young mistress earns them face among their peers. Gaining face is good for business. As with so many other things in China, the mystery of Shanghai mistresses can be explained by a collision of old culture with new wealth, underlain by the basic human impulses of lust and greed. As is the case, of course, the world over.

Jennifer and I walked by bushes pruned into so many triangles, rectangles and squares—and combinations thereof—I imagined the gardener had a degree in geometry. We passed a lone woman wearing large sunglasses. My head swiveled to watch her as she walked. I took in heels so tall I stumbled a step or two in sympathy. Above the heels and the sequined straps of her narrow-toed shoes rose calves as sculpted as the shrubbery that surrounded her.

"Concubine?" I asked Jennifer.

"*Kěndìng shìde.*" Most definitely.

Ah, to be an emperor in the new China. I took a few big breaths as we passed beneath supple boughs of freshly planted trees and I imagined this was all my domain, my Forbidden City. Flowers arranged in lines as orderly as Chinese schoolchildren added sprigs of color to the scene, and I was feeling good. I was rich and I was ready to move into Rich Gate. Every man in China can be an emperor and have his own golden columns and concubines if he works hard enough and pulls himself up by his bootstraps. All around the grounds of Rich Gate skulked the black Audis with darkly tinted windows that are omnipresent throughout the People's Republic—the private cars of Communist cadres. For all its recent reforms, the Chinese Communist Party is still the world's largest mafia.

Before we entered a tower of Rich Gate, I spotted a man sweeping a pathway with a broom of uneven bristles. The broom had a homemade look to it—not something you'd buy off the shelf at Wal-Mart. I walked over to talk to the man. He was from Sichuan Province and he spoke Mandarin with the slur of a Sichuan accent. We conversed while Jennifer looked on and listened. To make me work harder on my Mandarin we had agreed that she shouldn't interfere in my conversations with other people and give me the crutch of interpretation—and sometimes for fun we pretended she didn't speak a word of Chinese.

"*Tā shì shéi?*" the man asked, swinging his grizzled chin toward Jennifer.

"She is my little sister," I said. "She doesn't speak Chinese. She is from America. I have to translate for her." I told Jennifer in English what I had just explained to the man in Chinese and she nodded and smiled and waved at the man.

Why did I speak Chinese, he wanted to know, and why did I have a Beijing accent? For this man I had brought out my best *érhuàyīn*, the northern accent that emphasizes *r* sounds and makes Mandarin seem a pirate song filled with *ARRR!* If a high seas pirate with an eye patch and a parrot on his shoulder studied Chinese, this is how he'd speak. I explained to the man that my father had worked in the American embassy in Beijing and I had lived with him and learned Chinese. Jennifer had grown up with our mother in America and they had spoken only English, I said, gurgling my *r*s like a Beijinger. "Her English is really good," I told the man. "Better than mine."

"It's true," Jennifer said in Chinese, momentarily forgetting the rules of the game. "He was born in Beijing and grew up there." Her *r*s were nowhere to be heard, and instead were pronounced as the soft *l*s and *n*s of a Shanghai person—she was no pirate at all.

The man looked dubious, but he freely told me his story when I asked him where he was from and how he had come to be a groundskeeper at Rich Gate. Leaving behind a life of low-paid labor in the rice paddies of Sichuan, he had, like millions of other migrant workers in Shanghai, followed the Yangtze River from its sluggish brown waters deep in China's rural interior all the way to the booming coast, where the Yangtze meets the sea. Shanghai's growth has, of course, been fueled, along with favorable government economic policies and robust foreign investment, by immigrants leaving their rural lives to look for work in the city. Poor people had been doing this for hundreds of years, and Shanghai had always been a melting pot of different cultures throughout China, as wave upon wave of the rural poor swept into the city to raise its buildings, to fill its factories and brothels, to sweep its bustling streets. These workers, in theory only temporary residents of the metropolis because they lack the proper permits to settle there, are known as the "floating population." It is debatable whether this population will float away from Shanghai as they floated into the city, and their numbers confound the taking of an accurate census. As the constantly expanding size of Shanghai keeps mapmakers busy, so the floating population keeps census takers on their toes. Population figures for the city vary dramatically. You can read one source that says the population of Shanghai is less than twenty million; you can read another source that claims far more than twenty million—and both are right and neither is wrong depending on where the boundaries of the ever-expanding urban core are drawn and whether the floating population is added to the tally.

The groundskeeper at Rich Gate had lived in Shanghai for seven years, he said. He had floated in and showed no signs of floating back out. For several years he had worked on construction sites, but ten-hour days six days a week had left him with a twisted back. He stood hunched over his broom and laughed at the pain of lifting steel girders and working a rivet gun all day. (At this point I asked Jennifer for a hand with translation but my new friend didn't seem to mind when we exposed our ridiculous ruse. I guess he'd suspected as much. But I didn't drop my Beijing accent when I spoke, preferring to sound like a pirate, or a Beijing taxi driver clearing his throat of dust blown down from the Gobi, instead of an effete Shanghainese whose consonants have softened from a life filled with ease and finery. Spoken Chinese in general sounds very feminine with all its pretty tones and lisped pronunciation, which makes taking Chinese men with their sad machismo seriously when they brag about their liquor and mistresses, but *érhuàyīn* from the north is perhaps the language's most masculine incarnation.) This was a much better job, the Rich Gate groundskeeper said, bringing my attention back to the matter at hand. His back didn't hurt like it used to and he'd saved enough of his twelve-dollar-a-day salary to bring his wife to the city. That was a healthy amount, considering many construction workers in Shanghai were pulling in all of five bucks for a day of clinging to scaffolding far above the city to build the steel and glass citadels of commerce. The man and his wife had had a child many years ago but he had died. The man smiled when he said this.

"I tell myself to smile when I talk about my boy. If I smile, I remember good thoughts about him. If I don't smile when I talk about him, then I feel sad that he is gone. I wonder what he would have looked like if he'd grown up and been a man. I think he would have been strong like me." He rolled up his shirtsleeve and flexed his arm, stringy muscles bunching up into the lump of a bicep. "But he wouldn't have been a worker. He would have been a manager. Maybe a general manager. Maybe he would have lived here." The old man lifted his ragged broom and pointed it skyward toward the Roman temple atop a tower.

I gazed up with him, and then I looked at him holding his broom, and I realized I had lost my will to dupe the management of Rich Gate into believing I wanted to buy one of their ridiculous apartments. I didn't want to lie to this old man anymore, however much it was in the spirit of harmless fun. I didn't want to pretend with Jennifer that she was my concubine or my sister. I didn't want to be a pirate from Beijing. I just wanted to buy this man lunch.

"That's not a good idea," he said after I offered. The manager of Rich Gate would wonder why he was going to lunch with a foreigner, he explained. He could lose his job.

"It's just lunch," I said.

"Maybe they will think you are a journalist trying to find out problems with China. Or maybe they will worry that you are a manager from another apartment building like Rich Gate trying to get secret information about it."

"How old are you?" I asked.

He was sixty-five. He had lived through the famine of the Great Leap Forward and had come of age during the chaos of the Cultural Revolution. Perhaps he had been a Red Guard ratting out family members to the Communists; perhaps Red Guards had put a dunce cap on his head and denounced him as a capitalist roader and dragged him through the streets while his family looked on—perhaps both. In the madness of the revolution that aimed to turn society upside down, many had been both persecutors and persecuted. Perhaps this man's paranoia was a byproduct of those lunatic times; perhaps it was well founded. A foreigner taking an old man with a broom to lunch would get someone's attention, and attention was the last thing a person wanted in a country with a government that cracks the heads of those who step out of line.

"If the manager sees me talking to you here, I can say I was giving you directions or talking about the gardens—how I keep them beautiful. But if we are seen outside of the gates eating lunch together, that is very strange. I don't want to have any problems. I am too old to have problems."

If only this man had shown some form of disfiguration, a hand mangled and useless hanging limp by his side, tragic result of a blunder on a construction site and no workers' compensation, no socialized healthcare coverage to pay for his rehabilitation, he could have served as the perfect symbol of all that is wrong in China. But his hand wasn't mangled and he seemed happy enough, resigned to a life in which he had the good fortune to push a broom and not lift the steel beams of a building.

"You live in America?" he asked. "How much does it cost to fly here?"

All over China people asked me this. It is a common question and one difficult to answer. If I told him the true amount, say thirteen hundred U.S. dollars, he would calculate that in his head into Chinese currency, and the *yuán* it cost me to fly to his country might be more than he made in six months of work. And knowing that I had flown to China four times already that year would leave him shaking his head and smiling at the extravagant sum of money I must make. But instead of just imagining, he would actually ask me—he would want to know exactly how much I made: it was not at all uncommon in China to be asked your salary point-blank by complete strangers. Where are you from? Welcome to China. Do you like Chinese food? Are you married? Do you have kids? No? What's wrong with you? What is your job? How much money do you make? Many conversations progressed in this way. In a culture that values the collective above the individual, privacy is not a primary concern. Chinese people walk into rooms without knocking; they use squat toilets that have no stalls, walls or dividers; and discussing salaries with people they have known for all of five minutes is standard.

Tài guì le, I told the man in answer to his question about plane fare. *Tài guì le.* Too expensive. Many a foreigner has uttered this phrase in Shanghai; these are the first words a lot of people learn as soon as they arrive in China. The phrase is practical, to be sure, as so many things for sale do not have a fixed price and haggling for them is essential. When I taught China Travel 101 and survival Mandarin to MBA groups in the States preparing to embark on their first adventure to China, I gave them tips such as McDonalds and KFC are the best bet when trying to find a clean bathroom; take the Da Zhong turquoise taxis with 大众 on their signs in Shanghai and avoid maroon taxis; if you are a caffeine addict, pack a bottle of Excedrin in your dop kit, and when there is no coffee to be found, pop a pill to preserve your sanity. Then I taught them the tones, some basic pronunciation, how to say hello, and *tài guì le.* That was followed by—based on feedback I'd heard from people in past sessions regarding what they wanted to learn of the language—"bathroom," and then, "I want a beer." Bargaining, bathrooms and beer: the first three entries in the language survival lexicon of the American traveler. And during one of these sessions, or immediately after, invariably a man with a toothy grin would ask me how to tell a Chinese woman she was sexy. Not one MBA student had ever asked me to teach him how to ask a Chinese person about his hometown or his hobbies. Bargaining, bathrooms and beer—and chatting up Chinese chicks: that pretty much summed up the language interests of students in America's elite university business programs. Why not. I wondered if the old man with the broom, given a windfall of money and the chance to travel to America, wouldn't ask me to teach him how to ask for a bathroom, find a good deal, order a beer and chat up an American hottie.

I shrugged off the groundskeeper's inquiry about airline tickets and salaries in America, which was a bit rude of me considering he'd just told me how much he made and had basically given me his life story, but I felt so uncomfortable highlighting the wealth disparity between us that I could give no articulate answer. Which was pretty stupid when I considered it: Of course he didn't think I was his peer; he knew I made a thousand times more money than he did; he understood I lived a life of ease and luxury unimaginable to him. He knew it just as he knew that the people living in the Rich Gate towers were emperors and he was a commoner outside the gates of the Forbidden City. Or rather, he was inside the ridiculous golden columns at the gate and he was the eunuch who knew his place and served his wealthy overlords, posing no threat to their concubines in tall heels and large sunglasses who glided back and forth between their penthouse condos and their chauffeured BMWs. Or something. China is so clotted with history, so rich with lore and symbols, one can draw endless parallels between the dynastic past and the gritty present. Sometimes the parallels are instructive, pointing out continuities in Chinese culture that help explain what is happening now; sometimes the parallels are complete and utter nonsense. But even so, they can still provide great fun. One never grows bored with the banality of contemporary Chinese culture if everywhere one looks one sees echoes of emperors, eunuchs and concubines.

Jennifer and I left our new friend to his sweeping and I tried to leave Rich Gate behind and head off to our next adventure, but Jennifer was having none of it.

"Let's go inside," she said. "It will be fun. It was your idea."

About the first part I was doubtful, though the second part was true. I liked her feistiness. I usually had to twist her arm to participate in mischief such as this. So we turned around, walked past our perplexed friend with the broom, who was looking at us as though we were a few grains short of a full bowl of rice, and we entered the palatial space of Rich Gate's lobby, resplendent with chandeliers and marble floors so shiny one needed sunglasses to look directly at them. Gilt here, gilt there, gilt everywhere—there was a whole lot of gilt going on. Jennifer spoke with a manager first in Mandarin and then in Shanghainese and I stood there and smiled, trying to look rich. I looked white, I looked foreign, I most definitely did not look rich. And the manager looked skeptical. He examined me, taking in my running shoes and jeans, his eyes finally settling on my Billabong shirt, a T-shirt faded and torn that I had been wearing for the better part of a decade. He introduced himself in English clumsier than my Chinese. I glanced at Jennifer and realized that within our plan lay a gaping hole. I had no business cards with me. I took the card the man offered, studied it intently, then slipped it in a pants pocket and gave him an embarrassed grin.

Jennifer and I, before we'd stepped inside, had agreed that I would pretend I spoke no Chinese. We did this sometimes so I could concentrate on listening to conversations and then later tell her what I thought had been discussed. Sometimes I nailed it, sometimes I got the gist but missed the details, sometimes the people talking could have been speaking Arabic and I would have understood as much. Now was one of the middle scenarios, bordering on the last scenario.

When Jennifer and the manager spoke Mandarin I strained to understand their meaning but they were talking so fast my brain ached from trying to keep up; when they switched to Shanghainese I followed them around the building smiling and trying to look at things as a rich person might. Where will my chauffeured Mercedes park? Who will clean my condo each day? Where will my concubine shop?

Jennifer started translating for me, explaining in English everything the manager was telling her, but after a few minutes I wasn't even making sense of what she was saying in English. The banquet halls bright with chandeliers, the curlicues of curtains framing floor-to-ceiling windows, the gold-plated antique-looking phones, the grand pianos: it was all too much for me, and all I could do was laugh. This started Jennifer laughing, and by the time we made our way across one of the decorated demo units to a window as big as a billboard, our ploy was collapsing around us, and the manager, well, he did not look amused.

"This place is not renao," I whispered to Jennifer.

"Yes," she said. "It is rich, but it is not renao."

The city outside was hidden in mantles of haze and through the haze towers rose in faint and fantastic shapes like a city summoned in a dream. Amid skyscrapers with tops sculpted into ballistic missiles and spear points and blooming flowers lay the low-slung brick buildings of Xintiandi, and beyond Xintiandi was the lane where Jennifer's parents lived in their small house built close to the ground. All around Rich Gate were the ruins of mutilated neighborhoods and the mechanized paraphernalia of construction. Bulldozers and cranes were remaking the landscape into one of the hottest real estate markets in the world, and we stood now inside one of the planet's priciest condos. I felt giddy and a little sick. I looked away from the window and around the room. I don't know what the style of décor was called, but there was enough gold in gaudy shapes and oil-painted portraits in gilded frames to make me think I was in the Palace of Versailles. I walked to a window and watched my breath condense against the glass. Outside this gold-filled ode to conspicuous wealth was the future.

The science fiction thriller *Code 46*, a British film released in 2003, had been made without using computer-aided enhancement. Many scenes were filmed on location in Shanghai. Set in a future world divided into megacities where the rich reside and howling wastes of desert inhabited by the destitute, *Code 46* imagines a civilization with human cloning, a repressive state that presides over memory erasure procedures, and a ruined ozone layer that makes venturing outside during daylight deadly. None of this has anything to do with Shanghai. How could it? The movie is, after all, science fiction. But Shanghai itself seems science fiction, a city as strange as any created on a computer screen. To spend time in China observing the inner workings and not-workings of this nation, the contradictions so profound they can stop you in your intellectual tracks and permanently derail your thought, one must adopt a healthy sense of humor, lest one run the risk of going completely, incurably insane. Right now I was not laughing, and this concerned me greatly. How had we come to this place? Why were we here?

Jennifer wasn't laughing anymore either. The developer who would smash her parents' home probably had a mistress housed in this place. Shanghai's landmarks were falling each day to the bulldozer. In a matter of months or weeks or days there would be nothing left of a neighborhood that had stood a hundred years or more. There would be a shopping mall, or a car dealership, or a luxury high-rise beneath a riot of lights.

And in a flash of panicky realization I understood for the first time the nostalgia for Mao. So many people in Shanghai looked back to the days of the Great Helmsman and remembered a time when everyone was equal and there was a clear moral code, a distinct goal that society was working toward. Believing in Mao, for many, was better than believing in nothing. Shanghai was changing so fast one was left without moorings, and it was exhilarating to be adrift and moving toward who-knows-what, but it was also scary as hell. I could leave and go back to my stable life in America, but Jennifer was caught up in the tidal wave of change crashing through Shanghai. What to do but keep swimming like crazy toward the future.

Sometimes China's much ballyhooed claim to "five thousand years of culture" feels entirely relevant and reverberations from the ancient past appear everywhere. (Shanghai's massage parlors are filled with concubines! And the nominally male massage parlor attendants, those androgynous sprites that flit harmlessly about handing drinks to men waiting to enter the concubines' chambers and then offering them towels and rubbing their feet upon their return—they are like the palace eunuchs in the olden soul of China!) But most days "five thousand years of culture" seems as pointless as any other piece of propaganda, as silly as any other sales pitch. Shanghai is one big construction zone, as is every other city throughout China, regardless of the year of its founding. The Chinese flatten with abandon what little of their past is left to make way for new buildings—and any style, as long as it is new and stolen from the West without regard to referent or

The past is juxtaposed with the future in Xujiahui, where a stone lion gazes at lights laserbeaming across the night.

purpose, will suffice. China is a blank slate. It is the newest country in the world, a nation without a history inventing itself by appropriating whatever it can as quickly as it can while its cities materialize before our eyes as if generated by the silicon chips of supercomputers. And when the past does receive a nod from city planners in China, it is usually in the form of a structure that is bulldozed to the ground and then rebuilt with cheap materials and shoddy workmanship, or perhaps an ancient temple receives a crown of neon. And often these awful places are filled with performers from China's minority groups dancing in brightly colored clothes, and someone always makes a killing on the entrance fees or by taking a percentage of the profits from the retailers that fill these fabricated spaces—and that someone is often involved with the Communist Party. "Chinese culture" is dangerously close to becoming every bit the oxymoron that is "American culture."

I stood staring at the gold-crusted room around me. Why do I keep coming back to this country, this city? Perhaps it is because we are so similar and everything I hate in China I find harbored within myself, hiding behind my pointed criticism, lurking beneath my snarky comments. Perhaps the myth of Chinese "otherness" is as silly as the canard of "five thousand years of history," for when you strip away the patina of cultural differences, the unintelligible language and foreign concepts such as face and guanxi, we are very much alike, united by the great emptiness at our centers, and by a fear of this emptiness that forces us to scramble forward as fast as we can. The Chinese blather about owning the world's longest continuous culture, we drone on about freedom and democracy, and all any of us really wants is a gilded palace in the sky.

I entertained for a moment the possibility of changing my ticket so I could fly away from China as fast as possible. But then I realized I would miss the renao of the last remaining lanes in Shanghai. And I remembered that each time I had fled Shanghai swearing I would never return, after a few weeks back in the States I had begun to crave the loopy logic of China, where a country that desperately wants to be taken seriously has a box on its visa application form to check if you are a "businessman" (and no option for "businesswoman"); where government officials who refer to the Dalai Lama as a "jackal in monk's robes" earnestly scratch their heads and wonder why the world hates them; where people sucking on cigarettes tell you the mountain air in Tibet is bad for your health; where college graduates belting out Guns and Roses ballads in karaoke bars, cell phones swinging from lanyards tethered to their necks, these phones bejeweled with cartoon baubles and fringed with tassels of silk, insist that Chinese culture is superior to American culture; where people who have figured out how to build some of the tallest towers on the planet have yet to figure out how to form a line at a ticket window. Like a partner who infuriates you with endless bad habits but for whom your love flares all the brighter for these faults, Shanghai is difficult to like but easy to love. And once you have fallen in love with Shanghai, it is difficult to separate yourself from her, however much you want to, however hard you try.

Along the Bund

In the early summer, when the warm breezes of spring had given way to sticky heat and stillness, I invited Jennifer to go for a walk with me. Together we strolled along the Bund, past banks as grand as Greek temples, past the pointed roof of the Peace Hotel, past buildings boasting Art Deco shapes of sunbursts, wheels and gears. The Bund holds dozens of structures made of sandstone that between the world wars were home to banks and hotels, newspaper headquarters and trading houses, consulates and clubs. Shanghai boasts one of the richest collections of Art Deco buildings in the world, and many of them line the Bund. This museum of world architecture showcases, along with Art Deco, the styles of Romanesque, Renaissance, Gothic, Baroque and Neoclassical. The Bund's architectural charms can be difficult to appreciate, however, when dodging the legions of fake Rolex vendors lurking outside the handsome, storied buildings.

During Shanghai's heyday in the early twentieth century, the Bund was dubbed the "Wall Street of the Orient" for its thriving financial industry. For its thriving social scene it earned a reputation as the best party street in the East. Stella Dong, author of *Shanghai: The Rise and Fall of a Decadent City*, wrote this of Shanghai: "At the peak of its spectacular career the swamp-ridden metropolis surely ranked as the most pleasure-mad, rapacious, corrupt, strife-ridden, licentious, squalid, and decadent city in the world." The money flowed and the good times rolled until the humorless Communists ended the fun, stamping out vice and all things

Along Shanghai's Bund stand buildings of elegant stonework.

foreign, flipping off the lights of the Bund. But now the Party has loosened up, and the party along the Bund is back in full swing. The lights have been turned back on, and how they glow at night. Each evening the European colonial-era buildings send waves of light into the Shanghai night. But the flags fluttering atop the buildings of the Bund are not the Union Jack and the Stars and Stripes as once they had been. Now the flags show yellow stars upon backgrounds red as blood.

"Bund" is an Anglo-Indian word for an embankment. In the 400s AD fishermen built a village on a mudflat where the Yangtze and Huangpu Rivers run brackish and wide. In this nascent Shanghai (上 *shàng*; and 海 *hǎi*), which means "on the sea" or "to go to the sea," crabs were trapped from the salt marshes of the delta and fish were netted. Locals traded for rice and vegetables grown in the fertile soils along the banks of the Yangtze, and they hawked fresh water to seafaring junks. From these modest beginnings Shanghai evolved into a prosperous seaport under the Mongol governance of the Yuan dynasty, which in 1292 granted Shanghai county-level status. Shanghai's importance, however, was not assured; its fortunes throughout Chinese history have been influenced by the shifting weathers of the Chinese political climate. And the winds of political change, since Kublai Khan in the thirteenth century established his capital where present-day Beijing now stands, have generally blown down from the north. In the 1500s, the Ming dynasty, ensconced in Beijing's Forbidden City, in an act of reckless xenophobia, banned foreign trade, bankrupting merchants in Shanghai. Japanese pirates preyed at will on the weakened town until a circular wall was erected to protect it. After the Manchu-led Qing dynasty replaced the Ming imperial court in 1644, Shanghai's fortunes rebounded. Qing rulers lifted the ban on maritime trade and granted Shanghai increased administrative power. Shanghai's merchants did a brisk business in cotton, and the town again opened its ports. Boats arrayed in lines many miles long floated in, a forest of masts filled the sky, and once again the city boomed. Its strategic location at the mouth of the Yangtze River made it an ideal center for trade with the West. Tea and silk left Shanghai's harbor, and opium arrived on boats bearing the Union Jack.

Following the first British ships to penetrate Shanghai, foreigners came en masse. These Shanghailanders, as they called themselves, came with their gunboats; they came with their extraterritorial laws that allowed them to act with impunity on Chinese soil; they came with their bankers and lawyers and soldiers. China, unlike, for example, India or Zaire, was never colonized completely, but Shanghai certainly bore the imprint of European colonialism. At the conclusion of the First Opium War, China signed the Treaty of Nanking in 1842, turning Shanghai into a "treaty port," assuring a steady flow of British opium through Shanghai's wharves and into the interior of China, up the Yangtze and beyond. Like an artery swollen with drugs and sending them coursing through a diseased body, the Yangtze carried the cargo of raw opium that flowed upstream from Shanghai and spread throughout a nation too numb with narcotic bliss to fight back the foreigners who carved up Shanghai into sections governed by the British, French and Americans. While the rest of China was racked by civil war, Shanghai offered a safe haven for European businesses that flourished in the international "concessions": colonial enclaves built on rice and cotton fields in hinterlands outside the walled Chinese town. China conceded nothing; the Shanghai concessions were simply taken from the Chinese motherland where the Yangtze joins the sea. Governed by British and French magistrates, the concessions allowed the foreign powers to segregate themselves from the Chinese; Chinese officials, for their part, hoped that keeping the foreigners contained in their concessions would prevent their barbarian ways from contaminating China's superior culture, which held a prejudice against Western practices of large-scale trade—business in China had traditionally been limited to small enterprises run by families and local merchants.

As a treaty port under foreign control, Shanghai joined the East and West in commerce, and the West enjoyed the lion's share of the profits. So patently unfair to China was this "treaty port" arrangement, such a slap in the face to the ideal of national sovereignty, Mark Twain decried the imposition of taxation without representation on the Chinese people in their homeland, and he applauded the Boxer Rebellion, an anti-foreign uprising that swept through China and left scores of Europeans and Americans dead. Twain, in a letter to a friend, wrote: "[The Chinese] have been villainously dealt with by the sceptered thieves of Europe, and I hope they will drive all the foreigners out and keep them out for good."

A construction boom fueled by the money pouring into Shanghai's foreign concessions at the end of the nineteenth century and the beginning of the twentieth century turned the Bund into a major financial hub, and buildings of pillared grandeur were raised opposite the empty paddy fields of Pudong. With spectacular fortunes made in its shipping offices and trading houses, Shanghai grew to be the leading port in the Far East and the most important city in Asia. Shanghai became known as the "Paris of the East" and the "Whore of the Orient"—and both titles had merit. J. G. Ballard, in his novel *Empire of the Sun*, writing about the rowdy city in the late 1930s, noted that "life in Shanghai was lived wholly within an intense present." The Bund's gorgeous Neoclassical and Art Deco architecture became emblematic of a city that mixed money, glamour and vice in an addictive and villainous brew. British business tycoons in bowler hats blended with White Russian prostitutes and Chinese gangsters with names like Pock-marked Chen and Big Ears Du, and American women in flapper dresses drank Champagne imported from France and danced till dawn to jazz in ballrooms built of the finest Italian marble.

The Communists put an end to all that. The Chinese people blamed the Manchu-led Qing dynasty for allowing the humiliation of foreign occupation, and while Chinese patriots were putting down their opium pipes to rise up and topple the Qing, replacing the last dynasty with the Republic of China, Mao was using anti-imperialist fervor in Shanghai to build support for his revolution. The Communist Party, founded in the French Concession of Shanghai in 1921, gained control of all of mainland China in 1949 after forcing its rival, the Kuomintang (KMT) led by Generalissimo Chiang Kai-shek, to flee to Taiwan. When the Communists came to power, the Bund housed the headquarters of the major financial institutions operating in China. But as the Red Army descended on

Shanghai, foreigners fled. The Communists smashed statues of colonial figures along the riverside and they boarded the Bund's banks and businesses, its hotels and clubs. The lights went out—and stayed out for almost five decades.

Even in 1990 when Deng Xiaoping chose the farmland of Pudong on the shore of the Huangpu River opposite the Bund as a new development zone, the Bund was still neglected. Twenty watt bulbs struggled to light it at night so that a trickle of tourists could find their way along the gloomy waterfront. As the brash towers of Pudong rose across the river, spewing neon into the sky, the Bund's shuttered storefronts and empty office buildings lay in darkness, a relic of colonialism, a grim reminder of China's weakness and defeat. Many of the Bund's buildings had been given official preservation status by the government, which to its credit had recognized that this historic area, with its colonnaded banks and ornate hotels, had architectural merit and deserved a better fate than to be bulldozed over with skyscrapers raised from its ruins.

The first stirring of life in the dormant Bund came in 1999 when the restaurant M on the Bund opened in the pinnacle of the Nissin Shipping Building with an interior décor styled like a 1930s ocean liner, recalling the heyday of Shanghai's opulence. European haute cuisine, which had virtually disappeared from Shanghai's restaurants during five decades of Communist rule, won M accolades and a loyal following. It was named one of the fifty best restaurants in the world by *Condé Nast Traveler*, and *Zagat* dubbed it "the most popular restaurant in Shanghai." In the city that had given birth to Communism, the political movement that plunged China into a miasma of deprivation, asceticism and anti-Western hysteria, one could now sit atop a refurbished colonial-era building and dine on classic European dishes for one hundred dollars a plate while gazing along the Bund, where the European powers had set up their business empires to extract China's wealth while the country writhed in chaos. Beyond the Bund a diner could see the Huangpu River, once the entrepot for boatloads of British opium. And on the river's far bank, the towers of Pudong lifted skyward, announcing to the world that Shanghai was again open for business—but now on China's terms.

It is easy to forget that the quaint buildings of the Bund were created by the European powers as aggressive commercial statements. Opposite the thrusting shafts of Pudong, the Bund's squat edifices now appear no more potent than gingerbread dollhouses.

Manipulating public perceptions by crafting carefully designed symbols has always been a mainstay of the Communist Party's control over the Chinese people; preservation of the Bund can be viewed within the paradigm of Communist

The structures along the Bund seem quaint relics opposite Pudong's thrusting shafts of steel and glass.

symbol making. The Chinese government took the empty swampland of Pudong and raised a flash-forward skyline of futuristic towers complete with giant video screens and laser beams. But on the other side of the river it enacted height restrictions as part of the building codes that protected the Bund—perfectly sensible, given that aggressively tall skyscrapers could easily overpower the diminutive European buildings. The Bund remained intact through the government's historic preservation rules, and no one could argue that protecting the integrity of this treasure trove of classic architecture was anything but a good thing. The effect now, however, is for visitors in Shanghai to see the Bund on one side of the river with its low buildings with their stately stonework and Art Deco flourishes as a charming relic of the past, while across the river soars the mighty glass and steel metropolis of Pudong. Old Europe and New China. The twentieth century on the west bank of the Huangpu River, and on the east bank the twenty-first century and beyond. The past lies in the west, the future in the east. Kipling on one side of the river, Blade Runner on the other.

When M opened in 1999, China was heaving with change, and the Bund, like so many sectors of Shanghai's economy, was about to boom. The pent-up entrepreneurial energies of the nation had been released, and along the Bund the lights flickered back on. Soon plans were underway to repurpose virtually all of the Bund's fifty-two historic buildings. The Chinese government relocated national financial institutions in the structures that had formerly been home to British banks, and foreign investors flooded the Bund with money as they set up trendy stores and restaurants, lending the revitalized area an air of affluence reminiscent of its roaring days in the 1920s and 30s. Once again, foreign businessmen sipped cognac and smoked cigars, and women in diamonds and pearls danced till dawn. But now too female business tycoons met for power lunches and gay men gamboled through the night. And Chinese entrepreneurs flaunted their new wealth by ordering drinks that cost more than the monthly salaries of the migrant workers who brought bottles of imported liquor from the wharves of Shanghai to the clubs of the Bund. Not just the economy of Shanghai, but also the mores of its residents, had turned upside down. The new social contract in the new Shanghai was this: You could get rich, you could do what you wanted, you could indulge your every whim—as long as you didn't threaten the government's absolute control of society. Drink yourself numb, bang prostitutes in brothels, make a fortune by razing and rebuilding a neighborhood. Enjoy the party on the Bund; just don't question the Party. Guided by the economic pragmatism first proposed by Deng Xiaoping, the Communist Party now followed the tenet that whatever grew the economy was good, as long as it didn't challenge the government's monopoly on power. Foreigners and Chinese partying it up along the Bund pumped money through the Shanghai economy, filling the tax coffers in Beijing. The Communist government, based in Beijing, said let the good times roll. And roll they did along Shanghai's storied Bund.

Jennifer and I ducked into Three on the Bund, not to shop in its flagship Armani store or to relax in its spa that offered rivers of flowing Evian or to dine on foie gras and shark's fin soup, but to take in a few fresh breaths of air conditioning and escape the sticky heat outside. From damp shoulders my shirt hung heavy with sweat. As we stepped inside Three on the Bund, robotic doormen scanned us for signs of danger and monstrously beautiful sales associates swiveled their painted faces toward us and crimped their mouths into little scowling shapes. I shivered and peeled the sticky fabric of my shirt from clammy skin as I scowled back at the inhumanly perfect cheekbones and noses and chins sculpted with scalpels and shellacked with vivid palettes glowing fiercely beneath the showroom lights. We backed out of the hostile ground-floor store into which we'd wandered and then we found an elevator and set out to absorb the sights inside the re-vamped building.

Hollywood producer Josef von Sternberg, who directed the 1932 smash hit *Shanghai Express* starring Marlene Dietrich, recorded his rollicking visit to Shang-hai in his autobiography, *Fun in a Chinese Laundry*. Of one of Shanghai's notori-ous pleasure palaces, he wrote: "The establishment had six floors to provide distraction for the milling crowd, six floors that seethed with life and all the com-motion and noise that go with it studded with every variety of entertainment Chinese ingenuity had contrived. On the first floor were gambling tables, sing-song girls, magicians, pick-pockets, slot machines, fireworks, bird cages, fans, stick incense, acrobats and ginger. One flight up were . . . crickets in cages, pimps, mid-wives, barbers and earwax extractors. . . . On the top floor and roof of that house of multiple joys a jumble of tight-rope walkers slithered back and forth, and there were seesaws, lottery tickets, and marriage brokers."

Alas, today at Three on the Bund there were no tight-rope walkers to be seen, no earwax extractors. A stone tower with a Beaux-Arts façade built in 1916 and recently renovated by postmodern American architect Michael Graves (whose work I have a strong affection for because he designed the very cool Denver Pub-lic Library near my home), Three on the Bund says money. Its seven floors hold, along with the flagship Armani store and the spa with burbling Evian and hot-stone massages, four of Shanghai's top eateries, including a restaurant owned by French superstar chef Jean-Georges Vongerichten with retro-colonial flourishes such as eel skin sofas, pony leather armchairs, and more velvet than the Elvis paintings in a Mexican tourist town. The velvet, however, is crushed and red, and the food is affordable only for tycoons whose personal wealth equals that of the GDP of Mexico. When the sun goes down, the dining room is lit by skyscrapers, and jet-setting magnates feast on sea scallops with a caper-raisin emulsion while basking in the electric glow given off by the towers of Pudong. Atop the stone apex of Three on the Bund stands the domed dining room of the Cupola. The first floor of the Cupola seats a private party of eight; the highest point, and the highest-priced dining venue in all of China, is a cozy space for two with a 360-degree view.

"*Hěn làngmàn,*" Jennifer said when I mentioned the Cupola. Very romantic. "My ex-boyfriend told me he would take me to the Cupola but he never did. He said we would go when he got rich."

"You broke up with him before he got rich?"

"He will never be rich."

"He's not a good businessman?"

"He's an artist."

"Is he a good artist?"

"It is too hard for artists to get rich."

We skipped the Cupola and found a table at a café called New Heights. The view afforded a broad expanse of Shanghai's new heights, and the prices, too, had reached new heights. Not since I'd been in Italy with a disastrously dropping dollar had I paid so much for a cup of coffee. I had literally eaten breakfast, lunch and dinner in Shanghai for what a cup of coffee cost at New Heights; in rural villages outside the city I had eaten on the same amount for several days. There is something deliciously decadent about indulging in such extravagance while at the same time telling oneself, "This isn't me, I'm just going with the flow here, but really, I would never spend so much for a cup of coffee in a country where one billion of its residents could eat for days on what this cup of java cost, and I mean, really, look at all these obnoxious, oblivious foreigners, these new taipans of Shanghai—the whole thing just makes me sick." One not only gets the sharp jolt of hedonistic delight with that extravagant cup of coffee; one gets the reassuring warmth of smug moralism. Coffee with a big serving of self-righteousness always tastes better, and this cup was delicious as I sipped and gazed out at the new heights of China's grandest metropolis.

As I drank the curiously strong coffee, a rarity in this land of mild tea, Jennifer, picking up the thread of the conversation we'd been having before we got to the café, said, "Sometimes I wish I was interested in men who are successful."

"What kind of men do you like?"

"Rascals."

"Rascals?"

"Bad boys. It would be easier if I wanted a boyfriend who was boring but I want a boyfriend who makes some trouble. So many girls in Shanghai want foreign boyfriends who are rich—not me. I want a Chinese boyfriend who is . . . how do you say it in English?"

"Wild?"

"Wild!" Jennifer clapped her tiny hands. "Yes, wild. I like wild rascals."

"Do women in Shanghai find foreign boyfriends so they can get out of China?"

"Some of them do. Some of them do it to make their parents angry."

"You don't want to find a foreign boyfriend who can get you out of China?"

"I want to go to America but I want to go on my own. I don't want someone to help me. And I don't want to stay. I want to come back to China and make a family here someday."

"Do you think you could have a family with a foreign rascal?"

Jennifer was quiet a moment. "Perhaps it would not be possible."

"But your English is so good—you wouldn't have trouble . . ." I was about to say "communicating," but then I realized what I really meant was "talking." Jennifer's excellent English wasn't the point. She and her foreign rascal would have no trouble talking; communication would be another matter altogether. *Shuōhuà* and *jiāoliú*. There are different words for these things in Chinese, as I'm sure there are in every language. One can learn the words to speak in a foreign tongue; communicating across cultures is entirely different.

"Aren't you a romantic?" I asked. "Don't you believe that if two people are in love, then their different cultures, their different backgrounds—none of that matters?"

"No," said Jennifer. "I don't believe that. Those things matter a lot. I think it is better to love someone who is from your own culture."

"And that person should own a house?" I asked.

"*Dāngrán le.*" Of course.

There is a saying in Shanghai: A man must first buy a house, then he can get married. Without a house, no woman will marry him. *Méiyǒu fángzi, méiyǒu lǎopo.* No house, no wife. Simple as that.

I studied Jennifer a moment and then laughed. A Chinese woman fascinated with all things from the West, in love with reckless souls, but only if those souls happened to be Chinese and own a house. It was a puzzle, and part of me was determined to explore Jennifer's belief that love should be circumscribed by the boundaries of one's culture and should be dependent upon the object of her affection owning a house. But she was my friend as much as she was my gateway to understanding Shanghai, and sometimes friends don't need to understand each other, they need to stop asking questions and just listen. Jennifer continued to talk about dating and love and marriage, and about her parents, who she suspected liked each other enormously but were not now in love nor had they ever been, and had married, like so many from their generation, more from social pressure than from choice. She talked about all these things, talked more freely with me than she ever had (later she blamed it on the caffeine, which she said she still wasn't used to, and she blamed me for corrupting her with coffee). And I, for once in my life, shut up and stopped asking questions. I put away my notebook and listened. And the hour I spent listening to Jennifer before Marcus showed up to meet us at New Heights was one of the finest of all my time in China because for the first time in my travels I felt that a Chinese person had completely let her guard down and was talking to me without reservation, without hesitation, without whatever it was that always seemed to come between Chinese and foreigners when they talked in the same language but could not communicate. By the time Marcus turned up, I saw Jennifer not as a Chinese person but as a person, and that seemed to me no small thing. The exoticism and lure of the Other was gone; in its place was an honest affection that, for once, was not affected. We didn't have to joke around anymore about her being my little sister. As two people who flirt by teasing each other and feigning love eventually drop the joke because it has become real, so Jennifer and I reached a place in our relationship that day in New Heights café where the joke about her being my little sister was no longer necessary, because now it felt entirely true. To add one more play on words to a list of puns that has grown entirely too long, our relationship reached new heights.

"How's business?" I asked Marcus as soon as he sat down. "Have X-rated emoticons taken off?"

"I have a new idea."

"Let's hear it."

"A website for creatives."

"Creative what?"

"Creatives. You know, people who are creative."

"Like, what, writers?" I said.

"No, important creatives. People who come up with the ideas that change society. The creatives class."

"The creatives class?"

It is common for native Chinese speakers to fumble plurals when speaking English—there are no plurals in Chinese. *Péngyǒu* is friend. *Péngyǒu* is also two friends, or many friends. Unlike in English, plurality in Chinese comes only from context, not from adding anything to words or changing them in any way. This can, of course, cause confusion when one is conversing in Chinese, and it certainly leads to confusion for native Chinese speakers trying to unravel the mysteries of making words plural in English. They often apply *s* to everything: They speak of "reading feedbacks" and "sending mails" and "smoking pots." But I wasn't clear on what was happening here.

"The creatives class," Marcus said. "I just read an article about it."

"In a Chinese English-language newspaper?"

"Yeah. You Americans think Chinese don't get creativity, right? You think all we can do is copy your DVDs or make imitation clothing and electronics. You don't think we have any imagination. But we have a whole new creatives class."

"You certainly have a creative way of describing the class."

His grammar left me stumped until later I googled "creatives" and found that there is a class of people who do indeed call themselves "creatives." Apparently they are everywhere and they are changing the world as we know it. I had no idea.

"So what will your website do?" I asked Marcus. I noticed he was wearing a pair of very chic Gucci glasses with jade-green frames.

"It will give creatives a place to express themselves. They can post their ideas and their—like, their designs and their fashions . . . architecture, software, films . . . music . . . animation . . . anything that is new. Everything fresh in Shanghai will be on the site. And people will be able to post comments, and chat with each other about the ideas in forums and stuff like that."

"Will writers be featured on the site?" I asked. I just couldn't seem to let this one go.

"Maybe blogs, but not books. Books would make the site boring. I want it to be important. Important ideas from people in Shanghai who are changing China and changing the world."

I laughed and nodded and told him the website sounded like a good idea. And it did. I'd given up on the idea of books occupying a central place in globalized culture a long time ago and had resigned myself to the fact that they would most likely in my lifetime become relics as antiquated as the oracle bones of China's past. To be a writer in China once held great honor. To be a writer in China now is to be as relevant to the modern world as a blacksmith.

I saw Marcus fiddle with his mobile phone and a moment later Jennifer looked at hers. Fingers and thumb moving as deftly as those of a surgeon, with one hand she texted; a moment later Marcus was glancing at his handset. Call it caffeine-induced paranoia, but it seemed to me they were texting each other at the table.

"So the site is a way to build a community for . . . ah, creatives?" I asked.

Marcus slipped his cell into a pocket and Jennifer smiled and put hers away. Marcus said, "Its real purpose is to let them show off their ideas so that they have the chance to get contracts with advertising and marketing companies."

"And they'll pay to post their stuff on the site?"

"No, it will be free. I'll make money with Google ads."

"What about creatives who aren't interested in making money in advertising or marketing or whatever—what about creatives who just want to . . . create?"

"Everyone in China wants to make money. Creatives can make the most money of all. It's ideas that make money."

"What about art?" I asked.

"Art can make money too."

"Not the art my boyfriend made," Jennifer said.

"Hey," I said, remembering something from a few weeks before. "Let me ask you about this."

I fished my laptop from my backpack and powered up. Curious to learn more about Rich Gate, I'd found their website, stranger even than I had imagined it would be, and I'd copied and pasted pages from it into a Word doc for later study. Poor translations are commonplace in China, even in Shanghai with all its expats and so many Chinese who speak excellent English, and oddly worded signs add an element of fun to spending time in the city. Signs that warn, "Beware Slippy. The Pathway Can Be Crafty" make me smile when skies opaque with pollution are putting a frown on my face. It will be a dreary day in China indeed when signs in parks exhorting, "When you are getting off with your lover, pay attention to your bag" disappear. A sign in a Shanghai hospital had directed patients to the departments of "Fetal Heart Custody" and "Cunt Examination" until people pointed out the meanings to staff, who finally switched the sign—but not before pictures were snapped by foreigners and posted on the Web. There is a name for the butchered translations: Chinglish—Chinese English. Chinglish is everywhere in Shanghai: on the metro, on restaurant menus, in museums. And on the Internet. This is, word for word, what I found on the Rich Gate website:

The hat of international
New Territory a mark
Revive old customs, modern, hits to
hand over to melt
On the grace, history, the neon is bright
100 years elegance classic, future of
100 yearsdiagram
Here, enjoy all of Shanghai
Intravenous drop inside, extreme
achievement life of luxurious

That was on the front page of the website. As one drilled down into the site, it only got stranger:

> . . . exquisite art pieces are displayed one after another regularly, an air of noble families is unfolding calmly.

I read all this aloud, and then I queried Marcus. My question to him was this: Why, if a company was going to so much trouble to advertise to English speakers, wouldn't it hire a native English speaker to correct the copy and make sure it didn't sound completely nutty. My intent wasn't to make fun of the Chinglish. Lord knows if I ever tried to translate English ad copy into Chinese it would sound just as wacky—and that is exactly why I wouldn't even try. I'd have enough sense to hire a native Chinese speaker to make sure the translation was not loopy gibberish.

"They don't care," Marcus said.

"What do you mean 'they don't care'? They don't care that the website for the most expensive residential real estate in Shanghai is absolutely ridiculous to a native English speaker?"

"They aren't targeting native English speakers to sell to." Marcus paused to adjust his green Gucci glasses. "Most of the apartments will be sold to Chinese. Chinese just need to see that there is an English version of the website to be impressed. English is classy. It doesn't matter what it means. It's just decoration."

I thought of Americans getting tattooed with Chinese characters they didn't really understand because they thought they looked cool; I thought of framed pictures of Chinese writing in the homes of Americans who couldn't read Chinese, but who had been convinced by clever advertising that it made a sophisticated decoration.

"Okay," I said. "But what about Chinese companies in the U.S. marketing to American customers who do the same thing? Why don't they have a native English speaker proofread their copy? Why does a Chinese travel company in the U.S., on its website designed to attract American travelers say, 'For those who know how to appreciate the nature and want a little bit taste of adventure' or 'This activity packed itinerary is perfect for the energy group such as collage students.'"

No response from Marcus. Nothing from Jennifer. I pressed on: "And what about all the advertisements for banks and financial services and stuff you see all over Shanghai that have pictures of foreigners and then terrible Chinglish. If they're targeting foreigners—if they're saying in their ads, look at all these happy smiling foreigners that use our services, then why don't they get a native English speaker to correct the copy? They want foreign business right? When a bank advertises that 'Your money is more safety with us' that doesn't make me feel safe. Why not just have a foreigner proofread the ad before you slap it on a billboard?"

"Slap it?" Jennifer asked.

"Ah, it just means put it there. Look, Americans probably make fun of Chinglish too much—too many stories in the U.S. media basically laugh at Chinglish. How many of the people writing those stories can speak any Chinese, much less make perfect translations? But why don't Chinese businesses just proofread?" I nodded toward Marcus. "I think there's a business opportunity here for us. We could start an agency that eliminates Chinglish in ads and marketing. You could talk with Chinese businesses to find out what their intent is with the ad, then you could translate it, and I could check it to make sure the wording is correct and there isn't anything awkward or bizarre about it."

I sat back in my chair, folded my arms across my chest and smiled. It was by far my best business idea yet.

Marcus did not look pleased. He sipped his coffee and averted his eyes. "Why would I need you to help me?" he said. "I could translate it."

I uncrossed my arms and leaned forward in my chair. We had stumbled onto something interesting here. He was clearly offended by my suggestion that his translation wouldn't be adequate and I would have to come behind him to clean up.

"Marcus, look. If I studied Chinese every day for the next ten years and my Chinese somehow became as good as your English, I still wouldn't trust myself to translate Chinese and publish it in a business context. I'd still rely on a native Chinese speaker to edit my translation and make sure it sounded good to a native speaker. There's nothing wrong with that. There are subtleties of language that you simply cannot know unless you're a native speaker. You will never understand English as well as I do. I'll never understand Chinese as well as you do. Right?"

Wrong, the look he gave me said. His look said: I know your language better than you do because I am Chinese and my brain is infinitely more complex than yours, my brain being a product of a race that created the highest GDP of any economy in the world for nine of the past ten centuries, my brain being the product of a culture that built the greatest empire the planet has ever known, an empire that is poised to reclaim its dominant position at the center of the universe, and your barbaric language will soon take second place in importance to Chinese, and your inferior form of communication will eventually vanish altogether as your clumsy culture is absorbed by the superior civilization of the Middle Kingdom, and my people will do to your language whatever we please because we will soon have the power to do whatever we want, and your children will sit in classrooms in America struggling to learn Chinese so that they can survive in a Chinese world.

Or maybe I was reading a little too much into that look.

Jennifer sipped her coffee in the silence at our table, refusing to weigh in with word or with look, even when I tried to meet her gaze and encourage her to join the debate.

I really found this strange. Marcus knew how much I admired his language skills; I told him damn near every time we talked how amazing his English was and how I wished my Chinese were as good, and how I hoped I could someday slip between languages as easily as he did (and unlike with the first time I met him, I really meant it). But it seemed I had erased all that with my business suggestion—which to me seemed like a completely sensible plan to capitalize on a real need in Shanghai and not the least bit demeaning to anyone.

The more I probed, the more he tightened up; soon it was clear he wasn't going to articulate why my idea made him mad. I stared through his Gucci glasses at the folds of his eyes, tracing the shape of them with my gaze, and he seemed to me all of the sudden very Chinese.

The inscrutable Chinese. This had been a stereotype of the Chinese personality throughout the West's relations with the Middle Kingdom. The Chinese were inscrutable: so staid they were, so reserved, we Westerners could never truly know what they were thinking or feeling or what they believed. The Chinese are so exotic we can never get to know them: they are simply too foreign, this line of reasoning, which in some forms has prevailed to this day, seems to say. This had in the past always struck me as complete claptrap—nonsense manufactured by Westerners in the spell of the Other. But right now, in New Heights café atop Shanghai, I could not have felt more distant from Marcus. I searched my internal lexicon for a term that described him now and could come up with nothing better than "inscrutable." I felt like some bumbling British explorer delivering a pseudo-anthropological assessment of the Chinese people to the queen. "Your Majesty, the Chinese culture is exotic and its people are inscrutable."

More disturbing to me than my miscommunication with Marcus was that the bond I'd felt with Jennifer before Marcus joined us seemed to have suddenly vanished. By not commenting on the impasse Marcus and I had reached, she seemed to me complicit in his . . . inscrutability. I had never felt more foreign in Shanghai. I considered telling Marcus I was sorry if I had offended him and reiterating my admiration for his language skills, but I knew this formality would only further distance us. I had made some progress in terms of understanding Shanghai, delving into its history and diving beneath its glitzy façade, but I was, perhaps, no closer to understanding the people who lived there than I had been the first time I'd arrived in the city and gazed in gaping wonder across the river at the towers of Pudong.

Or maybe I was making too much of this. Didn't I have friends in America who perplexed me? Friends who said and did things that made no sense to me and who, when I said something I took to be benign, fell into bitter silence, suddenly rendering them inscrutable? Maybe Marcus's Chineseness was just an excuse for me to find his thinking unfathomable. Don't most people, whether born in a shikumen in Shanghai or a brownstone in Brooklyn, when we rush forward toward the mystery of who they are, recede further from us, rendering them inscrutable?

Maybe I just needed more coffee—or less. My half-empty cup sat on the table in front of me steadily losing heat. I felt the hollowness of a post-caffeine crash, and as I looked out the windows of the café I saw a very different view of Shanghai from what I'd glimpsed when Jennifer and I had first arrived. I saw Shanghai not as a vibrant blending of humanity, and I saw in the spires of Pudong not the hope of a prosperous future. Rather, the tall buildings now seemed to me Towers of Babel, their intent not to lift the Chinese people up from dismal poverty and into a more comfortable future but to worship the false god of wealth as an end in itself, as the goal instead of the means of improving peoples' lives. I saw each tower as a monument to loneliness rising from the dust of demolished neighborhoods. And I understood that nostalgia for those vanished neighborhoods was no antidote to the barrenness of the lives enclosed in those towers and the difficulty people would have talking with each other as their lives rocketed at warp speed toward a future of frantic communication. East meets West not in harmonious blending but in disastrous babble.

"Let's go look at art," I said.

Marcus glanced up from his coffee cup and met my eyes for the first time in several minutes.

"Yeah, okay," he said. "Let's check out the gallery here." Marcus's eyes suddenly went bright. "Some of the pieces there cost as much as art in galleries in New

York." His intent with this comment might have been inscrutable, but at least he didn't look pissed off at me anymore.

As we walked into the Shanghai Gallery of Art, Jennifer said, "My boyfriend and I used to go here all the time. He hoped his art would be sold here someday."

"Then he could take you to the Cupola and propose there," I said.

"Fèihuà," Jennifer said. Nonsense. Empty talk. She smacked me hard on my arm—a very Western thing to do. Chinese people are about as likely to engage in play hitting as they are to hug each other in public. Not likely. Unless they happen to live in the crossroad of cultures, the nexus of East and West that is Shanghai and are adopting Western ways. I wondered if slapping someone on the arm was something Jennifer had watched foreigners doing in Shanghai; I wondered if it had been something she'd seen on *Friends*—or on *Prison Break*.

Prison Break, in case you haven't been watching, is an improbable escape tale in which the tattooed hero orchestrates his own arrest and imprisonment to help break his brother out of prison. The show enjoyed modest success during its two seasons on American TV, but in China it is a phenomenon—every Chinese person I know in Shanghai is talking about it. I finally broke down and watched an episode to see what all the fuss was about. It was okay, just brainless fun in the same vein as *Lost* or *24*, but nothing special. Why was *Prison Break* watched by every twenty-something in Shanghai and not *Lost* or *24*, or any of the other zillion American TV shows? Some people credit a plot line that is easier to follow than that of *Lost* or *24*, making it more straightforward to translate; some (including Jennifer) credit the hotness of the lead actor, Wentworth Miller. Regardless of why this mediocre American TV drama is popular among Chinese people, what is fascinating is the way in which it has spread throughout China. Banned by the government, and with no publicity, marketing or advertising to boost it, it nevertheless appears each day on hundreds of thousands of computer screens throughout Shanghai. A translation of its second season received nearly ten times the number of views as *Desperate Housewives*, China's long-time Internet favorite, according to Evan Osnos of the *Chicago Tribune*, who reported on the phenomenon in 2007.

The government prohibited *Prison Break* from being shown on TV as part of a broader ban on shows containing crime or violence, under the guise that the programs were harming children's "living environment." This, of course, made people want to watch it all the more. And watch it they did—defying the government in droves and violating copyright infringement laws with abandon as they got episodes of *Prison Break* by downloading them from unauthorized sources or buying illegal DVDs. In Shanghai, bootleg DVDs of *Prison Break* are available on nearly every street corner for pocket change. In addition, people all over Shanghai are watching each episode online within hours of its airing in the West.

According to Osnos, one of the hottest trends in Internet use in China is the mushrooming popularity of underground file-sharing sites that let users download and swap foreign films and TV programs under the radar of censorship and with virtual impunity. *Prison Break* episodes are posted online by China's burgeoning community of "uploaders": young Chinese hipsters who gather, translate, and make available on the Internet media content not found on state-controlled TV—which broadcasts shows with production values so shoddy and writing so awful that *Prison Break*, by comparison, seems a Shakespearean drama.

A few months back, rumors about government censors approving *Prison Break* to air on state-run TV had been fueled by articles in Chinese newspapers. But the state-run Chinese news agency, Xinhua, quashed the rumors, and *Prison Break* remains underground. The Chinese government, always uncomfortable with people following trends not related to its propaganda campaigns and not part of its masterplan, has called for a crackdown on anything that is not part of "grand Chinese culture." This vague phrase used by President Hu Jintao leaves a lot of room for government censors to do their work. Some disaffected Chinese have argued that it is exactly the lack of "grand Chinese culture"—the cultural vacuum that exists in contemporary China—that allows crappy American TV drama to find legions of fans in a city like Shanghai, where Western-style materialism is the guiding principle, and Confucius, or any other traditional Chinese cultural icon, is about as relevant to a contemporary denizen of China's showpiece metropolis as Zeus is to a New Yorker.

Jennifer, like so many young Chinese people, had taken the basic English she'd learned beginning in grade school and had layered it with idioms and slang by obsessively watching American movies and TV shows. She had given me a couple of episodes of *Prison Break* to watch. One gets used to glancing for a few moments at inane American TV shows and predicting the demise of Western civilization; watching *Prison Break* in China left me feeling that the East is doomed as well. *Prison Break*, along with *Friends* and *Desperate Housewives,* had done wonders for Jennifer's English, but I worried that the shows were vacuuming her soul of anything worthwhile and would leave her with a deadened imagination and zombie-like stare.

Many Americans come to China, of course, only to make money. Utter "human rights" to the American MBA students who surge into Shanghai trying to figure out how to get rich in the world's hottest economy and they look at you as though you're speaking Chinese. Some Americans, however, come to China not to make money but to immerse themselves in the exotic lifeways they imagine they'll find in the fabled Orient. Dissatisfied with American mass consumer culture, they journey to the Middle Kingdom in search of something deeper. And when they arrive in Shanghai, they find everyone staring at their laptops watching *Prison Break.*

But not to worry: Jennifer, Marcus and I were now on a quest to stimulate our brains with high culture in the Shanghai Gallery of Art. The exhibit du jour involved installation projects of Gu Dexin, billed as "perhaps the most avant-garde and radical of China's leading contemporary artists." Known for filling rooms with piles of rotting fruit and using a blowtorch to turn plastic into tortured shapes, he is particularly fond of molding sex objects from meat. No sex objects made from meat were on display at the Shanghai Gallery of Art, though I heard a woman mention to a friend that the previous year a Gu Dexin installation had featured frozen pig brains. We had to settle for a pool of bright blue resin, which held, we could see when squinting closely at its surface, countless life-size models of flies, tiny wings asparkle in the glare of the gallery's lights. While I squatted down and peered into a drain wherein floated plastic maggots in red pools of muck, Marcus said to me in a loud whisper that filled the hallowed silence of the space, "Gu Dexin is the best marketing expert ever."

"What's his strategy?" I asked, sniffing the air cautiously for any hint of a decaying carcass.

"He does nothing to market his work."

I rose up from the drain and looked at Marcus. "Nothing?"

"Nothing."

"And that is brilliant why, exactly?"

"He doesn't even explain what his work is supposed to be about. It makes it mysterious. People want mysterious things. They want to own them, to buy them."

"Even if the mysterious things are plastic maggots?"

"He doesn't use any Chinese symbols in his work. Everything he does is completely new. He's a genius of marketing."

I nodded and glanced around the room at a recreated street complete with manhole covers. I suppose the exhibit was some kind of comment on alienation in contemporary society, or an exploration of identity, or a pointed statement about vulgarity and decay in the modern world, or an indictment of the ugliness lurking beneath lofty ideals, or a blatant rejection of standard ideas of art, and I have no doubt that the installation was profound. But I had no interest in looking at it, and neither did Marcus and Jennifer.

"Zǒu ba," said Marcus. Let's go. And we did. Perhaps plastic fruit flies and frozen pig brains can save us from the abyss, but I have my doubts.

When we got outside I noticed that Marcus and Jennifer weren't speaking much to each other and seemed to be making an effort not to meet each other's eyes. "Did you two get in a fight or something?" I said. They both mumbled answers that made no sense, and from the grin Marcus was trying to fight off his face, I guessed the tension between them had nothing to do with a fight but rather involved something they had done, or were about to do, that was not at all like fighting. Well, a little bit like fighting but a lot more fun.

Next to me walked a woman missing one hand. She thrust forward first her stump and then the hand she did have, palm cupped expectantly. I hurried past her, my brain overloaded with the horror show of stumps and tumors and sores I had witnessed in the streets that day, my stash of cash for beggars exhausted, and my compassion exhausted too. One can only register so much of strangers' pain before one simply becomes numb to it all.

We wandered away from the Bund's stone buildings to the riotous promenade across the street, where hawkers wearing shoes with hidden wheels skated next to us and tried to sell us trinkets. Chinese mothers and fathers pushed their children in prams along the waterfront, one child per each pair of doting parents. Men were flying kites on the walkway. I counted thirteen little kites tethered to a single string that bowed in the breeze as tassels of shimmering green rippled and stretched like dragons' wings.

A major renovation of the traficky eleven-lane highway that slices the Bund into two separate parallel strips had just gotten underway. The Bund waterfront was receiving a makeover to the tune of more than seven hundred million U.S. dollars to pretty it up in time for the Expo. An expressway would be routed underground, trees would be planted, and roofs would be covered in grass. Walkways would be bordered by tanks holding tropical fish, waterfalls, and special walls that change color in the wind. When the world came to the Expo, pedestrians would not have to negotiate honking, reeking traffic jams to get from the buildings of the Bund to the promenade overlooking the riverfront. The world would see, if all went according to government plans, a clean and green Shanghai with some futuristic flourishes. Cleaner and greener than it is now, anyway. Perhaps that's not saying much. A cynic might even claim that's like saying the temperature in Hell will be turned down two degrees. But there will be fish tanks and funny walls, so really, who's complaining.

I for one could not complain or even speak as my throat swelled with the effluvia of the city. While Marcus, Jennifer and I jogged between lanes of cars and construction barricades, I coughed and swallowed and fought the urge to spit out whatever it was in Shanghai's air that had just entered my lungs. Others had either not fought this urge or had lost the fight, for all around me the pavement lay spackled with glistening matter as green as alien slime. No tale of China would be complete without a mention of spitting. My god how Chinese people spit. Not just in rural places. Everywhere. Even in Shanghai. And not just outside. Everywhere. Even on the floors of restaurants. The practice certainly isn't as prevalent in Shanghai as it is in, say, Henan or Hunan or Gansu or Jiangsu, or in any of the other zillions of places where the streets are washed in saliva far from the cosmopolitan coastal cities, but even in sophisticated Shanghai there was enough spit flying through the air to make one think twice about walking into the wind; there was enough phlegmy spatter on the sidewalks to make one retch at so much as the thought of walking barefoot in public—the parks held minefields of sputum and snot, and strolling barefoot through the grass was not a pleasant proposition. There is a reason Chinese people take their shoes off inside their homes. They say it's tradition. I say it's spit. But the government had been cracking down on public expectoration. Eager to put China's best face forward for international events such as the Olympics and the Expo, propaganda campaigns had declared spitting forbidden. Tell it to the millions of migrant laborers from the countryside. Tell it to the Shanghainese in lilong who have been spitting for generations. Tell it to the foreigner with god-knows-what hurting his lungs. I took a quick look around to see if anyone was watching, cleared my throat with a resonant rumble, and spat whatever was blocking my airway toward the bare skeleton of a bush that looked not up to the task of taking on the perpetual exhaust fumes and providing a margin of greenery along the roadway. The gummy fluid I'd hawked from my lungs slipped down the dead brown branches of the bush.

Marcus shook his head and said, "You're a *nóngmín*." A peasant.

I laughed and listened to a nearby Chinese man, who seemed to be part of a tour group, engage in some of the most raucous, diaphragm-expanding clearing of a clogged windpipe I had heard in the fair city of Shanghai. It went on so long I resisted the urge to applaud when he finally spat out whatever he had just rattled loose from his lungs. The piece of airborne matter landed with a loud splat on the pavement, where it lay like a green amoeba sizzling in the noon sun.

The most interesting and attractive building in Shanghai is a slaughterhouse. Its original purpose was to serve as a slaughterhouse, anyway—soon it will serve as "one of Shanghai's leading creativity and innovation centers." Where once meat was made, now ideas are born.

Marcus and Jennifer talked about the place and decided they wanted to go.

"I'm in," I said. I'd heard that the building was arrayed like a mandala with a square exterior and circles moving inward toward a central axis. A slaughterhouse with stunning symmetry. Perhaps we'd find peace at the center.

"*I'm in*—what does that mean?" Jennifer said.

"It means he's going with us," said Marcus.

And off to the former slaughterhouse now home to hip culture we went, shouldering our way through mobs of tourists and weaving across a street clogged with cars and people, where two prostitutes in jeans tight as tourniquets appeared and flanked me, telling me I was handsome as we walked. I told them my wife agreed as I pointed at Jennifer, and they merged back into the mob.

Known as "1933 Old Millfun," or simply "1933," the building we were heading toward had been designed by British architects and constructed in 1933 by a Chinese development company in the Hongkou District just north of the Bund, beyond where the Huangpu River and Suzhou Creek converge in a medley of muddy currents. The slaughterhouse had been sited in an area thriving with art, politics and literature. In the early 1900s, Hongkou was a meeting point for cultures from around the world and home to many Chinese intellectuals, including Lu Xun, widely considered the father of modern Chinese literature.

When Lu Xun was living in Shanghai, Hongkou was crammed full of shikumen, and from behind their stone-framed doors came a fresh wave of creativity in Chinese letters. Inside many shikumen was a room located at the turn of the staircase between the first and second floors. The tiny, low-ceilinged room, known as a *tíngzijiān*, or a "pavilion room," generally faced north, making it chilly

in winter and sweltering in summer. Tingzijian often served as storerooms or ser-
vants' quarters; shikumen owners sometimes rented them out to earn extra income. In the 1920s and 30s, progressive artists and scholars who came to Shanghai
seeking cheap accommodations settled in these spartan spaces where they could
work in solitude and silence within the little rooms tucked above the kitchens and
beneath the balconies of shikumen. Sweating through summers and bundled up
in winter, they penned stories, many of which reflected life in Shanghai's lane
neighborhoods. Their works became known as "Tingzijian Literature" for the
rooms in which they were born, and Lu Xun is the most famous author associated
with the movement. He railed against traditional Confucian values—ancestor
worship, resistance to change, submission to authority, idealization of the past at
the expense of focusing on the future—which he saw as keeping the Chinese national character backwards and weak in the modernizing world. In one of his most
famous short stories, "Diary of a Madman," the protagonist, horrified at what he
perceives as the brutally repressive nature of Chinese culture that causes the strong
to cannibalize the weak, becomes convinced that the entire history of Chinese
civilization can be summed up in two words: "eat people." He gradually goes mad
believing everyone around him, including his family, is out to devour his flesh.

We wandered through neighborhoods collapsing with decay and filled with
children at play. Amid wooden beams shoring up walls, workmen raised bamboo
scaffolding and clashed and clanged their tools. Dampness hung so thick in the
sky the streets around us seemed to sweat. A fetid stench was in the air.

As Shanghai's fortunes declined in the latter decades of the twentieth century,
Hongkou deteriorated and many of its shikumen neighborhoods became part of
the district's slummy blight. The 1933 building was turned into a medicine factory, and then it was abandoned and fell into disrepair. Resurrected from the architectural graveyard and restored to its former grandeur, its Art Deco façade
now displays elegant geometric motifs, and the interior of the building is a
labyrinthine funhouse of sculpted concrete ramps, flaring columns, and walkways
in spirals and flyovers—all leading to the piece de résistance at the center of the
building: a theatre-in-the-round with capacious rooftop terraces and a massive
glass stage at its center. The abattoir in the heart of a once-vibrant Shanghai cultural center has now been repurposed into a crucible of invention and design
housing creative industry offices, artists' guilds and galleries.

But before we reached the trendy slaughterhouse, in order to escape the afternoon's searing heat, we ducked into a bookstore that offered everything from

Bibles to porn mags. Looking for a book by Lu Xun seemed a good idea, but none was in sight, and a quick survey of the bookshelves revealed the usual suspects: treatises by China's Communist Party politicians and biographies of American business titans. Business success books provide Chinese people who know nothing more than their jobs at Communist-controlled state-owned enterprises a blueprint for business success. In the past few years, aspiring Chinese entrepreneurs have, along with biographies of Andrew Carnegie and Bill Gates, devoured books with titles such as *The Legend of Jewish Wealth* and *Jewish Entrepreneurial Experience and Business Wisdom*.

As Marcus plucked a copy of *Jewish Entrepreneurial Experience and Business Wisdom* from a display island in the center of the store, he told me he wanted to read it. A lifetime of political correctness training told me not to laugh and to take this matter seriously. I could not stop from laughing. Of course broad generalizations about races, cultures and religions, however benign or even complimentary their intent, are unacceptable. But tell this to an aspiring entrepreneur in Shanghai.

"Have you ever met a Jewish person?" I asked Marcus.

"A lot of them."

"In Shanghai?"

"At Stanford. My roommate was Jewish. His family was rich. Really rich."

"I have a Jewish friend who is extremely poor," I said, fighting back a laugh and making a serious face. I wasn't sure what I was trying to achieve here. A part of me just wanted to have fun with this phenomenon, one that was perhaps no weirder than any other in this strange city; a part of me felt the urge to preach. These competing urges resulted in noises that came from my mouth sounding a little like laughter, a little like serious throat clearing, and a lot like choking.

"Do you really think there is some secret Jewish wisdom that you can learn from a book that will help you get rich?" I finally asked Marcus, who was staring at me with a look that seemed to waver between amazement and concern.

"We work so much we feel crazy," he said. "Today I have a day off because I worked the last two weekends. It's so hard to get ahead in Shanghai. Do you understand how much pressure people who live here are under?"

I did. In most countries the leading cause of death among young people is road traffic crashes. In China, it's suicide.

"It's hard just to survive," added Jennifer. "There are so many people, so much competition."

"*Rén chī rén,*" Marcus said. Man eat man. Instead of "dog eat dog," the Chinese say "man eat man."

"Like in Lu Xun's story," I said.

"You know about Lu Xun?"

"I've read 'Diary of a Madman.' You've read it?"

"Of course," Marcus said. "Everyone has to read Lu Xun in school. But I don't think you can understand Lu Xun's meaning. It is not possible for you to understand."

Marcus wasn't the first person in China to tell me this. Lu Xun advocated the use of *báihuà* ("plain speech" or "vernacular Chinese") in modern literature, and he employed in his writing an everyday form of language modeled after spoken Chinese and decidedly different from the Classical Chinese in use from the time of Confucius. His mastery of vernacular Chinese, I've been assured by many Chinese friends, makes translating his works in a way that preserves their original meaning virtually impossible.

It is interesting to note that while the Communists lionized Lu Xun because of what they saw as left-leaning sympathies in his writing, his works focus on individuals in a way that seems markedly Western and at odds with the collectivist mentality of Communism. Lu Xun, well read in Western literature, used what many have called an ironic tone in his essays and stories. That the word *irony* does not exist in Chinese did not stop him from twisting and turning language to attack the total sincerity that was at the heart of Confucian virtues. Regarding Lu Xun's ironic writing style, Mao noted, "[In a Communist society] we can shout at the top of our voices and have no need for veiled and roundabout expressions, which are hard for the people to understand." And then Mao and his cronies built memorials to Lu Xun and dictated that schools teach children about the importance of his ideas.

"Maybe I'll never understand Lu Xun," I said. "And you'll never understand *The Onion.*"

"I don't know why *The Onion* is funny," Marcus said. "I tried studying it to find out why it is funny, but to me it just seems stupid. But I used to carry a copy around with me on campus because all the Americans at Stanford thought it was so funny and so cool. I used to act like I was reading it and laughing at it so I wouldn't lose face."

Marcus laughed at this memory and then flipped open the cover of *Jewish Entrepreneurial Experience and Business Wisdom.* "If there's a chance this will work,

I'll try it," he said as he fanned the pages. He looked up from the book and stared at me a moment while I frowned. I was fighting the urge to scold him for stereotyping. "It's not just about business, either," he said before I could lecture him. "Chinese people are a lot like Jews."

He paused a moment, and had I been sitting down on a seat, I would have been on the very edge of it.

"How?" I said, having absolutely no idea what would come next but fully prepared to stifle my laughter.

"We both have long histories and cultures that are thousands of years old, and we both are good at business. We both move all over the world, but wherever we end up living, we keep our own . . . identities—that's the word. And Jews and Chinese both value family. And education—we both value education. And hard work."

Somebody call the Anti-Defamation League and let them sort it out. The books made me cringe, but Marcus's motives seemed harmless enough. And there was something delightfully fresh about throwing the political correctness playbook out the window and starting from scratch in a city yet to be patrolled by the PC police.

Shanghai was once home to tens of thousands of Jews, who ranged from Sephardic families from Baghdad such as the Sassoons and Kadoories, who made fortunes selling opium and real estate and left their mark upon Shanghai in the form of some of the city's most distinctive colonial buildings of palatial design, to desperate refugees fleeing the Russian pogroms and Nazism. During the Holocaust, Jewish refugees found a safe haven in the city when Shanghai was the only place in the world that did not require a visa. Jews who'd been refused entry into other countries made their way to Shanghai. In this "port of last resort," as it came to be known, more than twenty thousand Jewish refugees escaped the death camps of Europe. They created a thriving community dubbed "Little Vienna" that boasted German bakeries and Austrian coffee houses, symphony performances and theatrical productions, kosher butchers, synagogues, and Yiddish newspapers. The Japanese, after occupying Shanghai, interned most of the city's Jews in a ghetto in the Hongkou District, but Shanghai's Jews weren't persecuted as Jews in Europe were. Though the Hongkou ghetto was crowded and plagued by poverty and disease, most Jewish refugees in Shanghai survived the ordeal and their culture thrived. Following the Communists' takeover of China in 1949, however, Shanghai's Jews fled the country in a mass exodus to Israel and America.

In 2005, the Shanghai city government set aside a chunk of land in the Hongkou District as a historic area combining Jewish and Chinese culture. It has been scheduled to be redeveloped, and members of the international Jewish community are working with Chinese officials to preserve the area's cultural heritage. The development plan sounds a lot like the one that created Xintiandi: it calls for trendy dining venues, high-end retail shops, and historically accurate architecture—and the plan involves relocating thousands of Shanghai's families away from the path of progress.

Months after I held a copy of *Jewish Entrepreneurial Experience and Business Wisdom* in my hands in the Shanghai bookstore, I learned, while researching the Jewish business book craze in China, that publishing industry analysts estimate that at least half of the books are fakes: they aren't written by Jews, or by experts on Jewish culture, or even by experts on business—they are written by Chinese shysters with no legitimate credentials trying to cash in on a trend and make a buck.

After we left the cool refuge of the bookstore and headed back into the blasting heat outside, I glimpsed the Oriental Pearl TV Tower rearing strangely in the distance, its sticks-and-spheres shape like that of a chemical model of molecular structure in a laboratory cluttered with beakers and Bunsen burners. I recalibrated my attention on the historic slaughterhouse we were approaching. I was curious to see whether 1933's purported aim of fostering creativity would be trumped by commerce—rumors of stores squeezing out artists abounded, and word on the street was that the stylish slaughterhouse was about to make a lot of people with government connections very rich from a retail bonanza that included some of the world's biggest brands. But when suddenly faced with the panicky excitement of forcing our way through the crush of a mob, I had one of those moments you sometimes have in Shanghai when the urgency in the streets is so intense your heart could not beat any faster and you feel yourself being elevated to another plane, as if an adrenaline IV drip has been slipped into your vein.

Though I was living here and doing business in the middle of this maelstrom, I was still not completely a part of it. I was enjoying the constant frisson caused by the pressure that pervaded life in Shanghai, was mesmerized by the madness in the streets; but I was watching it all unfold at a bit of a distance—a distance caused by virtue of my ability at any time, for any reason, to pick up and leave, to go back home and hide in the Rockies and never return to this lunatic asylum of a city. But what of these people trapped amid the urgency, speeding through the streets in a desperate man-eat-man race for survival? I was thrilled to be among them, grateful not to be one of them.

When we finally arrived at 1933 and began exploring the building, I craned my neck in all directions to take in the sights, trying to catch a buzz from the creative vibe of the space. I thought this: Shanghai is anything you want it to be. It is a place of heady creative energy; it is a mecca for moneymakers that makes Wall Street look like an Amish town; it is a monument to technology that makes Tokyo seem a land of Luddites; it is a city where anything goes and everything happens at every hour of the day and night and the only rule is that you must move forward as quickly as you can and never linger in the present nor glance toward the past—unless doing so can make you money for your future. If there is a refurbished slaughterhouse full of Chinese hipsters, you check out the scene and then move with supersonic speed on to the next event. But really, after you've been to a slaughterhouse with chic boutiques, what's left? At some point a city must run out of surprises.

"So, what do you think?" Marcus asked me after we stopped to talk with one of his friends who was renting an office in the building and working with Marcus on his website for creatives.

I looked around at the tight corridors and cavernous spaces. The hidden nooks behind folds of concrete. The convoluted corners, the flaring overhangs. Mad spirals and zigzags of concrete ramps ran up and down the walls not unlike those of an M. C. Escher lithograph that shows stairs rising steeply floor by floor—and your eyes follow them upward to the top, and then you are, impossibly, back at the bottom where you started.

"It's very Shanghai," I said.

"It makes me want to play hide and seek," Jennifer said.

We all spent the next few minutes discussing Chinese hide-and-seek and American hide-and-seek and agreeing that they were basically one and the same, and then we hid, and we covered our eyes and counted, and we sought. We took turns hiding and seeking and we laughed until our bellies cramped. I'm no authority on architecture, but I will with confidence say this: 1933 is a world-class hide-and-seek venue. At 1933, as with all great hide-and-seek sites (old mansions, graveyards, abandoned factories), there is an element of creepiness. The ramps we ran along had no steps. Of course they didn't: How would cows have climbed steps as they were herded toward the killing floor? Smooth cement surfaces had once facilitated the washing away of blood. The real estate agents renting spaces in 1933 made no mention of the building's original purpose, other than occasionally using the word *abattoir,* which sounds French and cool—maybe a place where art is made, not meat.

So, what to make of the balance between art and commerce at 1933? That had been my main point of inquiry that had led me to this place, but as with so many other times in Shanghai, I got caught up in the furious energy, got lost in all the excitement. This happened while I was literally lost inside the madhouse matrix of the building. Roaming twisty corridors, I wandered from the outer square structure of the building toward its crazy circular center. I found myself at one point looking upward at a round window separated into a hodgepodge of panels. This looked exactly like the window on the pilot's deck of the Millennium Falcon. I swear I had done no drugs, and I promise you this was an exact facsimile of the cockpit from Han Solo's spaceship. Bright bursts of light filtering through the glass shined like distant galaxies viewed through the portal of a spaceship hurtling at warp speed into the infinite mystery of the cosmos. Or maybe I was just dizzy from running around all the circular pathways that corkscrewed upward.

I had read on the 1933 website that "1933 seeks to define true wealth: a holistic approach to life that is rounded and balanced and not simply material." I had vowed to suss out this claim, to see if it was just some government propaganda or savvy marketing nonsense aimed toward people who thought of themselves as too sophisticated to shop at the Xintiandi shikumen-themed mall but who would happily spend money at a "creative lifestyle center" in a slaughterhouse. But all that was moot, for the trippy opening in the roof above me had captured my full attention. It is not easy, as one is staring out the portal of the Millennium Falcon while the renegade ship tumbles through the galaxy, to ask important questions, much less to try to answer them. I just stood there. And to my compete embarrassment I am forced to admit that for several minutes the only thought in my head was this: "Wow. That is totally cool."

The stage at the center of the building was supposed to be closed off for renovation, but Marcus and I talked our way in. I can't remember what we said but it worked, and Jennifer came with us, giggling and telling us we were idiots as the guard waved us through. Our subterfuge was worth the effort because atop a round platform made of glass so thick it can—and has, I've been told—support the weight of a car, we stood and revolved together as a group in a slowly turning circle, looking between our feet through the glass slab at an open space that dropped down a few hundred feet, then gazing out beyond the stage at balcony tiers that appeared to float unmoored from any flooring in an area so boundless and surreal it seemed the setting for some imperial council in a future world based in space. I did what anyone would do in such a place: I sang a Chinese children's song about two tigers, one tiger without a tail and one missing an ear, set to the melody of "Frère Jacques." A butchered rendition of China's beloved "Liǎng zhī Lǎohǔ" bellowed across the center stage of 1933 Old Millfun and disappeared in the dark and empty places beyond. Another round of hide-and-seek ensued, beginning between the pillars and passageways around the stage, then turning into a game of tag that spilled out from the circular auditorium and onto the floors of the building's labyrinthine corridors and zigzagging ramps.

I forgot to ask the right questions and had entirely too much fun. Instead of interviewing Shanghai's creatives to find out what they made of 1933, I ended up playing endless rounds of hide-and-seek with my Chinese friends. A building that is part M. C. Escher and part *Star Wars* must be approached in a spirit of playful fun. I might not be a good journalist, but I'm damn good at playing hide-and-seek in a hallucinogenic slaughterhouse.

The building is beautiful in a fantastic, futuristic, fantasy-world way. It seems less an actual working building and more the rendering of a madman's dream. Why a British architectural firm would go to such lengths to add elegant Art Deco motifs to a slaughterhouse's façade and to create what is one of the coolest interior layouts of any structure ever conceived, is beyond me. And I have to hand it to whoever had thought, "Hey, let's take this dilapidated slaughterhouse and turn it into a haven for creative people." A bold leap, to be sure, and surely it had met with massive skepticism. Though the idea was not entirely without precedent. Manhattan's Meatpacking District morphed from a run-down slaughterhouse complex to a notorious bohemian haunt and finally to home of high-end boutiques. And making new creative spaces out of old buildings has recently been happening all over China.

Dashanzi Art District, better known as Factory 798, is a former military equipment manufacturing complex built in the Bauhaus style by East Germans in the 1950s outside of Beijing. The very cool vacant spaces with soaring arched ceilings awash with natural light were colonized by artists who needed a cheap place to set up shop away from the city center; soon 798 was earning international acclaim for the edgy art produced in its studios. Before long Sony was using the venue for a product launch and Omega was sponsoring a fashion show, and 798 now boasts a thriving retail and entertainment industry that caters to the tourists who

Its interior a funhouse of winding staircases and soaring ramps, 1933 served as one of the largest slaughterhouses in the world before falling into disuse. It was recently retrofitted with creative industry offices and high-end retail and entertainment establishments.

swarm there to sample Chinese avant-garde culture. Nothing new here: the avant-garde move into the Greenwich Villages and the SoHos of the world and set up their spaces in dirt-cheap places; the places become popular; real estate prices soar; soon yuppies are parking their Beemers in front of boutiques and Starbucks is selling lattes to tourists looking for a taste of bohemia.

1933 already offered, mixed with a few offices of creative industries and a smattering of workspaces for designers, a wine bar. Giant signs announced that Apple and American Apparel stores were coming soon. A chef from Three on the Bund was about to open a steakhouse. Shanghai's creatives could feast on slabs of fifty-dollar-a-plate prime rib while brainstorming ideas that would energize the culture and keep society vital. Either that or they could discuss how to make a boatload of money by selling "creativity" as a lifestyle.

Later, when the altered state of consciousness induced by 1933 Old Millfun wore off and I sobered up and settled down to the business at hand of researching

Shanghai, I began by looking at the uber-cool 1933 website, which makes this claim: "1933 will redefine what it means to be a 'person in full' by having all the elements to inspire in one location. Within its walls one can find all the pieces needed to be inspired and to become a fuller and more complete person." Empty and inane, certainly, but this was no Rich Gate Chinglish: The investors clearly had used a native English speaker to write the copy. The site plays up lifestyle centers, self-improvement classes and such—no mention is made of 1933 having been, back in the day, one of the three largest slaughterhouses in the world. Cows went in, packages of beef came out; now creative people go in and money comes out. This radical repurposing of the space is the result either of bold artistic vision or of shrewd planning that copies a financially successful model from the West— or like so many things in Shanghai, perhaps it is a messy mix of both.

What makes a place like 1933 different from other artist-community-turned-tourist-attractions is that it is all part of a plan. What happened incrementally at Greenwich Village and Dashanzi Art District—bohemian areas being commod-ified and creativity giving way to commerce—is often orchestrated in Shanghai by government planning. People in Shanghai don't clamor for a Starbucks next to the galleries; government planners put one there because it will line their pock-ets. Chinese Communists look at Manhattan's Meatpacking District and see bloated profits in designer boutiques; then they look at the derelict Art Deco slaughterhouse in their district and see dollar signs. Culture in Shanghai and else-where in China is often not something that sprouts organically; its seeds are planted by the Communist Party and its growth is nurtured according to a plan— the purpose of which is always to *zhuàn qián,* to make money.

As the Chinese invented so many things that the West found useful and per-fected, so the West invented capitalism but the Chinese could very well be per-fecting it, taking it to new levels as they forge ahead with their "socialism with Chinese characteristics," as they call whatever it is that they are doing. One of these "Chinese characteristics" seems to be a relentless determination to make money—okay, maybe we didn't invent that after all. Capitalism seems new in China given the Communist ideology that swept the country in the middle of the twentieth century, but competitive markets and making money are nothing new. *Gōngxǐ fācái* is a traditional Chinese saying that means, basically, "I hope you get rich." The Chinese were saying this to each other as a Happy New Year greeting before Adam Smith was born. To get rich was glorious in China long be-fore Deng Xiaoping proclaimed it was so in 1978, loosening up the strict govern-ment controls of the command economy that had strangled growth for a few decades—a paltry span in the vast timeline of Chinese culture. Perhaps the Chinese government didn't import the idea of capitalism from the West; rather, it simply set its people free to do what they had always done. The thriving economies of Singapore, Kuala Lumpur, Taiwan and Chinatowns throughout the world: these are all driven by the entrepreneurial spirit of diaspora Chinese, and that spirit is being unleashed right now in China in one of the swiftest economic expansions in history, one of the most frenetic periods of development the world has ever known.

But can a country that manages creative enterprises according to government planning truly free the full potential of its people? Is it just me, or is the Communist Party's hand guiding the repurposing of a slaughterhouse into creative spaces, designed to generate massive amounts of cash, as creepy as the killing floor of an abattoir?

So intertwined are creativity, commerce and government planning in Shanghai, seventy-five "creative industry compounds" similar to 1933 already exist, with many more under construction—all of them deemed to have potential economic benefits to Shanghai and planned by a special agency licensed by the Economic Commission of Shanghai Municipal Government and something ominously named Shanghai Municipal Administration of Social Organizations. The agency in charge of promoting creative industry in Shanghai, the Shanghai Creative Industry Center, has, according to its official website, this vision: "Creative industrialization Industry creativelize."

Allow me to translate. The Communist Party in Shanghai envisions a China of young, vibrant, independent-minded thinkers generating fresh ideas that won't turn society upside down, but will lead to businesses with missions more sophisticated than churning out knockoff consumer products or stealing the intellectual property of the West and mass producing it. China is not content to serve forever as the world's factory. Born of economic foresight or of cultural pride, or a combination of both, China's conviction that cheap labor alone cannot sustain its superheated rate of growth is causing some seismic shifts in the intellectual landscape. The Communist Party is pushing innovation in science and technology in the nation's schools, universities and government-sponsored think tanks, but Shanghai's leaders, aside from implementing state-driven initiatives aimed at fostering technological creativity, are encouraging pioneering efforts by individuals in areas such as fashion and design. To this end, the government has of late been aggressively preserving old factories and warehouses with historic merit and turning the abandoned buildings into creative industry compounds that are now home to—according to the Shanghai Municipal Government—more than three thousand five hundred creative industry companies from more than thirty countries with more than twenty-seven thousand art workers in the fields of design (industrial, interior, construction, clothing and makeup), advertising, game software, Internet media, fashion, and brand promotion. Art workers in brand promotion and makeup? That seems to be stretching the word *art* a bit far, but there's no denying that Shanghai is making a strong case for discarding the stereotype of Chinese people as automatons lacking creativity and able only to ape the ideas of developed nations.

All is not right in the Middle Kingdom, however. The problem, of course, is this: parents cannot force their children to be creative, because true creativity is always an act of rebellion. The day the Chinese people tell the Communist Party to stop abusing them will be their first creative act and the only one that matters—all else is simply clever schemes to sell Prada and Starbucks to the masses. The Chinese can cover their emperor in the flashy new clothes of hyper-capitalism, but their emperor is, in fact, wearing nothing but his birthday suit. The Communist Party controls China, and the Chinese masses kowtow to their naked lord. No matter how rich they become, the Chinese live in a nation run by thugs, a country in which freedom is the ability to make money, nothing more.

There are some things the Communist Party cannot copy. And there are many things it cannot stop, and the Chinese people's creativity, will, perhaps in time, be one of them. Perhaps in the funhouse corridors of Shanghai there are Lu Xuns lurking in the twisty passages next to the Apple store and waiting beneath the winding stairs of American Apparel. Perhaps there are people in Shanghai so radically inventive they can help us all find our way through the slaughterhouse maze into which we have wandered.

The 2007 Shanghai Creative Industry Week, which was held in 1933 Old Millfun, had boasted creatives from more than thirty countries, as well as homegrown Chinese creatives. And the Chinese media, which covered the event extensively, seemed quite pleased that Chinese people with ideas just as innovative as those of foreigners were represented. All of this is leading up to the 2010 Expo, in which Shanghai will showcase China's creativity to the world. As the 2008 Olympics was a coming-out party for the new and improved, kinder and gentler Communist Party that has put Tiananmen behind it, so China sees the Expo as its chance to show the world what it's thinking.

So what was it thinking at the 2007 Shanghai Creative Industry Week? One artist who hails from Shanghai displayed cartoons with dialogue balloons bereft of dialogue. The dialogue balloons were completely empty. The characters in the cartoon stories talked and talked but said nothing.

The Fastest Train on Earth

The next time that Jennifer and I went to her parents' neighborhood there wasn't much of a neighborhood left. The first thing I noticed was that the sentry at the stone gateway of the lane was missing. Then I saw piles of wood and tile inside the alley, materials stacked for salvage. Hot wind hissed across broken walls and lifted plumes of dust. The site was bordered by sheets of blue tin sheeting ten feet tall. These blue barriers that surround demolition and construction zones can be found throughout the city, sometimes, it seems, on every street. We peeled back a loose piece of the metal and peered inside. A few of the neighborhood's shikumen had been only partially demolished—just enough to make them uninhabitable in case anyone tried to move back in. When every family in the neighborhood was finally gone, Jennifer explained, then what remained of the homes would be smashed and cleared away. Beyond the construction site, where once there had been a series of little lanes lined with homes and shops, now a sprawling street cut a wide swath of emptiness through the neighborhood. At the edges of this boulevard new buildings soon would rise, each one a formidable statement of economic progress, each one as approachable as a castle keep. Gone were the street songs of hawkers selling snacks, replaced by the rumble of cars.

"Old Xu got moved," Jennifer said.

"Got moved?" I said.

"He lives by the airport now."

"Pudong?"

She nodded and then blew air from her mouth. "It's so far away."

"So nobody guards the lane now?" By the looks of things, soon there wouldn't be much left to guard. Instead of a few blank spaces scattered among the shikumen, now there were vast open places where long stretches of homes had been flattened. Rows of houses, instead of showing the gaps of a few missing teeth, were now dental disasters with only a couple of teeth left.

"Did Old Wang get moved too?" I asked Jennifer as we approached her parents' house.

Dust the color of bone covered my shoes. You could see past the alley now, beyond the wrecked walls. You could see too much and it made you feel exposed. Vulnerable. All around the last of the shikumen the city continued its quest for height, cranes raising colossal towers upward toward the clouds. The street vendors with their pushcarts of tasty treats were gone, and gone too were the peddlers with bamboo carrying poles slung across their shoulders bearing baskets weighted down with food. Gone were the men who had sat in the alley repairing bicycles and mending shoes. No one was selling socks or tea in what was left of the lanes. The laundry was empty. The tailor shop was abandoned, one of the two planks that formed its door hinging open and blowing shut in the breeze. The butcher was gone, the fishmonger. The dentist with his display of gleaming tools had fled. One shop was still open for business, a beauty salon wherein beauties with straining blouses and slender legs paced past the window. The first profession and the last.

Children scampered among the last scraps of the neighborhood, but their ranks had thinned. The ones who remained now had new spaces to explore in the piles of shattered stone, this the stuff of dreams for little boys in search of forts. I watched a group of kids, skin white with demolition dust, burrow their way into a mound of rubble and find peepholes through which they could watch their enemies. A rival gang surrounded the hideout and pelted it with chunks of plaster as crumbly as chalk. The soft missiles exploded against the brick fort, sending white smoke into the air above their battlefield. Two women bent with age sat in the lane playing mahjong, the tiles clicking in a rhythm that seemed some sort of music, a measured beat.

"Old Wang is gone," Jennifer said.

"Have you talked to her since she moved?"

"I don't know where she lives now."

This wreckage is from a shikumen marked by government officials with 拆 (*chāi*), the Chinese character that means "to tear down." The surrounding buildings also bear 拆, and they too will soon be rubble.

We walked past the little boys playing games of war. "You won't stay in touch with her?" I asked.

"She doesn't use email or MSN."

"Does she have a cell phone?"

"Probably she does. But she doesn't know how to text."

A man in a sleeveless shirt lifted a sledgehammer and brought it clanging down upon a pipe. I felt the concussion climb my legs and travel the length of my spine. The worker hoisted the broken pipe and tossed it behind him. It landed clanking in a cart heaped with other scraps of metal. Two more workmen shuffled like crabs, the weight of the air conditioning unit they were carrying twisting their faces into random shapes of pain.

"You'll call her?" I asked. "You'll stay in touch with Old Wang?"

Jennifer was silent a moment. "I don't know what we'd talk about. I can't think of what I'd say to her. I think she's gone forever."

We walked through the stone-framed door of the shikumen and onward toward a courtyard that rang with the silence of recent absence. Other families had already left the apartments surrounding the courtyard.

"The developers told my parents that if they don't accept the offer they will take the roof off their house."

"What do you mean 'take the roof off their house'?"

"That is how they make people leave. They break the roof apart with big hammers and then it is too hard to live in the house because it is raining inside and the people have to leave."

In the Confucian universe, the home was the basic unit of harmony. Each Chinese courtyard home had been designed to provide a quiet, guarded space to accommodate several generations of a family. Thick walls had been built along alleyways to shelter the shikumen dwellers within from the tumult without; the walls and the closely watched-over maze of alleys beyond had shielded families from rebels and thugs roaming the city. Chaos had found its way into the safe courtyards when families were forced to subdivide their shikumen to make money and, later, to appease the Communists, but several generations of families had often managed to remain together in the subdivided shikumen even as their world tilted toward dramatic change. As I sat eating lunch with Jennifer's parents in their tiny home, I learned that one of the women I had seen there each time I'd visited was Jennifer's mother's mother. She nodded to me now when Jennifer spoke of her. Her face was empty of expression. She rocked back and forth in a chair that did not move.

"Does she want to eat with us?" I asked Jennifer.

Jennifer spoke to her in Shanghainese and then told me her grandmother wasn't hungry.

Delicious frying smells filled the apartment. Garlic stung my eyes and ginger tingled my nose. I reached my chopsticks into a pile of cubed and stir-fried chicken, pinched a chunk and popped the hot morsel in my mouth. Temperature hot—not spicy hot. I reached for my water glass and drank, forgetting it was hot water. Even on the hottest days, cool water is not served with Chinese meals. The temperature in the apartment, even with the little air conditioner chugging, must have been in the nineties, and the muggy air clogged my lungs and clung to my skin in sheets of heavy wetness. Beads of sweat rolled down my forehead and dripped from my nose as I took a drink of steaming water. The shikumen of Jennifer's parents had been designed around Chinese notions of geomancy, or feng shui (literally "wind water"). It had been built to face south in order to gather *yáng* (positive energy), which was thought to come from the south, and to block *yīn* (negative energy), believed to emanate from the north. Chinese homes had been arranged this way throughout the ages, and her parents' belief in maintaining the balance of the body with the yin and yang of things that entered it informed what was served at their table. Cold water was traditionally never offered with hot dishes in China, because to mix cold liquid in one's body with hot food was to upset the balance of internal temperatures and invite disease. Even my most Westernized Chinese friends clung to the traditional Chinese medicine belief that mixing hot and cool substances in the body causes sickness. Marcus drank warm cola or tepid beer when he ate Chinese dishes on hot days.

I was dying for a glass of cool, refreshing water on this sweltery day while we dined on steamy food. I loved meals in China and participated fully in every feast. I ate chicken feet when they were put in front of me, claws scratching at my cheeks as I gnawed meat from the little knobs of toe knuckles. I swallowed cubes of coagulated duck blood and smiled at the host who'd served them. I was fine with crunching on fried scorpions, and I hadn't shied away from silkworm larvae seared to crispy goodness in a pan. I used chopsticks as though I'd been born with them in my hands. I slurped my soup. But I could not get used to drinking hot water on a hot day. It seemed . . . well . . . just plain wrong. And Jennifer thought drinking iced beverages with a meal was kin to madness. On days that were equal parts scorching and sticky, with heat indexes that made Bikram yoga classes seem arctic by comparison, Jennifer would say, "You'll get sick" whenever I ordered a chilled beverage with my food.

Jennifer's mom spread sheets of newspaper on the table for discarded bones. Then she pushed a platter my way, angling it so that I could take the sweetest, fattest chunks of red-braised pork. I scooped them into my rice bowl and then popped one in my mouth, chewing it thoroughly to extract every bit of goodness before I spit the bone onto the newspaper-covered table.

"Eat more," Jennifer's mother said. "You look too thin."

I raised my rice bowl and angled my head toward its rim as I closed my chopsticks on slippery beans and chunks of winter melon. Jennifer's mother studied me while I ate, making sure, I was certain, that I really was enjoying the food and not pretending. I helped myself to a platter piled high with pieces of fried pumpkin, and then I ate more pork between bites of rice, watching Jennifer's mom nod her approval. "Eat more, eat more," she said.

I spat out a shard of broken bone and smiled. I told her in Mandarin the food was delicious. She understood, and with flushed cheeks and her head shaking side to side she showed the embarrassed modesty of a Chinese person who has been given a compliment.

I remembered earlier that day when Jennifer, after I'd complimented her English, had said, "I know, it's getting really good. I'm ready to go to America."

"Your English was good enough to use in America when I first met you," I had said. "Now that you've lost your Chinese modesty and are starting to brag, you're definitely ready. You'll fit right in."

It made me sad, watching Jennifer change, watching her adopt Western ways. I had found the modesty of the Chinese to be one of their most charming features, antidote to our chest-thumping overconfidence. And the Chinese people had always seemed to me, on the whole, remarkably gentle. But China was on a mission to change, to develop into an assertive power, and modesty and gentleness do not serve a nation well on the world stage. Nor would they serve Jennifer well if she made it to America.

"They are still not accepting the offer of the developer," Jennifer said of her parents as I raised my rice bowl to my mouth and ate. "Two other families are not accepting either. All the rest have accepted."

Persistence: that was a characteristic of the Chinese people that would benefit them as they struggled to develop their country and claim their place in the world. Another thing I admired about the Chinese was that I found very little evidence of self-pity anywhere in China. People would tell me their tales of woe—poor treatment in the hospital, not earning a high enough mark on the national exam to go to a university, having their home confiscated and demolished—in the most matter-of-fact way. It was as though they'd seen so much, had endured so much, the latest struggle and indignity they faced was miniscule in the grand scheme of things and merited providing the facts and little more. That Jennifer's parents could sit in their home quietly eating as if nothing was happening, while at any moment they might be dragged outside by government goons and their roof would be ripped off and the walls would come crumbling down, was remarkable to me. I admired their stoicism in the face of disaster, their grace under pressure.

Everything I've just said in the previous paragraphs about facets of the Chinese character is complete nonsense. From Marco Polo onward Westerners have journeyed to the Middle Kingdom and returned with tales of the Chinese with which to regale their compatriots. The Chinese are this, the Chinese are that, they tell the citizens of the land they left in order to travel into the unknown realm of *Zhōngguó*. The Chinese are clever inventors, they eat dogs, they are modest to a fault, they spit in public. Beware of anyone who tells you about the Chinese character, about how the Chinese people think and what they feel and what they do. I know of the Chinese only what I know of myself. The things that I admire about them are the best parts of myself; if I criticize them it is only because I condemn in others that which I abhor in myself. I swore I would not write a book about China that falls into the category of "I went to China, and this is what I experienced, and I know the Chinese better than they do." I know nothing about the Chinese. But to claim that they are unknowable, some unfathomable Oriental puzzle that the Western mind cannot comprehend, is to dehumanize them by turning them into a mysterious Other.

I know nothing of the Chinese, but I do know Jennifer and I know her parents and Marcus. I know these people. And I think I understand them. I am starting to understand them because I am beginning to understand what they want. They want something—we all want something. And to understand what another person wants is to go a long way toward understanding that person, regardless of whether she is from St. Louis or Shanghai.

Soup was served last, as is usually the case with meals in China. I slurped my appreciation of the flavor as loudly as I could, and Jennifer's mother beamed her thanks back at me in smiles.

"Now do you know how the soup gets inside xiaolongbao?" Jennifer asked.

"You're not going to tell me, are you?"

"You are correct."

I laughed and lapped the rest of the soup from my bowl. "Does your father still want to go to the airport with me?" I asked. "You told him about how I like to go there and watch the planes take off and land, just like he does. You told him how I'd like to go together with him, remember?"

She spoke a moment to her father and then he smiled and nodded.

Shanghai's maglev is, quite possibly, the least convenient and least cost-effective conveyance in the history of public transportation. In theory, magnetic levitation trains ("maglevs" for short), are an excellent answer to the gridlock that plagues metropolises across the globe. They are relatively quiet and emit no exhaust, and they get people from point A to point B in a fraction of the time it takes traditional trains to cover the same distance. But in practice, the maglev line in Shanghai ends so far from the city center, and its infrastructure cost such an obscene amount to build, Shanghai's maglev makes virtually no sense at all. But it is fast. God is it fast. And it is fun. God is it fun.

Though riding the maglev is a waste of my money and my time, I ride it often. When the scenery is flashing past so quickly that I have to look away from a foreground fuzzy with speed and focus on a distant point on the horizon to keep from getting dizzy, I like to imagine that I'm in a future world—a China in which the skies are blue and I can board a maglev train in Shanghai and arrive in Beijing two hours later. And then I can transfer to the subway system and take the metro to the building where I have a meeting; and then, when my meeting ends, I can walk down a street open only to pedestrians to grab a bite to eat in the capital before hopping back on the maglev and gliding back to Shanghai above a frictionless rail. This could have been the future. It was supposed to be the future. But now Shanghai has a maglev train that travels in less than eight minutes between the Pudong International Airport and Longyang Road subway station, located in a "financial district" that looks curiously like a suburban wasteland and is at least a thirty-minute cab ride from downtown. The fastest train in the world goes nowhere. The skies in China are not blue, and the future of the maglev looks bleak.

China often seems like two countries, one First World, one Third World. Building a city like Shanghai in China is a lot like putting Berlin in the middle of Paraguay. And sometimes Berlin and Paraguay blend together in China, as with the maglev train lobby, where upon the floor lay shiny coins of spit, and overhead plumes of cigarette smoke billowed as the streamlined train from the future arrived. Jennifer and her father and I stepped aboard and sat down in plush seats near a group of Japanese people. At least, I think they were speaking Japanese. Jennifer and I discussed their language in Chinese and agreed it was Japanese. I asked her in Chinese what she thought of the Japanese. The chances of a Japanese person comprehending Chinese were no better than that of an American understanding German. That is to say, it was possible the Japanese passengers would know what Jennifer and I were saying but not likely enough that it prevented us from assuming we could talk about them without them understanding.

"Lots of people in China won't be friends with a Japanese person or even talk to one," Jennifer said. "In Shanghai it's different. People in Shanghai have modern views. We don't have prejudices against anyone and we can eat Japanese food and be friends with Japanese people. People outside of Shanghai are not as advanced as Shanghai people."

China and Japan fought a war over control of Korea from 1894 to 1895; the war concluded with a resounding defeat for China and a treaty that allowed Japan to join the Western nations in Shanghai as an additional foreign power residing in the city, furthering China's humiliation at its inability to maintain its sovereignty and to control its territory. Japan, after it joined the foreign free-for-all in Shanghai, built the first factories there; other nations soon followed and built factories of their own, and along with banking and trade, manufacturing in Shanghai boomed.

In 1937, after several decades of Japanese imperialist policy that aimed to dominate China politically and militarily so it could control its rich raw material reserves, Japan mounted a full-scale invasion. Chinese resistance was no match for the technologically superior Japanese, who had made a concerted effort to adopt the machinery of warfare and the military techniques of the West, looking outward for inspiration to modernize. China, convinced it was the cultural center of the universe, had made no such move to modernize and had avoided engagement with the outside world. China's stance toward other nations is famously exemplified in its response to Lord Macartney, whom England had in 1793 dispatched to China to negotiate better trade conditions with the Qing court. Macartney refused to kowtow to Emperor Qianlong, believing to do so would demean King George III; the emperor dismissed Macartney and sent him back to England with a letter that made clear China's belief in its superiority by stating, "We have never valued ingenious articles, nor do we have the slightest need of your country's manufactures. . . . Our Celestial Empire possesses all things in prolific abundance and lacks no product within its own borders. There was therefore no need to import the manufactures of outside barbarians in exchange for our own produce . . . ."

And China couldn't conceive of Japan as a threat, because it viewed Japanese culture as derivative of, and thus grossly inferior to, Chinese culture. While China was focusing inward and failing to integrate the technological accomplishments of the outside world, Japan was scrambling to reinvent itself into a modern war machine.

Japan quickly occupied the costal cities of China, steamrolling resistance. When the Japanese reached Shanghai and laid siege to the city, Chinese troops, outgunned but tenacious, managed to keep the invaders at bay for three months.

But eventually Shanghai fell, and China lost its financial center to the Japanese, whose army stripped everything of value from the city to fuel its war effort. Trying to pacify the Chinese through sheer terror, Japanese soldiers burned ancient landmarks, abducted Chinese women to be sold into sexual slavery, and executed civilians. Though Shanghai's international concessions were spared destruction, the Japanese bombed the rest of the city with abandon. Chinese fleeing this holocaust sought refuge in the French Concession and the International Settlement, both of which became horribly overcrowded. Starvation, exposure and disease took their toll on the refugees, and corpses lined the streets along the Bund.

But far more notorious than the Japanese occupation of Shanghai was their treatment of Nanking. The fall of Nanking (today known as Nanjing) led to what is widely considered one of the most brutal massacres in the history of warfare. The Japanese, after they gained control of the city, slaughtered more than three hundred thousand civilians and committed mass rape. The event, known as "The Rape of Nanking," is still fresh in the minds of the Chinese. Japan has never adequately apologized for the atrocities its troops committed, despite repeated prodding by the Chinese government. Many commentators in Japan refer to the Nanking Massacre as the "Nanking Incident," a semantic sleight of hand that slights the victims. And light treatment of the massacre in Japanese government-approved textbooks has been questioned by China's leaders. Not that the Chinese government would ever adjust history and gloss over atrocities of its own in the school textbooks it approves.

China has a legitimate gripe with its past treatment by the West and Japan, but the Communist Party exploits the emotions of the Chinese people, manipulating them with shame and fear to consolidate its hold on power. Along with resentment toward Western countries for "carving up China like a melon," condemnation of Japan's occupation of China is a major component of Chinese nationalism. In contemporary China, victimhood is an essential technique of mass control, as skillfully demonstrated by Susan Shirk, a former Deputy Assistant Secretary of State during the Clinton Administration, in her book *China: Fragile Superpower*. The Communist Party stokes the fires of nationalism by teaching about the evil deeds of the West and Japan in school curricula, and by regularly publishing in the newspapers it controls articles claiming Japan and the West are poised to once again prey on a weak China, to pry apart the motherland and commit further atrocities. Only the Party can keep China strong enough to remain a unified nation and resist the future brutalities of imperial bullies. The government foments fear and anger among its sheep-like populace—but only to a point. It closely monitors how its people valve the pressure of their hatred, and it quickly shuts down public demonstrations of anger toward Japan and the West, lest it lose control of a furious mass movement demanding that the government be more aggressive on the global stage.

Across the world it has become fashionable to refer to China as a new superpower, in large part because doing so stokes the fear of sheep-like Americans and has proven an effective technique to move newspapers, magazines and books. *China is waking, China is rising, China is a new superpower—be afraid, be very afraid, buy this book!* But China's stances on global affairs beyond its immediate sphere of influence in Asia aren't taken seriously by other nations, because an authoritarian government, regardless of the heft of its economy, has no real moral sway in the modern world. Furthermore, though China has for a few decades been assiduously building up its armed forces, it cannot yet project military power around the world in the manner of a real superpower. The Chinese government wants its people to hate Japan and the West, but it doesn't want them to hate Japan and the West enough that China is forced into a military confrontation, which its leaders understand would result in another punishing defeat and loss of face for China. It will be a few decades yet before China can go head-to-head with the West in a war and have a reasonable chance of winning: almost everyone in the Chinese government understands this, and so, for now, the Communist Party keeps anger toward the West and Japan at a carefully controlled level.

The Japanese occupation of China was horrific, but it pales in comparison to what Mao did to his own people. China killed far more Chinese people than Japan ever did. Yet Mao's face graces every denomination of Chinese paper money, and Chinese schoolchildren chant their hatred of the evil Japanese.

And China, for all its indignation at being treated badly by other nations, has its own long history of expansionist policies, its own legacy of colonial control over weaker states. Most of the Vietnamese I've met in Ho Chi Minh City and Hanoi are quick to forgive Americans and the French; but toward the Chinese, who occupied their country for a thousand years, they still hold long-burning resentment. And witness provinces such as Yunnan and Tibet on the fringes of the Chinese empire that were brought under control through brutal occupations— by the Chu Kingdom during the third century B.C in the case of Yunnan, by the People's Republic of China beginning in 1950 and carrying on to the present in the case of Tibet. And speaking of Tibet and trains, a new train that climbs from Shanghai to the frozen heights of Lhasa has been causing quite a stir. But before we board the highest train on earth, let's finish our ride aboard the world's fastest.

Shanghai's maglev train reaches a top speed with people aboard of 431 kilometers per hour (268 miles per hour); passengers can watch the current speed of the train on a digital readout in each car. As we pulled smoothly out of the station, green numbers began counting upwards. 60 km/h, 100 km/h, 110 km/h.

Maglev trains do not have engines—that is to say, they don't have the kind of engine used to pull conventional trains on steel wheels along steel tracks. What maglevs have is a "magnetic levitation propulsion system." A magnetic levitation propulsion system: try to say this without thinking of a futuristic utopia of ingenious robotic contraptions and whimsical inventions. What's next, you might ask—people commuting to work in flying saucer cars? Many people think *The Jetsons* was a cartoon. It was actually filmed on location in Shanghai.

Magnetic levitation propulsion was actually developed (seriously) more than fifty years ago, and the concept has been around for more than a hundred. The way it works is this: The maglev train runs on a guideway instead of a track. The guideway contains wire coils, through which electricity passes, creating a magnetic field around the charged guideway. The train cars have large magnets attached to their undercarriages. The juice is in the guideway, so the train needs no engine onboard, making it lighter than a locomotive with a burly motor, lighter even than a bullet train—which though shaped like an aerodynamic projectile to shoot through the wind, still has to haul a heavy engine. Lack of an engine makes the maglev faster than a conventional train, but what makes it really fast is that it floats. That's right—it floats. The magnetized coils running along the guideway repel the magnets on the underside of the train, allowing it to levitate a little less than half an inch above the guideway. Power is sent through the coils in the guideway walls to create a system of magnetic fields that pull and push the train along the guideway, propelling it forward. The maglev rides along on a cushion of air. No steel wheels on steel rails, no friction. No friction means fast.

The German company Transrapid proved on demonstration lines that maglevs can reach speeds of 310 mph with people on board—twice as fast as Amtrak's fastest commuter train. And to further put this speed in context, consider that a Boeing 777 commercial airplane used for long-range flights can reach a maximum cruise speed of 587 mph. Riding in a maglev is a lot like flying. Actually, it is exactly like flying because electromagnetism counteracts the effects of the earth's gravitational force, allowing the train to levitate. It leaves the ground when it starts its journey and doesn't touch back down until it pulls into the station at its destination.

China shouldn't be too smug about notching up another superlative—that of world's fastest train—in its showpiece metropolis of Shanghai for several reasons, above all because the system was designed entirely by German engineers and built by a German consortium that includes industrial giants Siemens and ThyssenKrupp. A maglev line was built in Germany in 1979—but it was a demonstration system only. Developing a maglev line demands enormous amounts of capital: because the maglevs can't run on retrofitted conventional rails, the entire guideway system of a maglev has to be built from scratch. And building new rail lines, whether they are of the steel variety or of the no-emissions environmentally friendly maglev variety, requires extensive environmental impact studies and public review. China had two things that made building the first high-speed commercial maglev line a reality in China rather than a pipe dream in Germany: piles of cash and lax environmental regulations. Public review to slow down the process in Shanghai? Forget it. While German citizens were demanding to know how the nests of bids might be affected by a maglev running through their habitat, the Chinese government decided it wanted the world's fastest train. German engineers and investors very much wanted to build the world's fastest train. And now said train takes you from Shanghai's Pudong International Airport nineteen miles to the dead center of nowhere in seven minutes and twenty seconds.

We were now more than two minutes into the ride and traveling at just under two hundred miles per hour. The maglev's guideway stood fifty feet above the ground, and we flew over freeways as billboards and a suburban horrorscape flashed by, big-box stores and gruesome apartment blocks painted in sick pastels distending and distorting as we rocketed toward the airport. Like the visual effects induced by eating magic mushrooms, cars gleaming in the sun turned to bright streaks of light and buildings stretched apart into long fuzzy blurs as the maglev approached its upper limit. Jennifer's father put his face to the window and tapped his black canvas shoes against the floor. I slumped down and spread out, filling my seat and the empty seat next to me as we went tearing toward the future.

The maglev, which cost more than one billion U.S. dollars to build, runs at only about 20 percent capacity because of tickets that cost six dollars one way

Shanghai's maglev is a thrill to ride but essentially goes nowhere.

(making a ride aboard the world's fastest train an unattainable luxury for all but the wealthiest Chinese), and the inconvenience of having to haul luggage along endless corridors and up and down escalators and through turnstiles when transiting to or from the airport. That the Longyang station, where you either pick up the maglev or leave it, depending on whether you are coming from or going to the airport, is in the outskirts of Shanghai far from the city center has not helped its popularity with travelers. I know of no Shanghainese who use it in their daily commute. At its current rate of revenue generation, it will take one hundred years for the line to recoup its massive investment costs. As it exists now, Shanghai's maglev is a mere tourist attraction, a glorified amusement park ride.

Shanghai had much bigger plans for maglev technology than its Pudong airport to Longyang station line. The reason those plans have not materialized highlights an utterly unexpected trend in Shanghai: public input about a proposed infrastructure project. Engineers insist a maglev cannot be derailed because its undercarriage literally wraps around its guideway system; plans to build a maglev line from Shanghai to Hangzhou in time for the 2010 World Expo were derailed by the unlikeliest of causes—public protest. That's right, public protest in China stopped the fastest train on earth dead in its tracks. But before we follow that line, let us note that Shanghai, in much the same way that its ambition to build the world's tallest tower was being thwarted by the United Arab Emirates, was having its fastest-train-in-the-world bragging rights challenged by the French. In 2007, the TGV train network centered around Paris set the record for the world's highest average speed for a regular passenger service. Maglev still holds the distinction of the highest recorded speed of a train—361 mph—but this record was not set in Shanghai. It is owned by China's archrival, Japan. Sometimes it seems China simply cannot win. Being the biggest and best at everything in time for the Expo has proved a challenge for China—and the people of Shanghai are not helping the cause when it comes to spreading maglev technology around the city to wow the world in 2010.

The grand plan had been to extend the maglev line into downtown Shanghai and then to the nearby city of Hangzhou. The line was to cover a distance of 105 miles, many of which would have been within the ever-expanding zone of Shanghai's urban sprawl. Four stations were to be built, including one at the Expo 2010 site in east Shanghai. The train would travel at more than 280 mph, allowing it to cover the distance between cities in a mere twenty-seven minutes. (I've done the trip between Shanghai and Hangzhou by bus, and while moving with painful slowness through an apocalypse of traffic and breathing noxious bus fumes, I had lost count of the many hours it took to traverse the hundred miles.) Construction, scheduled to be completed in time for Expo 2010, was budgeted at about four and a half billion U.S. dollars. Proponents claimed that the new maglev line would speed up development in Hangzhou and other cities in Zhejiang Province, spreading Shanghai's wealth to less-developed regions. Many economists argue that if China is to continue its staggering rate of growth, its boom has to spill outside a handful of areas like Shanghai and into the vast impoverished hinterland beyond; the new line, supporters argued, would fulfill this goal by speeding up urbanization and economic development in the Yangtze Delta region surrounding Shanghai. Opponents argued that the cost of a ticket to ride the train would be far beyond the budget of ordinary people, and the project would never recoup its initial investment. One additional benefit, and perhaps the most important of all, though its merits were not openly debated in the media, was that the new line would be the first inter-city maglev rail line in commercial service in the world—one more superlative to show off at the Expo.

But Xinhua, China's official news source, reported in May of 2007 that the Shanghai-Hangzhou maglev project had been suspended, due in large part to the "radiation concerns" of people living along the proposed route. The planned line was separated from some communities by a green-belt buffer zone only 22.5 meters

(about 74 feet) wide, substantially less than the 300-meter (984 feet) minimum
required in Germany. Crowds of people living along the proposed route in Shanghai and worried about the potential effects of radiation began registering complaints online and expressing their concerns in person to local officials. One
district office received more than five thousand petitioners in a single day. Government officials, because of this public pressure, had suspended the project, stating that it would not be completed in time for the Expo, and might not even be
built at all. They were considering an alternative solution: a high-speed rail link
almost as fast as the maglev but at only half the cost to build. There would be no
citizens anxious about radiation to contend with, and the trip between Shanghai
and Hangzhou would take thirty-five minutes, only eight minutes longer than
the maglev ride. But China is not content to simply catch up with the rest of the
world; it is determined to leapfrog past it.

The main drawback to the alternative plan to build a high-speed conventional
railway was, of course, that high-speed trains run all over the world all the time.
TVG trains rocket in and out of Paris; Tokyo sends its famous bullet trains speeding to distant cities. Shanghai would have nothing new to showcase at the Expo,
nothing to brag about. No face. Though I suspect that other countries attending
the Expo would be just as interested to learn that public protest derailed the maglev as they would have been in riding the line had it been constructed. China,
in not brutally suppressing public dissent, had perhaps made some progress in
catching up to the West in the one area in which it often seemed to have no interest in advancing—human rights.

After receiving scores of complaints from city residents concerned about the
new maglev line, the Shanghai Academy of Environmental Sciences released an
environmental assessment report. The report declared the maglev extension plan
posed no harm to public health. Who knows whether the report was accurate,
but that the government issued the report in response to citizens' input on the
proposed project is significant. In addition, government authorities announced
they would limit the maximum speed along the Shanghai section of the route to
a mere 125 mph, about half of the maglev's speed when it now travels between
the Pudong airport and the Longyang Road station, to decrease the impact of
noise on surrounding homes. They also conceded to rerouting the line to avoid
residential areas.

But the Shanghai Municipal Government didn't officially cancel the maglev
project, and when officials began discussing plans to extend the Pudong airport

line to the old Hongqiao airport west of the city, concerned citizens, mainly in middle-class neighborhoods that the line would pass through, continued to protest. They compiled petitions that they submitted to local officials and they hung banners from their homes. In January of 2008, many hundreds of maglev protesters took the fight to city hall, literally, as they gathered outside the Shanghai City Hall. They shouted that they didn't want the maglev because it would be a noisy nuisance in their neighborhoods and they carried signs that claimed the maglev was harmful to people's health. When police blocked off People's Square, the demonstrators marched down Nanjing Road through one of China's most famous shopping districts, and the protest swelled into the largest Shanghai had seen since its citizens took to the streets in violent anti-Japanese demonstrations in 2005.

Though dozens of protesters were herded into waiting vans and busses and many of them were roughly handled by police, the protest dispersed peacefully. Shanghai government officials issued a statement condemning the demonstration as an illegal disturbance to public order. But no shots had been fired on Nanjing Dong Lu, no tanks had rolled through People's Square.

Granted, this was no Tiananmen, either in scale or in content. The protesters were not demanding government reforms as students and workers had in 1989; rather, they were marching to protect their property values. And this was not the culmination of a nationwide movement that challenged the government, though China was, as the clock ticked down at the end of the first decade of the twenty-first century and toward the 2010 Expo, in the throes of rising unrest. In a 2008 Reuters article titled "Hundreds Protest Shanghai Maglev Rail Extension," Royston Chan and Sophie Taylor explain that people throughout the nation, driven by outrage at illegal land grabs, environmental disasters, widespread corruption, and an ever-widening gap between the wealthy and the destitute, were assembling to express their discontent—though large-scale protests in big cities such as Shanghai were rare. What was even more unusual was that the Communist Party had not crushed the maglev protest with brutal force, as it so often quashes demonstrations in rural provinces. No one knows the true number of protests that take place in China each year because the government not only puts a stop to them—it seldom allows the media to truthfully report them.

But in Shanghai, the eyes of the world were watching. There were too many foreigners milling around People's Square and shopping on Nanjing Dong Lu for the government to have marched in its goons and rolled in its tanks. Soldiers with assault rifles running amuck and armored war machines shoving through throngs of shoppers would not have been good for business. Nanjing Dong Lu is lined with Pepsi banners. One after another, the red, white and blue Pepsi flags drive home the message to visitors strolling along the pedestrian shopping street that in the new China, commerce is king. Few red flags with yellow stars appear among the Pepsi banners. And portraits of Colonel Sanders are everywhere, while pictures of Chairman Mao are scant, and usually relegated to the shelves of stores selling kitsch. The Communist Party must grow the economy to keep the people happy; as long as the people are building up their bank accounts and their living standards are soaring ever higher, they will not challenge the power of the Party that is making this bonanza possible—so the reasoning goes. Using overwhelming force to stop people from peacefully protesting amid shopping malls and Pepsi banners and KFC restaurants would have had serious repercussions for foreign consumer behavior.

In addition, the people protesting were not peasants from the countryside; they were middle-class property owners from the city. They were key players in China's frantic game to build its economy bigger than any other on earth. The protesters were savvy in their use of technology, sending text messages to coordinate their gathering and uploading video footage of the protest on YouTube. And they were also clever in their displays of discontent, carefully playing the Chinese propaganda game, as pointed out by Jeffrey Wasserstrom, a widely respected China specialist who analyzed the event in an article titled "NIMBY Comes to China" in *The Nation* in 2008.

The protesters said that they were pleased with China's economic development and proud of its increasingly prominent place in the world. They proclaimed themselves Chinese patriots, and they were careful not to challenge the legitimacy of the Communist Party's control of the country. The maglev protesters said that all they wanted was for their government to listen to the concerns of its citizens and take them seriously—which is exactly what the Communist Party had vowed to do in its latest rounds of propaganda, notes Wasserstrom.

The maglev protesters, in an Orwellian twist of language worthy of an authoritarian regime, called their actions at the Shanghai City Hall and on the streets of Shanghai not protests or marches, but "harmonious walks." The protesters handed out anti-German tracts to evoke the jingoism that had led to the anti-Japanese riots that the government had helped foment with its angry rhetoric against Japan a few years previous. By cloaking their actions in xenophobia and Chinese nationalism, which is precisely what the Communist Party so often does when it feels its grip on power slipping, the maglev protesters protected themselves from a brutal crackdown. With their education, technological sophistication, adroitness at public relations—and most important, their middle-class material assets—Shanghai's maglev protesters had perhaps ushered in a new era of Chinese civic engagement, if not civil disobedience, that proved virtually impossible for the government to eliminate in the same way that it vanished the grievances of illiterate farmers in poor provinces and disappeared the concerns of students who owned nothing save their ideals.

The student protests of 1989 are associated with Tiananmen Square, but tanks rolling toward Tiananmen were the culmination of a nationwide movement that started two and a half years previous in Anhui Province and in Shanghai's People's Square. The protests began with students asking for better living conditions on their campuses, then turned into pleas to curb corruption and to institute reforms that would lead to greater government accountability, and finally climaxed when students who owned nothing risked everything in the Tiananmen showdown to demand democracy. Deng Xiaoping, the chief architect of China's economic reforms, allowed a military crackdown to restore order. Bullets fired by the People's Army shredded the protesters' bodies, tank tracks pulped their flesh, and the students made no dent in the Communist Party's armor that shields it from accountability to its citizens.

In contrast to the student actions of 1989, middle-class Shanghainese took to the streets in 2008 to protest an infrastructure project that would lower their property values, and the government listened—the maglev project was put on hold. Distilling both of these complex events into a stark contrast risks oversimplifying them, but those who contend that swelling numbers of middle-class citizens in China will finally bring about democracy could take the Shanghai maglev protests and the government response to these events as evidence that they are right. Perhaps future political change in China will not take place because of democracy protests in the nation's political capital of Beijing, but rather because of people advocating for their economic self-interest in China's financial center of Shanghai.

Or maybe bureaucrats had been planning to cancel the maglev line anyway because the four-and-a-half-billion-dollar project wasn't practical, or maybe they simply decided to postpone the project because their infrastructure priorities shifted. Or maybe the government was waiting for its espionage team to steal

Transrapid's secrets so it could build a cheaper knock-off version of the maglev and claim that Chinese ingenuity was responsible for a new and better system—as some German officials have stated, accusing the Chinese government of technology theft. Or maybe the Chinese government was too busy stifling unrest in the countryside beyond Shanghai to muster the military force it needed to properly punish people engaging in civil disobedience in its modern metropolis. Perhaps the Chinese government had not had a change of heart; perhaps it had been too weak to do what needs to be done when citizens living under the rule of an authoritarian regime take to the streets.

The maglev rocked back and forth as it approached the upper limit of its speed. Numbers on the digital display at the front of the train car counted upward in kilometers. 380 km/h. 390. There was a conspicuous absence of clackety-clack sounds. No drumming of wheels against tracks, no clanking of steel. Nor did the windows rattle as they do on conventional trains; they seemed fitted as snugly to their frames as windows in an airplane. There was no dust in their corners, no grit along their edges, no greasy smears upon the glass. Everything about the maglev seemed sterile and silent. Like a capsule hurtling spaceward, like a coffin prepared to be buried in the earth.

A maglev demo train in Germany had smashed into a truck parked on its guideway a couple of years back and twenty-three people had been killed in the crash, but Chinese officials insisted that the Shanghai line had superior technology that would prevent a similar scenario from happening—the train was programmed to come to a halt if anything stood in its way.

I looked around the car at eyes watching the numbers change. 400 km/h. There was more rocking than I would have guessed. 410. Another maglev approached from the opposite direction and the relative speed of the two space-age conveyances torpedoing toward each other provided a visceral lesson in relativity. I fought the urge to make a loud whooshing sound with my mouth as the other train whooshed by and we shook in its wake. 420. Air whistled faintly in protest outside the sealed windows. 430. And then the magic number: 431 km/h. The top speed of the fastest train on earth. Everyone glanced around and gave small nods and shakes of their heads and grins that said, "Simply amazing." No one's hands came together in the maglev car that day but their faces were clapping loudly.

Jennifer told me it was the first time her father had taken the maglev. He gave me a grin and a nod that told me he liked it as much as I did.

We left the train and walked through a space so long and empty and silent it seemed we were moving in a dream. "What did your father do before he retired?" I asked Jennifer as we trundled down an endless passageway glowing softly with light that came from no source that I could see. I wondered if the maglev we'd ridden had derailed and we had died.

"He was a cloth worker."

"In a textile factory?"

"Is that to make cloth? Textile?"

"It is."

"Then yes, that is where he worked. My mother also worked there. In a textile factory."

Back in the days of the foreign concessions with their banks and trading houses, cotton had thrived as a cash crop near Shanghai and a textile industry had become big business around the Bund. Jennifer told me that the factory where her parents had worked had been owned by a businessman who'd fled to Taiwan when the Communist Party took power and nationalized Shanghai's textile industry. As with virtually every other industry in China, the textile business had been organized into *dānwèi,* or work units, by the Communists. Each *dānwèi* guaranteed its members housing, food, clothing, education, healthcare and pensions. Jennifer's parents were workers, so they were treated well during the revolution. They were made honorary members of the Party, and all they had to do in return for their cradle-to-grave benefits was to show their loyalty to Party beliefs by attending political meetings, memorizing gibberish, and repeating nonsense.

Textile workers heeded Mao's call and unleashed the Cultural Revolution in Shanghai by waging class warfare on anyone suspected of harboring rightist tendencies. They ransacked the city, destroying homes of suspected capitalists. Jennifer's parents had been caught up in the radicalism of their fellow workers at their factory and had committed their share of mayhem, I gathered from Jennifer as she talked with her father and translated for me. But eventually the mob turned, as mobs so often do, on some of its own. Jennifer's father had been suspected of having bourgeois sympathies—something to do with his parents being property owners, though I didn't quite understand the background, and it probably didn't much matter. It's a safe bet to say the mob didn't quite understand why they were turning against Jennifer's father, but turn they did, and he was "struggled against," as the process of being humiliated and abused was known.

What psychological indignities and physical pain he'd endured I had to imagine because Jennifer didn't provide details and I didn't want to pry. I knew that he hadn't been sent off to a work camp for a decade of "reeducation," which meant he had fared better than many. And he was alive while others had been beaten to death in the streets of Shanghai if they were found engaging in commerce of any kind, or if they came from families that had been anything other than poor peasants or illiterate laborers. Eventually the chaos subsided and he went back to work at the factory; he worked there until the mid 1990s, when it was bought by a wealthy property developer and demolished. Now a shopping mall stands in its place. He and his wife still receive small pensions and housing from the government, but the government had authorized the demolition of their home to make way for commercial development.

If one spends enough time in China, one begins to become blind to the lunacy that is rife in China's recent history and blind to the madness of the present. But every once in a while, when one meets the people caught up in the lunacy, its perpetrators and its victims, one cannot shake the feeling that an entire nation has been consumed by madness and will exist in madness forevermore.

We made our way down a monstrously long passageway. Eventually the sad monotony of it ended, and we passed through doors separating the surreal calm of the corridor from the frantic bustle of the airport. We were immediately surrounded by people ricocheting in all directions, bags in tow, eyes fixed straight ahead. Airports are not appropriate places for idle wandering, but we did plenty of wandering before we found what we were looking for. When I stopped walking to gaze up at an impressive arched truss roof, I was bumped into and given unpleasant looks by travelers representing at least a half dozen different nations, none of whom were in the airport to admire the architecture.

Pudong International Airport faces the East China Sea. The building is shaped like an enormous gull stretching its wings toward the water. Beyond one of these wings stands a control tower that is open to the public and in which you can feel the thundercrack of each plane passing. From the tower you can witness the entire elaborate process of jets arriving and departing, disgorging passengers and carrying them away. So many arrowed vessels heading in all directions, signaling their desire to turn this way or that, telling the tower they are ready to land, and the tower talking them in as radar bounces from their metal skin. Air traffic is a dance as fluent and beautiful as that of a bee. I stared in rapturous awe at planes arrayed on the aprons and taxiways, engines roaring as they waited. Planes angling upward, pulling frail banners of vapor. Planes shearing in for a landing, wheels nudging the tarmac. For a moment it all seemed the inner workings of some vast and fathomless mind and I disappeared in the mystery of it.

Next to me stood Jennifer's father. I peeled my gaze away from a runway and studied his eyes. Eyes that had seen famine and war. Eyes that had witnessed a revolution that had led his country into a nightmare from which it was just now waking. An old man who had seen so much now looking at the future.

I asked Jennifer to ask him what he was thinking as he watched the traffic at one of the busiest airports in the world. He said something in Shanghainese so quietly Jennifer asked him to repeat it and then she translated for me.

What he said was this: "I'm proud of Shanghai's development. I am proud to be Chinese."

Searching for Dongtan

The next time I came to Shanghai the sky had the coarse granularity of a photo taken with high-speed film, and the air tasted so thick upon my tongue I tried to chew it. I'd been meaning to visit Dongtan, another of Shanghai's megaprojects the city was planning to roll out for the Expo. Instead of being the longest, biggest, fastest something-or-other, Dongtan was being heralded as a first: the world's first eco-city. Today seemed a good day to experience what government planners had envisioned as a model of ecological harmony, a city powered entirely by renewable energy, where vehicles would release no emissions and there would be no waste because everything would be reused. Amid the endless murk around me, the tops of high-rises appeared and disappeared like phantom castles wreathed in mist. While I stood squinting through haze and breathing in choking draughts of lung-scalding smog in one of the most polluted cities on the planet, the carbon-neutral eco-utopia of Dongtan sounded too good to be true.

Dongtan is just one of many new communities planned by Shanghai. With its population now topping twenty million people, with masses of new residents scrambling to find housing and the city in danger of choking on its own growth, Shanghai has unrolled an ambitious masterplan to create satellite cities surrounding its urban center. In what seems an odd twist on Shanghai's colonial legacy and a bizarre expression of the city's eagerness to embrace an international future,

Shanghai has decided to build towns modeled after those in Britain, Italy, Holland, Spain and Sweden. These suburban theme parks are sprouting up all over Shanghai's outskirts and will eventually be home to a half million or more of Shanghai's residents. Anting German Town boasts gingerbread homes fashioned after Weimar, former home of Bach, Goethe and an infamous concentration camp. Designed by Albert Speer, son of Adolf Hitler's favorite architect, and located adjacent to Anting Auto Town, Anting German Town is one of the more bizarre variations on the East meets West theme. Though in sheer silliness it pales in comparison to Thames Town, a British-inspired Shanghai satellite city complete with a castle, a Big Ben replica, mock-Tudor pubs, James Bond film festivals, and a church where Chinese people can partake of the exotic Western ritual of being married by a pastor. I had traveled to Anting and seen nary a German; I had walked the cobbled streets of ye olde Thames Town and spotted no Brits. What I had seen were Chinese yuppies living in surreal microworlds orbiting the larger fantasia of planet Shanghai.

Shanghai's grand planning scheme can be seen in miniature—the world's largest miniature city. Inside the Shanghai Urban Planning Exhibition Hall one can stroll along an elevated walkway and look down upon a perfectly rendered scale model representing what the city will look like in 2020. Since Jennifer and I were in the neighborhood before we left for Dongtan, we decided to stop in and see said model. I had been there many times; Jennifer had never set foot in the Shanghai Urban Planning Exhibition Hall, which for my money was the coolest ode to city planning on the planet. She was not unlike a New Yorker who has never been inside the Statue of Liberty. Why visit a monument to liberty when you live in a city that screams of freedom every day; why visit a shrine to urban planning when you live in a colossus experiencing the greatest urban expansion the world has ever known.

I was forever showing Jennifer new things about her city, though the things I showed her were all marked on maps. Her family's neighborhood that she had shown me was not on the latest version of the Shanghai map I had picked up on this trip to the city. The map now showed a business district, shopping areas, grounds for the 2010 Expo and proposed subway lines where shikumen had been mere months before. But the neighborhood of Jennifer's parents had not yet vanished: a few homes still stood with their stone-framed doors and their stubborn residents playing mahjong while they declared the developer's compensation offers inadequate and refused the government's orders to leave, while all around them lay ruined walls, as in a ghost town. Everywhere was evidence of demolition and desertion, and they coughed without end from the dust.

Shanghai's monument to itself is contained in a starkly modern building made of microlite glass. (I'm not clear on what "microlite glass" is exactly. I've been told by an aficionado of contemporary architecture that it is a very high-tech building material. To me it sounds like something that kitchenware peddled on an infomercial might be made from.) Anyway, atop the building, embedded in an enormous lattice larger than the building itself, four steel caps are arrayed in the shape of a perfectly symmetrical white magnolia, the official flower of Shanghai. The roof forms, in effect, a mandala contained within an orderly framework. Harmony blooming inside the perfectly planned grid of the city's design—at least, that's what I think the architect was going for.

Above the entrance of the building was a sign that said, "Keep pace with the times. Blaze new trails in a pioneering spirit," and below these words a digital clock counted down the days to the 2010 Expo. Inside the city's cathedral of the future was an enormous atrium filled with light that fell upon a golden statue of Shanghai not unlike a gleaming Buddha in a temple. We bypassed the statue and headed straight for the third floor, which holds the scale model to end all scale models. It is a vision taken from the mind of a city planner in the throes of an amphetamine psychosis. The model, which covers most of the third floor, is 1:500 scale and spreads across an area the size of two tennis courts. An enormous miniature city within a monument to a gigantic city.

We climbed up to a raised walkway surrounding the model for views from above of the miniature Shanghai. This was like doing a flyover of the city, but without the sick pall of pollution. Within the model's staggering expanse you can spot every physical feature of Shanghai, from elevated highways to pocket parks, from jutting skyscrapers to sprawling blocks of homes. Colored buildings represent structures that exist today; clear ones indicate future projects. Some citizens of Shanghai come to this place to see if their homes will still stand in the future or will be replaced with something else according to plan. Each boulevard in the model is perfect and clean. There is no laundry hanging from windows, no oldsters playing mahjong in the alleys, no youngsters playing tag, no vendors calling out their foods, no citizens wearing pajamas in the streets. This is a Shanghai to be worshipped but there is nothing here to make one smile, nothing here to love.

As noted by Douglas McGray in a 2007 *Wired Magazine* article titled "Pop-Up Cities: China Builds a Bright Green Metropolis," Shanghai's urban planning is important to cities in developing countries across the globe. For the first time in history, the majority of the world's population now lives in cities. Within a few decades, two-thirds of the people on the planet will be city dwellers. The bulk of this urban growth will occur in the developing world. One hundred and fifty years ago London's population boomed; one hundred years ago New York City's urban core spilled outward; fifty years ago Tokyo ate up all its open space. The world will be watching Shanghai, not just at the Expo, but beyond. The way Shanghai grows will serve as a template not just for China's other megacities bursting with growth, but for all the world's booming urban centers—Rio de Janeiro, Dubai, Lagos, Mumbai. As Shanghai goes, so goes the rest of the developing world. And so goes the planet.

"What do you think?" I asked Jennifer.

"It is like a tiny toy city. A little city for little dolls. What do you think?"

"I think it's as beautiful as a Tang dynasty tapestry."

It reminded me of those model train sets that grizzled great uncles with gentle, restless hands construct beneath Christmas trees. A tiny world of clean details, a paradise in miniature where trains run through tunnels and over hills, snaking between trees and houses and towns. This Shanghai scale model was like that—but on an extremely pure and potent variety of crack. Instead of little rails with choo-choo trains circling around quaint towns from an arcadian past, elevated superhighways connect clusters of towers that power their way vertically above the landscape. The Shanghai scale model doesn't have a running train, but if it did, that train would float magnetically above its guideway and hurtle across the miniature city at half the speed of sound.

"I used to go to the Shanghai Museum when I came to the city," I told Jennifer. "I wanted to see ancient things—jade and bronze and calligraphy and stuff. Before I came here, urban planning made me yawn. But I think that if I had come here as a kid I would have devoted my life to urban planning."

"I don't understand."

"Neither do I. I used to hate cities. I stayed as far away from them as I could. But I'm addicted to Shanghai, and this model is one of the coolest things I've ever seen. It makes me feel like a kid to look at it. I look at this model, and I look at all the blueprints and masterplans here, the models and the movies and the computer-generated images of what the city will look like in ten years, twenty years, fifty years, and I think there is nothing more interesting in this world than building a city. But when I leave the museum, I lose that feeling. Outside it is . . . *luàn. Luàn qī bā zāo.*" A chaotic mess. I had been finding that each time I returned to China I was reaching for words and phrases to express myself and grasping not English words but characters from my Chinese lexicon.

"I understand," Jennifer said. She pointed at the model. "This city is too perfect. It is not a real place. It is like a city in a story."

The parks of the model were as green as astroturf, the rivers ran not black but a healthy blue. And most incongruous of all, the air was so clear you could see the tops of the buildings and the horizons in crisp relief. Outside the microlite glass of the Shanghai Urban Planning Exhibition Hall loomed a sky of fuzzy gray, and this cloud hung over my innocent enjoyment of a perfect city in miniature.

As we walked around the viewing platform searching for Jennifer's neighborhood among tall buildings and finding no low rows of homes arranged around narrow lanes, a worker crept out into the model, following the bright blue Huangpu River so as not to disturb any feature of the terrain through which he moved. He kneeled down in the center of the surreal river of cerulean plastic, maneuvering carefully so as not to bump the buildings on the banks as he went about his work adding trees and bushes to the model. Groups of grade-school-age Chinese children paused in their pointing at the future towers of Pudong and at their neighborhoods that did or did not exist in 2020 to watch the man work. When he turned to place a tree in a park, his feet brushed the buildings behind him. Towers toppled. The man hurried to right them and clean up his mistake while the children laughed at this clumsy giant run amuck in a fragile world of tiny playthings.

On the museum's other floors Jennifer and I perused the city's plans to triple its network of metro lines, to build new satellite towns to relieve congestion in the urban core, and to finish the infrastructure to host the World Expo in 2010. All of the development was laid out in five-year plans. The Chinese had learned about five-year plans from the Soviets. Stalin had been big on five-year plans. Mao's disastrous Great Leap Forward had been part of a five-year plan. Call me a five-year plan cynic, but whenever I hear about some glorious development plan the Chinese government is concocting that is scheduled to be completed in five years, I start to worry. Though when I saw in the Urban Planning Exhibition Hall a wastewater management exhibit as intricate and compelling as ancient calligraphy in the Shanghai Museum, I believed in the glory of greater China and in the inevitability of its prosperous rise.

The world's largest scale model of a city shows China's masterplan for the city of the future.

The Shanghai Urban Planning Exhibition Hall is, of course, one big piece of propaganda designed to convince people that everything is just fine in a city engaging in a delirious binge of development and chasing wealth at any cost. But I checked my conscience at the door of the theater on the third floor as I stepped into the middle of a video showing all around me and in what felt like three dimensions. Virtual Shanghai, a computer-generated flyover of the city projected onto a 360-degree movie screen, is as close to being in a virtual reality world as one can get in the year 2008. It might seem as outdated as Atari in a few years, but for now it is a visual experience unlike any other. Manic cartoon characters straight out of an acid trip narrate the journey in voices that sound as though they've been huffing helium. The camera zooms along highways and above the Pudong skyscrapers of a perfectly planned urban utopia preparing to host the largest Expo in world history. Viewers are flung across great sweeps of cityscape at gut-churning speed, and the visually frantic panoramic vistas are as unsettling as they are exciting. Railings circle the theatre for viewers to grip while they stand upright and feel themselves being hurtled through the future.

When the video ended and the lights came on, I stared at bloodless knuckles holding tight to rails slippery with sweat, and I saw eyes as wired as if the audience

Chinese schoolchildren are surrounded by a movie that zooms them above a virtual
Shanghai.

had just been bungee jumping. I stepped outside the theater and clutched at a
wall to keep myself steady; I swallowed hard to settle my stomach. Around me
on the floor were very clean places that I guessed had been scrubbed of vomit.
Thank you for riding the roller coaster of Shanghai and please exit to your left.

After Jennifer and I recovered from the sensory assault of the video, we worked
our way downstairs and found a decidedly staid map that marked the districts
scheduled to be cleared for new development, and we perused archives of historical photos chronicling the foreign concessions, the roaring twenties and thirties
along the Bund, and the Japanese occupation. Less space than I would have expected was devoted to the birth of the Communist Party in the backstreets of the
city, but there were a few choice pictures of workers' clothing hanging out to dry
among the repurposed buildings of the Bund after the Party took power and declared the British banks and foreign trading houses now home to the people.
There were archival photos of shikumen dwellings not unlike the one where Jennifer's parents lived. I tried to read her face, tried to imagine what she made of
the reality that the neighborhood where she'd grown up would soon be another
footnote in the city's history, perhaps meriting a mention in the historical archive,
a grainy photo in a museum amid the grainy air of a swelling metropolis.

"I applied for my visa," Jennifer said, apropos of nothing.

Her company had opened an office in New York. She had asked to be transferred there; her manager had approved her request. She planned to work in New York, to perfect her English while she was there, to learn everything she could about American marketing techniques, and then apply to MBA programs. With an MBA degree, experience working in America, and her English at a level impossible for people living in China to attain (even if they have me as their language partner), when she returned in a few years, Shanghai would be hers for the taking. She would send money home when she was in New York, perhaps as much as half her salary, and her parents would live well, wherever they happened to be living by then. But she wasn't celebrating just yet. There was the not-so-small matter of being able to leave China.

"Do you really think they'll make it difficult for you to leave the country if your parents don't sign the agreement?" She had just told me that the developers had again paid her a visit in her apartment.

"Of course."

"Are you angry?" I asked.

"It does not help to be angry."

"It's fucking crazy. *I'm* angry."

"This is the way it is in China. You don't understand our China."

Jennifer and I stared in silence at a sepia photo of the Bund in its bustling heyday, Brits in bowler hats strolling the parks and promenades along the river, the handsome row of buildings they'd raised like a movie set designed to give them the feeling they had never left London.

There is a story, a myth really, about a sign the British put up at a park in the International Settlement that read "No dogs or Chinese allowed." Though that exact wording of the sign never existed, the spirit of the message was certainly true. That the newly risen nation of China would be so angry at the injustices of its past that it would do everything within its power to best the nations that had once beaten it down makes sense to me. That the government would crush its own people—and that the people would allow this to happen to them—makes no sense to me at all.

So all-pervasive are the contradictions, so surreal are the crafty schemes of a government whose every move is calculated to keep itself in power, so hopelessly powerless seem the people to exercise any control over their world—one begins to see corruption and abuse in China as the normal state of things, and the petitioners and protesters who take their grievances to the government with the hope that the Communist Party will right the wrongs start to appear quite mad. Why would they even bother to ask the government to treat them fairly and let them stay in their homes or give them adequate compensation and a new place to live that isn't thirty miles away at the fringe of Shanghai's sprawling empire? Why would they go against the given state of things? Shanghai surely must grow; they are in the way and they must move. One might as well protest the law of gravity for all the good it would do.

Whenever I felt myself becoming this cynical I knew it was time to start thinking about going home. But I had just arrived and I had many weeks left before my return flight. Gone was any childlike glee at being caught up in Shanghai's headlong heave toward the future, the amusement park ride with a brief stop at the Expo in 2010 and then an accelerated rush through the twenty-first century. Maybe it was the weather today, maybe it was the air I could feel like scratchy fiber inside my lungs and taste like metal lozenges placed upon my tongue. Right now I didn't want to see any new megaproject, any new proof of Shanghai's superiority. What I wanted was to find the commie cadre responsible for crushing Jennifer's dream and beat him to a bloody pulp.

And speaking of bloody pulp, when we left the mecca to urban planning, my mood as ugly as the sky outside, I coughed from my lungs something, which had I spat it out in America, would have sent me racing to find a doctor. Here it was par for the course. If one were to seek medical attention every time one's lungs felt infected in Shanghai, one would be very busy commuting to the doctor's office. I sucked more air into my scalded windpipe, let the overworked cilia of my lungs scrub away the sulfur and soot, and rolled the clotted residue around my mouth, feeling its density on my tongue, tasting its chemical tang. The World Health Organization has determined that approximately three quarters of a million people die prematurely every year from respiratory problems in China. In Shanghai, it's easy to taste why.

This is the taste of an economy growing at 10 percent plus per year. It's also the taste of almost 10 percent of gross domestic product being deleted by resource depletion and environmental degradation. Many Western analysts have claimed that when the environmental costs of China's growth are factored in, the country's economy really isn't growing much, if at all. The Chinese themselves have toyed with this equation. In 2004, in an effort to determine the true GDP of China, the central government, with the help of the World Bank, launched the

Green Gross Domestic Product project with the aim of creating an index of economic growth that includes the environmental consequences—crop losses, healthcare costs, missed days of work from respiratory disease, etc. The Chinese premier announced that the Green GDP index would replace the Chinese GDP index as the main performance measure for the economy. The results, however, were so frightening to the Party that it quickly backpedaled and dropped the plan. The Party couldn't tell the people that the Chinese economy was stagnant. Economic growth keeps the Communist Party in power; environmental problems are curtailing growth. Something must be done—the Party knows this, and though it won't tell the people the Green GDP of China, it will tell them that one of its main priorities right now is greening the nation.

Apocalyptic pollution hadn't always been part of the plan. Traditional Chinese philosophy advocated living in harmony with the natural world. But Daoism didn't keep the British from barging their way into China. While the Chinese were contemplating how to achieve balance with nature, the Western powers were raiding their resources and the Japanese were using them for target practice. Chinese revolutionaries and reformers, horrified at their nation's impotence in the face of aggressive foreign incursions, blamed traditional Chinese belief systems for making China so much weaker than other countries. When Mao set the Communist revolution rolling, he tried to turn everything traditional upside down. He viewed nature not as something with which to live in harmony, not as something beautiful and profound to be appreciated, but rather as an obstacle preventing China from enjoying a prosperous future; he exhorted his countrymen to conquer nature and force it to serve the purpose of creating a paradise on earth. The Chinese people heeded his call. Forests fell and rivers ran black.

The Communist Party, when it began instituting economic reforms in the late 1970s and early 1980s, made rapid growth the top priority: it would develop the economy first and clean up the messes later. When foreign capital started flowing into China, the messes only got bigger. The West, hell-bent on making the most of the gold rush China's economic transformation afforded, jumped into Chinese markets and kept mum about sustainability. American stock portfolios fattened as factories rose from the rice paddies to puke inky clouds of poison into the atmosphere, and no effort was made to guide China toward a path of growth that avoided the mistakes made by the West. Now the ten most polluted cities on the planet all belong to China, and no tale of China would be complete without gawking at the environmental hellhole the country has become.

Instead of steering China with its one fifth of the planet's population on a sustainable course, foreign companies scrambled to outsource their pollution by setting up in China their most noxiously polluting industries. These factories fueled growth in cities like Shanghai, where the newly rich switched on the lights and powered up their computers, and peasants poured in, swelling the population and sending energy demands soaring. To feed the overburdened grids of cities like Shanghai, one new coal-fired power plant—sans sulfur scrubbers—opens on average every week in China. China has now passed the United States as the world's biggest source of CO_2 emissions. Another superlative for China in time for the Expo. Though they can't claim all the credit. Our demand for cheap TVs and tennis shoes helped them achieve first place.

I had been inside a single tower in Shanghai that contained within its soaring walls a supermarket, a school, a dating service, a barber, a brothel, college classrooms, a health clinic, a gym, corporate offices, and much more. I imagined a child could be born in such a tower, could grow up there without ever leaving its climate-controlled confines, could meet his spouse, get married, cheat on his wife, pursue a career, exercise, retire and die, all without ever leaving the tower. Maybe a life lived indoors amid filtered air is the answer to China's pollution problem. If Shanghai keeps raising towers, everything should be just fine.

I took a break from the snide pontificating that was whirling in my head to hand a water bottle I'd just drank empty to a man driving a bikecart piled with plastic refuse. He thanked me and grinned as though I'd given him money, which essentially I had. Recycling, as with virtually everything else in China, is driven by the marketplace, not morals. In America we recycle because we believe it is our civic duty to preserve the environment; Chinese people recycle because they need money. Trashpickers are considered the lowest of the low among Chinese: it is a job of last resort, an act of financial desperation—and it results in an extraordinarily efficient system of rescuing reusable materials from people's garbage, as pointed out by Adam Minter in his postings on his excellent website, Shanghai Scrap.

I watched the man with the bikecart pedal his environmentally friendly transportation (propelled by clean, sustainable power only by virtue of the fact that he was too poor to buy a car—which he surely would were he ever to make enough money from recycling to afford one) toward a public trash receptacle separated into two sections, one for recyclable materials, one for non-recyclables. These divided receptacles, which I had been seeing more and more of throughout

Shanghai, looked very Western with their emblems of revolving green arrows, that sign and symbol of our goodness, that icon that makes us believe we have atoned for our sin of overconsumption by doing what is right. Westerners throughout Shanghai stand before these receptacles like penitents preparing to confess their sins as they separate their refuse and place each sacrament in its appointed place. Then they congratulate themselves on having done their part to save the planet, and smiling beatifically, they return absolved to their lives of gluttony. Try explaining the civic duty of recycling to a Shanghainese stuffing his plastic bottle in the non-recyclable slot and watch his blank stare—ours is a faith they don't yet share.

But before all the trash from the divided receptacle is hauled off to the same landfill because there is no municipal recycling program in place, a trashpicker comes along and sorts through the garbage, salvaging what can be reused, and he earns money to feed his family by selling the plastic and paper and metal to a factory that wants to purchase cheaper used materials instead of more expensive new materials. Westerners sneer at the lack of recycling programs run by the government in China and mumble about the backwardness of the Chinese, their lack of faith in the moral mission to save the planet, but at the end of the day, landfills outside Shanghai are cluttered with far fewer reusable materials than are our own—thanks to the market and to the indefatigable trashpickers of Shanghai.

I bought three bottles of sweet green tea from a street vendor, gave one to Jennifer and handed one to the trashpicker up to his elbows in the recycling receptacle, and then I congratulated myself on doing my part to save the planet. I thanked the sweaty man wrapped in rags for his efforts; he looked at me as though I'd lost my mind as I guzzled green tea and drank the bottle empty in a few long thirsty pulls amid the concrete heat of the city. Then I handed the trashpicker another piece of plastic that was worth a certain price, and I glanced up at the sky, so heavy with filth it seemed to be collapsing and sinking toward the earth. It seemed a sky that had given up. A glum shrug of a sky.

NASA's satellites have imaged great brown clouds of soot, smog and other pollutants that begin as plumes of dust lofted into the sky by sandstorms in the Gobi Desert; these dirty storms pick up industrial emissions over China's megacities, and then they disperse across thousands of miles of the Pacific Ocean—all in a matter of days. The uppermost cloud layers sometimes travel across the entire North American continent to the Atlantic Ocean. These Chinese particulates find their way into North American lungs, and scientists are certain that the airborne particles block sunlight and alter regional temperatures and precipitation patterns across the globe.

Chinese pollution flows through our air; it also seeps into our soil and flushes into our waterways. Eat a wild trout fished from a gin-clear stream in Oregon and worry about toxins from China short-circuiting your central nervous system: a third or more of the mercury contaminating America's ecosystems comes from Chinese coal-fired power plants on the other side of the earth. Globalization has affected everything in our world—even pollution is global now, and China is by far the biggest player in the international production and exportation of pollution. They send us, along with our cameras and clothes, our computers and coffee cups, miasmas of soot and dangerous doses of mercury. We live in a global world indeed, and vast oceans cannot buffer us from the consequences of China's voracious appetite for energy. China's problem is our problem.

Airborne pollution, though threatening to change the climate of the planet, is only the beginning. The majority of China's forests have disappeared and clean water is becoming increasingly rare, especially in the northern portion of the country, where desertification could precipitate an environmental emergency as dire as that posed by dangerous air. Beneath China's fetid surface, underground fires rage, consuming two hundred million tons of coal each year, and heavy metals render aquifers toxic. Above it all, China's skies swirl with lead, mercury, and sulfur dioxide in a corrosive stew. China is starting to seem a lot like those planets that scientists tell us are uninhabitable—at least by carbon-based life forms. Perhaps some new species will evolve in China that is suited to the poisonous brew.

Until then, there is Dongtan, China's Great Green Hope. Or so it has been hyped—not just by the official Chinese news agency, which is to be expected, but by the Western media, which has gone gaga over Dongtan, perhaps in part because a Western company is leading the charge to green China one eco-city at a time. Dongtan caught the world's attention in 2005 when Britain's then prime minister, Tony Blair, alongside Chinese president Hu Jintao, attended the signing ceremony for the Dongtan contract between the British firm Arup and the state-owned Shanghai Industrial Investment Corporation (SIIC) at Number 10 Downing Street. Blair's successor, Gordon Brown, hailed the project as a shining example of cooperation between Britain and China, and the Western media was quick to herald Dongtan as a possible solution to China's—and even the rest of the planet's—environmental woes.

But was the West too late? Would Dongtan have any impact on Shanghai, much less on China overall? Would Dongtan be an agent of change, or would it merely serve as an island of green in a sea of gray polluted cities? Was it a beacon of hope for the planet, or was it a Potemkin village designed to divert attention away from the true scale of China's environmental crisis?

"Hey Marcus," I said into my phone when he answered. I had called him a couple of times since I arrived in Shanghai but I hadn't reached him—and I hadn't been able to leave a message. Citizens of Shanghai, for all their technological sophistication, rarely use voicemail systems. Chinese people find leaving messages socially awkward, so when someone is not available on his or her cell phone, you get a recording saying, simply, that the person is not available. How that is less awkward than being able to leave a voicemail message is beyond me, but there you have it: China is one big puzzle.

"Want to go with us to Dongtan?" I asked Marcus. "Want to find out if Dongtan is the solution to the world's environmental problems?"

"I want to find out about the real estate there. It's a hot market."

"The eco-city is a hot real estate market?"

"A friend of mine is investing in condos at Dongtan. It's going to be the coolest place to live in Shanghai once they finish the bridge."

The bridge to which Marcus was referring was yet another of Shanghai's megaprojects. Two of the world's largest slurry borers were, as we spoke on our cell phones, driving tunnels through the sludgy silt, sand and clay beneath the Yangtze River. When completed, the tunnels would be the longest soft-earth tunnels in the world (somehow that doesn't have quite the cachet of world's tallest tower or fastest train). But the tunnels were a key element of a direct link between Shanghai's city center and Chongming Island, home of the future Dongtan eco-city. The Shanghai-Chongming Expressway, scheduled to be completed in time for the 2010 Expo, would be the longest tunnel-bridge combination in the word (okay, that's a little more impressive). Visitors to the Expo would be able to drive SUVs forty-five minutes from downtown Shanghai to the world's first sustainable eco-city.

Until the engineering triumph of the Shanghai-Chongming Expressway is complete, visitors to the eco-city are forced to take a ferry. "This totally sucks," Marcus said as we waited to board a boat after spending an hour on the subway to reach the port. "It's so inconvenient."

Around the port, factories the size of small cities pushed steady streams of smoke into the sky. There was no wind to wobble the smoke from side to side. It rose straight up in perfect columns that merged with the great gray clouds hanging above the city.

"Would you rather own a car and drive to Dongtan?" I asked Marcus.

He looked at me as though I'd asked him if he'd rather starve to death or have food.

"When I get my Buick and the road is finished I'll go there on the weekends."

"To visit your condo in the nature preserve?"

"To get out of the city. I've heard you can breathe in Dongtan. Really breathe in the fresh air."

"Wouldn't that be something."

"It's good for your health," Marcus said. "And good for making money. My friend who's getting into the real estate market there says that nothing moves real estate in Shanghai like clean air. Clean air sells."

A vast wetland spreads across Chongming Island's southern tip. At the Dongtan Nature Preserve, great flocks of birds gather to migrate, following a flyway of instinct. The preserve provides rich food resources and safe nesting places, and it forms an important stop in the East Asian-Australian migratory shorebird flight path, one of the world's major bird migration routes. Dongtan is the birds' first station when heading north; it is the last place they stop when returning to Australia. While the migrating birds rest up and fatten on grass seeds, snails and crabs found among Dongtan's reedy pools and shallows, birdwatchers flock to Dongtan to see some of the 265 species that have been observed there, ranging from the diminutive Reed Parrotbill to the majestic Tundra Swan, from the increasingly rare Hooded Crane to the highly endangered Black-Faced Spoonbill. Green urban planners had vowed to preserve the wetland in its natural state and to build the Dongtan eco-city without disturbing the island's sensitive bird habitat.

As the ferry pulled away from port in a froth of dirty suds and chugged toward Chongming Island, Shanghai's skyline sank into the horizon behind us, gradually growing smaller. Shanghai is, in fact, sinking. The city with the name that means "on the sea," the city that for the past two decades has risen faster and higher than any other city in the history of the world, the city that is determined to fill with its towers every last bit of sky, is now sinking toward the sea, its buildings too much for the earth to bear. Ten thousand towers more than ten floors tall now stand in the city. And beneath this dense forest of skyscrapers the ground is subsiding, for Shanghai is situated on a soft and soggy plain. The city rests not on bedrock but on tofu. From 1921 to 1965, Shanghai sank by almost six feet, due largely to the draining of groundwater under the city. But the government put the kibosh on groundwater extraction and even pumped water back into the aquifer, putting a stop to the sinking—until buildings began to rise in the booming 90s. The city is again sinking, now at a rate of roughly a centimeter a year. This subsidence is at its worst in areas of the city center with the highest concentration of new structures. The further Shanghai reaches into the sky, the faster it drops toward the sea. As the melting of the polar icecaps accelerates, Shanghai on its low-lying alluvial plain will be one of the first cities in the world swamped by saltwater. Its towers will poke above the waves, bearing witness to the metropolis beneath the sea.

On the ferry we boarded, there were people packed inside the cabin, people swarming outside on the decks, people crammed in stairwells and smashed against railings, and it seemed this great press of humanity had filled the boat to flee some coming catastrophe in the city. I chatted with a Chinese man who in a voice hoarse from smoking told me he was a journalist. I think he assumed he was making idle conversation. But I was always floored to meet a journalist in the People's Republic of Disinformation, and with a glaring lack of tact, I charged right toward the big question: Did journalists in Shanghai, China's most open city, enjoy more freedom than journalists in other parts of China?

"The government has ordered Shanghai to be an open city," my new friend told me with not so much as a glance over his shoulder, as if to prove his point. "The openness is part of the central government's plan. They decided that an open Shanghai would be good for business. But it is a fake openness. We must report on the openness, but it can be very dangerous to report on the problems in Shanghai."

The Orwellian world in which he worked didn't seem to have dampened his spirits. He described his plight with an easy smile. He worked at least six days a week, sometimes seven, and the stories he submitted to his editor often had the truth edited out of them so the newspaper would not get in trouble with the government. I asked him if he knew the story of Sisyphus.

"Syphilis?"

"Never mind." It was too noisy on the ferry to speak of Sisyphean tasks. We exchanged business cards and a few minutes later an American interning at a five-star hotel struck up a conversation with me. He carried on about the spa in his hotel, which offered services that in America are legal only in Nevada.

"Can you believe it?" he said. "You can get a 'special massage'" (his fingers made quote marks) "for, like, sixty bucks? And you don't even have to tip! They don't tip here!"

"It is truly an amazing country," I said. "Have you heard of syphilis?"

"What?"

"Never mind." I wanted him to go away but he showed no sign of leaving. I told him I'd read that some specialists claim that a full 20 percent of China's economy is tied either directly or indirectly to prostitution. And we could definitely agree that America's economy is inextricably linked to China's—couldn't we? He nodded that we could. And of course America is the most important driving force behind the global economy, right? He nodded that it was. So, is it fair to say that if prostitution were suddenly to come to a stop in China, if the Chinese police and the Chinese army were to all of a sudden shut down the brothels they run in every city of the country, and prostitution were to just vanish completely overnight in China, the entire world economy could collapse, ushering in a period of economic depression more horrible than any that had come before it? He excused himself and went to go flirt with Jennifer, who blew him off by pretending she spoke not a word of English and stared at a soap opera blaring from a TV in the cabin.

"You could marry him and move to America," I told Jennifer in Chinese as the hotel intern shrugged and moved on to chat with another Chinese girl, whose face lit up at his advances as though she'd just discovered she had winning Powerball numbers.

"I don't want to go to your America that much," Jennifer said.

As I gazed out to where the Yangtze swells as it mixes with the sea, I thought that Shanghai is the only city in the world whose name is a verb. No one gets new yorked or pragued, but you might find yourself shanghaied. To be shanghaied is to be put aboard a ship by force, especially after being drugged, or more generally, to be put into an undesirable position by trickery. The term comes from the former custom of kidnapping sailors to work on American merchant ships heading to China. Many of these ships manned by abducted crews sailed to Shanghai. No coercion is necessary now. So many Chinese people in Shanghai are trying to get to the West, so many Westerners are heading to Shanghai.

I struck up a conversation with a Canadian. He told me he was in Shanghai because he'd grown bored with Brooklyn. "New York has already happened," he said. "Shanghai is still becoming."

"What it is becoming—that's the question," I said. He excused himself and went to flirt with a couple of Chinese men, including Marcus. Marcus seemed bored but unbothered.

"Do you know many gay people?" I asked Marcus when the Canadian gave up and left him alone. "I'm a creative," he said. "Of course. One of the clubs I go to is, like, at least half gay."

"You say *like* as much as an American," I said.

"Thanks," he said.

"It's not really a compliment."

"But I sound like an American?"

"How's the website going?" I asked. "The one that lets creatives post their content. Seemed like a good idea."

"It is a good idea. My partner stole it from me. He found some funding and he's going to launch it on his own."

"That sucks," I said.

"That's China," he said.

"What's next? Any other ideas? Is it back to X-rated emoticons?"

"I might launch my own site. My partner said I didn't have any good ideas, but the whole idea was mine. I can do it better than him. I just need some start-up money." He gave me a goofy used-car-salesman smile. "You want to invest in my site?"

"What's it going to be called?"

"I don't know. You have any ideas?"

"You're the creative. Come up with something creative."

He scrunched up his face and glanced around the ferry. The gay Canadian smiled at him. "Okay. How about 'Creative'?"

"That's what you want to call the site?"

"Why not?"

"Sure, why not."

"Maybe 'Creative China.'"

"You are nothing if not creative, my friend."

"Let's google it and see if it's been taken."

"As soon as we get back from Chongming."

"Let's find somewhere on the island."

"Where?"

"I don't know. An Internet café."

"You think there's going to be an Internet café on the island? Where—in the bird sanctuary?"

"Dongtan is an eco-city, not a caveman city. We'll find Internet somewhere."

Of course he was right. In Shanghai you could get broadband in homes with no indoor plumbing. Internet connectivity was a basic necessity in Shanghai. Breathable air and clean water were hit or miss, but you could always count on accessing cyberspace.

I walked around a deck of the ferry and then leaned over a rail and watched men sucking smoke from cigarettes. I counted seventeen Chinese men on the deck and fifteen of them were smoking. I considered asking the two without cigarettes pinched between their lips what was wrong. Perhaps they weren't feeling well as the ferry bucked against the waves. Plastic drink bottles and food wrappers rained down from all decks into the river and a dragon of trash lay twisting and coiling beyond the stern of the boat. At times like these I asked myself why on earth I was in China. Then I reminded myself that Americans not so long ago had considered smoking in public and chucking trash into the wind perfectly acceptable. And of course, many still do.

Brown waves bounced against the rusted hull beneath a sky so gray it seemed one shade away from black. Shanghai with its towers and teeming masses had vanished behind us in the pall. We had left the Huangpu River and merged with the larger flow of the Yangtze, the mighty river that begins as a clear trickle atop the Tibetan Plateau more than three thousand miles away and ends in the murky emptiness of the East China Sea. Once blind dolphins navigated the Yangtze by sonar. Venerated in ancient times, the pale mammal known in Chinese as *báijì* was turned from a river goddess to a villain during the Great Leap Forward and hunted mercilessly for its flesh and skin, and now the animal has vanished, its waters poisoned and blocked by dams, its habitat filled with the entangling nets of fishermen and the slashing props of boats. The ghostly beast is considered extinct, though every now and then there is a rumor of a large white animal sighted lolling in the Yangtze's soiled waters. A remnant population of the Yangtze Finless Porpoise survives amid the superpolluted goop. And the Chinese Sturgeon, a fish left over from the age of dinosaurs, still plies the river's currents, this relic's status as a national treasure and protected species taken nearly as seriously by the Chinese government as that of the Giant Panda.

Chongming Island, the last large piece of undeveloped land in the Shanghai municipality, slowly emerged from the haze ahead. Wildlife preserves often are not pretty places: what recommends them to animals doesn't necessarily recommend them to the human eye. Chongming was no Yellowstone. There were no dramatic cliffs. No waterfalls or mountains. In the silty mouth of the

The last large piece of undeveloped land in the Shanghai municipality is Chongming Island, a vast alluvial deposit rich with some of the planet's best bird habitat.

Yangtze, where the great river sludges its way into the sea, lies one of the world's largest alluvial deposits. Chongming is, in essence, one big mudflat, and its bounty of wildlife was nowhere to be seen. What we saw when we arrived was a grungy port city with smokestacks and taxi touts surrounded on all sides by mud. I stood on a dock watching brown foam push against the shore and slide back from the oily rocks. We found a driver to take us to Dongtan, though he didn't seem to know much about what China was touting as one of the biggest and most ambitious business projects ever undertaken. Apparently he hadn't gotten the memo about the Neo-Industrial Revolution that was about to shake his island.

"You want to look at birds?" he asked us.

"Houses," Marcus said. "We're going to look at houses."

Against a distant horizon, flooded rice paddies and fields of leafy vegetables lay in a limitless expanse, occasionally cut by an irrigation canal or marked by a leaning shed. For a moment no one spoke.

"Do you want to see birds?" I asked Jennifer.

"I don't know. Maybe. There's so much space here. It makes me feel dizzy."

This from a person who went to the highest point of the tallest towers in Shanghai and leaned against the glass, staring at the antlike people so far below.

Alongside the road we traveled, blonde grasses blew in waves as a breeze passed through them. I had the sudden disorienting sensation of being in a wheat field in Kansas. A metropolis of twenty million lay behind us across a bay of muddy water. A great emptiness stretched before us. We rode in silence. Explosions of flowers yellow, pink and white did little to lift my mood, and Jennifer and Marcus both seemed bored. In a field stood a row of turbines, blades blurring like propellers on a plane, then slowing to a lazy roll. We all turned to look at them, ducking our heads low to gaze up from the windows of the taxi at the topmost place where the spinning blades sheared the sky. The farmland and scruffy villages by the roadside seemed from an age long passed, but the wind farm with its towering turbines looked suitably futuristic for land that lay within the boundaries of Shanghai.

Our driver dropped us off near an enormous boulder inscribed with Chinese characters. We were at the nature preserve but we couldn't find the eco-city. Our driver either didn't know how to help us or didn't care. He drove away and left us standing in a Chinese wilderness of grass.

"I've never heard that before," Jennifer said.

"Heard what?" I said. "A taxi driver who doesn't know where the site for a future city of a half million people will be?"

"That sound." She pointed at grass that stood waist high. Wind and grass combined in an everchanging soundscape that ranged from gentle rustling to shrill whistling. But I think what Jennifer really heard was not a particular sound but the absence of a certain sound. There were no cars here. Even in Shanghai's parks, the murmur of freeways was always present. There was no traffic in this place of windy silence.

"I don't like it," Jennifer said. "The sound is strange."

"Where are the houses?" Marcus said. "Who would want to live out here. What would you do, look at grass?"

I looked at the grass. A burst of wind coming in off the water bent the blades, and then the wind sucked back toward shore, turning the grass to a riptide. When the gusty blowing slacked to a gentle breeze, silken currents stirred the tassels. I opened my mouth to taste the wind. It tasted brown, but not the dense, dark brown of the particulates and pollutants that sicken the sky of Shanghai. Rather, the wind tasted of grass that has gone crisp and tawny beneath the hot winds of summer and will green again with the first sloshy rain. I could not find the flavor of benzene and ozone that usually layered my tongue in the city, nor were my lungs filled with coal's fine soot or with scalding draughts of sulfur.

"I like it here," I said.

Marcus gave me the look he always gave me when he was feeling sorry for me for being an American of superannuated tastes who doesn't enjoy online gaming and thinks reading books is a worthy way to spend one's time.

We walked awhile, and when we found some farmers working in a field we asked them what they knew about the coming city that would have minimal impact on the earth. They stopped planting seeds a moment to stare at us. One of them moved from hunched to straight backed to better study us. The effort it took her to stand up and raise her head from her seed planting made it seem as though this might be the last movement she ever made.

I apologized for bothering them, and we walked on, past a froggy bog where a song of croaking rose from slimy waters. Past a stream that gurgled and slurped between rocks. We wandered into a small village that looked like one of those model villages you see in anthropology museums. Roads made of squashy mud, houses that look handcrafted, wickerwork baskets and chickens everywhere. Plastic bags hung up on bushes and flagging in the wind destroyed the illusion of stepping back in time. That and the Internet café Marcus found. It wasn't so much a full-on Internet café Shanghai style with hundreds of monitors and the blank faces of gaming teens glued to screens; rather, it was a couple of scuffed PCs in what looked like someone's living room. After Marcus paid the equivalent of a dime to find out if his website name would fly, Jennifer and I talked with the woman who'd collected the fee. The village had been there since the Cultural Revolution. This made sense: I'd read that many of Shanghai's intellectuals had been sent to the island for reeducation. They'd been forced by Red Guards to give up their bourgeois books and pick up a hoe to plant melon seeds. Only hard labor in the mudflats of Chongming shoveling piles of pig shit would reform their capitalist ways.

"We are standing right in the middle of one of the hottest real estate markets in China," Marcus said when he finished with his cyber sleuthing. "Developers are calling it the Shangri-La of Shanghai." My eyes moved toward a chicken pecking in the mud.

"Oh, 'Creative China' has been taken," Marcus said. "I'll have to think up a new name."

"It's not easy being creative," I said.

"And there are already sites selling X-rated emoticons. I was afraid someone else would figure it out first. But I found out we are in the right place. This is where the city is going to be built."

"Is it true?" Jennifer asked the woman who owned the computers and the chicken.

The woman said she didn't know much about the city the government was planning to build on the island but she knew that her village was being relocated. Apartment blocks were under construction a few miles away among fields filled with cabbages. She said she wasn't too worried about moving into a new home but she was worried about the people in the village losing their farmland. They'd been farming this area the same way for several generations; now the government wanted them to farm a new way, and maybe to farm in new fields. She didn't quite know what she was expected to do, but I guessed it would be organic and sustainable. Peasants living in harmony with nature on the outskirts of the eco-city seemed to be part of the plan. Another part of the master strategy for Dongtan was to make it as self-sustaining as possible. I imagined this woman's family would be growing food to help feed the city. Villages of peasants producing chemical-free melons would be an excellent selling point in the marketing campaign to move eco-friendly real estate, Marcus pointed out to me.

If one were to travel to the eco-city of Dongtan during a visit to the World Expo in 2010, after taking a gander at one of the largest construction projects in human history, which is being built on a mostly undeveloped island in the mouth of the Yangtze River, one could board a boat in Shanghai and travel upstream on the turbid waters of the Yangtze to the Three Gorges Dam—which holds more gigatons of concrete than any other structure on earth and is so massive that when the reservoir it holds was filling up, scientists detected a wobble in the earth's rotation. This megaproject of all megaprojects, the world's largest hydroelectric power station, had helped China lessen its need to build scores of dirty coal-fired power plants—and had resulted in the displacement of more than a million people as the waters behind the dam rose and inundated cities on the Yangtze's shores. Many of the displaced people had been relocated by the government to Chongming Island. And many of these relocated people were now being re-relocated away from the building site of the mighty green metropolis of Dongtan. In China it's not easy being green, and it certainly isn't easy being a peasant in the path of progress, be that progress measured in miles of concrete, or by the carbon footprint of an eco-city.

Half a million people: this is the government's target population for Dongtan by 2050. Fifty thousand are scheduled to be living in the nascent eco-city in time for the 2010 Expo. I walked outside the woman's home and scanned the horizon. It was flat and it was empty. Had I just arrived in Shanghai I would have thought the Dongtan scheme preposterous, but I'd spent enough time in China's show-piece metropolis to know that everything is possible. It took Boston twenty years to reroute a freeway underground. In less time, the towers of Pudong had risen, and Shanghai now had more skyscrapers than New York City and was finishing the most extensive subway system on the planet. From the mudflats of Chong-ming Island would rise a city housing half a million people: it was entirely possi-ble. In Shanghai, nothing is impossible because the Chinese people have endless ambition—and also, of course, because they have an endless supply of cheap labor and none of the constraints that slow massive building schemes in the West, such as pesky environmental restrictions, annoying labor laws, and progress-im-peding public review processes. When it comes to utopian construction projects, democracy is a drag. If the Communist Party wants to build an eco-city a third the size of Manhattan on a mudflat, planners draw up the designs, the government approves the project, and laborers work in three rotating eight-hour shifts around the clock seven days a week until the city rises from the mud.

I stood a moment and listened to the soft hush of wind moving through grass. I had no doubt that the Dongtan eco-city could be built by the Chinese. But about its eco credentials I had many doubts. Even if all of its eco-friendly features the government was touting were put in place, what sense did it make to have a self-sustaining, eco-friendly suburb in the midst of one of the most contaminated cities on earth? Shanghai has virtually no enforceable environmental protections in place. Instead of giving Shanghai yet another megaproject to add to its checklist when the Expo rolls around, wouldn't the saner course of action be to implement simple yet effective environmental measures in the city? How about better build-ing codes for the towers being raised each day in Shanghai? Many of these struc-tures are shoddily built without energy-saving windows or insulation in the roofs; they belch heat in winter and bleed air conditioning in summer. How about man-dating low-emissions vehicles on the streets of Shanghai instead of creating a sub-urb where cars are banned, but to get there citizens will drive from the city center on a gargantuan road that makes an L.A. freeway look like a country lane.

We made our way along a country lane through the villages and farmland and boggy grasses that held some of the world's best bird habitat, and eventually we found the Dongtan eco-city headquarters. There were no birds in sight, but there was a demonstration center with a scale model of the future city with which I fell instantly in love. It is an urban designer's dream—a built-from-scratch city where a half million people will live, work and play. And it is a green freak's wildest fantasy come true because those half million people will live, work and play in a carbon-neutral metropolis where nothing goes to waste. Much like the scale model of Shanghai in the Urban Planning and Exhibition Hall, the Dongtan eco-city model made me feel both very childlike and very serious. Serious like a god looking down on his domain; giddy like a child who has created from building blocks a city faultless and complete. The nerdy kid I'd been who had devoured all of Arthur C. Clarke's, Isaac Asimov's and Carl Sagan's books recognized Dongtan immediately—it was a city straight from the pages of a space utopia story. Perhaps the city was on a more perfect planet Earth, perhaps it was on a colonized moon beneath a dome that allowed a world of green trees and blue canals to flourish, but here it was—the city of the future. And my god was it beautiful.

A spokesperson for state-owned SIIC, which had partnered with the London-based engineering and design firm Arup—the brains behind the project that had designed Dongtan down to the last detail and orchestrated a PR campaign that had left Marcus and his friends lining up to invest—narrated the story of the eco-city while I walked around the model, lost in fantasies garnered from science fiction paperbacks.

Dongtan, which means "east beach," would be the world's first city designed from the ground up for total environmental efficiency. The wind farm we'd seen would generate green electricity, and a power plant would burn rice husks, creating so much surplus power that Dongtan would send juice to the Shanghai grid. And burning rice husks, a waste product from agriculture around the Yangtze River, would also create heat, which would be piped to homes and businesses to keep them warm in winter. Almost all trash would be recycled in Dongtan. Hollowed-out hills would be formed around the city to protect it from floods, and inside the hills hyper-efficient underground organic farms would grow piles of produce. Only zero-emissions vehicles would be allowed inside Dongtan; delivery trucks from outside the "green zone" would park past the city limits and load their goods onto shared zero-emissions vehicles. All buildings in Dongtan would be four to eight stories high, tall enough to minimize sprawl, but not so tall that they would sink in the squishy soil of the alluvial island. More than half of Dongtan would be dedicated open space for parklands and farms, and the entire city would be crisscrossed by pedestrian and biking paths. Sign me up. I want to live there—right there in that exquisite Dongtan diorama.

Our guide pointed out to us the canals of Dongtan: strips of glossy blue enamel bearing tiny boats across the model. People would be transported throughout the town on hydrogen-powered water taxis. Sagan and Clarke would be proud. As would the Chinese: the canals were not modeled after those of Venice, for the Venetians, compared to the Chinese, had lacked a sophisticated understanding of how to base a town around water. A couple of hours of driving from Shanghai took one to the famous water towns of China such as Suzhou and Tongli, where efficient networks of lakes, locks, dams and canals managed the water around which the communities were based, and boats powered by people with poles in hand plied the liquid routes between markets and homes. The British designers from Arup had drawn inspiration from these ancient Chinese water towns.

Looking at the Dongtan diorama, with its intricate parkways and canals, its perfect little houses like those of a model train layout, I could believe that Dongtan would be a paragon of ecological harmony, a carbon-neutral city powered entirely by renewable energy. I believed. I had no idea what the Dongtan spokesperson was droning on about—renewable this, recyclable that—but I looked at that flawless miniature world and I believed. I'm a sucker for miniatures. If we go into a museum together and there are dioramas in the building, you know where to find me. What is it about a scale model, everything tiny and tidy, that makes it so enticing? I looked at the model of Dongtan and believed China was moving from an industrial age to a post-industrial ecological age, and it was merely a matter of time before all of China would be as perfect and clean as the world of Dongtan in miniature.

Outside, in the decidedly imperfect and wholly disappointing life-size world, Dongtan was a mess. I clung tightly to my eco fantasies of a futuristic city, but once I was separated from the model in the climate-controlled office and I took in a few big breaths of swampy Dongtan air, something didn't smell right. Maybe it was the talk of heliports and cruise ship terminals, golf courses and marinas crowded with yachts. Maybe it was the plan to boost Chongming's real estate values by zoning part of the island for the construction of a Disneyland and a replica of Michael Jackson's Neverland Ranch. Or maybe it was the single-family demonstration homes we toured that looked to me big enough to house an American family in complete comfort. I could look past that they had huge living rooms and sprawling yards, but what about the garages? I guess the families had to have somewhere to park their no-emissions vehicles, but I began to suspect those garages might one day hold Buicks and that the people selling property at Dong-tan and promoting it as the world's first carbon-neutral city were a lot like the real estate agents in America who called the sliver of distant hill I could see if I stood in one corner of one room of my townhouse and raised up on my toes to peer over neighbors' roofs a "mountain view."

Maybe it was the disgruntled farmers and fishermen we met later that day who dimmed my enthusiasm for the green megaproject. The eco-friendly me-tropolis did not seem to be farmer friendly. "I won't go to the city," one of them told us. "They won't let me inside it when it's finished." Granted, he probably wouldn't have been let into a tower of Pudong either with his mud-crusted shoes and sour breath that could have knocked a dragon down, but at least Pudong had the decency to be overtly elitist. Dongtan's marketing team talked a lot about holistic living and balancing ecological sustainability with social responsibility, or fostering social sustainability and ecological responsibility within the context of integrated urbanism, or something. When Chinese Communists get hold of eco jargon, look out. The catchwords I had read in slick brochures and heard in sales pitches delivered by spokespeople in crisp suits were all muddled in my head.

Speaking of shrewd marketing, Marcus was burning minutes on his mobile talking about flooring with a friend. His buddy had good guanxi with executives in a flooring manufacturing operation in Shanghai, and Marcus and his friend were trying to get a contract with Dongtan to make flooring for its homes.

"The product is perfect for Dongtan because it looks like wood but it isn't wood," Marcus told me. "No trees are killed. It's a kind of plastic. It's made from petroleum instead of wood."

Petroleum is precisely why China is mucking around in Sudan and mixed up in Darfur and what has been called the first genocide of the twenty-first century. Mia Farrow and friends are having none of it and continue to hold China's feet to the fire, accusing them of bankrolling the Janjaweed, shadowy Arabic-speaking militias hell-bent on creating an African holocaust. Maiming, killing, raping, loot-ing and burning down villages is the daily work of the Janjaweed, and hacking off women's breasts with machetes is one of their signature tactics. But Sudan, the country in which they are running amuck, has oil, and China is there, pump-ing petroleum as fast as it can. Petroleum that might, in one way or another, make its way onto Chongming Island, whether from molecules engineered into flooring in the homes of the eco-city, or from gasoline to power the cars that will allow residents of Dongtan to commute from their ecologically sustainable and socially responsible suburb to their office towers in Pudong.

"What a world," I said. How could an American criticize another nation for morally questionable behavior in the pursuit of petroleum and keep a straight face? I shook my head and my face loosened as I laughed. "What a world," I said again.

"You are always saying that," Jennifer said.

"Sometimes I don't know what else to say."

"All the flooring for homes for half a million people," Marcus said. "And all made from oil—no wood." He shook his head and smiled. "Think about it."

I did. That was a lot of flooring. A lot of oil. And a lot of food—half a million people to feed, and Dongtan was claiming the majority of the food would be produced locally. It would take armies of farmers and fishermen to feed the eco-pioneers in Dongtan. And who would clean the homes of the green-minded hordes who would soon move here? Surely people who were shelling out a million U.S. dollars for an eco-mansion in Dongtan wouldn't be waxing their own shiny new flooring.

It's easy to be snarky about Dongtan with its British design company that builds airports and office blocks in a distinctly non-green way all over China all the time and is then hailed as an environmental hero for designing a green showcase project. Afloat in money from cashing in on the bonanza of China's messy rise, it's easy for Arup to unveil a model green city for the future and then brag about its eco credentials. And it's easy for a Chinese company with government ties to reap the profits of selling green to Shanghai's newly rich, who look to the West to figure out how to spend their boatloads of money and see that green is the new gold standard for sophisticated wealth.

Instead of applauding China for building a construction project on a scale unprecedented in human history right smack in the middle of an ecologically rich and fragile paradise for birds, let's share with China our practical technology. Let's talk with them about adding insulation to the roofs of the towers rising in Pudong. Let's talk with them about energy-saving windows and light bulbs. Let's find the simplest ways to reduce demands on Shanghai's grid—so those demands don't escalate to the point where, instead of occasionally breathing in an errant cloud of soot China has sent our way over the Pacific, we are cloaked in the perpetual creepy twilight that suffuses the Shanghai sky, no glimpse of blue by day, no glimmer of star at night.

China's once ubiquitous bikes are being replaced with cars as the nation hurries to wrap its cities in roads.

When the bridge-tunnel system to Chongming is finished, fresh ribbons of asphalt will be laid across the island, and cars will quickly outnumber the pedal-powered vehicles and pedestrians that now travel the muddy streets of Dongtan. When it comes to China's environmental disasters, what the Chinese government is guilty of most is mimicking the American model of economic development. Beginning in the 1980s, China started sending delegations overseas to figure out how the West had created massive growth. What they found, of course, was that the United States was enjoying the greatest prosperity in history in large part because it had adopted a model of development that encouraged an automobile-based lifestyle dependent on roads, sprawling communities, and unfettered energy consumption. And of course the Chinese, desperate to catch up to the West, promoted their automobile industry as a cornerstone of their economic development strategy. After all, it had worked not only for America, but also for China's Asian neighbors of South Korea and Japan. China's equivalent of America's Interstate Highway System was being built in the space of a few years, and China's auto industry recently passed up those of Japan and the United States to become the world's largest. My eyes sting with exhaust each day in Shanghai and my lungs convulse from fumes. About thirty-five million cars clog Chinese roads right now. Projections ten to twenty years out range as high as one hundred and thirty million cars. I imagine by then the air in Shanghai will be about as hospitable for human life as the atmosphere of Venus.

For the Chinese to achieve the same standard of living as Americans, two planet Earths will be necessary to provide the raw resources. Three planet Earths, seven, even nine—experts are forever announcing the number of planet Earths that will be needed to sustain China's rise. The exact metric is, of course, meaningless, as even two planet Earths is one too many. China has taken note: it is headed to the moon. Going into space gives China face; it also gives it a chance to mine distant worlds and gather the resources it needs to let its people live like Americans.

The environmentalism that will save Shanghai—and the rest of the planet, which is now connected to China's most populous city by the weather we share and the air we breathe—is not the convoluted engineering and marketing scheme of Dongtan. It is people parking their cars and riding their bikes to work among the elevated highways of the sprawling metropolis. It is people in the twenty-first century's most magnificent megacity dimming the lights. And this won't happen until people in Shanghai look to America and see citizens of the nation with the highest material standard of living in the history of human civilization doing the simple but effective things that lessen our demand for the earth's finite resources. At the risk of sounding like a complete nut, I say this: If you fear China's megacities that rise like mirages against a sky of industrial orange all aglow with amber waves of poison that ride the weathers of the world to our shores, if you don't want to breathe Shanghai's nastiness into your lungs, then turn off your lights, ride a bike to work, recycle. If you complain about China destroying life as we know it on planet Earth, know that China looks to you when deciding what to value and how to behave. One fifth of humanity is staring at you. They know us far better than we know them, for they are forever watching us, studying us. What they see will help guide their course in the coming decades. And the course they choose will determine whether our world looks more like the Dongtan diorama dreamscape or like the nightmare gathering in Shanghai as the city builds itself into oblivion.

There, I've said it. That's my earnest plea to save the planet. When I'm in the Rockies I don't want to breathe in that shit that I breathe in when I'm walking Shanghai's streets. And the Chinese government doesn't want its economy to fizzle and fade beneath the overwhelming weight of the environmental consequences of unchecked growth. The world is suffocating, but there is an open window.

"Will that work?" Jennifer asked. She was reading over my shoulder. I was writing the previous sentences in a notebook.

"Will Americans really ride a bike to work so that Chinese people will want to stop using cars and go back to riding bikes like we used to when we were poor?"

"I doubt it," I said.

"Then why did you write it?"

"Because writing it is better than not writing it."

She was silent a moment, her hand patting the air. "Why did you write, 'I was writing the previous sentences in a notebook'?" Jennifer asked. "You are writing it now."

"That's a good point. Tenses in English are confusing. They are much simpler in Chinese."

"You are going to write about Dongtan in your book?"

"I am writing about Dongtan in my book."

"But the book is about me and my parents?"

"That's part of it."

"Is it the most important part?"

I thought a moment. "Yes," I said. "You and your parents are the most important part."

"Why? Because my parents are having to leave their home?"

I studied Jennifer's face, so earnestly awaiting my answer. "Because stories can't be about cities or about the environment. Stories can be about people living in cities or living in an environment, but stories always have to be about people."

Jennifer raised up on her tiptoes and dropped back down and blew at her bangs. "And Marcus? Is he important too?"

"He's a minor character. You're the main character."

Jennifer smiled.

"Do you like being the main character?" I asked.

"*Dāngrán le.*" Of course. "Perhaps everyone likes being the main character."

"Not me. I'm happy to just be the narrator and a minor character."

"Narrator—*shénme yìsi*?" What does it mean?

"The person who tells the story."

Jennifer blew at her bangs, thinking a moment. "Then we are good partners," she said.

"That's right. We each have our job to do. Your job is to be you, my job is to tell about you."

"So what do I do now?" Jennifer said. "I haven't done anything at Dongtan that you've written about."

"Well," I said, "what do you make of Dongtan?"

"What do I *make of* Dongtan?"

"What do you think about it?"

"*Nèige . . .*"

Nèige is Chinese for "um" or "uh." It is a sound Chinese people make when they are thinking.

"*Nèige* . . . I don't know. It's very quiet. And I can see very far away. The air here is very clear. It seems strange to be able to see so far away."

"Would you want to live here?"

She shook her head side to side so hard I thought she might pop a tendon in her neck. "*Tài kōng kuàng le.*" Too empty. She quit speaking a moment, then said, "I want to live in Shanghai but I want the air to be clean there like it is here on the island. Like you," she said, grinning. "I don't want to breathe that shit in. It's not good for health."

"Do you think that will happen? Will the air be clean in Shanghai someday?"

"It is a problem now, but the government is working to fix it. It takes a long time. America and Europe did the same thing, right?"

"That's true. We had our industrial revolutions, and then we cleaned up the messes we made. We're still cleaning them up. It will take a long time."

"We will clean our air in China. It will also take a long time."

"How long do you think?"

"I think perhaps I will be so old I won't even know if the air is dirty or clean anymore."

I laughed and nodded. "You know what I just realized? When I was watching you speak? I've never seen you shrug your shoulders."

"Shrug my shoulders?"

"Like this." I demonstrated.

"Yes, in *Friends* they do that. Chinese people don't do that." She gave a giant shrug of her little shoulders. "Like this?"

"More casual," I said. "Like this." I gave a relaxed shrug.

"You do this because you don't know an answer?" she asked.

"Or if you don't care about something."

She practiced a few times. "How's that?"

"Better."

"Do you want to go look for birds?" I said.

She opened her mouth to say something, then she closed it, and finally she said, "Why?"

"We're right next to one of the most important bird sanctuaries in the world. Watching birds is what people do here. People from all over the world come here to look at birds."

Jennifer blew at her hair. "They just look at the birds?"

"Birdwatchers try to find different species, different kinds of birds. They watch them and they write down what kinds of birds they saw. They keep a list."

"This is strange," Jennifer said. "Why do they do this?"

"Because they like nature."

The look Jennifer gave me told me this was not a good answer. "Okay," I said. "Because they never have to worry about money or jobs or finding a place to live. Because they have time. They have time and money, so they look at birds."

She shrugged her shoulders. "Maybe when I'm old I will like to look at birds. Now I would rather look at people in the city instead of birds in the nature."

I considered correcting her: In nature—no "the." But it sounded pretty damn charming. I made no move to correct her and I wondered if my Chinese ever sounded charming by the accident of my fumbled grammar. Perhaps it probably did not.

"Do you want to look at birds?" she said.

"In the nature?" I said.

I turned and glanced around us at fishponds swirling with carp and at marshes thick with reeds. I saw no plovers, swans or cranes. The sky above the ocean in the distance wasn't exactly blue, but it lacked the sick hue of a nicotine stain that the horizon above Shanghai often holds.

One day a few years ago, beneath a dingy sky in Colorado, I had read an article about a brown cloud of soot and toxins that had drifted over the mountains of the West and could be traced on the jet stream all the way back to China. I figured I couldn't hide in the Rockies the rest of my life; I resolved to get out there and see for myself what on earth was going on in this frenzied nation of 1.3 billion plus people spewing poison across the globe and blanketing the world in its filth. There is no safe place left. We have no choice but to look toward China and to try to understand what is happening to all of us. And what better way to try than to travel with Chinese friends to the outer edge of the city of the future.

I stood next to Jennifer and together we looked across the marshes of Dongtan to where Shanghai lay buried amid the murk in the distance. Wind brushed the grasses and flowed against our faces. Behind us lay the East China Sea, and further out spread the salty bulk of the Pacific, its deep currents pushing toward distant shores, its endless airstreams wrapping round the planet. Jennifer was smiling. If this is how the world ends, I am grateful for that smile. For the peace it holds, the warmth. I will remember the way her mouth shaped her joy that day as we hurl toward the earth's unwinding. I will see the curve of her lips, the gentle divots of her cheeks, when the sun is finally snuffed.

Numbers of birds in the Dongtan wetland preserve have dropped precipitously the past few years. Construction of the enormous bridge-tunnel system connecting Chongming to the mainland might be contributing to the decline; the preliminary development of the Dongtan eco-city could be responsible. A culprit in the decreasing bird populations could be the shipbuilding industry being moved from the mainland of Shanghai to an island in the mouth of the Yangtze River next to Chongming Island, not far as the crow flies from the Dongtan wetland. Shanghai's shipbuilding industry, the largest in China and soon to be the largest in the world, is being pushed out to sea to make space for the Expo 2010 site. I have wandered the shipyards of Shanghai: industrial zones where the soundscape is dominated by a heavy metal cacophony of clanging and banging and the air ripples with gas fumes. I'm no ornithologist, but I'm going to go out on a limb and say the world's largest shipyard is not contributing to a healthy bird habitat.

Birds have had a rough time of it in China, beginning with one of the silly agricultural schemes devised in the days of Mao. China's chairman, ever the clever innovator, encouraged the Chinese people to kill as many birds as possible to keep their hungry beaks from cutting into the productivity of the country's crop harvests. Entire villages took to their roofs and other high places to bang together pots and pans. They made such a racket that the birds could find no peaceful place to land; they flew themselves in circles until they dropped from the sky, dead. Or so it's been said. It's a hell of a story, even if it isn't true.

And it is true that you rarely see wild birds in China. One of the things I'd first noticed when I came to Shanghai was the lack of life forms other than Homo sapiens. Pigeons flap through New York City, coyotes roam the canyons of Los Angeles, Chicago is crawling with squirrels. In Shanghai it seems the only animal species is human. And so few trees and green spaces brighten the urban core that it sometimes seems the only living thing is people.

A steel mill on Chongming Island has been there for many years amid the marshes and trees and what birds are left. The Chinese government could have built more steel mills and shipbuilding yards, transforming all the undeveloped land of Chongming into a manufactured landscape like the rest of Shanghai, replete with industrial zones and high-density housing projects. But instead it chose to preserve one of the world's major bird reserves more or less in its natural state, and it opted to build an ecological demonstration city, which has enjoyed the support of the highest levels of the Chinese government—all the way up to Chinese President Hu Jintao. However flawed Dongtan might be, it is heartening to see the Chinese government putting some brakes on pell-mell growth and taking the ecological consequences of development into consideration when issuing its economic plans.

While squinting through pollution-stung eyes at the apocalyptic spectacle of Shanghai's skies, it is easy to scapegoat China for spoiling the planet. But consider this: China recently adopted automobile fuel-efficiency standards more stringent than those in the United States. And Shanghai's public transportation infrastructure should be the envy of every American metropolitan area. Our cities' glaring absence of sophisticated public transportation speaks as powerfully to the Chinese of a country that is slipping downward as their polluted skies do to us of a newly risen nation that is choking on its own growth.

"America's airports are the first thing Chinese see when they come to your country, and your airports are a joke," Marcus had told me. He wasn't kidding. "And your subways are even worse. Maybe China can lend America money so it can build new subways." He had laughed experimentally at the last statement and I had joined him in his mirth. But a few weeks later, while I was lost riding BART in San Francisco, the maps defaced with graffiti and the announcement loudspeakers hanging uselessly from frayed wires, I had remembered the Shanghai metro with its plasma screens on every platform to show passengers the seconds until the next trains arrive, and Marcus's quip had seemed not so funny. While we wag our fingers at China for the messes they've made, we should remember that they are doing some things right—and they are doing some things better than we are.

When the Shanghai Economic Commission announced the city's top twenty goals for 2008, energy conservation and pollution control topped the list. Western governments should laud this kind of progress. Though not as glamorous as building the world's biggest eco-city, addressing Shanghai's environmental problems by issuing citywide guidelines and goals is a profoundly important step for Shanghai, for China, and for the planet. And Western businesses should take note. For the burgeoning American environmental industry, China offers a trove of messes in need of cleaning up. Pollution mitigation is a growth industry in China, and there are massive profits to be made filtering soot from the sky and purging aquifers of their poisons. There is money in them thar polluted hills.

China's great green hope might be market forces; or it might be its centrally planned economy, of which many elements are still in place. For all its free-market reforms, Shanghai is still a city controlled from above. What the Party wants, the Party gets. If the Party wants mega-development projects to showcase its economic and technological might to the world for the 2010 Expo, towers rise into the grotty skies and bridges span the rancid streams. If the Party wants a socially sustainable eco-city, it builds a socially sustainable eco-city for a half million people with none of the environmental review processes or citizen input sessions that would make the approval of such a mammoth undertaking in America or Europe impossible. Government planners in China don't answer to citizens at the ballot box; they answer to the Party. If the Party decides it wants a bright green future for the people of Shanghai, a bright green future those people will have. Whether they like it or not.

But can an ecological utopia be engineered by central planning committees? Can a green future be mandated from above? The Chinese have some experience with this top-down, authoritarian approach to creating a perfect world. It's called the Great Leap Forward. If any country knows about a utopian vision run amuck, it is China.

Take the case of Long Bow. A model collective farm designed by Chinese authorities to demonstrate the merits of Mao's agricultural paradise, Long Bow wowed the West when an American Marxist, William Hinton, waxed eloquent about its merits and glossed over the myriad failings and crimes of the Cultural Revolution. Perhaps it is not a stretch to view Dongtan within China's history of Potemkin villages, outrageous propaganda jobs by the Communist Party, and incompetent reporting by Americans. Rather than signaling the start of environmental sustainability, Dongtan perhaps indicates the end of any meaningful discussion about how to implement practical measures to clean up the messes China has made. As Paul French, the China Editor for *Ethical Corporation* magazine, points out in articles such as "Arup and Dongtan, Worthy Winner of Greenwasher of the Year," British and American journalists have traveled to Dongtan to meet with Arup spokespeople and returned with stories of "China's Bright Green Future." These William Hintons of our day have seldom a word to say about the disconnect of a clean, green suburb for rich Shanghainese being built at immense expense while millions upon millions of people in Shanghai's urban center and its new satellite cities choke on the air they breathe and are poisoned by the water they drink in an unregulated world of growth at any cost.

It is hard not to be awed by Dongtan: its scale and the scope of its vision are phenomenal. Yet it is the duty of members of a free press to exercise healthy skepticism, to not let themselves be enthralled by the smoke and mirrors of corporate marketing schemes and clever dioramas wrapped in Communist Party propaganda. It is their duty to visit a Potemkin village and then restrain themselves from telling the world that all is right. While Hinton praised the cooperative agricultural endeavor of Long Bow, Chinese who disagreed with Maoist doctrine were imprisoned and tortured, and peasants starved to death en masse. While corporate press releases from a British company sing the merits of Dongtan and hold it up as an exalted example of China's commitment to a clean world, coal-fired power plants without sulfur scrubbers rise across the nation, and each year three quarters of a million Chinese people die prematurely from pollution. What will save these people is not a model city at the Expo designed to make the world gasp at China's vision of a perfect future. What will save China's future scientists and teachers and innovators—who are now children gasping from asthma attacks—is the wholly unglamorous and tedious work of making policy changes and implementing those policies in every city of every province across China. Somewhere between the catastrophe of China's current environment and the futuristic utopia of Dongtan eco-city lies a middle ground—a middle ground of sensible environmental polices guided by the government to steer China toward a greener future that ensures its continued economic growth. A future perhaps not as perfect as the Dongtan diorama, but also not as debilitating as Shanghai's toxic atmosphere is now. Somewhere in the middle between these two extremes lies the only hope the country has of giving its young people enough air to breathe and water to drink so that they can fulfill their potential and build China into the world leader that the nation envisions itself becoming. And the Western media, instead of lauding China for making ludicrous leaps forward into an impossibly perfect future, should praise China for taking small but crucial steps toward sustainability in the imperfect present.

I tried to convince Marcus and Jennifer to spend the night on Chongming Island and return to Shanghai the next day. Respite from the riotous city would do them good, I said. Marcus agreed to stay, telling me he'd have more time to assess the property values and investment potential of the real estate market. Jennifer was more hesitant. The mud would ruin her boots, she said. I told her we could go shopping when we got back to Shanghai and she could buy new boots. This brightened her mood, and soon we were planning our stay. We skipped the "Happy Farm Households Tour" a taxi driver tried to sell us as we roamed dirt roads through a patchwork of paddy fields at the edge of the Dongtan wetland. The tour offered visitors from the city the chance to try their manicured hands at a little farm work, eat a genuine farm dinner, stay in a genuine farmhouse, and enjoy some genuine farmers' folklore. It sounded genuinely ridiculous to me, and the corners of Jennifer's mouth turned down at the idea of her boots squishing through a rice paddy while she rolled up her sleeves to pluck vegetables from the muck.

"Maybe we should do that so we can talk with the farmers and find out how we can buy their land," Marcus said.

"Maybe we should eat crabs," Jennifer said. "They're famous here."

Did we want to watch a goat fight, the taxi tout who was following us around enquired. We most definitely did not want to watch a goat fight, I told him. He gave me a look that said, "Are you crazy? Who doesn't like a good goat fight?"

We all agreed to eat crabs. Chongming's famous crabs are called *héngpá* (crawling sideways) or *bāzhījiǎo* (eight feet). After finding two farmers selling crabs at a street stall, we selected some choice crustaceans and then dined on them until our stomachs ached.

After finding a place to stay for the night, we set out into a wetland, following twisting footpaths beneath a red stretch of light as the sun dipped down in the west. A moist and salty sea wind pressed against our cheeks, our lips. At a crossroads where two paths converged we stopped to glance skyward. Clouds on the move, high winds aloft. Jennifer dragged her feet back and forth, scuffing the soles of her boots through sand and toeing its delicate furrows, handiwork of the wind. These ridges and waves so fragile, so fine, they seemed crafted by a race of tiny artisans. Crabs the size of a child's thumbnail crawled around the roots of plants and disappeared in little holes.

Marcus lifted his leg and then smashed his shoe against the ground, raising into the air sprinkles of sand. Jennifer told him to knock it off as she blinked sand from her eyes and used her forefinger to brush specks from her lips. We took off our shoes, rolled up our pantlegs and waded into a clear and shallow stream. After climbing across a sandbar, we pushed through sticky muck that sucked at our legs, threatening to hold us in place if we stopped moving. Marcus stumbled forward and splatted in the mud. Jennifer and I laughed as Marcus picked himself up, took a few unsteady steps, and then sank in up to his knees. He held his phone high to keep it dry. Slathered in mud, he looked like a swamp beast. Some strange creature risen from primordial ooze bearing the latest in cellular technology.

"You look like a monster," Jennifer said.

"That's nothing," I said. I ran across a mudflat until I'd picked up some speed and then I dived face first and slid like a baseball player charging home plate and scooting under the tag of a catcher's mitt. When I stood up, Jennifer was clapping. With my fingertip I smeared little globs of mud on her cheeks; she screamed and fled. Marcus chucked mudballs at her as she ran away into the reeds.

We made our way off the mudflat and searched down narrow paths in the jungle grasses for a place to rinse off. Small birds teetered and wheeled against the purpling sky as we pushed our way through a thicket of reeds. Before us was a pool. In its center, stones ten feet under looked the same as those lining the shore. The pool water so clear it seemed a thing of dreams, a thing imagined. At a far edge floated swans. So still, watching. We stood motionless and watched back. The swans all in a row, six of them, necks straight, heads high and steady and staring. A council assembled to judge what threat there was. Their beauty made me shiver. Their white plumage and slender necks.

"Don't move," Jennifer whispered. "Don't make sounds."

Soon the swans were swimming, the webs of their splayed feet paddling, necks curved and elegant, white breasts gently plowing as they circled through the pool. Water lipped against their bodies and small waves spread behind them as they passed. Into the wake of one stepped Jennifer. Ripples sloshed against her ankles, each ripple like an echo of the birds' passage that faded in the larger silence of the pond.

Marcus bent down and touched the water. He recoiled when his fingers dipped into it, as if surprised that it was real. He grinned and then stepped onto the pebbled floor and waded in up to his hips. Mud melted from his pants, sending a brown cloud spreading through the pool. I walked in, the warmth of the water rising above my knees, my stomach, bubbles lifting toward the surface. I watched the bubbles wink and vanish and then I pushed forward and slowly stroked, dogpaddling above the center of the pool, suspended in bathwater warmth, the swans circling, indifferent to my swimming. Their territory invaded perhaps a thousand times, the days of angry wing flapping and snapping beaks long passed, so used to this intrusion they'd grown.

I jumped up and then with outspread arms fell backward, my body smacking the water and raising fans of spray. The swans moved as if to rise, then tucked their wings at their sides, and their circling did not cease. Through the still waters they moved in loops of silent elegance and the story says they will never sing until the moment of their dying. Around us and between us swam the swans, pale and ever-moving toward their final song. As if they must circle for their lives entire toward one thing, a song so perfect its consonance will earn them what little immortality the earth allows.

"I think my phone might be broken," Marcus said, peeling a glob of hardened mud from his handset after he'd stepped dripping from the pond and retrieved his phone from the nest of leaves in which he'd set it. Then he said, "Do you think they will build houses next to this water?"

"Luxury condos with a view of the swan pond?" I said.

"They would be very expensive condos," Marcus said.

Jennifer said, "I saw on TV about rich people in France who put mud on their faces to make their skin beautiful."

"My parents won't believe it," Marcus said.

"Believe what?" I said.

"They won't believe expensive houses are being built here."

"They've been here?" I asked.

"They were sent here."

He told me that his father was an economics professor. An economics professor who had not preached the virtues of Marxism as forcefully as the Party would have liked. His mother's family had owned a bookstore in Shanghai.

"They were sent here in 1969 to dig irrigation ditches," he said. "They lived here for seven years. Now my dad's a professor again in Shanghai."

"And the bookstore?"

"The government didn't give it back to my mom's family. They sold it to a developer who made it into a massage shop. It's on Zhapu Road in Hongkou."

"So it's a brothel?"

"No, they really give massages there."

I'd been helping Marcus develop a sarcastic sense of humor, and the smirking tone with which he delivered this statement gave me hope that, in time, we could move on and I could help him appreciate satire and irony. Lessons using *The Onion* as a teaching resource would commence upon our return to the city. Perhaps someday he'd laugh when he read *The Onion*, not because he didn't want to lose face by failing to understand our strange Western ways but because sometimes in this world there is nothing left to do but laugh.

"They dug ditches here for seven years," I said, mainly to myself, trying to make sense of the senseless. The wackiest imaginations in the world could not conjure up tales as utterly odd as the stories from China's recent past. I had been in China long enough to know better than to trust that my understanding of logic could illuminate everything, but sometimes I indulged myself in the belief that there were perfectly sensible reasons for things like university professors being banished to an island to dig in the mud where a few decades later luxury homes were built in a nature preserve and billed as Shanghai's Shangri-La, and a book-store becoming a brothel as red banners trumpeting a harmonious society brightened the city's streets. Up was down and down was up, Chinese say of the Cultural Revolution when explaining the chaos that ensued.

I dived down into the water, rolled over in a circle and watched up turn to down and down to up, and then I broke through the surface of the pond, blinking my wet eyes, shaking my hair dry.

"I was born here," Marcus said.

I had no idea what to say. Sarcasm failed me, empathy was impossible. Irony seemed some invention of a distant world, and nothing I had ever read in a book had any relevance right now. I just stood there nodding and staring at the swans.

Orange rays of afternoon sun fell upon the water the swans rode in their endless passing, black masks upon their faces, with black eyes that bulged unblinking, as if to better see the darkness at the end of their circling. And in their breasts of purest white lay the buried notes of song.

We left the swan pond and passed through marshes and through fields. Quiet as cat burglars we hiked straight toward the sun to thieve the last angles of light. As the sun's color drained into the dusk, we huddled close together, damp backs goosebumping in the chill, faces tilted toward the last bright place in the west. Lights in little houses winked on around Dongtan like phosphorescence in a sea of black, and the wind moved in eternal waves through the reeds around us. We found a dry patch of dirt in a cluster of trees and lay on our backs and looked up at the dark plumes of trees tipped with moonlight, and we stared into the galvanic black beyond. We stared so long I believed I could see the streak of the stars in their slow revolving, the bleed of their light as the world rolled upon its axis.

"Do you like the nature?" I asked Jennifer.

"I like the stars," she said. "In Shanghai it is not possible to see them." She was quiet a moment and then said, "It is strange that the stars are always there even when we can't see them. We are watching them, but maybe they are watching us, too. Maybe they can always see us, even when we can't see them."

"Maybe they wink like that because they are laughing at us," Marcus said.

I rolled onto my side and studied Marcus, his face turned toward the sky, his eyes closed, the faint wash of the moon bright against the bones of his cheeks, the crest of his brow.

"Why are they laughing?" Jennifer asked.

"Because we are funny to them," Marcus said, his eyes still closed.

"Why are we funny?" I asked.

"Because we are so slow."

"Slow?"

"We are so slow to go to the stars," Marcus said. "We are all running around buying things and building things and breaking things on this earth, and they are waiting for us."

"The stars are waiting for us?"

"If we cooperated we could go to the stars. They are waiting for us, but we are too slow. We are funny to them. They watch us and they wonder why we don't hurry up, and they are laughing at us." Marcus opened his mouth in a moon-bright smile, each tooth gleaming in the light. "When I was a little boy and I lived here on Chongming I saw the stars every night and I wanted to study space."

"You wanted to be a scientist and study the stars?" I said.

"Of course. Stars are the most interesting thing there is. The stars are the biggest mystery in the world. They are the coolest thing. When I was little my father gave me an American encyclopedia—*World Book*—you know this?"

"Sure," I said. "Before Wikipedia there was *World Book*. You can see them in museums now."

"My father kept his *World Book* during the Cultural Revolution. When he was sent to Chongming he hid it under the floor of his brother's home in Shanghai. It was dangerous to keep it but he did. He gave it to me to help me practice my English when I was fourteen and I read it."

"You read the whole encyclopedia?"

"Most of it. I read it every day before I went to school and I read it on the weekends. I read about space and planets and stars—those were the best parts. When I was in high school I read *Cosmos*. Carl Sagan was the coolest person ever. He wanted us all to go to the stars."

"So why didn't you become a scientist?"

"My scores weren't good enough."

"On the National Exam?"

"I had to study marketing and business."

"There is a saying in the West that comes from this scholar—his name was Joseph Campbell. He said 'Follow your bliss.'"

Marcus turned to look at me. "I saw this on a bumper sticker at Stanford once. I asked someone what it means. I understand it, but it doesn't mean anything to me. In China we have a saying: *shēng yú yōu huàn, sǐ yú ān lè.*"

"*Shénme yìsi?*" I asked. What does it mean?

"It basically means you should worry about practical things."

"It's not easy to follow your bliss in China."

"It is much easier now than it was for my parents. When I am rich I will study space and teach students about space."

I stared a moment at Marcus, his eyes sealed shut, the light of the stars in their countless numbers bright against his face. "Remember when I asked you what you thought would happen when all the nations of the world are rich?" I said.

"You ask so many questions."

"You said there wouldn't be wars anymore. What will people do when there aren't wars?"

"They will go to the stars." He opened his eyes and smiled. "They are waiting for us."

When we finished watching the sky we weaved our way through paths lit by the moon and sometimes we parted thick reeds as if parting curtains. Tickly grasses touched our cheeks and we laughed our way back toward the house where we had rented rooms. Once again we were covered in dirt. Near the house lay a path that ran to the shores of another pond, and in the air above the dark water mist unfurled, laying a hush upon the world. I stripped down to my boxer shorts and tread my bare feet across a floor of mud, plants pressing their rubbery leaves against my legs as I waded into the pond. The bottom fell away, not in a gentle sloping but in a sudden end and now I was swimming in silken waters. The dirt of Dongtan rinsed from my body. The pond was warm, heated perhaps by some fiery wellspring buried deep beneath its floor. Marcus and then Jennifer followed me in and we splashed around and lingered in the waters, for they were warmer than the night. I told Marcus and Jennifer stories of hidden hot springs in the Rockies, how they were filled with natural sulfurs and salts that had healed my body from the battering it took on long runs over mountain trails, and how when I was young I had believed that if I bathed in those places on the other side of the world I could run in the mountains forever and I would never tire. As if those mountain ponds welled from a magic seam in the fabric of things.

"Maybe this pond is magic too," Jennifer said. She shrugged her shoulders a few times. "My shrugging," she said. "It's getting better?"

"Much better." I laughed and rolled over on my back to watch stars winking overhead. Marcus sat upon the reedy shore plipping pebbles in the pond. Jennifer swam next to me, and when we spoke our voices carried far in the silence of this place. Between us stars lay on the water as steady as where each hung in its place above, and when one fell from the sky it fell through the water, the pond like some lens focused on another night world, one visited perhaps in dreams. Our legs pedaled through the depths beneath us and our arms slowly fanned. Ripples fled from our fingers and wobbled the reflected stars. From a far edge of the pond came the soft clatter of duck wings and other noises. Scratchings and gruntings in the dark, a cooing birdsong, small dogs talking in yips and barks. Marcus threw a rock across the pond and suddenly all around us were frantic beating wings and crazy splashing as ducks rose. The water dripping from their lifting bodies plinked back into the mended waters of the pond and the commotion vanished as quickly as it had started.

Jennifer closed her eyes and rolled onto her back, hair fanning out from her face, legs kicking softly, arms in gentle churn as if careful not to disturb the world as it was. Her movements were steady and precise and the stars lay still upon the water. The knowledge that this perfect moment could not last caused my breath to catch for a moment in my throat. I longed to know the inside of her mind, the Chinese puzzle of her mind, and for an instant I believed I could.

Babies, before they learn to form words, babble every sound within the human vocal range. Whether we are born in St. Louis or Shanghai, whether our parents' eyes have epicanthic folds or blue irises, we enter the world babbling English sounds and Chinese sounds; we acquire our native language by narrowing the vast spectrum of noises available to us into one limited band. Perhaps learning to speak Chinese and to think in Chinese is not so much a process of acquiring something new and exotic as it is an act of remembering what we have always known, what we have always understood.

Not a word passed between the three of us for several minutes, the silence we shared in this sheltered place louder than any spoken sound, so loud against the stillness of Shanghai's last wilderness.

The Bridges of Shanghai

Had an atom bomb exploded in the alleyway the destruction would not have looked any worse. Piles of rubble everywhere, shattered bricks and boards. People had vanished as if vaporized. Jennifer and I tromped through a graveyard of doors. These doors, large and lacquered, had once hung in the stone frames of the shikumen that had lined the alleys. One of those doors belonged to Jennifer's parents. Their home had been knocked down and bulldozed over. The demolition crew had come in the night with four policemen. They had given Jennifer's parents and her grandmother one hour to pack their belongings and leave. Her parents and grandmother had done as they were told, and now they were living in a temporary apartment until the residential complex out by the airport where they were being relocated was completed.

"Don't feel sorry for them," Jennifer had told me that morning when she explained what happened. "If you show them you feel pity for them they will lose face."

I had nodded.

"You can write about them, but they don't want you to make an example of them. They are not an example of anything. Do you understand?"

I had nodded that I did.

"My dad wants to find his door," she'd told me. "He thinks he knows where it is. Can you help him?"

"Why does he want the door?"

"He wants to keep it," she'd said. "I don't know why. Will you help him?"

And now we were looking for the door. Jennifer and her father were wearing surgical facemasks to protect them from the dust raised by demolition. A bandanna covered my nose and mouth train-robber style. Jennifer's father stood up straight every few minutes to stretch his back and then he bent again to his task, sorting through the wood slabs for the one that was his own. Our hair was white with dust, our clothes stiff with grime. We were alone in what was left of the alley, bounded by a few crumbling walls. A haggard band of searchers. Survivors of some nameless cataclysm clawing through the rubble of a ruined land.

I had said nothing to Jennifer's father of his plight nor would I ever. A few errant words from a sympathetic foreigner and he could lose the one thing he had left—face. I won't pretend I completely understood this, but Jennifer had led me this far into Shanghai and I would trust her advice to guide me through the scattered remains of her family's life. Our cultural trainings run deep; it had been difficult for me to learn not to offer a hearty handshake to every Chinese person I met. My instincts often sent my eager hand reaching for another's and I had to pull back my hand with my brain. And now I fought the urge to offer my condolences, my brain telling my mouth to seal itself shut.

I pried the great slabs of the doors up from the ground, lifting with my back instead of with my legs, using the pain of the labor to block my frustration. I was pissed at the Chinese government for colluding with developers to tear down an old man's home. And I was pissed at the Chinese people for allowing such a government to exist. It is easy to say I love the Chinese people but I hate their government—it is too easy to say this. The Chinese Communist Party rules the Middle Kingdom in much the same way that emperors before it did. Mao was right about one thing: if there is not continuous revolution in China, the country will revert to old ways. As Qin Shi Huang, the first emperor of China, burned books with ideas inimical to totalitarian rule and buried alive dissidents who did not support his regime, so the Communist Party has created the Great Firewall to block material on the Internet that threatens its absolute hold on power and imprisons anyone who questions the legitimacy of its rule. It is easy to say that the Chinese people are basically good and their government is inherently bad, but this has been going on for thousands of years. Perhaps the Chinese people have chosen their rulers as surely as we have elected ours. Perhaps they have willingly allowed themselves to be imprisoned by the repressive control of one-party rule. From the beginnings of their history they have been governed by regimes with monopolistic powers, sometimes benevolently when Confucianism held sway, sometimes not so benevolently if Legalism or Communism was the rule of the day. They are so proud of their five thousand years of civilization. But as I knelt next to an old man whose home had been taken from him by force by Party functionaries who were rewarded for building new things as quickly as possible and not for preserving objects of quality from the past, I had to wonder what thousands of years of culture had brought the Chinese people.

I bent down next to Jennifer's father and lifted the final door that revealed his own.

"That's it," Jennifer said, identifying the door of their disappeared home. To me it looked like any of the other doors, but first Jennifer and then her father ran their fingers along a small set of characters etched in the black paint, pale wood beneath showing bright in the sun.

"It's a poem," Jennifer said. "From the Tang dynasty. I wrote it on the door when I was a little girl." She said the poem first in Chinese and then in English.

> *Goose, goose, goose*
> *Curves its neck to the sky and sings*
> *White feathers on green water*
> *Red feet paddle the clear waves*

I didn't recognize any of the characters on the door. I asked Jennifer to again recite the poem in Chinese, and while we carried the door through the rubble of the neighborhood and toward a waiting truck that would transport it to the apartment where Jennifer's parents were staying, I said the poem in Chinese over and over, parroting it back to Jennifer. I reproduced the sounds accurately, my tones correct, my pronunciation perfect. My spoken Chinese had improved dramatically—to the point where I was speaking better standard Mandarin than a lot of Chinese people in Shanghai—but my goal of reading Chinese characters fluently was still a long way off. I had been slacking in my studies, preferring to focus on speaking everyday language at the expense of studying characters.

"You speak very well," Jennifer's father told me in Mandarin. I almost dropped the door we were carrying. I looked at Jennifer for an explanation.

"He speaks a little Mandarin," Jennifer said. "He understands it pretty well. But it's hard for him."

"You should learn to read Chinese characters," he said in Mandarin and then he switched to Shanghainese and Jennifer translated into English for me. "It's too bad you can't read yet," he said to me. "You only know the sounds. If you don't understand the characters, your Chinese is like a child's. Characters are the heart of China's culture. They are its soul."

We paused to rest, leaning the door against a chunk of concrete and sitting down atop a pile of shattered stone. As Jennifer and her father had done a few minutes previous, I ran my fingers over the characters that composed the poem. They seemed as strange to me as all characters had my first day in Shanghai. Random lines and squiggles, as cryptic as hieroglyphics.

Written Chinese characters are the same in each dialect throughout China, regardless of the spoken sounds. Jennifer's father reads and writes the same characters that a person in Beijing reads and writes, though their spoken languages are mutually unintelligible. Characters are, as Jennifer's father had said, the heart and soul of Chinese culture. I'd made such a display of my spoken Mandarin, had taken great pride in making the effort to communicate in the native language of the land. I was no ugly American—I had convinced myself of this, and I had taken every opportunity to remind myself and everyone around me by speaking Mandarin. I spoke Mandarin with Jennifer more when monolingual Americans were around, showing them I was different from them, showing them I was better. I had taken the time to learn, they hadn't. But my Chinese was little more than a party trick. I could talk like a Chinese person, but until I recognized the characters I would never think like one, and I would not touch their culture in any deep and meaningful way. And maybe I had been slacking in my studies of written Chinese because I wasn't that motivated to think like a Chinese person. Maybe I didn't really want to know why so many Chinese are content to place the collective good of social stability above personal liberty. Maybe I didn't really want to dig too deeply into why they have created societies for thousands of years that allowed authoritarian rule and valued unquestioning obedience and submission to power above all else. Maybe I was content to have my American thoughts while I spoke Chinese. There was a part of me that I was either too lazy to change or too stubborn to give up. There was a part of me that treasured my Americanness, however ugly it was. I learned this about myself carrying that door with Jennifer's father through his demolished neighborhood, and I didn't necessarily like it, but I did like that I was being honest with myself, and I was grateful for the time I'd spent in China, which had helped me learn as much about my country as I had learned about a nation on the other side of the world. Funny how we have to stray so far from home to understand the home we've strayed from.

After we'd loaded the door into the waiting truck, it pulled away from the curb and blended into a trickle of traffic on a side street; then it flowed toward a boulevard where we merged with a surging swell of cars, buses, trucks and taxis; and we were carried along in the furious current toward a highway larger yet. We rode in silence as somber as if the door we'd recovered had been the remains of a family member. I pressed my face to a window and focused on the spectacle outside. The huffing trucks, the electric bikes threading silently through traffic. People on motor scooters with no helmets, but their faces covered by iridescent shields. People in pajamas with shopping bags in hand. People moving in great masses as though something terribly large and meaningful was afoot. The first day I'd arrived in Shanghai I had thought something was happening, some event, perhaps a rally or a festival. It seemed everyone was moving toward something, frantically pushing their way in the direction of a distant venue where all would gather and an important truth would be revealed. But this had been one of many quasi-hallucinations induced by the city, by its fumes and crushing crowds, by its amphetamine intensity and LSD lights. There was no single event happening, no great gathering or endpoint toward which the crowds were moving. People were simply moving, each in his or her own direction, and nobody knew toward what.

In the days when Shanghai was a treaty port carved into foreign concessions, Chinese people had come to the city to see modernity, to be transported into a future of gas lights and telephones that was a world apart from their rural villages untouched by the Industrial Revolution that had swept Europe and America. Now Westerners swarm to Shanghai hoping to witness the height of the Information Age, hoping to glimpse the Chinese future, but what they see often leaves them disappointed. Though everything in Shanghai is loud and fast and bright, there is nothing new in the megacity, just more of everything that exists in every other city in the world. After the initial thrill of Shanghai's delirious energy fades, the city starts to seem amped but empty. Pretty but pointless. "Shanghai looks like the future!" Paris Hilton proclaimed in 2007 at a news conference for the MTV Style Awards.

Outside the window I saw China's largest city, but I also saw America. I saw America spread out before me as clearly as I saw thousands upon thousands of Chinese faces staring blankly as people passed in vehicles and on foot. I saw that a free and open press is a precious thing. I don't know why of all the things to value in America this one struck me at that moment on the crowded Shanghai street, but it did. Perhaps it was because so many of my Chinese friends had told me a free press is impossible in China because there are too many people. If all of those 1.3 billion people began thinking for themselves . . . . *luàn qī bā zāo*. A total mess. Another popular chengyu, the set phrases of Chinese characters passed down through the ages, is *rén shān rén hǎi*. Literally, "people mountain, people sea." People are everywhere: this is the meaning this phrase conveys, and many foreigners learn it as their first chengyu when they come to China. Or their second—say *mǎ mǎ hǔ hǔ* and try not to smile, both because forming the sounds makes you feel like a happy kid and because the literal translation is "horse horse tiger tiger" but the phrase means "just so-so," or "only average." However poetic and fun the language of chengyu, too many people seems to me a lame excuse for not allowing people to think for themselves.

The Industrial Age is fading fast, though the smoke of it lingers above Shanghai, suffocating its citizens. The Information Age is, of course, the future. The Information Age is dependent partially on technology, which China can copy, but also largely on the freedom to spread information. Perhaps Shanghai is but smoke and mirrors. Perhaps China, as it exists now, is not the future, and anyone who says otherwise is selling something. Or they are Paris Hilton.

We have done so many things wrong. In America I had scoffed at patriotism, had refused to hold my hand to my heart during the Pledge of Allegiance or sing along to the national anthem, had never owned an American flag. This day in Shanghai I felt more comfortable being an American than I ever had at home. I knew I would still not buy the Stars and Stripes to wave at the Fourth of July, nor would I rush to an open-stack library to read about John Locke's theory of natural rights and government by social contract, but I understood that when I returned to America I would be grateful for a free press and for so many other things. And perhaps more important, I understood that instead of telling my Chinese friends that they had to change their way of life to mimic ours, the best thing I could do was to share with them why I believed a free press was a good thing. I would tell them that in America we can go to any library or surf the Internet and see pictures of tanks rolling toward the man standing defiantly near Tiananmen, the Gate of Heavenly Peace, and then each person can decide for himself or herself what this means. And we can read of our own leaders' follies and make fun of the people who run our country and we can criticize them and participate in their choosing, or we can choose to do nothing at all; we can choose to be oblivious to the world around us and to try to spend and consume our way to happiness by filling our empty lives with boxes of junk made in China, but at least we will be responsible for our choices—at least the great plague of human apathy will be revealed for what it is, something that lives in each of us rather than a curse imposed from above. Better to fail as adults than to succeed as children guided by an abusive parent. I would tell my Chinese friends that I thought a free press was a good thing because I believe that maintaining the stability of society at the expense of individual freedom is a bad thing, and will, in the end, lead to the stagnation of our species. I would have no way to prove that I was right, and many of my Chinese friends would not agree with me. But that is to be expected. There is, after all, a world between us.

The Nanpu Bridge spans the Huangpu River, a waterway so murky, the Mississippi by comparison seems a crystalline stream. Behind us as we drove lay Puxi with the Bund and its legacy of colonial meddling in China; ahead of us stood Pudong, the city of skyscrapers that the Chinese had raised at a pace that crackled and hissed. Staring at the giddy spires, I remembered the first time Jennifer and I had met to exchange language lessons on the bank of the Huangpu River. We had stood looking across the grubby water at a city of towers and light, a shining metropolis that had risen from the swampland nothingness of Pudong. It had seemed a dream then and it seemed a dream now. A city propelled by such massive force it would swell to swallow all of China and then fill the world with its neon. It was a beautiful, horrible dream, and I knew that when I woke my heart would shove against my ribs and sweat would spill in cold rivulets down my cheeks and I would be grinning like a madman high on meth. Onward to the World Expo of 2010. Momentum can be a wonderful thing, and Shanghai shows no signs of slowing down.

Neither did our driver, who attacked the on-ramp of the Nanpu Bridge with a confident recklessness that made me wonder if I should be wearing a helmet. I reached for my seatbelt but found nothing. As the road approached the bridge, instead of gradually rising in a straight line, it spiraled steeply upward in three tight loops. As we sped around a corkscrewing ring, centrifugal force pressed our bodies against one side of the vehicle for what seemed several minutes as we rose toward the top of the on-ramp. Had Shanghai decided to build an elevator that dropped people in freefall from the top of one of its supertall towers to the ground floor I would not have been surprised. Had safety belts been included in that elevator, I would have been very surprised indeed.

The Nanpu Bridge, with the overlapping corkscrews of its on-ramp, is one of Shanghai's many public works projects that seem less a functional piece of infrastructure and more a showpiece conceived simply for shock value.

The Nanpu Bridge, with its on-ramp that seems more an amusement park ride than a functional public works feature of a bridge, is a much-photographed landmark in Shanghai. I had taken a picture of it on my first trip to Shanghai, had gawked at it like any other tourist. And now I was traveling in a truck with Chinese people transporting a salvaged door from the razed lanes of an old neighborhood across the Huangpu River to the new metropolis of Pudong, where Jennifer's parents waited in their temporary home for the construction cranes to finish assembling their new apartment block out by the international airport and the terminus of the maglev train. I wondered if anything had really changed in the two years that had passed and the ten or so trips I had taken to Shanghai. Perhaps I was still that tourist shooting a photo of a cool bridge that made me think I was on the set for a science fiction movie.

After I'd grown numb to so many spectacular sights in Shanghai, I had started to wonder what the lives of the people living in this futuristic fantasy-land were like. I had found my way into an antique shikumen in a lilong neighborhood and now the neighborhood was gone and in its place more space-age structures would rise to slash the sky and spread their light across Shanghai. And tourists would take more pictures, and old men would bear the remains of their alley homes across fantastic bridges toward a landscape that inspired awe but not love.

Pudong with all its magnificent towers felt as cold to me as the government buildings of Beijing, where Jennifer's father was preparing to go to petition the government for fair compensation for his demolished home. In decades past, monolithic Soviet-inspired shrines to the Communist Party had been erected throughout China's capital city. When one stood before these massive edifices with their slabs of brutally blank concrete, one felt small and powerless—exactly what the Communist Party designers had intended. It was hard to even see the openings where one could enter. How could one challenge the power of the government if one could not even see a way into these monstrous buildings? They were hideously ugly and dehumanizing, and they had been wholly successful in their intended effect. The towers of Pudong had been designed to symbolize Shanghai's participation in the global economy, its openness to the world—and, of course, its staggering prosperity. As we drove between these towers and I crimped my neck to gaze upward toward their airy heights I felt as small and unimportant looking up at these phallic wonders of corporate might as I did standing before the great windowless, doorless concrete blocks of Beijing's architectural ode to authoritarian power. I'm no expert on architecture, I'm no expert on China. I'm just a guy who stumbled into Shanghai, took a few pictures, and now two years later found himself riding in a truck with a man who wanted to keep the door to his demolished home, the dust of which covered my shoes.

I came to China like so many Westerners before me in large part because I felt there was something missing in myself, and I thought I might discover what I was lacking amid the mysteries of the Middle Kingdom. But I had discovered no hidden wisdom of the Orient, no pearl of Eastern knowledge. What I'd found were friends. Friends who at times seemed very much like me, and who sometimes seemed to me utterly foreign. But our friendship, unlike so many other things in the transitory world of Shanghai, would endure. When I went back to America I would not miss the city's towers and shopping malls and lights. I would miss sharing meals with Old Wang. I would miss playing jianzi with kids in the alley. And most of all, I would miss Jennifer and Marcus.

Our truck pulled up in front of a bare concrete building that looked like the dismal barracks of some bedraggled army. As we unloaded the door, the hand of Jennifer's father found my own. It was an awkward gesture, a fumbling approximation of a Western handshake. It was his way, I think, of trying to thank me in the way he thought I would want to be thanked. His fingers brushed against my own, his skin thick and smooth from years of working thread through machines in the textile factories of Shanghai. No words passed between us as our hands touched and each of us found the other's eyes. His grip was soft, and I had one of those moments I sometimes have when the world slows down and is filled with a gentle green glow like the light that, when I was a little boy growing up in Missouri, came before tornadoes. Something shivery and electric moved from the hand of this old man into my arm and worked its way along my spine, and I understood that all the monuments to government power in Beijing, all the tall towers of Shanghai, did not define these cities, nor did they explain what was vital within them.

After we dropped the door off at the apartment, propping it against a wall of an empty room, I invited Jennifer to wander the city with me. It was my last day in Shanghai. I was flying back to the States in the morning and I wanted to walk.

I had a feeling this would be a day of epic wandering: the urge to explore had been nagging at me the past week while I'd been stuck doing business in the sealed rooms of towers and the sterile lobbies of hotels. I needed to move, I needed to see it all and breathe it in. Watching Jennifer's parents in their temporary apartment with their shikumen door had made me want to wander all the more. Shanghai only began to make some sense to me when I was moving, when my heart was pumping blood to my brain and my feet were being bruised against the pavement and the scenes were gliding by.

"Can we take a taxi?" Jennifer asked.

"I need to walk."

"Perhaps I should change my shoes?"

I looked down at her feet and saw a pair of high-heeled boots that just about disappeared completely beneath the flaring cuffs of her long jeans. She hiked up a pantleg to show me a boot. I don't know much about women's footwear but I could see that those boots weren't made for walking. Off they came at a shoe store where Jennifer bought a pair of fake Nikes. The Nike swoosh was a little off—that is to say, the upturn of its curving swoosh was not as upturned as that of the real Nike swoosh. . . . I wrote the previous sentence about six times in six different ways and none of them made much sense. Suffice it to say that something was just not right about that swoosh.

In any event, now Jennifer had shoes for walking, but what to do with the boots? It was a long way back to her apartment and I didn't want to revisit old ground—I wanted to hike to places I hadn't yet been. I offered to carry the boots. It was the least I could do after convincing Jennifer to walk with me. Walking around the city was a very non-Shanghainese thing to do. I had learned to never tell any of my business clients in Shanghai that I had walked to an appointment— they associated walking with being poor. Peasants walked, sophisticated Shanghainese took taxis. I was tickled that the decidedly sophisticated Jennifer would accompany bumpkin me on one of my peasant wanderings to gawk at the bright lights of her big city.

We walked. Spaceship high-rises rocketed upward, their highest reaches wrapped in gauzy smog. Every street we traveled, every alley we explored, every marketplace we wandered offered sights and sounds and smells and textures so many and so intense my senses gave up. Without Old Wang or Jennifer's parents, without the community bonds of a neighborhood holding it all together, it meant nothing to me. Each tower was taller than the next, each elevated freeway system had more levels than the one before it, each alleyway was crammed with more people selling more products and more services. It was just spectacle, and there is a point at which spectacle becomes . . .

"Banal," I said to Jennifer.

"What?"

"You asked me earlier today for a new word—*banal*. It's a good word."

"Is it useful?"

"No, not really. But it's a wonderful word."

"What does it mean?"

"It means containing nothing new or original, nothing fresh."

"Oh."

She didn't repeat it, didn't write it down.

"Are you okay?" I asked.

"I will miss the way they used to yell through the alley, the sound of their voices when they were selling food."

"I'm sorry, what?"

"You asked me what I would miss most about the lane. I didn't answer you before because it makes me sad to think about it, but maybe it is okay to be sad for today. After today I will finish being sad." She was staring up at a tower, its metal skin glinting in the sun. She was either squinting or trying very hard not to cry.

"The people who sold food in the alley, so many kinds of food, I will miss their yelling, the way they would call out what they had to sell, the way they carried little kitchens on their shoulders when they walked through the lane, and I will miss all the delicious foods. There were people carrying baskets of fried bean curd, and there were fresh green olives and cherries." She was smiling and crying. "Wonton soup and sesame cakes and *zòngzi*. So many delicious foods." She wiped at her eyes and looked at me. "Sometimes late at night they would yell out their foods in the lane and we would lower a basket down from a window with money in the basket and they would fill the basket with snacks."

Together we stared up at the tower, windows rising far above. No baskets would be lowered down to be filled with snacks as street vendors peddled their treats in the streets below.

"Shanghai is getting rich now," Jennifer said, "but it is not renao. Now we buy things and sing karaoke to try to feel happy but it is not the same. Sometimes I don't know how to feel happy. The lane is gone, our home is gone, but even if it wasn't gone, everything would still be different. It is easier to be rich in Shanghai than it is to be happy. And it is very hard to be rich. Can you understand my meaning?"

I nodded that I could.

"I'm glad it is finished," Jennifer said. "My stomach hurt because I worried what would happen. Now it has happened and my stomach can stop hurting."

Sarcasm had been my shield for as long as I could remember, had been a stance that kept me safe from caring. One of the things I like most about China is that when I'm there I can't rely on a sarcastic sense of humor, both because it is difficult to translate, and because many times I am faced with situations when sarcasm fails me and I am forced to feel something without the protection of a snarky comment, without the safety of an ironic tone. Right now was one of those times.

"Are you worried about your parents?" I said. "About your dad going to Beijing to protest?"

"*Méi bànfǎ*," she said beneath her breath. Nothing can be done. Her eyes were dry now and her face was as steady as a face can be.

"You don't want to talk about it?" I said.

"It's not your problem. It is a problem in our China. It is a problem for me and for my parents, and we don't need you to help us. I don't want you to write about our problem anymore. Okay?"

"Okay."

Jennifer started walking. "Do you understand?"

"No. But if you want me to stop, then of course I'll stop."

"I want you to stop."

"Can I finish the story today? Can the story continue for the rest of today—and then that's the end?"

Jennifer stopped walking and blew at her bangs. "The Americans in *Friends* are not as strange as you. And I don't think the Americans in my company are as strange as you, but they don't talk to me too much, so I don't know. Maybe they are as strange as you."

"Probably not."

"Yes, okay. Today is the last day. After today we are just friends, and no more stories about me or my family. Okay?"

"Okay."

From a ruinous sky emerged the hulking outlines of structures paneled in glass and large beyond measure. We wandered boulevards lined with perfect rows of ranked buildings where a decade before there had been ragged farms and run-down fishing villages. The entire area had been built anew from a blueprint, had been planned from the top down. And now sprawling precincts held great slabs of nothingness arranged in modular units along wide avenues that swept away to nowhere, and each horizon was smudged with the grim haze of eternity. Neighborhoods that evolve over time and grow up from the ground have layers, and each layer holds stories. The story here was of a government designing a residential area without any semblance of life. The straight streets and perfect apartment blocks seemed built of enormous interlocking bricks, like some demented giant's plastic playworld where people don't shit and piss and fuck and fight and hold each other tight against the dark descending night. I suppressed the urge to scream.

Jennifer's cell rang. It was Marcus. He was in Puxi and wanted to meet up with us. We were in Pudong, on the other side of the Huangpu River. I warned him I was in the mood to walk.

"That's too far," he said when I spoke to him on Jennifer's cell.

I passed the phone to Jennifer. "Don't be banal," she said to Marcus. She handed the phone back to me and asked me how she'd done.

"Not bad."

"I didn't pull it off," she said.

"We'll work on it."

I spent several minutes telling Marcus to quit whining about walking and join Jennifer and me on our aimless transit of the city. He was having none of it: "It would take you till like tomorrow to walk all the way over here."

My Chinese friends couldn't believe that my boss in America rode his bike to work. He must be a poor boss, they said. Maybe his company was failing. Marcus had viewed my penchant for walking as some strange affliction of which he had constantly tried to cure me, offering to give me money for taxis, showing me maps of the metro and telling me how convenient it was. The Shanghai subway system was convenient, to be sure, but it was also insanely crowded, and taxis sat snarled in traffic, and sometimes the only way I could escape from being crushed beneath a feeling of claustrophobia, the only way I could really breathe, was to walk. Of course, walking briskly, heart and lungs moving Shanghai's air through one's system, is not good for one's system, but what can one do.

I conceded to take a taxi to meet Marcus, and before Jennifer and I jumped in, she grabbed my sleeve. She had never done this before, a gesture so common in America, where we are forever tugging and pawing at each other and slapping the backs of friends and crashing together our knuckled fists. But even in Shanghai, where it sometimes seems every Chinese person is trying to outdo every other Chinese person at making a display of their Western ways, there is little deliberate contact. Strangers grind against each other in crammed subway cars, people exchange elbows as they board busses and push each other's backs as they shove their way toward ticket counters, but friends rarely touch their friends, and lovers seldom hold hands in public, much less kiss. All this was changing, of course: there were occasional cheek kisses and high fives, and Chinese hipsters sometimes twined their tongues beneath the romantic glow of the Bund at night, but it all seemed a bit forced. Amateur actors moving stiffly through a stage act.

Jennifer grabbed my sleeve and tugged at it and held it tightly in her little fisted hand. She told me three things so quickly they all jumbled together and it wasn't until after we were in the taxi and I had told the driver to take us to the Bund and we were passing through a tunnel beneath the Huangpu River that I fully understood what she had said. She thanked me for helping her father find the door and for not making an American ass of myself by telling him how sorry I was for him. She told me she would pretend in the taxi that she spoke no Chinese so I could practice talking with the driver. And after that relatively meaningless piece of information, which she had apparently offered so she could pause a moment to prepare for the next important bit of news she was about to throw my way, she told me this: She and Marcus had been dating and she thought she was in love with him. "I am too busy to love someone," she had said to me. And she had laughed and looked as though she would cry at the same time, her face moving more in a few seconds than I had seen it move since the day I'd first met her. As if all her stoicism had been an act of storing up for this moment. As if for many months she'd let her face rest and prepare itself for the facial gymnastics she was engaged in now. And then we had stepped into the taxi and I had told the driver where to go, and I had apologized to him that my wife didn't speak any Chinese because she was American. He had said in the slurred Mandarin of a southerner that my wife was very beautiful. I had agreed that she was.

Now the lights of the tunnel passed across Jennifer's face and played brightly on her tears. "I am afraid that maybe Marcus is not bad enough," she said. "He is too good, too nice to me, and maybe I won't be happy because he is not a rascal. I tell myself that maybe I will meet someone better but I don't believe it. I believe perhaps I love him."

Her small hands resting on her knees. Her wet and trembling cheeks. I did something I had never done with her before and haven't done since. I slid next to her in the backseat of the taxi and pulled her to my shoulder, and she did not stiffen or pull away. Once in a rural province where I'd made a Chinese friend I had hugged her when I left to return to Shanghai. I had known that it was inappropriate, had understood that it would make her uncomfortable, had reminded myself that we were in Henan, not L.A. or New York—or even the Midwest for that matter—but I had done it anyway. And in my arms she had gone rigid as a board. Husbands and wives did not hug in public in Henan, much less men and women who were friends. My gaffe had embarrassed both of us terribly, and it marked the beginning of many blunders I would make in China.

But this seemed right, hugging Jennifer now in the taxi. Whether because we were in Shanghai with its worldly ways and not out in the countryside, or because Jennifer and I had known each other longer and she'd grown used to my American shenanigans, she did not stiffen and resist as my friend in Henan had; she leaned into me and pressed her face against my shoulder, and the moisture of her tears spread through my shirt and touched my skin. "He doesn't own a house," she said. "I should find someone to love who owns a house, but I don't want to. I think I'm happy, but I don't know. Most days I want to hit Marcus. Sometimes I want to hit him very hard."

We rode in silence, each body leaning into the other, her head resting against my shoulder, our taxi moving through darkness and through light as we traveled the tunnel beneath the river. When we reached the other side we blinked our eyes in the brightness and the driver dropped us off along the Bund. He asked me if my wife was okay.

"She's fine," I told him. "She's in love, that's all. She's in love and she'll be fine."

"You're lucky," he said, tossing his grizzled chin in Jennifer's direction. She stood on the curb looking out toward the river, the elegant buildings of the Bund behind her.

"You're right," I said. "I am lucky."

"You should treat her very well," he said.

"I will, shifu."

There is no tradition of tipping taxi drivers in China. Though in Shanghai, as more and more foreigners flood the city, taxi drivers are getting the hang of working over foreigners for a few extra *kuài*. One of my greatest pleasures in China has been chatting with taxi drivers, practicing my Chinese with a captive audience. Sometimes they were simply angling for a tip, telling the foreign devil his Chinese sounded authentic and answering all his stupid questions in the hopes of buying an extra bowl of noodles and a bottle of beer when they turned off the meter and collected the rewards of my American largesse, but more than once I had put something extra into the hand of a driver and he had given it back to me, thinking I had accidentally overpaid him. A couple of them had looked as confused by my tip as the woman in Henan had by my hug.

On this driver's dash, beneath a dangling medallion that held the face of Mao, was a picture of a woman with a pigtailed girl snuggled into the cozy basket of her lap. "That's in Hangzhou," he said.

"West Lake?" I asked, looking at the water and the boats behind the woman who held the little girl.

"Yes, my wife and daughter at West Lake. Our family went there for vacation last year."

"Is your daughter very clever?" I asked. Chinese people like this word *clever*, and I had adopted their fondness for it. It made me sound clever to say it in Chinese.

"*Hái hǎo*," he said.

"You are so modest," I told him. "I'll bet she is very clever. And your wife is very beautiful."

He waved away my compliment with one of his white-gloved hands. "She is waiting for you," he said, moving his chin toward Jennifer, standing on the curb. "We are both lucky," he said.

I tried to give him a tip but he told me it wasn't necessary. I considered hugging him but realized he would probably punch me. Sometimes Shanghai just made me plain crazy. Something in the air, I suppose. I do not hold an advanced degree in neurology, but it is my belief that air so thick you can chew on it surely must do a number on your mind.

The taxi driver saw me staring at his picture of West Lake and his face brightened as he thought of something. He asked me if I liked to drink *Lóngjǐng chá*, "Dragonwell tea." I told him it was my favorite tea, both for the flavor and for the story of how it had been named, as Old Wang had once explained it to me—the swirling waters of a deep well had appeared to villagers as a twisting dragon that could grant their wish for rain. The driver smiled and nodded. The streets around us lay mantled in gathering mist, and Shanghai at that moment seemed to me as ancient as any other place in China, and its towers not something from the future but rather pillars raised in some faraway past. And these towers would one day tumble and rot, and something else would rise from the ruins, and two people would meet in this place along the river, and one would give the other a gift, and then both would be absorbed back into the crowds that fill the pulsing streets of China like some great and nameless beast.

"Wait a moment," he said. In a cup holder attached to his console was a plastic bottle filled with pale green fluid. Below this bottle, tucked beneath his seat, was a box, its dark wood carved with writhing dragons, its top clasped with a latch of silver. I imagined this box held some fabulous treasure and perhaps great danger too, as in some timeless story. He raised this box and slowly hinged it open, showing me the leaves that the Chinese say are shaped like the tongues of sparrows. I breathed in their honeyed fragrance as he pinched a fat quantity with his gloved hand and dropped them into a plastic bag. He rolled the bag closed and then flipped shut the lid of the box and fastened the latch.

"For you and your wife," he said as he handed me the rolled bag bulging with tea leaves. "Because she is sad, and you look sad too. Maybe this will make you both happy."

I took the bag from his fingers sheathed in white cloth. He gripped the steering wheel with two gloved hands and grinned and then he drove away. I stood staring after his car as it merged into a mass of traffic, and I remembered exactly why I had traveled to China again and again after each time swearing I would never return.

Young Chinese lovers on the Bund were kissing, defying millennia of tradition. As they turned their backs on Confucian restraint and propriety, they faced the river and their tongues probed each other's mouths. Beneath a hazy sun the waters of the Huangpu crawled out to sea in glittering waves of sludge, and the stonework of the buildings along the Bund showed in stark relief as the Custom House clock ticked the hours of the afternoon away. I grabbed Jennifer and lifted her from the ground, her tiny body no heavier in my arms than a few sacks of groceries. I spun her around and told her not to worry. I told her she was young and in love and everything would be just fine.

Easy for me to say. My parents weren't fighting Communist cadres to receive fair compensation for the home that had been bulldozed. Being in love in China, as with anywhere else, is seldom enough. But isn't it pretty to believe it is, if only for a moment. I believed it was enough as Jennifer and I spun in the misty sun along the Bund. When I finally put her down, Jennifer's hysterical laughter was making a wet mess of her eyes, and with my thumb I dabbed at her streaked mascara. We laughed our way down the promenade to where Marcus leaned against a railing, waiting for us.

"What's so funny?" he said.

"Are you ready to walk?" Jennifer asked him.

"Can we take a taxi?" Marcus said. "Or at least the metro—how about the metro?"

"No subway," I said.

"Today we are walking," Jennifer said. "Taking a taxi is banal. The metro is banal. Sometimes you are banal." She punched Marcus in his arm. Hard.

She looked at me. "I pulled if off?" She took her boots from me and handed them to Marcus and told him to carry them. He looked down at her bright white fake Nikes, which promised not to stay white very long as they tread the city's streets.

And walk we did, Jennifer keeping pace with me, Marcus lagging behind and every block or so reaching for his footwear to adjust buckles. He was wearing some kind of trendy man-boots with shiny buckles, footwear that would have screamed homosexuality in St. Louis and would have signaled good taste in Manhattan. To me they simply said *uncomfortable*.

"Let's get you some walking shoes, my friend," I said to Marcus as I guided our group down Nanjing Dong Lu, one of the busiest shopping streets in China. To the peroxide blonde Chinese hooker with fake eyelashes and a tiny leather skirt who immediately accosted me, propositioning me with everything from "happy massages" to "good long fucking" I said that my wife would not approve and pulled Jennifer close. So Marcus would not feel jealous, I told a couple of the ladies of Nanjing Dong Lu that my husband would not approve and pulled Marcus close. This being Shanghai, they were about as shocked as Scandinavians hearing talk of the myriad ways in which humans fit their bodies together, and the unfazed sex workers moved on to the next white face passing through this street of infinite commerce, where everything could be purchased, from dumplings to fake Rolex watches, from one-dollar handjobs in back alleys to children sold into lifetimes of sexual slavery.

"What a world," I said aloud as I stood staring up at the biggest portrait I had ever seen of the man who had arguably done more to change China than any other. Colonel Sanders stared back at me, and all along the famous shopping street, Pepsi banners wrinkled in the wind. I'm not saying the good Colonel had anything to do with Shanghai's sex trade. How on earth would he be involved in that? And of course Pepsi wasn't the official corporate sponsor of Nanjing Dong Lu's bustling sex business for lonely Westerners. Marcus asked me if I was hungry. I slowly turned away from the stenciled mug of Colonel Sanders to stare at Marcus.

"Do you want to eat chicken?" he said.

"I think I might be going crazy," I told him in Chinese. My voice was torn apart and scattered by the crowd's grumble and roar.

"Are you hungry?" he yelled.

"No, crazy," I said in English. "I think Shanghai has made me completely nuts."

Or maybe it was the travel business. Burnt out on MBA students, I'd led a group from a Chinese cultural institute based in America around the Middle Kingdom, hoping people with a professed interest in Chinese culture instead of Chinese business would provide some relief from the drivel of aspiring American executives. No luck. The wife of an investment banker had slurred her way through China on the cultural tour, swilling liquor and spewing nonsense from the moment she stumbled off the plane in Beijing until I bid her farewell as she dizzily boarded the jet in Shanghai that would take her to make a fool of herself in some other place. She'd loved the time she'd spent in China, in large part because the Chinese guide who had been assigned to her trip was in the later stages of alcoholism. His hands shook so violently he could hardly work his cell phone, and he had trouble holding down his food each time he ate. Emaciated and jittery, he began drinking each day in the early afternoon, and by bedtime every night he was stumbling drunk. The wife of the investment banker thought the guide was the greatest thing since bottled gin. The guide's job, essentially, was to keep her cocktail glass filled for two straight weeks, a task he completed with perfect diligence.

I'd gotten into the travel business because I'd believed it was important for Americans to experience China firsthand instead of learning about it through the filter of the American media, which has none of the constraints placed upon it by government censors that the Chinese media does, but instead self-censors the stories it chooses to tell, weeding out small stories of people living their lives and trying their best to find meaning in the modern world, in favor of large stories about large spectacles in the country with the largest population in the world and soon to have the world's largest economy and *blah blah blah*. It is no wonder Shanghai is addicted to superlatives. How else to gain the attention of Americans, how else to earn our respect. We have created Shanghai, the city of the future, as surely as the Chinese have.

I had lost count of the people I'd taken to China who'd told me the trip had changed them, had influenced the way they saw China and saw themselves, and I had believed I was doing something worthwhile. But for every one of those people, there was a hopelessly shallow MBA student who spoke only the language of money, or there was the dimwitted wife of an investment banker boozing her way down the Yangtze, and I could not get these people out of my head. I feared that, instead of adding something of value to the world, I might be helping to make more of a mess of things.

"Are you okay?" Jennifer asked me.

That she cared enough to see past her own problems and notice I was having some of my own made me smile. I shrugged my shoulders and said, "I don't know what I want to do with my life."

"What is the problem?"

"I'm halfway through my thirties and I still don't know what I want to be when I grow up."

Jennifer looked away, and then she looked back at me and smiled. "Do you know how the soup gets inside them?" she said.

A man was hunkered down on his haunches atop a concrete stoop, working chopsticks into a steaming bowl of xiaolongbao.

"Are you going to finally tell me?"

"Gelatin."

"Gelatin?"

"Gelatin is put inside the dumpling skin with the meat. When the xiaolongbao is steamed, the gelatin melts and makes hot soup for you to drink when you bite the dumpling open. Do you know why I didn't tell you?"

"I give up."

"Because I didn't know the word for *gelatin*. Last night I looked it up online."

"A mystery of the Orient revealed."

Jennifer started walking and I followed her. "Let's buy shoes," she said. "I know where to go." She took my hand and she took Marcus's hand and she led us through a puzzle of interlocking alleys, past whispering hookers and shouting touts, until we ended at a shoe store that made no effort to advertise its wares.

"This is the place," Jennifer said. "They have the best deals on shoes in Shanghai. You have to know it's here."

Marcus bought a sweet pair of Nikes with a very real-looking swoosh for less than a chicken dinner and a cup of Pepsi at Kentucky Fried Chicken, and then we were on our way. His laggard pace improved, but he was still moving too slowly for my liking. I offered to carry Marcus's boots along with Jennifer's. My arms full of fashionable boots, I led our little group in a beeline away from Nanjing Dong Lu. I didn't know where we were going but I wanted to put some distance between us and that godforsaken street. There was something about the ridiculous commerce of Nanjing Dong Lu that made me want to wave Mao's Little Red Book in the air and proclaim a revolution of the proletariat.

Down pathways slippery with spit we passed, through air foul with smoke. Past beggars with grabby hands clutching at our clothes. We walked in endless alleyways till finally we arrived at Huangpu Park, which contains a lovely public garden that had been closed to Chinese when the foreign powers that invaded Shanghai had entrenched themselves in their colonial buildings on the Bund. Atop a flight of steps in the park was a broad and open place with a commanding

Nanjing Dong Lu is a frantically busy shopping street crammed full of pimps and hookers, scammers and touts, and each night the scene is bright with neon.

view of the Huangpu River sulking its way toward the sea beneath a glum sky. And in this vast space, the massive concrete columns of the Monument to the People's Heroes rose, memorializing those who'd given their lives for the Communist struggle in Shanghai. Across the river reared the buildings of Pudong. I squinted at the Aurora tower with its shiny gold coat that gleams by day and at night serves as a forty-story screen to show commercials to the city, its light working its way into the last of the city's collapsing lanes. Within a dense cluster of towers the Shanghai World Financial Center stood tallest of all, metal and glass burning incandescent in the sun, a vision so beautiful you are forced to shield your eyes. Once we built toward the sky to honor gods and kings.

History is, of course, a series of stories we tell ourselves to explain how we've arrived where we are. The Chinese tell themselves stories such as their culture is older than any other on earth, they are the tragic victims of foreign aggression,

Mao was a great man, and their nation has not been fully appreciated or respected by the world's established powers. These stories are everywhere, on the lips of the Chinese people, on their television screens, in their films, in the textbooks they read as children. To understand a nation we must understand its stories, and to understand its stories we must listen to its people tell them. I have tried to understand China by listening to the stories my friends in Shanghai tell. From their telling I have gathered fragments, and from these fragments I have assembled my story, a story of the places I have seen and the Chinese people I have known in the city of Shanghai. Shanghai is built of fragments. It is a city of splintered stories that do not fit smoothly into a linear narrative.

Another story the Chinese people tell themselves is that one of the things they want most is peaceful cooperation with the international community. They speak of their nation's nonviolent rise with such earnestness it is impossible to snicker. This is the central narrative of the World Expo: peaceful development. It is only a story. But just as history is a collection of stories, so the future of a rising nation begins with stories, and these stories guide its course. At the Columbian Exposition held in Chicago in 1893, we told stories of Freedom and Democracy. China says that the World Expo in 2010 will be the first World's Fair held in a developing nation, and China tells this story: It is a country sympathetic to all developing nations, for it understands the pain of their colonial humiliation and exploitation, and it will help them rise along with it. It sees itself at the center of the developing world, and then it sees beyond this. It sees a time in the twenty-first century when it regains its rightful place as the Middle Kingdom and the nations beyond its borders bow before its greatness, its cultural supremacy. The West is powerful, but it is also shallow and decadent, violent and depraved, so the story goes. China invented paper and printing, the compass and gunpowder. It sailed the world's seas hundreds of years before the Europeans left their continent to explore beyond their borders, but China, a nation of peaceful people, became an easy target for barbarian countries that adapted their invention of gunpowder to modern weaponry and applied their nautical innovations to vessels of war. Now it is time for China to take from the West what it needs so that it can develop and once again be a great empire, a great civilization. And what it will teach the world in the twenty-first century when it is the planet's leading power is a Confucian value rooted profoundly in its past: Harmony. The deep genius of ancient Chinese culture will show the barbarians with stunted histories how to create a Harmonious Society, how to build a Harmonious World.

This story, this grand and hopeful saga, guides the Chinese people through their lives each day and propels their nation forward. But it is only a story. Communism and capitalism were borrowed from the outside world, and of Chinese culture, is there anything left? Through sheer economic clout China might regain its empire, but what of its civilization? When a culture engages in a decade-long frenzy of destruction that aims to annihilate every principle upon which it was built, perhaps there is no way back. The only way is forward, and the faster the better.

Near Huangpu Park, Suzhou Creek merges with the larger flow of the Huangpu River as it pushes toward the Yangtze. Spanning Suzhou Creek is Waibaidu Qiao, known in English as "Garden Bridge." Or more precisely, there was once a Garden Bridge here, and there will be a Garden Bridge here again in time for the World Expo. Built by a British businessman, the bridge connected Shanghai's British settlement south of Suzhou Creek with the American settlement to the north. The Chinese name for the bridge, Waibaidu, is sometimes translated "foreigners cross for free," and the bridge has been used by Shanghainese as evidence of their exploitation by evil imperialists, who could pass without paying, while Chinese people were charged a toll: so goes the story, one that doesn't jibe with the tales told by British chroniclers of Shanghai's colonial history such as F. L. Hawks Pott. Who to believe, colonizers or communists? Garden Bridge was the name given by the British to the span at the edge of their manicured public garden. Constructed in 1907 with long trusses that crossed Suzhou Creek, it held claim to the title of the largest steel bridge in Shanghai. The Japanese added another chapter to the Garden Bridge story in 1937, when after invading and occupying the Chinese sections of Shanghai, they posted guards on both sides of the bridge to harass Chinese who tried to pass.

As Shanghai swelled into a megalopolis in the 1990s, traffic clogged the Bund, and the Waibaidu Bridge was too narrow and too old to bear the burden. A new road bridge was built to handle Shanghai's heavy traffic. But the Waibaidu Bridge with its stately trusses remained, one architectural constant that anchored the ever-changing cityscape. In the spring of 2008, as part of an enormous public works project to reconfigure traffic flow along the Bund in order to help restore some of its past grandeur and ready it for the World Expo, the Waibaidu Bridge was sliced in two; the sections were detached from their pylons and floated on barges to a shipyard. The bridge will be restored and replaced in time for the Expo.

The Waibaidu Bridge is beautiful, its latticework of steel testament to human ingenuity spanning the problem of water that blocks the flow of traffic. But the bridge is more intriguing for the stories that cling to its beams. The Chinese hold fast to these stories. They are determined to keep intact the bridge that has served as a symbol of their humiliation, for it occupies a central place in their narrative of their past.

Huangpu Park is a place of cool green respite in the concrete heat of the city. Marcus, Jennifer and I walked away from Suzhou Creek and the absent Waibaidu Bridge into the grassy heart of the park. Beneath a canopy of trees lay a tiled square. In this square Chinese people danced with practiced ballroom steps to music flowing from a portable CD player. Some of the dancers were elderly, some were middle aged, and all of them danced as though they had been practicing these steps for a hundred years—feet never stuttering across the paved floor, hands never fumbling across their partners' waists and arms. Some wore looks of grim determination, others smiled as though today were their birthday. One woman, smiling the splendid smile of one who is doing exactly what she wants to be doing, danced with a partner who owned a handsome jaw, and he was grinning so fully, so forcefully, it was hard to imagine there was anything on earth that could provide him more pleasure than this dancing. He looked as though he'd erupt with laughter at any moment, or perhaps he'd combust with joy. And why not: The woman with whom he danced wore boots up to her knees, and her jeans followed the curves of her waist as though she had been born in them, and her blouse was moving in the breeze along with the dark and furling banners of her hair. Her eyes were smiling as brightly as her mouth and she was the most beautiful woman I had ever seen.

"What's the date today?" I asked Marcus.

"Why?"

"Because I want to remember today. I want to remember the exact day that I saw the most beautiful woman in the world." I pointed with my eyes toward the twirling couple.

"Do you really think she is so pretty?" Jennifer asked.

"No, but I think she is beautiful. God is she beautiful."

"Do you want to dance with her?" Marcus asked.

"God no."

"Because she already has a boyfriend?" Jennifer asked.

"I would ruin her with my awful dancing. My clumsiness would kill her."

"Do you want to talk to her?" Marcus asked.

"God no."

I just wanted to remember her as she was, as a vision, a blissful vision. I fell instantly in love with the idea of her, with the image of her, and I wanted her to dance in my head for the rest of my days. One word from her to me or from me to her and the vision would vanish.

I remember her dancing in the park with that music playing, those trees above, her boots sliding over the tiles of the patio, that smile of drunken love upon her face. She makes me smile wherever I am in the world, whatever I happen to be doing. I remember

People dance each day in Shanghai's parks.

the people around her, all of them dancing as unselfconsciously between flowerbeds as if they were behind the drawn curtains of bedrooms. Women wearing gray buns of hair upon their heads, men whose hands trembled with age touching the backs of their lovers. Practiced fingers pressing the silk of their wives' dresses. Dresses they'd had to hide when down was up and up was down and everyone in Shanghai donned the baggy blue garb of the revolution. But the revolution had ended long ago, and now these people in the park showed their gorgeous dresses and handsome suits and danced in public the perfect steps of partners who have practiced together for so many years that they now move together as one.

They danced and danced and I fell into a trance so deep only the stammering steps of Marcus and Jennifer brought me back to my place on the bench in the park. They had handed me their boots to hold. In their new tennis shoes they tried to mimic the ballroom moves of the crowd. They were the youngest people

dancing in the park, perhaps the only people under forty. What they lacked in elegance of movement they made up for in laughter. Jennifer jiggled in Marcus's
laughing arms and their feet bumped against each other's as they tripped their
way across the park.

This is a love story. It is a tale of two people who fell in love in a city that is
being ripped apart and rebuilt on a scale unprecedented in human history. And
it is the story of a narrator who fell in love with the characters in the story he was
telling. As with all people in love, the narrator cannot be trusted. He is smitten,
he is not objective. He understands the faults of the objects of his love, but he
chooses to look past them. He is filled with hope. Against all reason, against good
sense, he dreams the delirious dream of one in love and he believes there will be
a happy ending.

Speaking of love, Shanghai is in love with bridges. The city has gone completely
bridge-crazy of late. Bridges to this, bridges to that: new bridges are being built
everywhere. Shanghai's Donghai Daqiao, or East Sea Grand Bridge, completed
in 2005 to connect mainland Shanghai to the offshore Yangshan deep-water port,
became the longest transoceanic bridge in the world—until the completion of
Hangzhou Bay Bridge two years later displaced it as the world's longest
transoceanic bridge. The Hangzhou Bay Bridge links the municipality of Shanghai with the Ningbo municipality in Zhejiang province. Whether these munici-
palities really need to be connected by a highway at such astronomic expense is
a matter of debate. What is not debatable is that having very long bridges makes
the people of Shanghai very proud.

As the Nanpu Bridge we had driven across earlier that day served as an emblem of Shanghai's urban renaissance a few decades past, so Shanghai's Lupu
Bridge, built in 2003, is a monument to the city's ambition to reclaim its title of
Pearl of the Orient, the most prosperous and powerful city in the East. What
better way to announce to the world Shanghai's greatness than to build the
world's largest arch bridge to connect the fairgrounds for the World Expo. The
grounds will be sited on both sides of the Huangpu River and they will be linked
by a bridge so cool it will forever be associated with NBA star Yao Ming, the
Michael Jordan of China, who christened the city's face project by jogging across
it in the opening ceremony, connecting Shanghai's past filled with impotent submission to the West to its virile future, in which it sends its athletes to compete

with the big boys of the NBA, and its MBAs run the boardrooms in the towers of Pudong.

The Nanpu Bridge, one of the first bridges to span the west and east banks of the Huangpu River, joined the European architectural museum that is the Bund of Puxi with the postmodern playground of Pudong. It is the fourth longest cable-stayed bridge in the world. Yawn. . . . It had been labeled "a wonder in world bridge construction" in the breathless description typical of China's Xinhua News Agency and Shanghai's tourism bureau. And it is pretty damn cool, especially at night with its circular approach lit up like the flashing corkscrew ramp in a pinball machine—but really, how much face is there in having the "fourth longest cable-stayed bridge in the world"?

The World's Longest Arch Bridge: now that's the kind of face project a city on crack craves—that's exactly the kind of megaproject it needs to keep the adrenaline rush going deep into 2010. And speaking of keeping the rush going, I need to get up from this park bench I'm sitting on and walk. I don't want to stay in any one place; I want to keep moving on this, my final day in Shanghai. I'll be back, I'm certain, but I have no idea when, and I want to devour as much of this shifting feast as I can before the menu changes. I must keep moving. *Zǒu ba.* Let's go, let's walk.

I pulled Jennifer and Marcus from the patio and carried their boots as they leaned into each other and told me we should ride the metro. After I conceded to take the subway a few stops, we were sucked by a surging crowd into the vortex at an entrance, and after a crammed car with advertisements showing on LCD screens rolled us to where we wanted to go, we were pushed toward daylight by a mass of people that poured forth from an exit. We squinted and blinked and breathed lungfuls of air that hadn't already passed through the lungs of subway travelers in the sealed world below. We walked by a Rich Gate billboard, upon which a slim woman with heavy cleavage rode in a black sedan, a handsome cityscape rising behind her. "Kinging the Shanghai buildings" the billboard proclaimed, and it boasted a crest with a giant "R." Beneath the billboard a man wearing pajamas and slippers walked with a confident stride. I stepped in line behind him, following him into the heart of the Luwan District.

Part of the old French Concession, Luwan is blessed with genteel streets and gorgeous villas draped in ivy, beauty from an age that has passed. We strolled the pleasant boulevards of Luwan lined with lovely London plane trees, a hybrid bred by the British to withstand the polluted skies of cities. The mottled trunks of plane trees are similar to those of sycamores, and their broad leaves with three large lobes atop and two smaller lobes below, all with toothy edges, are reminiscent of maple leaves. This foliage hung in robust clusters from wide-spreading boughs on both sides of the road. Arching overhead, mingled branches formed green tunnels of shade, and humidity pearled the leaves. The plane trees had been imported from Europe more than one hundred years ago—just yesterday on the China timeline, yet long enough for the trees to grow into mature pillars that anchored the twisting roads and spread a sheltering canopy beneath Shanghai's baking sky. Sun Yat-sen, Mao Zedong, Zhou Enlai: they had all lived and worked in this district when the trees were half as high.

Aside from historic residences and regal trees, Luwan holds one of the swankiest sections of Huaihai Lu, formerly known as Avenue Joffre, and once dubbed "Champs-Élysées in Shanghai." Along this boulevard legendary for its wealth and glamour, White Russian émigrés had once set up shops next to French merchants. Violin music had floated over the street and blended with jazz, the smells of croissants and borscht had wafted from windows, and elegant storefronts had boasted haberdasheries and clothing boutiques, florists and perfumeries. Now Huaihai Lu is home to the massive multi-level House of Barbie Shanghai Flagship Store, which boasts not just dolls but Barbie clothes and Barbie jewelry and a Barbie spa offering Barbie Plastic Smooth Facials and Barbie Bust Firming Treatments.

Marcus and Jennifer forced me to enter. "One of my friends is involved in the launch," Marcus said as he stood beneath a lurid pink Barbie banner and nodded toward a plastic case two stories tall and filled with endless rows of Barbies, each doll ensconced in a little square space. Women ranging from teens to middle aged, some with children in tow and many without, massed in front of the dolls suspended in their compartments stacked atop each other in the towering display. "My friend is really smart," Marcus said as he studied the frenzied women, each jostling for position by the Barbies. "He's a marketing genius."

Jennifer posed in front of the display and told Marcus to use her phone to take a picture of her. "My friends and I knew about Barbie when we were little girls but we couldn't have them," Jennifer said as she grinned toward the phone and Marcus counted to three and told her to say *eggplant*. *Eggplant* in Chinese is *qiézi*, which sounds very much like *cheese*.

Huaihai Lu is a boulevard legendary for its wealth and glamour, where White Russian émigrés and French merchants once established elegant storefronts. Now the swanky street is home to the House of Barbie Shanghai Flagship Store.

"There were no Barbies in China," Jennifer said. "Now we have so many Barbies, and we are so happy."

Joyous women of every age and description knifed my ribs with their elbows, and with outstretched hands they pushed me to the side as they charged forward, shoving their way toward molded plastic dolls. "Five thousand years of culture," I said as I was nearly trampled in the stampede, smoke from a man sucking on a cigarette in front of a NO SMOKING sign stinging my eyes. It is a strange state of affairs indeed when Americans decry the philistinism of another nation and curse the crass materialism we have unleashed upon the world.

Jennifer grinned at a picture of herself holding a Barbie that she had just made the screen saver on her phone. "The world's longest continuous civilization," I said, shaking my head.

"I read today that soon Paris people will be looking at Shanghai to find out what to wear and eat," Jennifer said as we left the store and walked through the heart of the Huaihai haute culture scene, Shanghai's glitterati all around us. For an instant I glimpsed, squeezed between department stores, the stone archway of a lilong. I shook my head and blinked my eyes to clear my battle-fatigued brain of any hallucinations, but there it was, within sight of the House of Barbie. One of Shanghai's last lanes lined with shikumen. From these dark and narrow places revolutionaries had risen, great literature had been penned in pavilion rooms, and people to this day wore pajamas as they perused the crowded markets. I sighed. If only my feeble mind could invent a world as peculiar as Shanghai.

"And America will have to look at China to find out what technology is the best," Marcus said as I hurried to catch up to him. "America is *tài lǎotǔ le*." Too out of date, too backwards. "Our companies applied for more patents than American companies did this year. China owns IBM and pretty soon we'll have our own brands that are better than American brands."

Lenovo, a Chinese company, had indeed purchased IBM's PC division—as anyone in China could tell you. They could not have been more proud of their acquisition of an American icon.

"Maybe," I said. "But we'll still have the ballot box." Possibly a cardboard ballot box made in China from America's number one export. Along with democracy, we were sending to the world scrap paper. It's true: Scrap paper is now our number one export. China takes it in by the boatload, recycling it into cardboard boxes that are crammed full of the junk that is shipped back to our shores to fill our shopping carts in America. Chinese laborers benefiting from the manufacturing bonanza of creating our junk save their wages at an extraordinary rate, and the government's savings rate is off the charts. These savings allow China to purchase staggeringly huge amounts of U.S. Treasury notes—which allows us to enjoy the massive consumer credit that lets us buy all the junk that Chinese laborers manufacture and put in the cardboard boxes made from our scrap paper. China finances our debt; we drive China's manufacturing boom. Poor people in China get factory jobs; we get endless boxes of stuff to buy, and upwardly mobile Chinese can now purchase the Barbies they were deprived of in the past. I'm no economist but I'll tell you this: When it comes to the global economy, it's a mixed-up crazy world. You can quote me on that.

"What are you writing in your notebook?" Marcus asked.

"I was writing about you two dancing in the park," I lied.

"Why?" Jennifer asked.

I thought for a moment. "Because it was one of the coolest things I've seen in Shanghai," I said with complete honesty, my voice so earnest tears wobbled in my eyes.

"Why?" Marcus asked.

"Because when I watched you dancing in the park, I believed that maybe this isn't the end. Maybe there is some hope after all."

"What the fuck are you talking about?" Marcus said.

"Never mind," I said. "Let's keep walking." I rubbed my wet eyes with the back of my hand. "Fucking pollution," I said.

We kept walking until we reached a place where we could see the Lupu Bridge. We stopped and stood staring at the world's longest arch bridge.

"We have the world's longest arch bridge," Marcus said. "You used to have the longest—in your Virginia."

"Yes," I said. "Your bridge is longer than our bridge. But our bridge is in our West Virginia, not our Virginia. And really, Marcus, does the size of a bridge matter?"

He stared blankly back at me. There were many things Marcus had not learned in America, and the double entendre was one of them.

Marcus checked the facts of bridge length on his new smartphone that allowed him to connect to the Internet anywhere in Shanghai. Jennifer had started using her smartphone to record words from our language lessons—no more notebook and pen for her. Together the happy couple had purchased matching phones boasting features that wouldn't turn up in electronics shipped to America for several months. I wrote about their smartphones in my notebook, black ink bleeding onto bleached paper, while Marcus consulted Wikipedia and Jennifer searched her electronic dictionary for *double entendre*.

I pushed my timeworn notebook back into a pants pocket and looked at what was, for now, the world's longest arch bridge. According to Marcus's research gleaned from the new computer he held cupped in his palm, the city of Chongqing upstream on the Yangtze was building a longer one, and Dubai had announced plans to one-up China in the world's-longest-arch-bridge competition. While Jennifer giggled as she googled "size doesn't matter," Marcus told us that the Lupu Bridge had been designed by Chinese engineers, pride beaming from his Chinese face.

Along Shanghai's waterfront, structures made of steel tell several stories. The iconic building Three on the Bund, much like Garden Bridge, once served as a wonder of contemporary engineering. Back in the day when its structural steel frame had been designed by Europeans, Chinese had gawked at the modern marvel. But Shanghai's Lupu Bridge is the brainchild of Chinese engineers. Infrastructure specialists had told the local government that a bridge was needed for the further development of Shanghai. Experts had advocated choosing a bridge design that was simpler than that of the current arch bridge and much less expensive, but city officials, led by Chen Liangyu, decided that Shanghai needed the world's longest arch bridge. A superlative designed entirely by Chinese engineers—a perfect showpiece for the city. And another construction project to line the pockets of Communist Party leaders with kickbacks.

The bridge was one of many megaprojects championed by Chen Liangyu, Shanghai's former Communist Party secretary. A close ally of former Chinese President Jiang Zemin and a rival to the current Hu Jintao administration, Chen was stripped of his position by Party leaders in Beijing and then sentenced to eighteen years in prison for misusing money in Shanghai's social security fund and other abuses of power. Before his fall, he set in motion a series of face projects to be finished in time for the Expo. Like an emperor of old, Chen Liangyu had used his power to create fantastic and frivolous monuments to his kingdom's grandiosity. He'd decided Shanghai needed a beach: he'd shipped more than a hundred thousand tons of sand to Shanghai's suburbs to build a beach. Under his direction a two hundred and ninety million dollar tennis complex and a three hundred million dollar Formula One racetrack had been added to Shanghai's ever-growing list of assets. The proposed Shanghai-Hangzhou maglev line was his most controversial project, followed closely by the Dongtan eco-city and the Lupu Bridge. Shanghai's residents will be paying for the world's longest arch bridge far into the future as the city struggles to recoup the investment costs of yet another superlative.

Being the preeminent city of the future does not come cheap, and being a little emperor in the new China is not easy. Some see in Chen Liangyu's fall from power evidence of an incipient rule of law in China; most simply see the machinations of a paranoid regime that feared the growing influence of Shanghai in Communist Party politics. If there is an emperor metaphor for the new China, this metaphorical emperor resides not in the twenty-first century boomtown of Shanghai but in the Chinese Communist Party headquarters in Beijing. Shanghai is but one showpiece in the Party's vast domain. And it is a blueprint for the empire's future.

After Mao died, a clutch of powerful Shanghai engineers schooled in standards of Western efficiency rose to power in Beijing and placed urban improvement at the top of the nation's agenda. Jiang Zemin, former Shanghai mayor and Party chief of Shanghai, became president of the People's Republic of China; Zhu Rongji, another former Shanghai mayor and Shanghai Party chief, ascended to the position of premier. The tech-savvy, development-happy Shanghai crew replaced leaders who hailed from rural provinces and who had ruled continuously and, by Shanghai standards, sluggishly, from the days of Mao. In the new China,

The enormous steel arch of
the Lupu Bridge casts a long
shadow over Shanghai.

run by sophisticated technocrats instead of bumpkin ideologues, Shanghai's enduring fascination with borrowing from the West and with pushing material progress forward shimmered with renewed energy. China's central government shifted money from rural projects to urban infrastructure overhauls, injecting huge infusions of cash into the economies of its many metropolises. Shanghai's Chen Liangyu had been slapped down by Beijing. But Hu Jintao, the current president of the country, though he does not hail from Shanghai, holds a degree in hydraulic engineering, and massive infrastructure projects surge forward in Shanghai and throughout China with ever-increasing force.

And speaking of unrelenting force, to get to the base of Lupu Bridge we had to cross a highway on-ramp surging with traffic and crazy with construction. This place of perfect disorder offered no pedestrian overpass or underpass, just a crosswalk with a flashing green person signaling the okay to go. I hate that little green man, his LED legs calmly walking. Easy for him: he doesn't have busses and trucks barreling down on him and not so much as slowing for people in the crosswalk, just swerving around them at the last second.

When the nightmare of crossing a Shanghai street ended we were faced with 367 stairs to climb.

"Are we going to climb all of them?" Jennifer asked.

"There's no point in going halfway," I said.

"We could not climb any of them," Marcus said. "That's an option. We could go to the Nanpu Bridge and take the elevator there. It goes all the way to the top."

"I think we should take the elevator here and then climb the rest of the way," I said.

"Why?" Jennifer said. "Is the elevator at Nanpu Bridge broken?"

Marcus and Jennifer had grown used to my walking escapades, but climbing stairs when there was a perfectly good elevator that went to the top of another bridge was just plain nuts. They weren't having any of it.

"*Nǐ nǎozi jìn shuǐ le*," Marcus said to me. Say this to a stranger and get punched in the face; say it to a friend and have a good laugh. Literally: Your brain is in water. You are brain-damaged. You are completely and hopelessly stupid. This is considered incredibly offensive—and also hysterically funny when you say it to a good friend in the right context.

I laughed. Then I coaxed and I goaded, and eventually Marcus and Jennifer agreed to climb the stairs to the top of the Lupu Bridge. After the glass-fronted elevator deposited us on the deck of the bridge, and before we began our ascent to the apex of its arch, we were greeted by a giant statue of the Expo mascot, HaiBao, bearing the official slogan of the 2010 Shanghai World Expo: "Better City, Better Life." HaiBao is a cartoon version of the Chinese character that means *person*, but he looks an awful lot like Gumby painted blue. According to China's official World Expo English language website, HaiBao's design philosophy can be interpreted as, "Vivid and lively mascot standing for the city and interactions between urbanians and urban planets profoundly express the internal relation between footprints and dreams." After one digests this, one can go on to read about the mascot's "Theme manifestation," of which the website has this to say: "HAIBAO embodies ideal of the coexistence of different cultures in cities; embodies the appreciation of economic development and environmental sustainable development; embodies the wish to remodel the city communities, embodies the anticipation of the well-off both urban cities and countryside. HAIBO is the wish to colorful life and the warm invitation to friends from all over the world to Shanghai."

The website's copy, composed of equal parts sincerity, sweetness, crazy ambition, and wild hope, seems to me to be quintessentially Chinese. It should not be made fun of, nor should it be corrected or improved. It is perfect as it is. "The highest good is like that of water," the website tells us. "Water is the source of life.

The main character of the mascot is water. The blue color stated Chinese brand-new gesture to embrace the world."

On the deck of the world's longest arch bridge, the HaiBao statue stood against a sky of industrial gray, above a river the color of raw sewage, and next to the big blue cartoon mascot, cars rushed past in endless fuming waves. Better City, Better Life. Marcus and Jennifer noted nothing strange in this scene, and for a moment, neither did I. For a delirious instant Shanghai made perfect sense to me and I believed we were all headed toward a fine future indeed. Sometimes China can do that to you—it can murder irony and kill your sense of reason. It can fill the shriveled carcass of your heart with hope. Must be something in the air.

In the filthy air we panted as we walked past HaiBao and climbed the steps to the highpoint of the bridge. On the viewing platform at the top, the sun boiled overhead and the steel of the massive arch threw off heat like a sizzling skillet. The Huangpu River flowed hundreds of feet below, boats heavy with cargo pushing through its waters. Amid the riot of development on the riverbanks, empty spaces that held pits and pile drivers lay waiting to be filled with buildings. On the Puxi side were the last rusted remnants of an old shipyard, one of the sole remaining pieces of Shanghai's heavy industry within its city limits. Most of the city's smokestack-belching industry had been moved to the outskirts to lessen pollution in the city center, and by the time the Expo rolls around, the reeking, clanking shipyard will have been relocated to an island, where the great buffer of the Yangtze's mouth that opens to meet the sea will muffle the noise and soak up the fumes. Moving the shipyard to the outskirts of a city with air unfit for human lungs made me think of a saying that I taught Marcus and Jennifer while we stood on the platform of the Lupu Bridge looking at the boats below: "rearranging the deckchairs on the Titanic." They discussed this in Chinese and understood it quickly because every Chinese person has seen *Titanic*. Marcus started to sing the movie's cloying theme song, one of his favorite selections in karaoke clubs, to Jennifer. If I hear someone in China sing the theme song to *Titanic* one more time, so help me god I will hurl myself from the observation deck atop the Lupu Bridge.

On the Pudong side of the Huangpu River, fairgrounds for the World Expo were being finished. The colossal outline of China's national pavilion was visible through the murk, the structure's stepped and flaring crown as gorgeous and as goofy as anything else in Shanghai, as grand and as unapproachable as the towers of Pudong. The plot of land China had set aside for the U.S. pavilion remained bare.

The tiered crown of China's national pavilion rises from the World Expo site in Pudong according to schedule.

One of the most important of all the World's Fairs was held in New York City in 1964 and 1965, when America was at the height of its economic power and global prestige. The fair's most popular exhibit, sponsored by General Motors Corporation, was "Futurama," a show in which visitors sat in moving chairs and were propelled past scenery depicting what life might be like in the future: a lunar base, underseas exploration, and a city of tomorrow—a metropolis composed of very tall towers, endless miles of elevated highways, and all of it covered in lots and lots of lights. In 1965 China was on the cusp of the Cultural Revolution; the country was about to spasm with ten years of chaos. The Chinese were too busy building themselves into a frenzy that would allow them to murder each other in the name of Mao to pay much attention to the New York World's Fair. But apparently somebody had been paying attention: China three decades later had begun building the Futurama city of tomorrow in Pudong.

"I heard today that the United States can't afford to build a pavilion at the Expo," Marcus said.

"That's true," I said. "The effort to finance it was terribly mismanaged, and now we can't raise the money. We may not have a pavilion."

"I heard that Shanghai offered the United States a loan so it can build a pavilion," Jennifer said. "So it can be part of the Expo."

"I read that too," I said. "That was very generous of Shanghai to offer."

There are two very different stories here. Americans tell themselves they aren't interested in the Expo and participating in it isn't important: We have everything we need already, and our products are coveted across the globe—there is no point in sharing our vision of the future with the world at the Expo, no need to learn what other countries are up to. . . . *The Chinese emperor dismissed Lord Macartney and sent him back to England with a letter that made clear China's belief in its superiority by stating, "We have never valued ingenious articles, nor do we have the slightest need of your country's manufactures. . . . Our Celestial Empire possesses all things in prolific abundance and lacks no product within its own borders. There was therefore no need to import the manufactures of outside barbarians in exchange for our own produce. . . ."* The Chinese tell themselves that America's arrogance and complacency have crippled it and our nation is now too poor to participate in the Expo, too weak to lead the world, and America's momentum is slowing—soon it will be passed by China. Few people in the United States care about having a pavilion at the Expo; every single Chinese person in Shanghai will note its absence. Some Chinese call it a snub to their nation, but they are acutely aware of our bungled effort, and all of them understand that China offered America financial aid to raise a pavilion in their city of the future.

In the place where we once helped to colonize China's shores and to turn Shanghai into a pleasure dome for Western powers, in view of the towers of Pudong, we have committed an act of deep national shame. We have lost face in front of China. Everyone in Shanghai knows it, and we have no idea what just happened. Face is at the center of the cultural divide between the West and China, a divide that sometimes seems to me a fracture fine as hair, at other times a chasm.

I stared at Marcus and Jennifer; something felt different, and suddenly I realized what it was. The three of us had just felt the axis of the world shift, had felt it tilt toward Shanghai. We stood together on that bridge, one country rising and the other falling, equal for a moment as the trajectories of our two nations crossed, and for the first time we were peers in each other's eyes.

Or at least that's what I think they thought.

"You aren't kidding when you say you feel sorry for Americans, are you," I said.

"No," Jennifer said. "We are making a joke, sort of, but not really a joke. Chinese know what it is like to be the most powerful country in the world and then for it to break apart into little pieces."

"Do you really think that's what's happening?" I asked.

"What do you think?" Marcus said.

"The jury is still out," I said. "We've made some mistakes, some enormous ones, but I wouldn't write us off just yet. We might build that pavilion—we might pull it off."

"Yeah," Marcus said. "With Chinese money. Your whole country is financed by Chinese money."

"Jury?" Jennifer asked.

I laughed. "It's something that old-fashioned Americans once believed in—it was a part of our barbaric civilization with a brief history before we were absorbed into the Middle Kingdom. Maybe your one child will read about it in a history book written by your government someday."

Marcus and Jennifer didn't laugh. They thought my world was crumbling and I stood there making jokes. I recognized something in the way Jennifer looked at me. It was the same look I'd given her when bulldozers smashed shikumen in the lane where she'd been raised, when the brick walls around her family were reduced to cindery dust.

I turned around, my eyes crawling over the panorama. Elevated highways shot across Shanghai in great swooping curves and endless straightaways that arrowed off into crowded emptiness and vanished in haze. I looked downriver toward the Yangtze, where on an island a carbon-neutral city would rise, fully realized, from nothing. Somewhere out there buried beneath the heavy gray blanket of sky, amid the wasted rivers and the tired land, would be a spot of green, a perfect eco-city on an emerald island. I could not see it. My eyes squinted in the toxic air.

Above countless building zones, construction cranes loomed like birds of prey too heavy to fly, their shriveled wings useless to lift them into the sky, these great metal creatures tilting and swiveling as they clutched at skeletons of steel. Past the fairgrounds, in the distance to the north where the river turned in a broad arc, stood the towers of Pudong. A mélange of every strange shape spat from the human mind strained skyward through the haze. I looked at the other side of the river in the direction of the Bund. A nostalgic museum on one side, a futuristic dreamscape on the other, muddy waters gliding out to sea beneath us—where was the now in Shanghai?

Marcus and Jennifer were kissing. There they stood on the observation deck, the city spread out around them, holding tight to each other, lips bumping together as clumsily as their feet had when earlier that day they'd danced in the park. They pulled apart when they saw me staring. Marcus busied himself adjusting a control knob on his camera and Jennifer worked at her pant legs, turning up the cuffs. The sun was morphing into the swollen red disc it becomes at the end of days in deserts and in the defiled skies of cities.

"The lights won't be turned on tonight on the Bund," Marcus said. "A friend told me today. He works for the power company."

Shanghai had been putting a stop to the evening lightshow to relieve pressure on the stressed grid. Somewhere outside Shanghai, coal-fired power plants were being built to feed a city hungry for power, to sate its ravenous craving.

"Maybe they'll turn the lights on tomorrow," Marcus said.

"But he'll be gone by then," Jennifer said to Marcus.

"You're leaving?" Marcus said.

I nodded. "What will happen to you?" I said to both of them. I cleared my throat and looked away from their faces.

From atop this platform on the Lupu Bridge, the buildings of Shanghai did not appear as fantastic or as intimidating as they did when viewed from the teeming streets below; nor were they as small and tidy as they appeared from the glass encasement at the apex of a tower. The city at this moment seemed to me neither an apocalyptic vision of choking fumes and screeching machines, nor the utopia of a perfectly planned scale model in a museum. For the first time, Shanghai did not seem to me larger than life. It was backdrop and nothing more. It was simply a place where people lived.

"What do you mean 'what will happen to us?'" Jennifer asked.

"Your parents, you, everything," I said. "Will you be okay?"

"China is changing so fast," Marcus said. "You had your development in America and now we have ours."

"Things will get better here," Jennifer said.

"It's true," Marcus said. "I know they will."

I pointed at Pudong, and I swept my finger back and forth, across the towers and the bridges, the endless highways, the boats and planes and cars. The ubiquitous cranes and the swarms of construction workers, laboring with efficiency relentless and rote. "Would all this be possible with democracy—I mean, building all this in less than two decades?"

"Of course not," Marcus said.

"Is it worth it?" I asked.

"We don't have a choice. It has already happened."

I looked away from the sprawling cityscape and narrowed my focus on the faces of my friends. "What do you want?" I said to Jennifer. "I mean, what do you really want?"

"I want to go to America and learn about marketing," she said.

"Why? So you can get a better job? So you can make more money? So you can help China be rich and powerful?"

"So I can have a good job." She patted the air with her hand as she thought a moment. "And so I can understand more things. I want to understand about the world outside of our China—not just by watching movies and looking at it on the Internet. I want to live in it and understand it. I don't think it will change who I am. Deep inside I am very Chinese. But I also want to understand what is not Chinese. Maybe I won't understand it—but trying to understand it is important. It is important to try. If I don't try, then my life . . . my life will be small. I don't want my life to be small."

"What do you want?" Marcus asked, his eyes holding mine in his stare. "You are always asking us what we want, but what do you want?"

"What do I really want?" I said. "I want to know this city. Not from the drive-by media reports that we see in America every day, not from the groups with their business plans and shopping lists that I bring here to stay in five-star hotels. I want to be swallowed up by this city. I want to disappear into it, I want to be right in the middle of it, I want to be everywhere inside of it. I want to eat every inch of it, I want to crunch it between my teeth and smash it beneath my feet. I want to breathe all of it in until I'm coughing up blood and covered in dust and then try to make sense of it. Like you, Jennifer—I know it won't change who I am, but I want to try to understand it. I feel like I have to keep trying."

"We are the same this way. But you are much crazier—perhaps because you are an American." She smiled at me. There is a certain Chinese smile that makes me believe all is right in this bizarre nation and all is right in my soul. That smile, the warmth of it, I saw every day in China, and I saw it now, on the bridge above the Huangpu River.

"And I want other Americans to decide for themselves," I said. "I want them to turn off their TVs and switch off their computers and put down my book and come here and meet people like you and then make up their own minds about China."

Marcus said, "Before I went to school at Stanford I was afraid of America and I hated it because of everything I'd ever been taught and everything I'd learned. But after two years living there, I changed. I still don't like America, but now I don't hate it."

We both laughed.

"You have to go back home?" Marcus said.

"I don't know how long it will be before I come back to Shanghai. I don't think I can work in the travel business anymore. I need to figure out what to do with my life. Maybe I won't be back until the Expo."

Jennifer had stopped smiling, and judging from the way her mouth was moving she was very close to crying. "Everything might be different when you come back," she said. "I don't know what will happen to my parents. I don't know what will happen to me. Sometimes I wish they would stop fighting the government and just accept what has to happen. Shanghai has to change. . . . I don't know. Sometimes I'm proud of them for not quitting. Sometimes I wish Shanghai doesn't have to change. I'm confused, but I think everything will be okay." She nodded and rubbed her eyes. "I think things will get better." She shrugged her narrow shoulders and smiled.

"Things will definitely get better," Marcus said. "The world will see at the Expo. All the countries of the world will come to Shanghai and then they'll understand."

"Understand what?" I asked knowing full well what he would say but wanting to hear him say it, wanting his words to fill my ears for my flight back to America.

"They'll see that China wants its people to be happy. They'll see that China wants better lives for its people. They'll understand that we want what developed countries have—and we want peace."

"And they'll see how much anger China has toward the West and Japan?"

"They'll see that we have not forgotten what happened to us here in Shanghai. But they'll also see that we are focused on the future. They'll see that we're ready to forgive the world for the way it treated China."

Perhaps the cowed can never truly forgive, and their wounds will always fester as long as they are weak. The ability to forgive, to let go of a bitter past, is a luxury owned solely by the strong. A mighty nation can move beyond the injustices it has endured. Its citizens can stand atop the world's longest arch bridge and look forward as they forgive those who have trespassed against their country. They can believe their future will be better than their past. And perhaps they can even begin to forgive themselves for the violence they visited upon each other, for the mistakes they made that sent their nation into freefall.

"Perhaps you are confused?" Jennifer said.

I was looking over the side of the bridge at the roiling waters below, talking to myself as I often do in Shanghai, muttering words in Mandarin, babbling thoughts in English, speaking beneath my breath like a man afflicted. "I've been confused since my first time in Shanghai and I'm confused now. But I'm happy to be here on this bridge, in this city, with both of you. Because of you my life does not seem small."

Chinese people are forever taking pictures of themselves, snapping self-portraits wherever they go—as if the pictures of them standing in each place are necessary to prove where they have been, what they have seen. As if someone, someday, will demand photographic evidence of their travels, and if they don't produce it, then for the record they will never have been there. Our journey to the top of the Lupu Bridge was no exception. It demanded documentation. Marcus straightened his arm and held his camera in front of him, pointing its lens toward himself and Jennifer and me as we stood together on the platform far above the river, Puxi on one side, Pudong on the other, the future Expo fairgrounds all around us. Arms draped across each other's shoulders, we grinned at the silver camera shining in what little light the hazy sky allowed. After Marcus took our picture, we looked at the image on the digital screen, towers paling away behind us in endless shrouds of gray, grins frozen forever in the bright matrix of the screen.

Buddhist monks are imprisoned for owning pictures of the Dalai Lama; Falun Gong practitioners are tortured because their ability to organize protests threatens the government's grip on power; China will go to war in a heartbeat if it believes Taiwan is being taken from the motherland. I knew all these things—we all know these things. But there is a central story threaded through the larger narrative of China, and I did not know this story until I spent time in Shanghai. It is the story China wants to tell at the World Expo. It is the story of a nation trying its best to provide better lives for one fifth of humanity, a nation that believes things will get better. Amid the canyons and towers of China's largest metropolis I heard this story often, and sometimes I believed it. I believed it because my Chinese friends so earnestly believed it. Surrounded by problems that would give any people pause, the Chinese look past their country's social horrors and trashed environment and again and again they tell themselves this story. Things will get better.

My friends in Shanghai believe this story. It is a beautiful story. I want to believe it too. I have no reason to believe the lives of the Chinese people will improve, no real rationale. I am not an expert, I don't know all the facts. But I am moved by stories: I am weak this way, I am human.

I believe things will get better because I have seen them dancing. I took video footage the day I watched the people of Shanghai dancing in the park, and whenever I am in the States and I hear the latest report of China's gloom, I open my laptop and look at the video. In the pixels of my screen I see Shanghai's polluted skies. I see a manufactured landscape of concrete and steel, and within this cramped and dismal world there is an open place with grass and trees and the sweetest smiles I have ever known. Music rises up to the trees' branched crowns and spreads through the gritty air, the poisoned sky.

They are dancing. I see them dancing and I believe things will get better.

Bibliography

Listed below are the principal works referred to in the text, as well as others that shaped the background for this book.

Anderson, E. N. *The Food of China*. Yale University Press, 1988.

Ash, Robert F. and Y. Y. Kueh (eds.). *The Chinese Economy under Deng Xiaoping*. Oxford University Press, 1996.

August, Oliver. *Inside the Red Mansion: On the Trail of China's Most Wanted Man*. Houghton Mifflin Company, 2007.

Baker, Barbara (ed.). *Shanghai: Electric and Lurid City: An Anthology*. Oxford University Press, 1998.

Ballard, J. G. *Empire of the Sun: A Novel*. Simon & Schuster, 1984.

Baum, Richard. *Burying Mao: Chinese Politics in the Age of Deng Xiaoping*. Princeton University Press, 1994.

Becker, Jasper. *Hungry Ghosts: Mao's Secret Famine*. The Free Press, 1996.

———. *The Chinese*. Free Press, 2000.

———. *Dragon Rising: An Inside Look at China Today*. National Geographic Society, 2006.

Beech, Hannah. "Ye Olde Shanghai." *Time*, February 7, 2005.

Birns, Jack (ed. Carolyn Wakeman and Ken Light). *Assignment, Shanghai: Photographs on the Eve of Revolution*. University of California Press, 2003.

Bo Yang (trans. Don Cohn and Jing Qing). *The Ugly Chinaman and the Crisis of Chinese Culture*. Allen & Unwin, 1992.

Bonavia, David. *The Chinese*. Penguin, 1982.

Buck, Pearl. *The Good Earth*. Washington Square Press, 2004 (Originally published in 1931).

Burtynsky, Edward. *China: The Photographs of Edward Burtynsky*. Steidl, 2005.

Chan, Royston and Sophie Taylor. "Hundreds Protest Shanghai Maglev Rail Extension." *Reuters*, January 12, 2008.

Chang, Gordon G. *The Coming Collapse of China*. Random House, 2001.

Chang, Iris. *The Rape of Nanking: The Forgotten Holocaust of World War II*. BasicBooks, 1997.

Chang, Jung, *Wild Swans: Three Daughters of China*. Simon & Schuster, 1991.

———— and Jon Halliday. *Mao: The Unknown Story*. Knopf, 2005.

Chang, Leslie T. *Factory Girls: From Village to City in a Changing China*. Spiegel & Grau, 2008.

Chen Guidi and Wu Chuntao (trans. Zhu Hong). *Will the Boat Sink the Water?: The Life of China's Peasants*. Public Affairs, 2006.

Cheng, Nien. *Life and Death in Shanghai*. Grove Press, 1987.

Cherry, Steven. "How to Build a Green City." *IEEE Spectrum*, June 2007.

The China Beat website: http://www.thechinabeat.org.

"China Maglev Project Suspended Amid Radiation Concerns." *Xinhua News Agency*, May 26, 2007.

"China's Infrastructure Splurge." *The Economist*, February 14, 2008.

ChinesePod website: http://chinesepod.com.

Clissold, Tim. *Mr. China: A Memoir*. HarperBusiness, 2005.

Cohen, Paul A. *China Unbound: Evolving Perspectives on the Chinese Past*. RoutledgeCurzon, 2003.

Crozier, Justin. "5,000 Years of History." *China in Focus*, Spring, 2001.

Dalton, John. *Heaven Lake: A Novel*. Scribner, 2004.

Danwei website: http://www.danwei.org.

Dong, Stella. *Shanghai: The Rise and Fall of a Decadent City*. William Morrow, 2000.

"Dongtan." Shanghai Industrial Investment Company website: http://www.siic.com/en/business/business_01_01.htm.

Dutton, Michael (ed.). *Streetlife China*. Cambridge University Press, 2008.

Economy, Elizabeth C. *The River Runs Black: The Environmental Challenge to China's Future*. Cornell University Press, 2004.

————. "GDP: Accounting for the Environment in China." China from the Inside, U.S. Public Broadcasting System, January 3, 2007.

Elvin, Mark. *The Retreat of the Elephants: An Environmental History of China*. Yale University Press, 2004.

Eunjung Cha, Ariana. "Jewish 'Success' Sells Big in China / Boom in Books Purporting to Reveal Business Secrets." *Washington Post*, February 9, 2007.

"Evolution and Revolution: Chinese Dress 1700s-1990s - Mao Suit." Powerhouse Museum website: http://www.powerhousemuseum.com/hsc/evrev/mao_suit.htm.

Expo 2010 website: http://en.expo2010.cn.

Fairbank, John King and Merle Goldman. *China: A New History, Second Enlarged Edition.* Belknap Press, 2006.

Faison, Seth. *South of the Clouds: Exploring the Hidden Realms of China.* St. Martin's Press, 2004.

Fallows, James M. *Postcards from Tomorrow Square: Reports from China.* Vintage Books, 2009.

Farrer, James. *Opening Up: Youth Sex Culture and Market Reform in Shanghai.* University of Chicago Press, 2002.

Fenby, Jonathan. *Generalissimo: Chiang Kai-shek and the China He Lost.* Free Press, 2003.

———. *Modern China: The Fall And Rise of a Great Power, 1850 To The Present.* Ecco, 2008.

———. *Penguin History Of Modern China.* Ecco, 2008.

Fishman, Ted. *China, Inc. How the Rise of the Next Superpower Challenges America and the World.* Scribner, 2005.

French, Howard W. "Ire Over Shanghai Rail Line May Signal Turning Point." *New York Times,* August 10, 2007.

French, Paul. "Arup and Dongtan, Worthy Winner of Greenwasher of the Year." Ethical Corporation website: http://www.ethicalcorp.com/content.asp?ContentID=5552. December 4, 2007.

———. "Dongtan: China's Eco-Potemkin Village and Arup's Political Connections." Ethical Corporation podcast: http://www.ethicalcorp.com/content.asp?ContentID=5113. June 4, 2007.

——— and Matthew Crabbe. "China's Dongtan Eco-Village - and How the Press Fell for It Hook Line and Sinker." Ethical Corporation blog: http://ethicalcorp.blogspot.com/2007/04/chinas-dongtan-eco-village-and-how.html. April 19, 2007.

Gifford, Rob. *China Road: A Journey into the Future of a Rising Power.* Random House, 2007.

Girard, Greg. *Phantom Shanghai.* Magenta Foundation, 2007.

Gittings, John. *The Changing Face of China: From Mao to Market.* Oxford University Press, 2005.

———. *Real China: From Cannibalism to Karaoke.* Simon and Schuster, 1996.

Gluckman, Ron. "The Ghosts of Shanghai." *AsiaWeek,* June 1997.

———. "In Shanghai's Bund, They're Partying Like It's 1939." *AsiaWeek,* June 1997.

————. "Bright Lights, Beautiful Bund." *AsiaWeek*, March 2001.

Goldberger, Paul. "Shanghai Surprise: The Radical Quaintness of the Xintiandi District." *The New Yorker*, December 26, 2005.

Greenspan, Anna. "Shanghai, The Becoming Thing." Asia Times Online website: http://www.atimes.com/atimes/China_Business/HA07Cb01.html. January 7, 2006.

Guariglia, Justin. *Planet Shanghai*. Chronicle Books, 2008.

Han, Bangqing (trans. Eileen Chang; ed. Eva Hung). *The Sing-Song Girls of Shanghai*. Columbia University Press, 2005.

Hanssen, Beatrice (ed.). *Walter Benjamin and the Arcades Project (Walter Benjamin Studies)*. Continuum International Publishing Group, 2006.

Hessler, Peter. *River Town: Two Years on the Yangtze*. HarperCollins, 2001.

————. *Oracle Bones: A Journey Between China's Past and Present*. HarperCollins, 2006.

Hewitt, Duncan. *China: Getting Rich First: A Modern Social History*. W.W. Norton, 2008.

Hinton, William. *Fanshen: A Documentary of Revolution in a Chinese Village*. University of California Press, 1997.

Hsu, Immanuel C. Y. *The Rise of Modern China*. Oxford University Press, 1995.

Ishiguro, Kazuo. *When We Were Orphans*. Knopf, 2000.

Jacobs, Jane. *The Death and Life of Great American Cities*. Random House, 1961.

Jacques, Martin. *When China Rules the World*. Penguin Press, 2009.

Jeffries, Stuart. "Where Blade Runner Meets Las Vegas." *The Guardian*, November 8, 2004.

Johnson, Ian. *Wild Grass: Three Stories of Change in Modern China*. Pantheon Books, 2004.

Johnston, Tess and Deke Erh. *A Last Look: Western Architecture in Old Shanghai*. Old China Hand Press, 1998.

————. *Frenchtown Shanghai: Western Architecture in Shanghai's Old French Concession*. Old China Hand Press, 2001.

————. *Shanghai Art Deco*. Old China Hand Press, 2006.

Kahn, Joseph and Jim Yardley. "Choking on Growth: As China Roars, Pollution Reaches Deadly Extremes." *The New York Times*, August 26, 2007.

Kane, Frank. "Shanghai Plans Eco-Metropolis on its Mudflats." *The Observer*, January 8, 2006.

Katz, Peter. *The New Urbanism: Toward an Architecture of Community*. McGraw-Hill, 1994.

Kingwell, Mark. *Concrete Reveries: Consciousness and the City*. Viking, 2008.

Kristof, Nicholas D. and Sheryl WuDunn. *China Wakes: The Struggle for the Soul of a Rising Power*. Times Books, 1994.

Kynge, James. *China Shakes the World: A Titan's Rise and Troubled Future—and the Challenge for America.* Houghton Mifflin, 2006.

Land, Nick (ed.). *Urbanatomy: Shanghai 2008.* China Intercontinental Press, 2008.

Lee, Jennifer 8. *The Fortune Cookie Chronicles: Adventures in the World of Chinese Food.* Twelve, 2008.

Lee, Leo Ou-fan. *Shanghai Modern: The Flowering of a New Urban Culture in China, 1930 – 1945.* Harvard University Press, 1999.

Leslie, Jacques. "China's Pollution Nightmare Is Now Everyone's Pollution Nightmare." *Christian Science Monitor,* March 20, 2008.

Li, Zhisui (trans. Tai Hung-chao; ed. Anne F. Thurston). *The Private Life of Chairman Mao: The Memoirs of Mao's Personal Physician.* Random House, 1994.

Linebarger, Paul. *Sun Yat Sen and the Chinese Republic.* The Century Co., 1925.

Lu, Hanchao. *Beyond the Neon Lights: Everyday Shanghai in the Early Twentieth Century.* University of California Press, 1999.

Lu Hsun. *Selected Stories.* W. W. Norton, 2003.

Macartney, Lord George (ed. J. L. Cranmer-Byng). *An Embassy to China: Being the Journal Kept by Lord Macartney During His Embassy to the Emperor Ch'ien-lung 1793-1794.* Archon Books, 1963.

McGray, Douglas. "Pop-Up Cities: China Builds a Bright Green Metropolis." *Wired Magazine,* Issue 15.05. May 2007.

McGregor, James. *One Billion Customers: Lessons from the Front Lines of Doing Business in China.* Free Press, 2006.

Mackerras, Colin. *The New Cambridge Handbook of Contemporary China.* Cambridge University Press, 2001.

Meisner, Maurice. *The Deng Xiaoping Era.* Hill and Wang, 1996.

———. *Mao's China and After: A History of the People's Republic, Third Edition.* Free Press, 1999.

Merkel-Hess, Kate (ed.), Kenneth L. Pomeranz (ed.) and Jeffrey N. Wasserstrom (ed.). *China in 2008: A Year of Great Significance.* Rowman & Littlefield Publishers, 2009.

Meyer, Michael. *The Last Days of Old Beijing: Life in the Vanishing Backstreets of a City Transformed.* Walker & Company, 2008.

Mian Mian. *Candy.* Little, Brown, 2003.

Minter, Adam. "Return of a Shanghai Jew." *The Los Angeles Times,* January 15, 2006.

———. "The Pavilion Wars." *The Atlantic,* April 9, 2009.

———. Shanghai Scrap website: http://shanghaiscrap.com.

Mitter, Rana. *A Bitter Revolution: China's Struggle with the Modern World.* Oxford University Press, 2004.

——. *Modern China: A Very Short Introduction*. Oxford University Press, 2008.

Needham, Joseph and Colin Ronan. *The Shorter Science and Civilisation in China: An Abridgement of Joseph Needham's Original Text*. Cambridge University Press, 1978-1995.

O'Connor, Joanne. "The Most Exciting City on Earth." *The Guardian*, September 18, 2005.

Osnos, Evan. "A Breakout Hit Sweeps China." *Chicago Tribune*, January 23, 2007.

Pan Ling. *In Search of Old Shanghai*. Joint Publishing Co., 1997.

——. *Old Shanghai: Gangsters in Paradise*. Cultured Lotus, 1999.

Pearce, Fred. "Greenwash: The Dream of the First Eco-City Was Built on a Fiction." *The Guardian*, April 23, 2009.

Pei, Minxin. *China's Trapped Transition: The Limits of Developmental Autocracy*. Harvard University Press, 2006.

Perry, Elizabeth and Li Xun. *Proletarian Power: Shanghai in the Cultural Revolution*. Westview, 1997.

Pomfret, John. *Chinese Lessons: Five Classmates and the Story of the New China*. Henry Holt, 2006.

Pridmore, Jay. *Shanghai: The Architecture of China's Great Urban Center*. Abrams, 2008.

Ristaino, Marcia Reynders. *Port of Last Resort: The Diaspora Communities of Shanghai*. Stanford University Press, 2001.

Salzman, Mark. *Iron & Silk*. Random House, 1986.

Schell, Orville. *To Get Rich Is Glorious: China in the 80's*. Pantheon Books, 1984.

——. *Discos and Democracy: China in the Throes of Reform*. Pantheon Books, 1988.

——. *Mandate Of Heaven: A New Generation Of Entrepreneurs, Dissidents, Bohemians And Technocrats Lays Claim to China's Future*. Simon & Schuster, 1994.

——and David Shambaugh (eds.). *The China Reader: The Reform Era*. Vintage Books, 1999.

Sergeant, Harriet. *Shanghai*. John Murray, 1998.

Shanghai Creative Industry Center website: http://www.scic.gov.cn/english.

Shapiro, Judith. *Mao's War Against Nature: Politics and the Environment in Revolutionary China*. Cambridge University Press, 2001.

Shaughnessy, Edward L. (ed.). *China: Empire and Civilization*. Oxford University Press, 2000.

Shen, Rujun. "Shanghai Highrises Could Worsen Threat of Rising Seas." *Reuters*, October 5, 2008.

Shirk, Susan L. *China: Fragile Superpower*. Oxford University Press, 2007.

Spence, Jonathan D. *The Gate of Heavenly Peace*. Penguin Books, 1981.

———.*The Search for Modern China*. W. W. Norton, 1990.

———.*The Chan's Great Continent: China in Western Minds*. W. W. Norton, 1999.

———. *Mao Zedong*. Viking, 1999.

"The Tank Man." PBS *Frontline* Documentary, 2006.

Tata, Sam. *Shanghai: 1949, The End of an Era*. New Amsterdam, 1990.

Terrill, Ross. *The New Chinese Empire: And What it Means for the United States*. Basic, 2003.

Torchia, Andrew, "Rising Middle Class Fuels Shanghai Maglev Protest." *Reuters*, January 14, 2008.

Tu Wei-ming (ed.). *The Living Tree: The Changing Meaning of Being Chinese Today*. Stanford University Press, 1991.

Von Sternberg, Josef. *Fun in a Chinese Laundry*. Macmillan, 1965.

Wasserstrom, Jeffrey N. *Student Protests in Twentieth-Century China: The View From Shanghai*. Stanford University Press, 1991.

——— (ed.). *Twentieth-Century China: New Approaches*. Routledge, 2003.

———. *China's Brave New World: And Other Tales for Global Times*. Indiana University Press, 2007.

———. *Global Shanghai, 1850–2010: A History in Fragments*. Routledge, 2008.

———. "NIMBY Comes to China." *The Nation*, January 18, 2008.

———. "Shanghai's 2010 Expo: the 'Economic Olympics.'" *The Christian Science Monitor*, May 14, 2009.

Wei, Betty Peh-T'i. *Old Shanghai*. Oxford University Press, 1993.

Wei Hui. *Shanghai Baby: A Novel*. Washington Square Press, 2002.

Winchester, Simon. *The Man Who Loved China: The Fantastic Story of the Eccentric Scientist Who Unlocked the Mysteries of the Middle Kingdom*. HarperCollins Publishers, 2008.

Wong, Jan. *Red China Blues: My Long March from Mao to Now*. Anchor, 1997.

Ye, Sang. *China Candid: The People on the People's Republic*. University of California Press, 2006.

Zachary, Robin. "As Business Rolls In, the Western Suit Makes a Comeback in China." *New York Times*, March 5, 2005.

Zha, Jianying. *China Pop: How Soap Operas, Tabloids and Bestsellers Are Transforming a Culture*. W.W. Norton, 1995.

Zhang, Ailing. *Love in a Fallen City*. New York Review Books, 2007.

———. *Lust, Caution: The Story*. Anchor Books, 2007.

Zhang, Xinxin and Sang Ye. *Chinese Lives: An Oral History of Contemporary China*. Pantheon, 1987.

Zhong, Wu. "China's Dented Image Projects." Asia Times Online website: http://www.atimes.com/atimes/China_Business/IF13Cb02.html. June 13, 2007.

Acknowledgements

Thanks to Aron Rosenthal, my *hǎo péngyǒu*, for introducing me to China. It all began on a small stream hidden in the Rockies where the mountains wear clean robes of snow and trout with pearly sides hold in the current and dimple the surface of deep green pools. Aron told me about the pollution in China, how if it didn't kill you, you might wish you were dead, how he had seen the end and the end looked a lot like China, how he loved the people there all the same—and I knew I had to go and see for myself.

I am indebted to Dave French and the Orbis Institute for sending me to teach and to learn in Luohe. Cheers to Hank, the king of Zhengzhou, for helping Aron and me when we washed up in that cursed and wicked land along the Yellow River. Thanks to Nick Wang for giving me an opportunity to learn the ropes of the travel business. Thanks to Yi and Selina for letting me crash at their places in Shanghai. Thanks to Jing for keeping my interest in China alive while I was in Boulder—you are one of your country's finest cultural ambassadors. Thanks to Niu for the language lessons and for exploring Hongkou with me. My stomach owes a debt of gratitude to Ada and Avon for introducing me to some of Shanghai's best eateries. Thanks to Fabrizia, my language genius friend, for patiently parsing *pǔtōnghuà* for a *wàiguórén*.

Many thanks to Marcus and Jennifer: without you, Shanghai would have been spectacle and nothing more. 我祝你们快乐.

I would like to thank whoever figured out how to brew the coffee bean into a tasty beverage that boosts productivity and makes the dreary skies of *Zhōngguó* a bit more bearable.

I am immensely grateful for the hard work and dedication of the many China specialists and scholars who have tried to understand China by paying attention to how its citizens live and what they want.

My sincere thanks to Connie Shaw for believing I had found a story worth telling, and for her limitless patience.

The only grant I received while writing this book was from my wife, Amy, who granted me permission to work less and write more. I'd like to thank her for that. While I was practicing Chinese, she was putting on purple scrubs and heading off to the hospital to save lives.

About the Author

Stephen Grace is the author of the novel *Under Cottonwoods*, a BookSense 76 selection, about which the *Los Angeles Times* said, "...Grace writes with a lyrical power, celebrating the healing power of the human spirit set free in the wilds." He is also the author of three nonfiction books, including *Colorado: Mapping the Centennial State through History: Rare and Unusual Maps from the Library of Congress*.

Stephen has traveled extensively throughout China, where his experiences range from trail running in Tibet to teaching English as a volunteer in Henan. He has developed customized China travel programs for Harvard Business School, Stanford Graduate School of Business, UCLA Anderson School of Management, and the School of Engineering and Applied Science of Columbia University. He has also designed and led cultural immersion programs in China for high schools, a media company, and various nonprofit organizations, and he has worked with Aspen Skiing Company and Vail Ski Resort to bring groups of Chinese skiers and snowboarders to the United States. He lives in Boulder, Colorado and commutes to Shanghai.

Sentient Publications, LLC publishes books on cultural creativity, experimental education, transformative spirituality, holistic health, new science, ecology, and other topics, approached from an integral viewpoint. Our authors are intensely interested in exploring the nature of life from fresh perspectives, addressing life's great questions, and fostering the full expression of the human potential. Sentient Publications' books arise from the spirit of inquiry and the richness of the inherent dialogue between writer and reader.

Our Culture Tools series is designed to give social catalyzers and cultural entrepreneurs the essential information, technology, and inspiration to forge a sustainable, creative, and compassionate world.

We are very interested in hearing from our readers. To direct suggestions or comments to us, or to be added to our mailing list, please contact:

SENTIENT PUBLICATIONS, LLC

1113 Spruce Street
Boulder, CO 80302
303-443-2188
contact@sentientpublications.com
www.sentientpublications.com